GOOD TIMES AND BAD TIMES IN RURAL JAVA

VERHANDELINGEN
VAN HET KONINKLIJK INSTITUUT
VOOR TAAL-, LAND- EN VOLKENKUNDE

195

JAN BREMAN and GUNAWAN WIRADI

GOOD TIMES AND BAD TIMES IN RURAL JAVA

Case study of socio-economic dynamics in two villages towards the end of the twentieth century

2002
KITLV Press
Leiden

Published by:

KITLV Press
Koninklijk Instituut voor Taal-, Land- en Volkenkunde
(Royal Institute of Linguistics and Anthropology)
P.O. Box 9515
2300 RA Leiden
The Netherlands

Cover: Creja ontwerpen, Leiderdorp

ISBN 90 6718 187 0

Printed in the Netherlands

Contents

Preface

The coastal plain of West Java is the site of the research reported in this monograph. Our investigations on the dynamics of work and income in the rural economy were carried out at the beginning and towards the end of the last decade in the twentieth century. The two villages selected for our micro-level studies had already been visited from the late 1960s onwards by the staff of the Survey Agro Ekonomi (SAE), a rural research agency affiliated to the Ministry of Agriculture. The benchmark data built up over a long period were a major consideration for our focus on these localities. For Jan Breman, an additional motive to include the village called East Cirebon was a historical account he had published earlier on the dynamics of land and labour relations in this region which became dominated by agro-industry during the late-colonial period (Breman 1983).

By contrast, North Subang, although much closer to Jabotabek, the metropolitan zone around the city of Jakarta, looks far more like the peasant village one is apt to associate with the Javanese countryside. In 1990 most inhabitants still earned their livelihood by farming and the village was also monitored on and off by the Agro Economic Survey for changing practices in foodcrop cultivation. The locality gained more policy fame when Hayami and Kikuchi included this *kampung* in their case studies of the transformation caused by the green revolution in the Southeast Asian countryside towards the end of the 1970s (Hayami and Kikuchi 1981).

Labour circulation, both intra-rural and rural-urban, was the theme of the fieldwork which Breman conducted in East Cirebon in 1989 and North Subang in 1990. His investigations then formed part of a more comprehensive research project on non-farm employment within the rural economy of Java (White 1986). For the duration of his stay in North Subang he was accompanied by Setiawan, a staff member at Bogor Agricultural University. Agrar Sudrajat, at that time associated with *Akatiga* (a non-government agency located in Bandung) went with him as a fieldwork assistant to East Cirebon. While the findings in the latter village have been kept in portfolio until now, the outcome of the local-level research in North Subang was first published in an earlier version in Bahasa Indonesia in *Prisma* (Breman 1994) and subsequently in *Modern Asian Studies* (Breman 1995). For the renewed publication of the results of this first round of investigations Breman has produced a more elaborate and revised text.

When the first author happened to be in Jakarta for a short visit at the end of October 1997, the exchange rate of the rupiah registered a massive fall. Overnight, all construction work in the national capital which, for many years, had been one big building site, came to a standstill. The next day Breman went to the outskirts of Jakarta, to neighbourhoods where workers from his fieldwork villages were accustomed to lodge in a *pondok* (boarding house) or around one of the *warteg (warung tegal)* (foodstall) which cater to the daily needs of this floating mass. The owners told him that all the workers had left, *phk*, dismissed instantly with the message not to come back until further notice. Gunawan Wiradi, a senior staff member of Bogor Agricultural University, was as eager as Breman to find out what had occurred to this huge army of labour migrants on their return home. We decided to team up for investigation the impact of *krismon* in the rural hinterland of Jabotabek. We went to East Cirebon and North Subang which both of us knew from earlier local-level research which we had conducted separately. A first, mainly survey-based, round of investigations took place in July-August 1998 in which we concentrated on how the loss of urban employment and income had affected the village economy until then. Wiradi went back alone for a short visit towards the end of that year when the economic crisis was at its worst. Adding to the data gathered, we followed up with another round of investigations in March-April 1999, concentrating then on the various schemes executed under the label of government-sponsored social safety net provisions. In this round we also revisited half of the households earlier surveyed in North Subang and East Cirebon, which provided us with quantitative and qualitative information on the further onslaught of *krismon*. The empirical part of our study was concluded over a year later, in the summer of 2000, when we went back for a final trip to both localities. By stretching our endeavours over a period of almost two-and-half years we were able to examine the effects of the economic crisis and the resulting political upheaval on these villages in West Java as an ongoing process and not simply at one moment in time.

The Prologue was delivered as the Dies Natalis Address 2000 at the Institute of Social Studies in The Hague. We would like to express our gratitude to Prof. S.M.P. Tjondronegoro of Bogor Agricultural University for his advice and support at various stages of our research, to Teun Bijvoet of the Amsterdam School of Social Science Research and for their assitance in sending the manuscript to press. All photos reproduced in the book were taken by Breman in the course of the fieldwork.

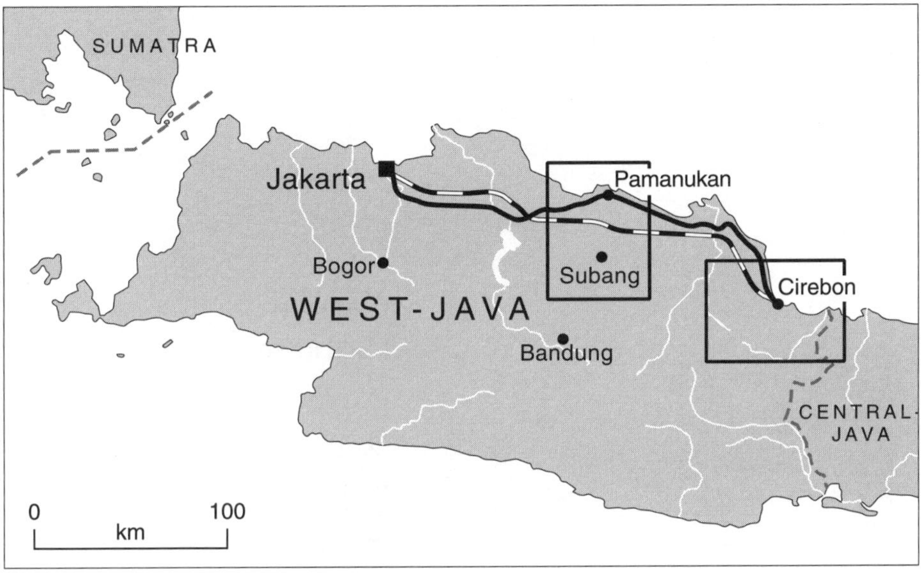
SUMATRA
Jakarta
Pamanukan
Bogor
Subang
Cirebon
WEST-JAVA
Bandung
CENTRAL-JAVA
0
100
km

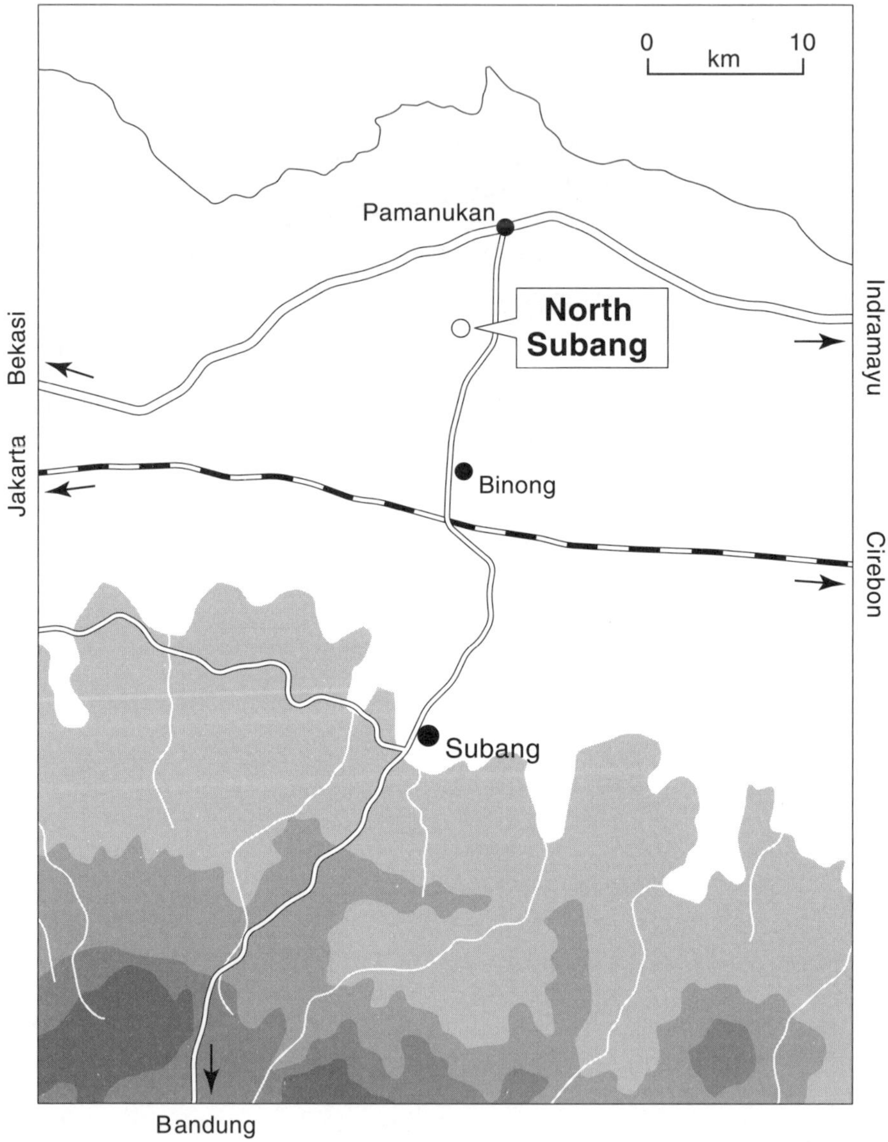
0
km
10
Pamanukan
North Subang
Bekasi
Indramayu
Binong
Jakarta
Cirebon
Subang
Bandung

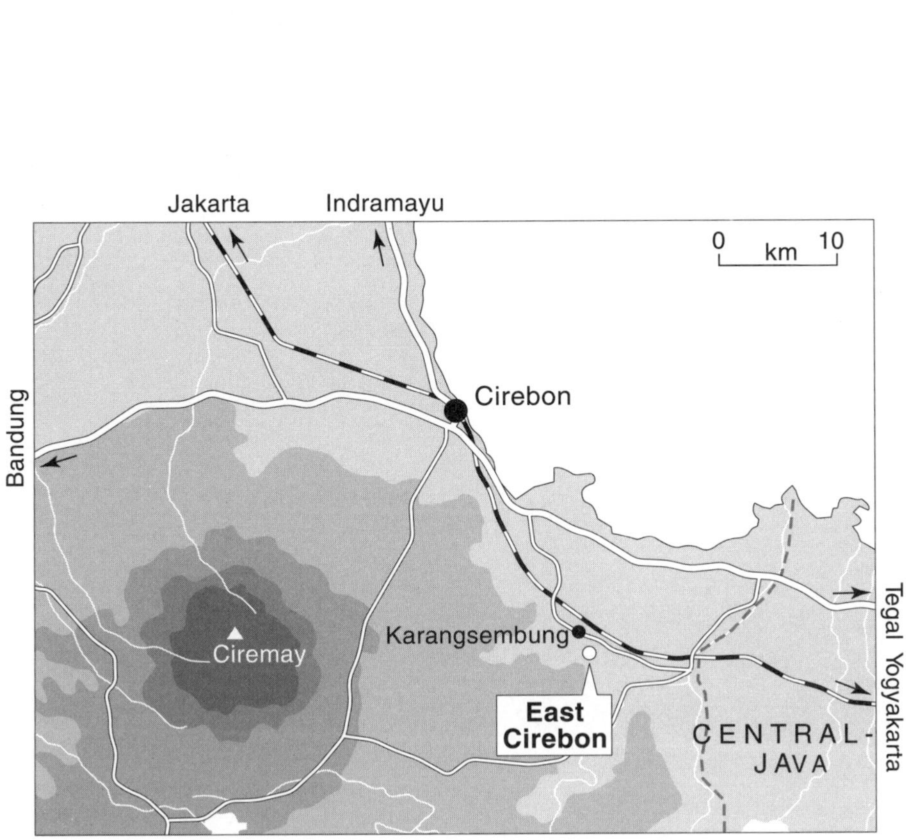

Jakarta
Indramayu
0 km 10
Bandung
Cirebon
Ciremay
Karangsembung
East Cirebon
CENTRAL-JAVA
Tegal
Yogyakarta

CHAPTER I

Prologue

Introductory note

The crisis which hit the regions of East and Southeast Asia in 1997-1998 gave rise to instantaneous and fierce debate. Differences of opinion focused in the first round on the causes of the sudden halt to the long-time boom that had led the economies on a trajectory of high growth rates and, in the second round, on the impact on levels of employment and welfare for the peoples involved. This study does not address the origins of that economic crisis but rather its effects on work and welfare in two localities of rural Java. The factual evidence presented demonstrates that, although the crisis caused major setbacks for the whole region, their scale and intensity differed considerably. From the beginning Indonesia has been singled out as the worst case. While some affected countries already showed signs of recovery in 1998, the most populous nation in Southeast Asia seemed to collapse into further chaos. As elsewhere, the downward slide began with depreciation of the national currency starting in the autumn of 1997. In contrast to, for example, Malaysia, Thailand and South Korea, where inflation was brought under control and financial institutions were cleaned up, the monetary crisis in Indonesia deepened and triggered a political crisis. Suharto's fall in May 1998 signalled the end of the New Order regime which had lasted for more than three decades. The economic malaise also affected other spheres of life: the *krisis moneter* or *krismon* turned into *krisis totàl* or *kristal*. Later, the slump was overshadowed by political turmoil, religious strife and ethnic violence but, in my opinion, the recession was a major factor in aggravating the general state of disorder.

From alarmist to revisionist assessments

Early on, an alarming increase in impoverishment and unemployment was predicted. The Minister of Manpower then in office went on record saying that 22% of Indonesia's total workforce would be unemployed by the end of 1998. Backed by official statistics, produced by the Central Board of Statistics

(Badan Pusat Statistik, BPS) on the basis of calculations that had never before been disputed, the ILO regional office estimated that the combination of wage stagnation and high inflation might cause 37% of the population to fall below the poverty line by mid-1998, with a further spurt to 48% before the end of that year. In comparison to the all-time low of 10.1% reported for the period before the start of *krismon* in mid-1997, this implied a three to fourfold jump in the incidence of poverty. It was an acceleration that threatened to undo much that had been achieved in raising the standard of living for all and sundry since the mid-1970s. The ILO (1998) further argued that lack of improvement in household incomes and the likelihood of more price rises might even result in two-thirds of the population dropping below the poverty line in 1999.

Other international agencies produced more conservative appraisals or forecasts, vehemently rejecting the ILO's doom scenario. In February 1998 the World Bank conceded that absolute poverty might eventually rise to 17%. A year later, a Bank-commissioned study reported that the poverty rate had gone up but only marginally so, from the pre-crisis figure of barely 10% to not more than 14% (Poppele, Sumarto and Pritchett 1999:13-4). The authors stated that the lower income classes in particular were actually quite successful in coping with the crisis. In their considered opinion, *krismon* had a sharper negative impact on the urban than the rural economy; secondly, it hit the better-off harder than the poor; thirdly, it reduced waged work in the formal sector of the economy while employment in the informal sector expanded. Jellinek and Rustanto, another World Bank-sponsored research team, carried out a rapid appraisal mission and summarized their findings in early 1999 by claiming that what had been written up as a crisis instead had created a veritable economic boom. They lauded the transition to 'a mini-communal-capitalist system' under which petty producers made good, stepping in to substitute for high-cost commodities that had been driven out of the market.[1] Their story, consisting of a series of glimpses and based only on a two-week tour around a number of urban and rural sites in Central and East Java, sounded too good to be true and, due to lack of solid substantia-

1 Products which were formerly imported or made in the formal sector are now being made by indigenous small-scale enterprises. Small enterprises, killed off during 20 years of economic boom of the New Order period (1975-1995), are being revived. Old traditions of artisanship and trade are being rediscovered. Rich and middle class consumers who formerly bought from the formal sector are now buying from traditional markets on the street. Markets which were formerly restricted to big traders are now open to masses of small traders. Capital is being accumulated in the informal sector through a combination of traditional social networks and modern cooperative techniques. This has resulted in new and diversified types of capital accumulation which vary from hamlet to hamlet and city to city. In contrast to the economic crash depicted in the official, national and international media, we are witnessing an unprecedented economic boom in the small-scale sector (Jellinek and Rustanto 1999:1-2).

tion, carried little weight. The assumption, however, that many of those pushed out of formal-sector employment could find refuge in the informal sector, was in line with the persistent notion of an infinite capacity for absorption in the lower realms of the urban economy. And what about those who failed to find a niche in this sector of last resort? There was always the possibility to return to the place of origin in the rural hinterland. Idul Fitri in February 1998 witnessed the exodus from the cities of a large labouring army that had for long been kept footloose. Municipal governments facilitated the departure of these migrant workers to their home villages, with which they had stayed in close contact, by handing out free one-way tickets for public transport. The idea was to get this mass of partially or fully unemployable people out of the cities lest they should turn restive, instigating food riots and fuelling political turmoil. Underlying this attempt to defuse an acute threat to public order were thinly veiled references to the social-Darwinist notion of *'la classe dangereuse'*, a mob alienated from society which, at any moment of time, might turn violent and destructive.

The Asian crisis has had a differentiating impact not only among but also within the affected countries. It has frequently been asserted that the economies of Indonesia's islands other than Java remained fairly untouched by, or even benefited from, the huge depreciation of the rupiah. In 1997 the province of East Indonesia suffered from the El Niño drought, a temporary setback which helped to hike food prices; in the following year, however, rainfall was back to normal and agricultural yields were satisfactory. In various parts of the country cash-crop cultivation and artisanal manufacture for export rose, resulting in increased employment and handsome profits for old as well as new producers.

By and large, towns and cities faced far more hardship than the countryside, but even in this respect urban Java was said to bear the brunt of *krismon*. Many sources maintained that the floating workforce that had been pushed back to the hinterland on this densely populated island, had managed successfully to find shelter in various sectors of the rural economy, above all in agriculture. One prominent observer reported a dramatic increase in agricultural work (Manning 2000:123). What did he mean exactly? Output per agrarian worker probably fell by 10% overall, a phenomenon that Manning attributes to progressive crowding, long a characteristic feature of land-scarce Java. The cultivation was resumed of dry fields and home gardens which, in the preceding years, had been left idle by owners who had gone in search of jobs in the urban economy where their labour power commanded a much higher price.

Summing up, Manning (2000:126) insists that 'a high proportion of displaced workers found work in agriculture', a point of view that was also corroborated by several other commentators. Comparing the composition of the labour force between February 1997 and 1998, Poppele, Sumarto and Pritchett (1999: 20) report that agrarian employment grew by 15.2%, much more than any other economic activity. They conclude that 'agriculture more than expanded to pick up the slack'. These and similar statements imply not only a reversal of the substantial loss of jobs experienced in this sector from the 1980s onwards, but also suggest that the erstwhile migrants who returned to food production were at least able to safeguard their basic needs. The assumption that agriculture acted as a catchment reservoir for labour made redundant in other sectors of the economy is inspired by the widely held notion that the army of migrants moving back and forth between the rural hinterland and urban growth poles have never ceased what had always been their prime occupation. It is the tenacious myth of Java as an on-going peasant society dominated by a compact and subsistence-oriented mass of petty owners, tenants and sharecroppers who cultivate a piece of land primarily to supply their own food requirements and who, in the slack season, go away to earn the non-agrarian wages that they need for cash expenditure. In view of this received wisdom, it is hardly surprising that members of peasant households who lost their urban jobs were expected to face no difficulty in falling back on their age-old identity as tillers of the land.

The same type of wishful thinking has it that the rural economy at large operates as a safety valve for migrants driven out of the cities. Petty trade provided ample space in which men and women thrown out of employment could manoeuvre. Activities such as peddling and hawking helped to provide one out of five displaced workers with a new living. Also, various types of petty commodity manufacturing in small-scale ateliers flourished in different parts of Java, and were able to add to their workforce labour dismissed from the metropolitan zones (Manning 2000:125, 128; Hüsken 1999). Such positive signals exhausted the array of good news that could be marshalled, however.

In 1998, gross domestic product contracted by 14% and prospects for 1999 were bleak, anticipating zero growth at best. Among the multitudes made redundant in a wide variety of occupations, especially those who had a secondary school education, many were unable to find gainful work again. Statistical data show that one quarter remained unemployed in 1998; in particular, a high proportion of females (44%) was laid off (Manning and Van Diermen 1999: 128). The adverse repercussions of *krismon* afflicted urban as well as rural Java, to the extent that poverty figures had to be raised to reflect the sharp drop in income. On the basis of National Labour Force Surveys carried out towards the end of 1998, the Central Board of Statistics declared that 49.5 million people, or 24.2% of the total population, had sunk below the official poverty line. This downward trend, the report suggested, was caused mainly by the fall in living standards of the workforce that had been engaged in the formal sector of the urban economy. The percentage of people unable to satisfy their basic needs was higher than earlier estimated, but had not risen to the dramatic apex foreseen by alarmist scenarios.

To overcome the information vacuum on what happened during the crisis the World Bank and other international agencies helped to establish a research NGO to assess the impact of *krismon* and the dubious efficacy of state intervention. The first bulletins and working papers broadcast by this Social Monitoring and Early Response Unit (SMERU) continued to dispute the figures made public by the ILO on the expected rise in levels of poverty and unemployment.

What inspired revisionist commentators to adhere to their far less pessimistic point of view? In the first place, as I have mentioned, the argument that the workforce retrenched in the modern sector could find an escape in the lower and informal circuits of the urban economy. This assumption of reabsorption at a more modest level of employment was actually part of the scenario drawn up by the ILO (1998:28). On second thoughts, however, it was conceded that the economic crisis also played havoc within the informal sector. Workers in construction, trade, transport and other services who had become jobless, tried to earn a living in other branches. Since occupational multiplicity is considered to be a feature of the lower economic echelons where skills or training are said to matter little, it is suggested that men as well as women, old and young, are quite accustomed to roam around searching for paid work in various branches of activity. Cross-sectoral mobility was possible, not least because of 'the remarkable flexibility of Indonesian labour markets and the capacity of people to find new jobs after being retrenched from wage employment' (Manning 2000:121). In Manning's view, this phenomenon of horizontal drift explains why the predicted de-urbanization, a massive return of dismissed workers to the rural hinterland, never took place. Under such a scenario, the informal sector economy would merely swallow up the labour surplus pushed out of higher-paid, regular and protected employment, enabling the displaced workforce, through income-sharing arrangements, to stick it out in all kinds of odd jobs until the economic tide would turn again in their favour, when they would be reinstalled in their former occupations. This bright prospect already seemed to be just around the corner. At the beginning of 1999 there were already signs that real wages had begun to recover from their earlier fall (Papanek and Handoko 1999; Booth 2000b:10). The third reason why alarmist forecasts were toned down was that circular migrants who did not succeed in finding another niche in the urban informal sector simply returned to their villages of origin, there to retreat into agriculture that had always been the mainstay of their livelihood. The possibility of this escape route seemed to confirm the preconceived idea that the rural economy has indeed done much better in resisting the onslaught of the crisis and that, in comparison to the urban workforce, the rural one has been much less adversely affected (World Bank 1999:2; Suryahadi et al. 2000:28).

The successive fall-back scenarios outlined above, three in all, account for a reportedly low rate of increase in open unemployment, understood as not working although seeking work, from an initial figure in August 1997 of 4.7% to not more than 5.5% in late 1998 (Manning 2000:121; Booth 2000b:9). The majority of those whose labour power became wasted after the crash of the rupiah were said to be mainly the well-educated and better-paid workers retrenched in the modern industrial economy. This suggestion was justified with the old dictum that the poor cannot afford to remain unemployed and will always manage to find jobs at lower wage rates. Work and income-sharing mechanisms helped them to cope with the adversities of the current economic crisis. The revisionist stance is bolstered by hints that falling wage rates may actually have created more work in the urban and rural informal sectors, including agriculture, than was lost.[2] These commentators share the conclusion that the rise in unemployment and in the incidence of absolute poverty has been much smaller than was anticipated at the outbreak of krismon. Assuming a poverty level of not more than 11% in May 1997, Suryahadi and Sumarto (1999:11) calculated that poverty rose to 18% by August 1998, but by December had already fallen back to slightly above 15%. Such messages of hope and relief are often substantiated by the argument that absolute deprivation had diminished so rapidly in the preceding years that even the workforce at the bottom of the economy was able to build up sufficient reserves to deal with the crisis.

My opinion differs on almost all of these scores. For a start, official statistics on economic growth and equity prior to mid-1997 were biased by political correctness, the result of collusion between the government of Indonesia and leading international agencies, which underestimated the magnitude and intensity of the poverty that still existed throughout the country. I would agree with a recent statement that a quarter of the population of Indonesia was unable to meet basic needs even before the crisis (Dhanani and Islam 2000:21). Secondly, *krismon* has caused not only much more misery and loss of employment but has further widened the divide between the poor, whose numbers have rapidly swollen, and the non-poor. Thirdly, the coping mechanisms with which people who have sunk below the poverty level can deal with life's vicissitudes highly exaggerated. Fourthly, notwithstanding some signs of improvement in terms of employment and poverty levels, in mid-2000 *krismon* is by no means over.

2 Jellinek and Rustanto 1999:29-30; Poppele, Sumarto and Pritchett 1999:18; Manning 2000: 125-6.

What has been the impact of the economic crisis on work and welfare in rural Java? This is the theme elaborated upon in Sections II and III of our monograph. Two villages have been selected with which both authors were already familiar on the basis of earlier research carried out by them in these two localities. North Subang and East Cirebon, the names given to their recurrent fieldwork sites, are situated in the coastal plain of West Java. As an introduction to these micro-level studies, which are presented in a longitudinal perspective, I shall first discuss our main findings in the context of the changes which became manifest in the rural economy of Java towards the end of the twentieth century.

Work and welfare during the last phase of the New Order regime

In the last decade of the twentieth century the significance to the rural economy of agriculture as a source of income and employment declined further, a trend which coincided with neglect in government policies of what had always been the prime sector. In this respect, Booth's comments are pertinent:

> 'Since 1987, the manufacturing and modern service sectors have been the principal engines of growth in the Indonesian economy; the agricultural sector has been relegated to a secondary role in policy debates, and receives a falling share of budgetary resources' (Booth 2000a:89).

Since the green revolution in the early 1970s, agriculture has experienced no new breakthrough in rice cultivation which might have resulted in higher yields per hectare. Although demographic growth has slowed down considerably, the high pressure on land has made it necessary for increasing numbers of rural dwellers to slacken their ties with agriculture. Moreover, a first phase of light mechanization and the use of insecticides and pesticides have greatly reduced the quantity of labour required in field operations. With activities concentrated around the beginning and end of the crop cycle, work in agriculture became even more unevenly spread. More than eight out of every ten households in the two villages own no cultivable land at all, and access to agrarian capital through tenancy or sharecropping arrangements is also severely restricted. In East Cirebon agro-industry, in collusion with the local administration, continues to lay claim to a large part of the total acreage for sugarcane cultivation, providing yet another reason for the reduced demand for agricultural labour among households that are still in business as cultivating producers. Under the so-called *ceblokan* system, the management of agro-industry engages in contracts with landless households which accept responsibility, without pay, for pre-harvest tasks in paddy cultivation (especially transplanting) in exchange for one-fifth of the harvest yield.

In contrast to this closed field system in East Cirebon, customary practice in North Subang is different. The open field system is an arrangement under which cultivators are obliged to allow access to all labourers, whether local or not, who want to take part in cutting and threshing the rice crop. The harvest wage is paid in kind, the *bawon*, a share amounting to one-tenth of the yield. For all other operations throughout the plant cycle tillers of the land hire labour as and when necessary, for cash payment. While real wages in agriculture stagnated in the 1980s, they tended to grow moderately in subsequent years (Manning 2000:113-4). There is no doubt whatsoever that this upward swing was driven by the strong demand for labour outside agriculture during the booming years of the New Order.

To all practical purposes, employment opportunities in other sectors of the economy implied migration from the village. Only in East Cirebon did brick manufacture, organized in small-scale enterprises, provide full-time work for an increasing number of land-poor and landless households. This labour-intensive industry prospered because of better housing conditions in most rural settlements, a reflection of the decrease in poverty combined with an insistence on urban-style comforts which circular migrants brought back to the village after their exposure to city life. Brick, tiles and glass, together with a cemented or even tiled floor, replaced bamboo, wood and thatch as building materials. Work in the brickfields is arduous and requires the involvement of all household members, that is, husband, wife as well as half-grown children, and even then the wage rate is extremely low. The standard labour arrangement is a *kontrak*, a sum of money paid in advance which then has to be worked off by the production team. Labour power, in other words, is sold in a modality of debt bondage. As a form of petty commodity production the owners of the brickworks appropriate the benefits out of all proportion.

Apart from a modest range of trade, crafts and services, no economic ventures have emerged in either village capable of absorbing the growing workforce that could not be accommodated in agriculture. The only alternative was to move out and join the army of migrants heading for Jabotabek. Indeed, in both East Cirebon and North Subang half or more of the household budget of the land-poor and landless was provided by earnings realized from work outside the village. The labour force drained away from the local economy, used to being kept in a state of perpetual mobility, thrown out and then pushed back again because of employment modalities at the point of destination. Not more than one-quarter depended on self-employment, usually in petty trade and services, the other three-quarters were engaged in waged work, predominantly in the construction industry, but casual in nature and with constant changes of site as well as of employer. Only a handful managed to penetrate into the formal sector of the urban economy, achieving more permanent and better-paid jobs with regular hours of work in private enterprise or public establishments. The majority lacked the higher schooling and social contacts needed to enter such privileged zones of the metropolitan labour market. Women were a small minority among the migrant workforce, in most cases engaged as domestic servants or as waitresses in *warung*. Young males predominated in the trek to the city. Beyond the age of forty or so, migrants opted out and resettled in their place of origin, not only because they found the monthly-to-two-monthly rhythm of toing and fro-ing too strenuous, but also because employers or their agents preferred to hire young adults with greater physical stamina. It rarely happened that workers moved on to other branches of activity, while upward mobility in the same branch of employment was also quite limited. Newcomers who started as *kenek*, helpers, in the building industry learned skills from their workmates, often relatives, and might eventually be taken on as *tukang*, craftsman. Others, however, remained navvies for as long as they worked outside the village, that is, fifteen to twenty years at maximum. The best-paid job was that of *mandur*, the middleman who recruited and supervised the members of his gang for the duration of the *proyek*. The circulators not only found employment on far more days than if they had stayed on in the village but also earned higher wages. Out of these earnings, however, they had to pay travel costs back and forth every few weeks, while daily life in the city was far more expensive than in the hinterland. When they visited their village the workers brought back what was left of the wages received for the preceding weeks, and the households to which they belonged had to depend, mainly or even exclusively, on those savings for their livelihood. On reaching home the migrants first settled the outstanding debts with shopkeepers and moneylenders. Usually, all money had been spent when they left again a few days later. A high rate of interest was charged on loans extended to finance lifecycle events or durable consumer goods. In other words, a state of indebtedness was for all those years a common feature within the workforce, which had to remain constantly on the move in order to make ends meet.

In the shifting emphasis from local to outside employment female labour has steadily been marginalized. Agricultural work has, to a large extent, lost its gendered balance. Women's participation in paddy cultivation is nowadays restricted to transplanting and helping in the harvest. The brick industry in East Cirebon would not be able to operate without the involvement of wives and daughters of brick-moulders, but other than that there is little scope for women to earn an income in the village, particularly those who belong to land-poor and landless households that lack the capital required for petty trade. Their expulsion from agriculture has only slightly been compensated by a new demand for their labour power in Jabotabek. Several young women from our fieldwork villages have agreed to work as domestic servants, waitresses or prostitutes, but their numbers are quite low. A recent option is to go to Saudi Arabia, and more lately also to Malaysia, to be employed as domestic maids on two-year contracts. These young women have to work extremely hard and, far away from home, are ill prepared for the ordeal they have to face, which may include sexual abuse. Heavy deductions from their wages are made by the recruitment agencies responsible for their emigration. Nevertheless, in their opinion, the handsome amounts they send or bring back home amply outweigh the low esteem in which such type of employment is held, mainly resorted to by female members of low-income families.

For more and more inhabitants of East Cirebon and North Subang work outside agriculture and away from the village has thus become of increasing significance in providing a livelihood. Their circulatory trek to Jabotabek has brought them higher incomes than they would otherwise have been able to earn. Manning has rightly pointed out that, during the decade before the economic crisis, real wages rose rapidly in all non-agricultural sectors and more moderately in agriculture (Manning 2000:113-4). Consequently, policy-makers started to worry that the upward trend in minimum wages might have a negative impact on job generation. The World Bank warned that 'caution must be exercised in raising them further for fear of eroding competitiveness, lowering employment growth and paradoxically of increasing poverty and labour unrest' (World Bank 1996). The size of the population below the official poverty line is, accordingly, reported to have fallen sharply. Is that really so? The rapid growth experienced between 1987 and 1996 certainly helped to improve the material conditions of those workers who were stuck in the bottom ranks of the economy; at the same time the decline in numbers living in poverty slowed down, especially in rural areas (Booth 2000a:86).

The impression that deprivation had become a residual problem found in rather remote pockets of the archipelago, which essentially persisted because these backward parts happened to be beyond the reach of government programmes, was in line with the late-colonial myth that suggested that poverty was closely bound to so-called 'minus areas'. In contrast to such geo-ecological exceptionalism, I would posit that poverty has remained widespread in Suharto's Indonesia, including rural Java. Without a shadow of doubt, the land-poor and landless have managed to dignify their lifestyle and these gains were reflected in a better quality of housing and the possession of consumer durables. However, the existence of working-class households has always remained precarious. The dynamic ratio between productive and non-productive members has made all the difference between living slightly above or below the poverty line. A category of ultra-poor could be identified even before *krismon* began to make its impact. These were the people who had no labour power or were unable to use it fully: the old, the physically or mentally handicapped, and widowed or divorced female heads of households in charge of young children. The New Order regime kept a great deal of misery carefully hidden behind its propaganda statistics. The incidence of poverty was also understated in the reports of the World Bank and other international agencies.

Major segments of the working classes living close to or in a state of poverty have shared only marginally in the benefits of economic growth. The gap that already existed between the elite and the subaltern classes in East Cirebon and North Subang at the time of my prior fieldwork in 1989 and 1990, has since widened further. Contrary to the cherished policy view of rural society on Java as a communal-oriented social order based on patronage and reciprocity between strong and weak, our perception of the processes at work is that polarization and exclusion should be emphasized. The growing inequality in the late 1980s and early 1990s has been acknowledged insofar as widening rural-urban disparities are concerned (Booth 2000a:89). Nevertheless, the fallacy continues that the striking divide between rich and poor is mainly due to the concentration of wealth in the primary cities.

Similar stark contrasts in levels of welfare, however, can be found within the countryside. More noticeable than the reduction of deprivation in the land-poor and landless milieu is the newly gained wealth of the rural elite. That affluence is expressed in the conspicuous lifestyle of a fairly small cluster of notable households among whom most of the village's capital assets, both agrarian and non-agrarian, are concentrated. Little light has been shed on the size and identity of the *orang kaya baru*, a privileged social formation owing the elevation of its members to their role as local agents of the New Order regime, which has consistently opted for a 'betting on the strong' development policy. In an essay based on his fieldwork in a West Javanese village, Antlöv has highlighted the features and functions of this intermediate class between the state and the people. His observations fit into a more general pattern.[3] This set of local notables has been an important instrument in the control of law and order over 'the floating masses'. Their subordinated loyalty to higher powers has guaranteed that organized resistance from below could not erupt and that even the paltry weapons of the weak could be pre-empted by close supervision and the registration of all acts of defiance

3 'Through a strategy of "civilian patronage" the Indonesian government has recruited nearly all local notables and leaders into state functions [...]. These leaders-cum-state-clients are expected to be loyal to the government and to promote extension programmes and state directives faithfully. In exchange, they get privileged access to credit schemes and government programmes, and the ideological support of the higher authorities in their search for increased wealth and power.' (Antlöv 1999:191.)

or disobedience. The old colonial myth of 'village elders' who acted as representatives of people with no voice of their own, the *massa bodoh*, became a lever by which a base of legitimacy was created for the exploitation and suppression of subaltern classes in the countryside. Progressive landlessness in the recent past was not merely a consequence of ever-increasing demographic pressure on agrarian resources, but also of the fact that the large majority of households in North Subang and East Cirebon were excluded from cultivating land. The Basic Agrarian Law introduced in 1960 was never implemented. In fact, this effort to ensure the more equal distribution of land by imposing a ceiling on ownership became a bone of contention which ended in the military takeover of 1965.

It is against this background of a progressive divide between rural rich and rural poor that we need to understand the impact on village Java of the economic crisis which started a few years before the end of the last century.

Krismon in the village

After the crisis broke out most circular migrants from North Subang or East Cirebon started to come back from Jabotabek. In the last months of 1997 those who returned were mainly construction labourers laid off instantly because work had suddenly come to a halt. Many did not even receive their final pay. Subsequently, the price explosion in early 1998 caused many, although not all, of the self-employed petty traders to return home because their daily sales and profit margins had fallen below the critical level. Additionally, the intermittent street riots that broke out in the cities at the end of the New Order regime scared them away. Rather less than half of this mobile workforce tried desperately to hang on to whatever they were doing in the urban economy. They continued to pay their recurrent visits to the village and stayed perhaps a little bit longer, but were nevertheless anxious to go back to Jabotabek in order to keep in touch with their shrinking occupational niches. Among the minority who had managed to find semi-permanent work in the lower echelons of the formal sector in the metropolis some were dismissed forthwith, usually without any severance pay, while the few who were able to prolong their employment had to accept fewer hours of work or lower wages. In view of the persistent contention that the urban middle class bore the brunt of the crisis and that their lifestyle was impaired more than that of any other class, it is noteworthy that out of all the migrants who were forced back to the village not a single one had been employed as a domestic servant. Prostitutes, however, were among the repatriates.

What employment opportunities were available for workers who were pushed back into the rural economy? Hardly any. As it turned out, agriculture was not directly affected by *krismon*. In the wake of the enormous hike in rice prices that consumers were made to pay from early 1998 onwards, farmers received a much higher floor price, on average twice the amount per quintal which they had received for their last harvest. In terms of the net result, however, they came out no more than even at best since the cost of inputs increased by 300% for fertilizer and by 700% for pesticides (for similar observations, see Hardjono 1999:3 and Ahmed and Dhanani 1999:26).

Could the workforce expelled from the urban economy be re-absorbed into agricultural production? Over the years cultivation has, if anything, become less labour-intensive. Members of the large majority of land-poor and landless households were progressively pushed off to other economic sectors, usually outside the village. In many cases they combined such off-farm activity with ongoing participation in field operations at the peak of the agricultural cycle, particularly harvesting. Staying on in the village for the time being implies that their urban income has largely or fully ceased, but it does not mean that these erstwhile migrants have found significant employment in agricultural production. From occupational multiplicity their economic status has changed, not into a purely agrarian one, but into part-time unemployment. The idea that workers who have repatriated to the countryside can be reinserted into agriculture seems to overlook, in the first place, the simple fact that they initially constituted a redundant part of the rural labour force, thrown out of the prime economic sector because of lack of sufficient income opportunities in tilling the land. In the second place, it is misleading to assume that all ex-migrants were either willing or able to reduce their vulnerability by engaging in agricultural work. In only a few instances did we find that repatriates managed to get access to land as self-cultivating producers, that is, as owners, tenants or sharecroppers. We have already made it clear that most men and women who took up employment outside the village were members of landless households when they became circular migrants. Not all of them opted to seek occasional employment as agricultural labourers on their return home. The younger generation in particular, although born and bred in the village, claimed to have no knowledge of field operations, or even said openly that they found such work demeaning. A more important reason than lack of familiarity was the farmers' preference for what they called 'genuine' agricultural labourers with whom they were accustomed to work, and who had gone to Jabotabek only in the slack season, if at all. The closed field system practised in East Cirebon caused ex-migrants, who were ready to accept whatever they could find, to be excluded from harvest work.

Could workers who had become obsolete elsewhere turn to non-agrarian sources of income in the village economy? Again, such niches were few and far between or, to the extent they had existed, were also forced to shed labour due to the economic crisis. In East Cirebon, a fall in demand forced the formerly booming brick industry to reduce production. Several small owners had to close their works because they were unable to mobilize the necessary capital to remain in business. Under such circumstances it was nigh impossible for returned construction workers to find employment as brick-makers, partly due to their lack of technical as well as mental aptitude. Brick manufacture is teamwork, involving the labour power of the wife and one or more children. The quite different employment modality to which the ex-migrants were accustomed, almost all males, made them inclined to eschew such work as not gensi, or below their dignity. At best they allowed themselves to be hired as casual hands for carrying bricks from the oven to the roadside, or as members of small transport gangs accompanying trucks as loaders-unloaders and scouring the countryside for paddy husk to be used in large quantities in the burning process.

Otherwise, transport did not provide an outlet for the redundant workforce. Pedicabs have increasingly been replaced by *angkot*, small vans that carry passengers more quickly and more cheaply from the village to the neighbouring market town. Young men who own motor cycles ferry passengers on their back seats, but lack of customers and fierce competition cause *ojek* operators to remain inactive for the best part of the day; they usually hang out together at various meeting places. Petty trade is another occupational niche of the last resort, but newcomers who have become jobless find it difficult to start up any business without at least a small amount of capital. Exceptions are squalid trades such as collecting waste, that is, old paper, plastic sheets, used bottles and tins, and the buying and selling of second-hand goods.

Local services and tradesmen operating from fixed sites have dwindled, an effect of the loss of income earned outside the village. Many *warung*, the smaller in particular, have closed because of lack and loss of capital. The clientele were accustomed to buy on tick *(bon)* and would settle their debts whenever the men came home from Jabotabek. Owners of big *toko* also tried to cut down on credit and refused further sales when the debt rose above a hundred thousand rupiah. This was already much more than small shopkeepers could afford, and those who were still in business reduced both their stock and their profit margin. At the worst of the crisis they stopped selling rice in order to avoid having to supply this most common daily consumption commodity without cash payment.

In North Subang, many households have managed, at least partly, to compensate the consequences of unemployment and impoverishment by sending young female relatives to work as domestic servants in Saudi Arabia or Malaysia. By August 2000, female emigrants contracted as *tkw (tenaga karya wanita)* for a two-year period numbered nearly sixty. The sharp fall in the exchange rate of the rupiah has made working as a maidservant far away from home a very attractive option. These women remit or bring back with them sizeable amounts of money, up to twenty-five million rupiah, although considerably less if they had to take out loans to pay for the cost of recruitment. In low-income households, most of such savings are spent on daily necessities; those who were already better-off before their departure build new houses, buy ornaments and other high-expense consumer durables, and are also able to budget more productively, for example by renting in land. In several cases these married or unmarried women have become their family's main breadwinners, and soon after their return home leave again for a second or even third time. The stigma that used to be attached to domestic service is still there, but apparently does not apply to foreign destinations. This change in view is reflected in the growing numbers of women from well-to-do families who are willing to be recruited. On the other hand, low-class households these days have difficulty in borrowing the increasing sum of money required to go abroad. There is little open discussion of the negative side of sending young females away from home to employers with whom they find it difficult to communicate and who make them work for very long hours in a milieu of subordination. The more ugly consequences are there for everyone to see: divorce in the case of married women, babies and children growing up without the care of their mother, and the not infrequent instances of return before the end of the contract because of rape or other forms of abuse.

When the crisis deepened in North Subang and East Cirebon the sliding scale between employment and unemployment was of striking importance. The idea that unemployment is a phenomenon to be found only in the formal sector of the economy is misleading, held by economists who do not fully comprehend the intricacies of informal sector work modalities on the basis of knowledge gained by observation from close quarters. Conventionally, the cutting edge of the distinction is softened by referring to underemployment. And indeed, this was precisely the predicament in which we found a very large part of the male and female workforce in our fieldwork villages at the height of *krismon*. In July 1998, 40% of all heads of households in both localities had not been involved in gainful work 'today' and roughly the same applied to 'yesterday'. 'Gainful' was understood as including work that lasted for more than one hour, also when no cash wages were paid but only allowances in kind, such as meals in return for tasks done on behalf of employers or relatives and neighbours. Even on these two consecutive days, the pattern of economic activity among respondents showed remarkable fluctuations, so much so that to collect data based on a longer recall period would have resulted in information of questionable validity. There were also the somewhat older men, most of them ex-migrants accustomed to working as casual labour in the construction industry of metropolitan Jakarta, whom we have included without hesitation among the openly unemployed. They said that they were quite willing to return to their earlier work sites and that, in or around the village, there was nothing for them to do. 'Waiting at home', was how they summed up their current work status. In contrast to the fatigue shown by middle-aged workers among the tribe of circular migrants, the younger generation refused to give up hope and continued to search for work at some distance from the locality. Lacking any better alternative, their desperate sorties did not seem to discourage them from continually trying to land a job, however short it might last.

On my return in August 2000 for a final trip to the fieldwork sites in West Java, good news awaited me in Jakarta. On my usual round along the offices of international and national agencies dealing with the economic crisis, I was invariably reassured that the worst was definitely over and that recovery had already set in over a year earlier. Indeed, petty traders from North Subang were back on the streets of Jakarta and the surrounding satellite towns, selling their *goreng* (fried cassava and plantains). They complained, however, that daily transactions were much fewer than before *krismon*, and that they could peddle their wares at prices only slightly higher than those of the cost of the ingredients. As a result, the amount that they take back to the village every few weeks is far below the level of their earlier savings. In East Cirebon the brick industry has also picked up, stimulated by the building of houses paid for with the money that young women have earned abroad. A little construction activity, mainly repair work, is again going on in Jabotabek. However, contractors and *mandur* (bosses of labour gangs), still vainly wait to complete the big projects that were often left in an unfinished state on the outbreak of the crisis. What we found in East Cirebon seems to be a standard pattern: young men going on short expeditions to Jakarta. Bus conductors on the journey to the city know that their customers are short of cash and charge less fare for going than for coming back. On arrival, the migrants find accommodation in one of the many hostels adjacent to the sites of possible employment. The sleeping place is free and the *pondok* owner provides food on credit until the workers manage to sell their labour power for a couple of days or weeks. When the waiting time between these petty jobs becomes too long, the migrants have to leave with hardly any money to pay the fare back home.

On the basis of these empirical findings, I conclude that the flexibility that many economists proclaim to be such a remarkable feature of Indonesian labour markets is much exaggerated (Manning 2000:106, 121). The simple truth is that many people have not been able to find new jobs since being thrown out of waged work, either in the formal or informal sector of the economy. There are some signs that circular migration along the arteries from Java's hinterland to the main cities and surrounding zones is starting anew, but the trek will remain below par for a long time to come. In my opinion, the pattern of long-distance work migration at present, that is, the end of summer 2000, more than ever reflects a serious lack of gainful employment at rural points of departure rather than that it indicates a rising demand for labour at urban points of destination. Many industrial establishments in Jabotabek's formal sector are still in shambles, and the concomitant spill over is a low level of activity in the manufacturing, trading and servicing sectors of the informal economy as well.

Impoverishment

In addition to the loss of employment the real wages of the working class collapsed by a huge 40%. This downward spiral occurred in all sectors, even more harshly in the informal than in the formal economy. It has correctly been pointed out that the collapse was less severe when wages continued to be paid partly or wholly in kind, as for instance in agriculture during harvest time. Nevertheless, according to Papanek and Handoko (1999:4), real wages for agricultural labour fell by 40% all over Java between June 1997 and September 1998. Although a slight recovery occurred in subsequent months, these authors conclude that in the first quarter of 1999 the real wage level in agriculture was lower than it had ever been since 1976. In their calculations, the fall during the crisis in real income for workers engaged in bricks and tiles was even bigger, 43%. For the brick-making men, women and children in East Cirebon it cannot have been less. While there is no doubt that the loss of jobs has been of overriding significance for construction workers, real wages in this industry show the same dynamics as in other trades, that is, a massive fall. Nominal daily pay indeed rose on average by 15 to 20%, but the waves of inflation in 1998 in particular meant that that rise could not even begin to match the rapid decline in money value. Irrespective of the subsequent reduction in the rate of inflation, in mid-1999 the real earnings of workers in industry and agriculture and all other economic sectors may still have been 40% lower than the pre-*krismon* level two years earlier (Ahmed and Dhanani 1999:22).

My estimate is, that between mid-1997 and mid-1999, the gross local product contracted by roughly one-quarter in East Cirebon and by rather less than one-sixth in North Subang, where the negative impact of the economic crisis was moderated by the inflow of remittances from female workers overseas. Loss of employment, in combination with the decrease in real income, led to a sharp fall in living standards. The purchasing power of households with few if any capital assets decreased very sharply. People were aghast when, as a result of the policy decision imposed by the IMF and the World Bank that the subsidy on consumer rice should be eliminated, the cost of this staple exploded. The shop price per kilogram of 800-900 rupiah in June 1997 shot up to two thousand five hundred rupiah and, for a short time in late 1998, rose to even more than three thousand five hundred rupiah. Since that peak, the price has stabilized between two thousand one hundred and two thousand two hundred rupiah per kilogram *beras*, but that is still two-and-a-half times higher than before *krismon*. The provision of cheap food had been an inevitable concomitant of the extremely low wage rate for a very large part of the labour force. Apparently, nobody had bothered to think how the living standard of working-class households was going to be affected by the price explosion for basic needs.

In our fieldwork villages we witnessed what several other commentators have also noted, namely, that the cost of food consumption rose more rapidly than that of non-food consumption. This basically meant that the poor were harder hit by the runaway inflation in 1998 than the non-poor. People with the smallest budgets saw their food expenditure increase to over two-thirds to three-quarters of their total monthly income. Frequently, such households had no money left for anything but rice. Even then, they could not afford to buy the same quantity as before. The idea that rural dwellers live in an environment where food is produced does not make adequate allowance for the plain fact that the village economy is thoroughly monetized. Most economic transactions among inhabitants are in cash only. Certainly, agricultural wages at harvest time are settled in kind, and on days of employment artisans as well as various service specialists usually receive prerequisites such as meals, drinks and cigarettes, in addition to their cash remuneration. This does not detract from stating the fact that, for the better part of the year, most people in North Subang buy their food requirements (including rice) in the local shops; in East Cirebon this even applies to nine out of ten households (see also Hardjono 1999:25). The crisis does not seem to have led to de-monetization, as happened during the economic recession in the late-colonial era.[4]

The economic recession has had a differential impact on social classes among the village population. This contradicts the World Bank's argument that, al-

[4] 'One of the most interesting temporary changes to be observed during the 1930s was that monetization, a long-term process that by 1929 had reached a rather high level, was all of a sudden reversed. Barter took the place of selling and buying for cash, wages were no longer paid in cash but in kind, or mutual help took the place of wage-labour.' (Boomgaard 1999:7.)

though poverty and living standards have been adversely affected, the impact on distribution may well have been positive. Estimates published early in 2000 suggest that the Gini coefficient fell slightly between 1996 and 1998 (World Bank 2000:Table 6.2, quoted in Booth 2000b:13). Several commentators suggested that *krismon* had an equalizing effect on people in various walks of life. In these representations of the popular mood emphasis was laid on the crisis as a shared experience, strengthening rather than weakening cohesion in society (Jellinek and Rustanto 1999). Again, this was not our finding in either North Subang or East Cirebon. While the fruits of economic growth were mainly digested by affluent households in the two villages during the years preceding *krismon*, the brunt of the current malaise is borne out of all proportion by the far more numerous households in the lower echelons of the local economy. The net outcome has been a further impetus to the already wide income disparities existing between top and bottom. Booth presents nationwide figures for 1998 showing that upper-income households in urban society had a disposable income per capita over nine times that of the poorest in rural society, that is, farm labourers. She adds that, in view of the higher incidence of inflation on lower income budgets, the gap could well have been greater (Booth 2000b:13). Investigating rural households between April and May 1999 in a corridor close to our own fieldwork villages along the northern coastal plain of West Java, Hardjono found that people at the top of the income scale were seven times better off than those at the bottom (Hardjono 1999:15). In North Subang and East Cirebon rich families appear to have increased their distance from the poor. The average ratio separating the least and most prosperous deciles, a magnitude of 1:7 in 1989-1990, rose to more than 1:10 in 1998.

Has the employment squeeze induced by *krismon* led to increasing competition among job-seekers or, conversely, to a division of work and earnings in line with the notion of shared poverty once so popular among colonial policy-makers? At the end of the twentieth century the village in Java can less than ever before be characterized as a homogeneous peasant community (Breman 1980). Although circular migrants have never renounced their rural identity, the social fabric within the local community is both looser and more contractual than previously, due to the strong external orientation of the younger generation among the inhabitants. Petty traders and construction workers who went away to Jabotabek returned to the village once monthly or so, but kept a low profile outside the domain of their own household. They played little part in the cycle of rituals and festivities or institutionalized arrangements such as prayer meetings, which give meaning and articulation to the collective dimensions of a locality.

The absence of a communitarian ethos is emphasized by class lines that divide households according to their level of welfare. Such socio-economic boundaries, of which housing quality and the possession of durable commodities providing material comfort are good indicators, have become sharper and more visible. These demarcations expressing modernity owe their weight to new lifestyles shaped by consumption patterns that originate in the urban milieu. As *krismon* deepened it became clear that many more inhabitants of North Subang and East Cirebon had sunk below the poverty level. Was their immiserization alleviated by cash or transfers in kind from the more well-to-do households? Such social security arrangements, said to have been characteristic institutions of rural Java in the colonial era, are nowhere in sight. Their disappearance is certainly not a recent phenomenon. Hayami and Kikuchi (1981:207), who included North Subang among their sites of investigation in various parts of Southeast Asia at the end of the 1970s, maintained that the poor and the rich in the *kampung* shared equally in the gains of the green revolution which raised production and productivity per land unit. Neither Pincus nor I were able to confirm that conclusion in our successive researches in the same locality (Breman 1995; Pincus 1996). We both concluded that the trend was not only towards increasing inequality, but also that relations between the few landowning and the many landless households could not be expressed in the patron-clientele paradigm which, at least in the minds of the two Japanese economists, was still the organizing principle on which the political economy of rural Java rested. In fact, our predecessors in these village-based investigations drew attention to the lack of mutual help and insurance systems along vertical lines. If anything, the social and economic bonds connecting the better-off segment of the population with the impoverished households at the bottom of the village economy have since become shallower in substance and duration. The *orang kaya baru* have decided to liberate themselves from all sorts of 'traditional'obligations which stressed norms of reciprocity. They do not seem to consider the deprivation around them, which is in such sharp contrast to their own well being, as an unfortunate and intolerable human condition to which they were morally obliged to respond with support and protection.

The prolonged and recurring absences from the locality of many workers belonging to low-income households must forestall any possible claims to share in whatever is left of the common good in the dire times that have now reappeared. Antlöv (1999:198) has recently argued that a moral community based on intimacy and social order still lingers somehow in his West Javanese fieldwork village. He concedes, however, that to the extent it still exists, this distributive ideology comes close to a mere façade behind which assertions of equality are essentially rejected.

Do the well-off in North Subang and East Cirebon also suffer from the economic crisis? Although our informants in the elite milieu emphatically insist that they are affected much more than the poor, we find it difficult to accept the veracity of such statements. There are no indications of any remarkable changes in their lifestyle. Members of better-off households complain in the same way as the less privileged about the price explosion, but do not seem to have cut down on their daily expenditure. The quantity and quality of their food intake is the same as it used to be, and they do not economize on non-essentials such as snacks, soft drinks, cigarettes, cosmetics, clothing and the like. We did not come across instances where they have been obliged to dispose of consumer durables because of acute distress. If some have sold ornaments, it was because the rising price of gold made it attractive for them to cash in on earlier investments. It is difficult to perceive whether or not the value of their property has kept up with the depreciation of the rupiah. Respondents among elite households showed anxiety about the career prospects of their educated children, however, and were concerned lest sons in particular should not find employment appropriate to their level of schooling. Nonetheless, they did not impress us as being unduly worried about declining living standards for themselves or their offspring, let alone about any eventual drop into the ranks of the poor.

Have the impoverished households no social capital at all that they can mobilize in case of acute need? They are certainly not without a modicum of support, but the networks in which they operate usually have a smaller reach than those of the well-to-do and, moreover, run mainly along horizontal rather than vertical lines. The safety net surrounding the poor consists predominantly of relatives, friends and neighbours. Kinship ties in particular are an important channel for redistributing whatever income and employment can be pooled between or even within households. The problem, however, is that poor people tend to be related to kinsmen who are equally deprived, implying that the capability for sharing the meagre resources at the bottom of the local economy is quite limited.

Manning is one of those mainstream economists who seem eager to give a positive interpretation to what they are apt to call the 'crowding' of labour in the informal sector of the economy. In describing this phenomenon in his various reports on the social impact of *krismon*, he emphasizes 'flexible employment and income-sharing arrangements' (Manning 2000:131). This jargon is meant to convey a kind of solidarity among those who are the principal victims of the economic crisis, that is, all those who have lost their employment, wholly or partly, and with it their major source of livelihood. The implied notion of solidarity is even stronger when explicit references are made to the culture of 'shared poverty', a state of mind that is supposed to have been a prominent feature of the Javanese peasantry, portrayed as a rather undifferentiated lot, during as well as after colonial times. I would add the rider that this cultural norm does not claim that those who are vulnerable have, for that very reason, a prior right to support. The basic assumption of 'shared poverty' is one of homogeneity and, in that context, the need to divide the spoils evenly.

Can the economic behaviour of the working poor in North Subang and East Cirebon at the outbreak of *krismon* indeed be understood in this stylized manner? Paramount to the idea of such a strongly sanctioned code of conduct that is accepted by all and which acknowledges that everyone, in supreme disregard of the ever-growing number of people seeking to be accommodated, should be given equal access to the scarce quantity of available resources is, of course, the absolute prevalence of a normative willingness to share. Such a situation is not a feature of social life in our fieldwork villages. Firstly, there is no legitimate way by which the non-poor can be held accountable for their refusal to come to the aid of the underprivileged majority living in the same locality. Secondly, in the milieu of the poor any sign of at least a horizontal type of solidarity is also non-existent. At the height of the crisis, when work and income were extremely difficult to find, people were indeed in daily competition for the few available jobs which could in no way accommodate all those who sought employment. For example, elderly men were made to understand that they should not join gangs waiting to load and unload trucks; young men hastily grabbed hot bricks straight from the oven with their bare hands and carried them running to the roadside, thus trying to outdo their equally assertive competitors; finally, *becak* drivers fought a regular street war in East Cirebon to resist the intrusion of *angkot* into their domain.

Growing inequality

While most high-income households managed to adhere to their strategy of accumulation and a good number among the middle-income households faced severe problems in realizing their strategy of consolidation, those at the broadened base of the village economy had to rely on the strategy of sheer survival. In this last category, to which in mid-1998 the majority of inhabitants of North Subang and East Cirebon belonged, coping mechanisms were structured more or less in successive stages, from the moment the crisis broke out until the deepening of the shock when costs of daily necessities spiralled beyond the budget of most households.

In the first instance, of course, all savings that had been stored in one way or another were consumed, a drain which was soon completed. Simultaneously, the people cashed in on all possible sources of credit: shopkeepers, moneylenders, neighbours and friends. This option was also quickly exhausted.

The second phase was one of disaccumulation, that is, pawning or selling valuable goods. This was only possible to a limited extent since many poor households had always been living beyond their budget and had often purchased new or second-hand commodities on credit. Unless all instalments had been duly paid, such items had to be returned to the original seller or moneylender, usually without compensation. As was to be expected, ornaments such as earrings or bracelets were paramount on the list of disposable goods, and agents of the urban-based *toko mas* (gold shops) roamed the countryside collecting whatever gold was now for sale. Next went TV sets, radios and cassette players, but also furniture, crockery and clothes. Apart from consumer durables, means of production were also traded in for cash: bicycles and motorcycles, pedicabs and handcarts, a bascule or *pikul*. The saddest distress sale that we heard off concerned a toolbox. The former owner, a middle-aged carpenter, told us how he had struggled for many years to bring together its contents, a variety of tools which enabled him to raise the price of his labour power. The man realized that once the building industry started again in Jabotabek, he would have no alternative but to go as *kenek* and no longer as the skilled craftsman that he is.

Cutting down on food consumption was an early priority. Initially, this was restricted to doing away with *lauk pauk*, all that goes together with the main dish of rice. Subsequently, not only were proteins taken out but the quantity of staple consumed also lessened. Households with few working members reduced their meals from three to two, while people who had no productive power whatsoever, had to make do with one meal a day. The evidence from our fieldwork villages shows that the Minister for Food and Agriculture in no way exaggerated when, in autumn 1999 he went on record saying that 17.5 million families could still not afford to eat twice daily (Booth 2000b:19).

Living from hand-to-mouth caused the occasional avoidance or even open refusal of claims by old-aged parents, living apart, for the regular assistance that they formerly received from their children in cash or kind. It further meant that investments to improve and dignify the future quality of life had to be abandoned. This was the inevitable course of action to which the large majority of impoverished families were forced to resort. By not celebrating minor lifecycle events in their own household and by inviting fewer guests or, alternately, by not attending ceremonies and rituals held in the neighbourhood, people were able to minimize or avoid expenses they would otherwise have had to incur. To include such costs in the category of non-essentials, however, ignores the fact that the decision to refrain from such expenditure scales down the investment of social capital needed to keep intact networks through which economic resources are mobilized.

Economies in health costs were achieved by not seeing a doctor or paramedic at the primary health centre and by using palliatives instead of patent medicines in the attempt to remedy ailments. Serious diseases which could have been brought under control at an earlier stage, were aggravated due to the lack of timely professional aid. Hospital care was far beyond the reach of poor patients who were cut off from their usual sources of credit on which they would otherwise fall back in cases of emergency. As for education, early predictions that school-age children would drop out en masse did not materialize. At least, not at the primary school level. Although the official decree abolishing entrance fees for public schools was disregarded without discussion in North Subang and East Cirebon, parents tried to pay whatever they were charged. Over the year this represented quite a sizeable amount of money. Many families could ill afford to do it but, in one way or another, they persisted as far as elementary education was concerned. They were unable, however, to send their children to lower and then higher secondary school. At that stage parents were not only confronted with much steeper school fees and far more expensive school uniforms, but also had to bear the daily transportation cost to and from school. Barely literate, a very large part of the new generation faces a future in which the modest skills in which they have been formally instructed will only qualify them for the sort of low-paid work that has kept their parents in poverty for most of their lives.

Frustrated by being unable to provide the daily income required for even a minimal living standard, men have deserted their families, saying nothing of where they would be seeking employment or simply returning to their own birthplace. Young couples, whether on the basis of agreement or conflict, have broken up their households for the time being, each returning to their parental home.

Finally, *krismon* has helped to create insecurity in the sense of a threat to law and order. The food riots that broke out in the wake of the price explosion early in 1998 were an expression of popular discontent. The street violence, however, soon turned into attacks on shopkeepers of Chinese descent who dominated the pasar trade in small towns such as Pamanukan and Sindanglaut, the commercial centres for North Subang and East Cirebon respectively. The looting and burning of their shops were wanton acts which may well have been committed or instigated by elements close to, or even from within, the New Order regime. In retrospect, the downfall of that authoritarian rule was hastened as a result of these riots.

Once the legitimacy of the state had successfully been contested, criminality did not abate. Petty crime has become a problem even within the village. Thefts of bicycles, but also of chickens or goats and even of clothes hanging out to dry, show that such crimes are not always committed by outsiders who, anyway, are beyond the pale. Disgruntled at not being able to find suit-

Table 1. Classification of households in North Subang and East Cirebon according to welfare level, 1989-1990 and 1988-1999 (in % share)

	North Subang				East Cirebon			
	1990		1998-99		1989		1998-99	
Social class	of hh	in welfare	of hh	in welfare	of hh	in welfare	of hh	in welfare
high	18	55	14	58	17	45	13	50
middle	31	25	23	22	33	35	20	30
low	51	20	63	20	50	20	67	20
of which:								
nearly poor								
to poor	37	15	41	15	35	16	43	16
ultra poor	14	5	22	5	15	4	24	4

Note: The surveys on which the reported data are based were conducted during fieldwork in 1989 and 1990 by Breman, and in 1998-99 by Breman and Wiradi. The figures for the latter refer to all households (216) in North Subang and to nearly one-third of all households (hh) (179 out of 582) in East Cirebon. The main survey in both villages was carried out in July-August 1998; the findings were checked in March-April 1999 by revisiting half of all households in North Subang and half of the households included in the stratified random sample in East Cirebon.

able employment, young men take to drinking and other 'bad habits', which they finance by committing harvest thefts in nearby villages or by extorting money from people who travel by motorcycle or car along the highway. When caught in such pilfering, the more rowdy among them turn aggressive. Feelings of mutual distrust reflect the erosion of the cohesive forces that formerly held village inhabitants together in what appeared to be a common front. Local authorities now increasingly have to cope with the problem that the spirit of commonality which they keep trying to impose is no longer endorsed by the people.

The dynamics of welfare and poverty in North Subang and East Cirebon are summed up in a time perspective in Table 1. Deprivation is a relative term and, of course, has not remained constant over the years. The state of welfare and poverty enjoyed or suffered is not merely a matter of temporal perception that can be deconstructed by finding out how respondents reflect on their economic condition 'then' as compared to 'now', and vice versa. Experiences of changing levels of welfare relate equally if not more to the widening diversity in living standards among households within the same habitat.

Although prior to *krismon* the percentage of families in our fieldwork villages living below the poverty line was much higher than shown by official statistics, many more people sank into deprivation once the economic crisis started in mid-1997. Our findings are actually very similar to those reported by

Hardjono on the basis of her investigations in the same period, and carried out close to North Subang and East Cirebon. Her empirical research in a rural corridor along the northern coast of West Java, stretching from Purwakerta in the west to Cirebon in the east, show that in April-May 1999, out of a total of four hundred and fifty-five households, four-fifths had dropped below the level that she had fixed as the poverty line. They were unable to pool a monthly income of three hundred and fifty thousand rupiah, needed to satisfy the daily minimal requirements for five to six members per household on average (Hardjono 1999:15). In fixing the poverty line in our fieldwork villages during 1998-1999, we used the somewhat lower income of two hundred and fifty thousand to three hundred thousand rupiah per month, albeit for fewer members (an average per household of 3.4 in North Subang and 4.7 in East Cirebon). According to our calculations, around two-thirds of the inhabitants in our fieldwork villages were living in poverty. A uniform label for such a large majority would disregard the sharp divides that exist even among the lowest ranks in the countryside. To draw attention to those distinctions, I have introduced the under- class of ultra-poor, characterized by a condition in which they have hardly any means of production or none at all, and are also starved of access to any means of consumption. Their misery is intense and tolerates no cash expenditure other than on food. Such underprivileged individuals or families have always been present, consisting invariably of all those who had lost any former capability to work: men and/or women in old age, physically or mentally disabled, and female-headed households with small children. This category has been swollen by the recent influx of workers who can sell their labour power only occasionally instead of regularly, and even then, are paid wages that are barely sufficient for survival. Hardjono found in her survey that this extremely vulnerable segment accounts for not less than one-fifth of all households; my calculations show that the percentage of this residual category at the rural bottom is somewhat higher.

The data presented in Table 1 contradict reports suggesting that *krismon* has levelled out former disparities in income (Suryahadi et al. 2000:29-30).[5] I want to repeat, however, that from the start of the economic malaise, inequalities have increased rather than decreased. How, then should we interpret the hopeful news that since the beginning of 1999 the crisis, in the phrasing of economists, has bottomed out? No doubt some recovery has taken place in various branches of urban and rural economic activity: a turnaround for the

5 Some of the authors referred to in this book have managed, within a short space of time, to co-publish articles that express opposite views about rising or falling levels in income inequalities (see for example Suryahadi, Sumarto, Suharno and Pritchett, March 2000:29-30 and Skoufias, Suryahadi and Sumarto, August 2000:107-8). Such contradictory observations seem to illustrate the fluidity in the minds of researchers rather than the real life situation.

better which has somewhat reduced the incidence and intensity of poverty. Nevertheless, the conclusion that the worst is over and that for most people currently living in deprivation poverty is a transient phenomenon, needs to be qualified in several respects. Firstly, it is too early to suggest that the magnitude of poverty is in the process of falling back to pre-crisis levels. Secondly, job opportunities have not increased across all sectors, whether organized on formal or informal lines, but only in particular branches of economic trade and industry. The resumption of construction in Jabotabek, for instance, is still mainly limited to the building and maintenance of private housing. For the army of navvies waiting in the rural hinterland, employment prospects in August 2000, the latest round of our research, were almost as dismal as during the previous one-to-two years. Thirdly, although real wages have started to rise, they are still about 30% lower than before the crisis (see also Dhanani and Islam 2000:15). As has been pointed out, Indonesia has returned to a type of economy in which labour is superfluous to demand, a trend that is of major significance to the structure of the labour market (Feridhanusetyawan 1999:3). Fourthly, instead of frittering away time in the countryside or going on short trips to the metropolitan zones where jobs remain in scarce supply, the younger generation among the huge and growing rural reserve army desperately searches for better options. In North Subang in particular, youngsters have set their hopes on employment abroad. Malaysia is a much-preferred destination since that country can be reached without official and expensive permits. Increasing numbers of male workers risk travelling illegally, while most young women are recruited on legal two-year contracts. Applicants for factory jobs in Taiwan or Korea require a secondary school certificate, but there is another reason why boys and girls from lower-income classes cannot apply for such work contracts. Only well-to-do parents are willing and able to invest the money, 16 million rupiah in mid-2000, that has to be paid in recruitment cost prior to departure. It is a sad comment on the state of labour in Indonesia that workers without skills are considered for employment abroad simply because they can be fobbed off with lower wages than the workforce in most other parts of Asia.

Policy-makers who in the past have understated the magnitude of poverty for reasons of political convenience, seem inclined to continue to do so. After all, empirical studies that conclude that the majority of the rural population subsists below the poverty line could be seen as illustrative of the need to redistribute the resource base of the economy. In a rural context, that objective must inevitably include land reform. This was not how the New Order policy-makers wanted to address the poverty issue at all. Their successors – if indeed they are successors – talk more about increasing the productivity of the poor than about giving them access to the means of production that will enable them to do so.

Finally, the shock with which *krismon* made its impact felt towards the end of the twentieth century, should not allow us to overlook the fact that many people trapped in a survival strategy at the bottom layer of society in rural Java have been exposed to economic crises several times before, if not throughout their working days. '*Krismon*? I have known *krismon* all my life!', was the forthright reply when I questioned an old woman regarding the past and present state of her landless household.

The social safety net that failed

As the economic crisis took much longer to bring under control than had initially been expected, it had to be decided whether or not a state-sponsored system of social provisions should be introduced to provide even minimal cover for the increasing numbers falling below the poverty line. Initial reactions in policy circles were negative. A non-subsidized scheme had operated only in the formal sector of the economy, financed by compulsory contributions by employers and employees. Due to large-scale fraud practised for many years by the management of the Jamsostek (Worker Social Security) fund, many workers dismissed at the outbreak of the crisis received little if anything of the savings they had been compelled to make. This misfortune must have reconfirmed the dominant view that Indonesia sadly lacks both the economic wherewithal and the administrative transparency considered pre-conditional to sponsoring an all-inclusive state-backed programme of social welfare. Following these critical appraisals came the optimistic message that the countryside had no need of such schemes, since 'rural people have access to a greater range of coping strategies, including extensive family networks, subsistence farming and work in the informal sector' (Manning and Van Diermen 1999:144).

In opposition to those who argued that informal arrangements, to the extent that they existed, would be totally inadequate for helping the poor to deal with their loss of income and the rising prices of basic needs, other observers warned against doling out cost-free assistance. These and more dominant voices exhorted the Indonesian government and major international agencies not even to explore that option because, once introduced, it would be very difficult to discontinue public provisions to which people had become entitled. Proponents of economic policies favouring the unfettered interplay of free market forces even postulated that the informal sector had no need of welfare and social security programmes. Such interventions were said to be counterproductive, since they would destroy 'the dynamic mini-communal-capitalist systems currently being created by the people for themselves' (Jellinek and Rustanto 1999:2).

In their early 1999 report, based on a quick tour around urban and rural Java, these authors prescribed the good old medicine of reliance on hard work and individual initiative.[6] With such ideological notions playing a role in the background, the more sober policy assessment was that a comprehensive welfare packet for poverty alleviation might easily lead to mistargeting and misappropriation at all administrative levels of the huge amounts of funds that would have to be mobilized for the purpose. In the full awareness that such waste on a very large scale would be difficult to avoid, steps were nonetheless taken to set up a Social Safety Net Programme (Jaring Pengaman Sosial, JPS), with the economic and political objective of redressing the immediate threat to the livelihood of massive numbers of people. This was because the phenomenal price increases of all basic needs, triggered by the withdrawal of subsidies on consumer rice under strong pressure from international agencies, gave rise to alarming explosions of popular discontent in large cities and small towns throughout the country. The possibility of further food riots resulting in political turmoil that might become unmanageable, motivated the authorities to change their stance. They now started to persuade foreign donors to underwrite the cost of the 'return to social security' operation.

Ultimately, even the provision of ample loans by the IMF and the World Bank failed to shore up the dwindling legitimacy of the New Order regime. To maximize the inflow of 'donor dollars' there was an urgent need for fresh stocks of data that would reflect the escalating dimensions of the poverty problem. Their production was entrusted to the National Family Planning Coordinating Board (Badan Koordinasi Keluarga Berencana Nasional, BKKBN). Field staff at the sub district level supervised door-to-door investigations which classified all households into five categories, dependent on their state of welfare. In the course of our empirical research, we checked on the procedures for collecting and processing these data by local officials in the village and at the sub district level.

The number of households that had fallen below the poverty line rose abruptly and hugely in autumn 1998 because government needed to 'update' the figures in order to increase pressure for massive foreign loans. While earlier head counts had understated the magnitude of indigence, the new instructions were intended to maximize the number of people living in a state of acute deprivation. In both cases the statistical zeal was inspired by the political convenience of the moment. Just as Suharto, the father of devel-

6 The authors gave their populist language an undiluted social-Darwinist twist when they argued that 'the crisis has forced people together to overcome their poverty. Poverty, where the poor are lazy, incompetent, stupid, spendthrift, unable to think about the future and unable to organize, has been wiped away by the crisis. It has forced them to work together to overcome their difficulties.' (Jellinek and Rustanto 1999:33.)

opment *(bapak pembangunan)*, had produced 'wealth for all', statistics were now also delivered in accordance with the command-style of administration. The assumption was that no one would bother to look behind the Potemkin façade, whether past or present.

In unswerving adherence to the typical newspeak jargon of the New Order, in the Social Safety Net Programme the ultra-poor were identified as people in the 'pre-prosperity' stage. They were singled out to become exclusive beneficiaries of the Special Market Operation (Operasi Pasar Khusus, OPK), intended to improve the food security of this most vulnerable segment of the population. The distribution of cheap rice, at a thousand rupiah per kilo, did not proceed according to plan in our fieldwork villages. Monthly consignments were irregular, of bad quality in the beginning, and were divided unevenly among the various hamlets, with inhabitants residing in and around the centre received a much bigger ration than those living on the periphery. Of much greater significance than these shortcomings, however, was the immediate and downright refusal by most well-to-do households to agree that the cheap rice should be set aside for the poor in the village. They ensured that quota were evenly apportioned among all. This mode of 'fair and equal sharing' also failed, however, because several of our respondents in the pre-welfare category stated that they did not have the cash – ten thousand rupiah – in hand to buy their standard share of ten kilos. This was somewhat more than one dollar, or a full day's wage for an agricultural labourer. The rations to be distributed, fixed on paper at twenty kilos per month for targeted beneficiaries, never reached that amount and were subsequently cut further from ten to five kilos. In mid-2000 even that reduced quantity was no longer made available on a regular and timely basis.

Other components of the Social Safety Net Programme were also not specifically earmarked for the most underprivileged far below the poverty line, who were exposed to the impact of *krismon*. All that materialized under the heading of employment creation in North Subang and East Cirebon were some minor public work projects which invariably took the form of road improvements. Wages represented a mere 10% of the total budget; the biggest part of the outlay was spent on raw materials and 'overheads' or fees nominally paid for supervision to the local authorities and to their friends. To distribute employment evenly – and here, again, the non-poor insisted on their right to share – new gangs of workers were recruited each day, with the result that, in East Cirebon, the employment period averaged no more than three or four days. In North Subang, households had to contribute their labour power in rotation and as *gotong royong*, that is, without any wages at all. Only men could participate in these public work projects. Our suggestion that *padat karya* might also help to alleviate unemployment among female workers was not readily acknowledged by local officials with whom we discussed this issue. Their argument was that, in times of crisis, public works had always been male-based. They saw no reason to change that practice; moreover, no orders had come from above instructing them to do so.

Announced as a people's empowerment programme, a micro-finance scheme was launched for small entrepreneurs who could not afford to pay the high interest rates charged on regular bank loans. In North Subang and East Cirebon, some petty traders and shopkeepers, farmers, artisans and brick manufacturers received credit in order to strengthen their business activities. On the basis of occupational identity, recipients were clubbed together and encouraged to work with one another in a cooperative spirit. This scheme proved abortive even before it started. Firstly, apart from sharing the same occupation, the members of a group had absolutely nothing to do with one another and the assumption that they would act as partners in the same venture was senseless. Second, the loans provided were so low, ranging from fifty thousand to two hundred thousand rupiah (six to fifteen dollars), that it was clear from the beginning that the money would neither be spent for productive purposes, nor would it be repaid. Thus, the loans did not come back in the form of instalments needed to build up the revolving fund which the chairmen of the various groups were supposed to run. The budget, apart from being wasted in most cases on consumption, was also spent on beneficiaries who were selected not on the basis of economic vulnerability but of social proximity to the local power mongers. However small the amount of capital distributed, it went only to people who already owned assets and who were in the higher income brackets. We did not encounter a single jobless migrant or landless labourer who had qualified for receipt of the cheap credit.

The final link in the Social Safety Net Programme was meant to provide protection to impoverished households that were forced to cut down heavily on costs of health and education. To prevent them discontinuing the schooling of children or forgoing medical care, scholarships were granted to poor students and a special health card *(kartu sehat)* was introduced which guaranteed free access to the primary health centre. In East Cirebon parents were allowed to send their children to school free of charge in some cases, but this eligibility was restricted to boys and girls who continued their education beyond the primary school level. Village officials in North Subang decided to spend this part of the budget on maintenance and repair work. The allotted money was then diverted from the much-needed repair of the school building, however, to renovation of the *masjid* in the centre of the village. As for free medical care, in both localities that provision was reserved almost exclusively for old people. Although their vulnerability was mostly beyond dispute, it meant that among the working poor men, women and children in ill health could not benefit from the facility.

The total performance was thoroughly disappointing, but not unexpectedly so (see also Breman 1999a, 1999b). At the end of 1998, in view of warning signals received from all over the country, the World Bank decided to postpone a loan of another six hundred million US dollars for the next round of the operation until after elections scheduled for June 1999. As reasons for doing so, the Bank listed political abuse and lack of transparency in expenditure. A substantial part of the budget disappeared in the delivery process before reaching the grassroots. A critical reappraisal now being circulated by the Bank argues that the SSN schemes were actually quite small and that, other than with OPK, less than 15% of households benefited. The document, still in draft format, goes on to say that aid distributed through public channels did play a role but that, according to one study quoted, less than a quarter of the people who were questioned considered 'government' as their primary means of coping with the crisis. The conclusion drawn from these findings is that 'poorly designed SSN programs can weaken both "informal" safety nets of family and community relations and undermine existing poverty efforts and institutions' (World Bank 2000).

In other words, not only have the various schemes delivered under the umbrella of the JPS failed to accomplish what they promised, they were also counterproductive in the sense of destroying or damaging coping mechanisms at individual, household and community level. In view of that apprehension, it is not surprising that the World Bank has decided to stop funding the public provision of social security in its present shape. Expenditure for the current financial year has already been scaled down and will be phased out from 2001. Welfare entitlements are no longer on the international agency agenda, and not only because of leakage and mistargeting. As far as the World Bank is concerned, the emphasis is again on making the poor more productive. Nothing, of course, is amiss with empowerment of the poor. The disillusionment shown by the World Bank and other foreign donors, however, is stated in rather rhetorical terms and tends to overlook the empirical evidence that, for poor people in particular, the so-called informal social security arrangements are both inefficient and ineffective. In more ways than one, these mechanisms are inadequate to provide badly needed coverage against the ongoing impact of the economic crisis for large parts of Java's rural population. I could not agree more with Dhanani and Islam (2000:22) who in a recent paper argue that 'a fiscally sustainable social protection policy that is able to reinforce household coping mechanisms and social capital should become part of Indonesia's medium-term strategy for battling poverty'. Such a strategy, however, would require far-reaching changes in the political setting. What are the prospects for transformation to a political order that is not authoritarian but participatory and to policies that are bottom-up instead of top-down?

Reformasi from the bottom up

The chances of such a turnaround seem rather remote in the near future, even though the New Order has been eclipsed. The policy-makers in charge of the Social Safety Net Programme have declared that a truly participative style of development was what they had in mind in implementing the new public care arrangements. Active participation of the community should guarantee the targeting of beneficiaries on a needs basis, while such popular monitoring mechanisms would increase the transparency and accountability of the operation and thus help to suppress costs. With the heavy-handed style of government administration acknowledged as being counterproductive, emphasis was placed on self-reliant organizations at the local level, for example the Village Community Resilience Institution (Lembaga Ketahanan Masyarakat Desa, LKMD).

Since the state had clearly failed to deliver development for all, NGOs were invited to accept a consultancy role in activating the people in cooperative endeavours. The JPS became the vehicle for this new approach. As laid down in the general guidelines for the Social Safety Net Extension Programme 1998-1999, coordinating teams were established to manage the programme, consisting of local officials, representatives of the people, and voluntary agents acting on behalf of qualified NGOs. Their modus operandi was to emphasize 'the active and full participation of the community through counselling and partnership' (Sumodiningrat 1999:30-1). Grassroots 'facilitators' were appointed to organize community meetings at which projects were identified and people were helped to arrange themselves into activity groups. What happened in actual practice was very much at odds with the paper presentation which underlined the need for mobilization and socialization, training and capacity building. Still, that discrepancy was beyond the comprehension of the planners who had designed the new shape of policies.[7]

In a critical reappraisal of local level power politics and the command style of administration practised under the New Order regime, the World Bank seems to have changed to a view that is sceptical of the community façade which for so long has been deliberately manipulated to suggest that all rural people have shared equally in the development process.[8] Why

7 Staff of the National Development Planning Agency (Badan Perencanaan Pembangunan Nasional, BAPPENAS) in Jakarta were invariably surprised to hear that most people in our fieldwork villages were not consulted or counselled in the decision-making process on the distribution of JPS benefits. They insisted that general meetings must have been held at which community members sat together to discuss various options on what to do and how to proceed. If such meetings were not held, it must have been because of the unanimous decision not to hold them.

8 An example of the critical reappraisal is the following passage. 'The "villages" in the structure of government are not necessarily natural communitiesî nor, in many cases, a unit of com-

express such devastating criticism, so unexpectedly and in stark contrast with the earlier praise for Indonesia's model of economic growth led by Suharto, at this moment in time? Doubtless because now that the New Order state has finally lost all legitimacy, it is well nigh impossible to uphold the communitarian pretension any longer. That realization seems to have inspired the unreserved approval with which the World Bank now quotes comments made by poor men and women regarding their experience of exclusion, in a manner which is both guarded and matter-of-fact: 'Although many institutions can be influenced by the community, not all levels of the community can influence them. Those who are able to have influence are only people with high social status, the village officials or the rich.' (World Bank 2000.) The Bank's draft report supports that statement with many illustrations.

The illusion that 'everyone – both rich and poor – are in the same boat, experiencing the same difficulties during the economic crisis' (Jellinek and Rustanto 1999:30) has still not lost its charm for some observers, but it was certainly not a widely shared sentiment in North Subang and East Cirebon.

I would like to advocate more case studies similar to those which we have carried out, and to suggest that the contribution of such micro-level monographs should not only be understood in terms of checking on baseline data that are aggregate in nature and which aim at quantification in a macro-level analytical framework. As Mehta and Venkataraman (2000) have argued in the context of anti-poverty policies in India, a fresh approach is needed to review the current methodology of poverty estimation. Far more than the government of India, in the recent past the Indonesian state has used statistics not to ascertain objective reality, but to camouflage the deprivation in which a greater part of the population continue to live than has officially been acknowledged. The risk of distortion and misrepresentation on this score is still present.

In an apparent effort to revoke earlier measurements which deliberately

---

munal or social affiliation. Rather the existing desas were created as an administrative conven ience as a means to impose order and control. These were intended to supplant and co-opt – not cooperate with – existing social structures. So Inpres schools replaced community schools – and their associations which sponsored them, official irrigation systems created new water user associations – often supplanting pre-existing arrangements. New groups for "women", for "co-operatives", for "farmers" were arranged along a quasi-corporatist model of organization by "interests" – but with all of these organizations down to the local level based on vertical hierarchical structures that were centrally driven and controlled. These locally based but centrally controlled 'community' groups interacted with locally based but centrally controlled government officials (every member of the 'local' government hierarchy was employed by one single, Jakarta-based ministry – Ministry of Home Affairs).' (World Bank, 2000:15.)

understated the number of people working and living in poverty, the World Bank is on the verge of going on public record with the news that 'poverty is a reality that faces in one form or another half or more of the Indonesian population' (World Bank 2000). How can this truly Pauline conversion be explained? The line of reasoning signals an interesting turnaround from earlier policy views, beginning as it does with the statement that the poverty line is a social and political decision, and cannot be fixed by experts exclusively based on any 'technical' criteria. The Bank document then goes on to argue that the absolute level of the poverty line is not of crucial importance, but that in its fixation, standards of living should be comparable over time and across households. And then comes the sleight of hand: that it would be fallacious to assume that 'the poor' constitute an identifiable and relatively stable group which is different from the 'non-poor'. Not at all, since a large swathe of the Indonesian population may very well not be 'poor' today but is nevertheless 'at risk' of poverty. Any adverse shock to their incomes (or necessary expenditures) could easily force such people over the (arbitrary) line into poverty.

What is the moral of this insight? Firstly, that 'the poor' are definitely a very fluid group, changing from year to year in size and composition, and second, that any comparison with previous estimates would be misconceived. And this is precisely the rationale of the World Bank exercise: to deny the relevance of critical reflection on earlier calculations that suggested that the official poverty level in pre-krismon days had fallen to close to 10%. The marvel of the Bank's solution is that, on the one hand, it makes it possible to reiterate that, prior to krismon, only one out of ten households was still below the poverty line while, on the other hand, it may now be conceded that poverty has since increased by whatever multiplier you care to choose. It all depends on where and how that arbitrary line is fixed.

The anthropological research that we recommend enables us to focus at close quarters on the background, dynamics and context in which poor people live, and upon their social identity. Such studies make it much more difficult to imply that, granting the fluid nature of poverty, many people who happen to live and work in deprivation are not transient in that status, weathering a temporary setback and waiting for good fortune to return. Because of their lack of economic assets and adequate social protection and, last but not least, due to policies that do not aim at direct improvement of their plight, this substantial segment of the population has consistently been, is now and, in all likelihood, will remain in the foreseeable future, condemned to experience the shortcomings and defects in their well-being which are associated with poverty.

My final observations are based on the earlier conclusion that the economic malaise has escalated into a more encompassing and lasting crisis, one that, by overturning the political order, has also affected the social fabric of society. The time has not yet come to draw up the balance of all these changes, but the outcome may very well be not entirely negative. How have the forces of *reformasi* made their impact felt in our fieldwork villages? The *lurah* in East Cirebon, who was forced to step down, told us that he was an innocent victim of *reformasi*. He did not confess to, and was not openly accused of, malpractice. He argued that the decision to remove the leader of the nation from office, was bound to be followed up by urging low-ranking members of the government cadre like him to resign. In his view, it was not something to feel guilty or embarrassed about. Long-standing enemies among the local elite had simply made use of the political turmoil to engineer his downfall. The script is persuasive – the idea of turbulence higher-up becoming a means with which to settle old scores at the grassroots – but the change of scene may be rather more complicated than just a matter of rivalry among local notables. The youth of the neighbouring village had written 'down with the *aparat desa*' on the signboard in front of the local office. Such slogans seemed to reflect a new mood which was not merely critical of petty officials for their misdemeanours, but of the state power at large which they represented.

The run-up to the elections saw the return of political life to the countryside. For the duration of the campaign village streets were decorated with coloured party flags. Youngsters constructed booths from which activists hailed all passers-by with loudspeakers to cast their vote in favour of the respective candidates. The floating mass, thoroughly demobilized under the New Order regime, was supposed to have become politically articulate again in, and as a result of, the 1999 elections. Is this indeed what happened? During our stay in the villages in March-April that year it was interesting to note that local officials invariably predicted that Golkar would return to power. Perhaps with a reduced majority but, so they said, any other outcome was highly unlikely. They could not have been more wrong. In both North Subang and East Cirebon an overwhelming number of votes, nearly two-thirds, went to the Indonesian Democratic Party of Struggle (PDI-P) of Megawati Soekarnoputri. Golkar finished only in third place, after the PKB led by Abdurrahman Wahid. In my opinion, the results indicated massive distrust by most village inhabitants of the party which, until recently, had been so dominant in the political landscape; they should not be read, however, as a vote of confidence in the parties which had become active in order to oppose continuation of the New Order. The political formations that have come to the fore are still very much leader-centred. So far, they lack a programmatic base and, in most cases, do not even have a consistent set of policy objectives with which to attract followers. In the wake of the New Order, politics and politicians seem to be active only in the urban domain. What will be the organizing principle for mobilizing political support in the rural hinterland?

'Village reconstruction' was the title of the 1952 lecture in which J.H. Boeke expounded his views on the urgent need for a person-centred village policy which would be neither authoritarian nor autocratic. In his address before an academic audience nearly half a century ago, the colonial policy-maker began by conceding that, due to what he chose to call the disintegrative influence of capitalism, it would not be possible to bring back the *ancien régime* of homogeneity that used to exist in Asian agrarian societies. He made a plea, however, for restoring the traditional communal sense as much as possible. For that challenging task in the new era that had come, experts would have to be trained to empower and give voice to the 'little man' who, under colonial rule, was given 'no chance to follow his own insight and initiative' and was left without 'opportunity for self-activity and self-responsibility'. Such experts had little room for manoeuvre in early post-colonial Indonesia and none at all in the aftermath following that first period of Independence. The authoritarian regime that came to power in 1965 ruthlessly wiped out whatever self-activity and self-responsibility had so far been built up by and for 'the little men'.

W.F. Wertheim started his career in the colonial civil service of the Netherlands East Indies. In his scholarly work on changing Asia in the second half of the twentieth century he favoured a different and more radical approach for overcoming the problem of mass poverty in the Javanese countryside. In vehement disagreement with what he called the 'betting on the strong' principle, Wertheim spoke out against the 'community development' type of rural policies that had become dominant in various parts of South and Southeast Asia in the course of the 1950s and 1960s. Such policies which targeted the better-off in the rural economy were, according to Wertheim, bound to fail to lift the majority of village people out of the backward state in which they were held. 'Betting on the many' – to make those who were weak strong, mainly through organization and education towards efficiency and self-reliance – was his prescription for a development trajectory that would benefit this major, though heavily underprivileged, part of mankind. His essay ends with the proclamation that those who had sided with the subordinated masses in the development process and who were actively promoting their emancipation from all kinds of bondage, were patently on the winning side (Wertheim 1964:277).

In retrospect, Boeke's pessimistic scenario of the development path has been proved wrong, while Wertheim's optimism turned out to be ill-founded. Looked at from the perspective of what the two scholars wanted, the first a revitalization of the community and the second a rural policy that would favour the rural poor, prospects for the immediate future do not appear bright.

The government apparatus at the village and sub-district level has by and large remained loyal to Golkar, and the administrative style of petty officials is also pretty much the same as during the last three-and-a-half decades. The 1998 election results reflect a shift in the local power balance, but competition for the not-so-negligible spoils seems again to be limited to factions among the village elite. At the moment, political and administrative decentralization is a high priority on the agenda of central government. Much will depend on the concrete shape given to the devolution of executive, economic and political power to the district level. It might provide a new opportunity for bottom-up reformasi, but it could also legitimize the closed shop practices of local wheeler-dealers. When all is said and done, the floating mass is still floating. It will take a long time to build up the reform movement that is needed to articulate the interests of the majority of underprivileged and marginalized segments of Java's rural population.

SECTION 1

North Subang

CHAPTER II

Work and life in Java's coastal plan

Introductory note

The choice of North Subang as a research location dates back to the introduction of new methods for cultivating rice in around twenty villages on Java between 1968 and 1973. The project was undertaken by the Survey Agro Ekonomi (Agro Economic Survey, AES), which was based at Bogor Agricultural University. As the research evolved over the course of time, the focus shifted from the original agronomic to a more agro-economic approach, a change that was reflected in the name of the new programme: Rural Dynamics Study. An AES re-survey conducted in 1981 in some of the same villages, including North Subang, provided data for a study of the agrarian and non-agrarian causes of the observed socio-economic inequality at this local level (White and Wiradi 1989). Referring to only a part of the results of these previous studies, the Japanese economists Y. Hayami and M. Kikuchi included North Subang as one of a small number of case studies in their analysis of the transformation of village-level institutions in Southeast Asia at the end of the 1970s. Their book on the effects of the green revolution on rural communities in the Philippines and Indonesia – *Asian village at the crossroads; An economic approach to institutional change* (1981) – received great international acclaim and became a favoured reference work, particularly for policy-makers. The availability of this monograph was one of the reasons why I decided to locate my fieldwork in rural West Java in 1990 in the same village, which I then referred to as S. (Breman 1995). For similar reasons, the British agricultural economist Jonathan Pincus took up residence in the village immediately after my departure, using the name that his Japanese predecessors had given it – North Subang.[1] Pincus' study *Class, power and agrarian change; Land and labour in rural West Java* (1996) was intended as a critical response to the conclusions reached by Hayami and Kikuchi and the theoretical assumptions on which they were based. My decision to visit North Subang in 1990 was related to the start of a new research project carried out

[1] Shortly before my departure, Pincus completed his fieldwork in two neighbouring locations, one of which had also been the subject of a case study by Hayami and Kikuchi.

in a number of the former AES villages and concerned with the dynamics of non-agrarian employment in rural Java (White 1986). The core of my critique of the neo-classically tinted work of the Japanese economists was their failure to consider non-agrarian employment and labour migration in North Subang, in spite of the undeniable importance of both phenomena, including during the period preceding my fieldwork.

North Subang's location on a plain known as the rice basket of Java was one of the main reasons why agricultural labourers went in search of work far from their home village. Many of the landless and landpoor were recurrently absent from North Subang, following the harvest schedule throughout the region, while there would be a massive influx of labourers from elsewhere when the peaks in the agrarian cycle reached the local area. In addition to this rural circulation of labour, there was also an increasing tendency for labour to shuttle back and forth between the village and Jabotabek, the conurbation around the Jakarta metropolis.

The expansion and extension of both the rural and urban labour markets was closely linked to the increasing ease with which people could move around. Since the 1970s, there has been a genuine transport revolution on Java which has connected underdeveloped regions, characterized by a high population density, to urban growth poles. The metropolitan agglomeration of Jabotabek in particular absorbed large quantities of labour for which no regular or permanent employment was available in the rural hinterland. Migration – whereby labourers leave and settle for an indefinite period of time wherever they can find work – has been replaced by circulation, a continual coming and going, as the dominant pattern of intra-rural or rural-urban labour flows. This form of mobility became particularly characteristic of localities such as North Subang, situated in the immediate periphery of Jabotabek. The *kampung* of my research belongs to the sub-district of Binong in Subang district and lies at a distance of twelve kilometres from Pamanukan along the national highway. A provincial road connects this coastal town to the district capital up in the hills.

Location

North Subang is situated on a plain that is known as the rice basket of West Java. Surrounded by fields on which paddy is cultivated for a large part of the year, the village appears to the visitor as the prototype of agrarian settlements that fill the landscape along the northern coast of Java: a cluster of houses hidden amongst trees and farmyard crops, whose inhabitants have for centuries lived in the shelter of their community and depend for their living largely or even entirely on cultivating the local land. This is the classical image of peas-

North Subang as a typical village along Java's north coast.
The settlement is marked by trees, surrounded by paddy fields.

ant society on Java as laid down in the literature but one that is in need of revision, also in this particular case.

For a start, North Subang's past goes back no more than two generations. The region which later became the Subang district formed part of the Pamanukan and Tjiasem estates in Krawang, the private property of a Western large-scale agricultural enterprise dating back to the beginning of the nineteenth century. Ever since, the corporate management had restricted its operations to higher ground, growing rubber, coffee and other cash crops by making use of waged labour which was brought in from the surrounding areas for the various operations during the crop cycles. In order to promote the cultivation of rice for export, the plain was drained and a railway constructed across this empty area in the early 1920s. Under a scheme of peasant colonization settlers were encouraged to open up the lower-lying plains for cultivation. There was a standard procedure for distributing land to these new pioneers, most of whom were from Indramayu and other areas with a predominantly Sundanese population, with which marriage ties are still maintained. Each settler received one *bahu* (0.7 hectare), enough – according to colonial standards – to run a viable farm. The homogenous social structure that arose as a result of this policy did not last long. Some of the older informants told us of the hardships they had to endure in the early days. The first thing to be done by the newcomers was to build a house, or at least shelter of some kind. They had to spend the first few nights after their arrival in the trees for fear of the wild animals that inhabited this inhospitable region. Clearing the land they had been allocated was heavy work and the varying degrees of success – greatly influenced by the availability of sufficient labour power in the household – led to early differentiation even among the first wave of settlers. Colonists who left were replaced by others hoping for better fortune. By 1940, a settlement of around forty households had grown up, which fell under the administrative control of the next larger village. The influx of migrants continued at a modest pace after the opening-up of the vast coastal tracts. For rice cultivation, the villagers were dependent on rainfall. The construction of the first irrigation system at the end of the colonial period improved the situation somewhat but not sufficiently to allow more than one harvest. The yield was low, around 1.5 tons per hectare, and subject to strong fluctuation, condemning the majority of the villagers to live in a permanent state of poverty. Settlement and departure continued to be spasmodic. In the fight for national independence after World War II an adjacent *kampung* came under artillery fire by the Dutch military. Houses still left standing were burnt down by the enemy shortly after their inhabitants had fled. Several of the families who sought temporary refuge in North Subang have since remained there. In this way the number of households in the locality increased over time from no more than ten shortly after the opening-up of the region, to about fifty in the mid-1940s. During the 1950s harvest workers started coming to the village from Tegal and Pemalang along the northern coast of Central Java. A number of these seasonal migrants have stayed, mostly because they married local women. Their arrival augmented the emerging landless underclass in the village which grew disproportionately during this period. In addition to immigrants who came in search of a better life, spatial mobility also took the shape of an outflow whenever survival in North Subang was threatened. Such a crisis occurred in the early 1960s when a long draught led to a succession of failed harvests. The people were forced to eat cattle fodder, stinking red millet imported from the USA which was actually unsuitable for human consumption. At this time of the *bulgur* (called Ben Hur by some informants, after a famous film shown at the time) the poorer peasants in particular left the village. They had lost their land to moneylenders with whom they had taken out loans in the early phase of the drought hoping for a return of better times. Several of these economic refugees went to kinsmen in Banten, where farming had not been so badly affected by the drought, to work as tenant-cultivators or agricultural labourers. With no one interested in buying, they sold their land for a pittance. Some received no more than twenty kilograms of rice for a part of a rice field (Pincus 1996:22), others received only enough to pay for their journey. The buyers were often fellow villagers who themselves had a few more reserves. Some returned in later years when agrarian production in North Subang increased due to improvements of the irrigation system. The transactions that took place at times of misery laid the basis for the extremely unequal land distribution that now determines relations so strongly in North Subang.

The genesis of the settlement and the changes in the local economy that have taken place over time, clearly demonstrate that North Subang has never been a closed, inward-orientated, peasant community. The lifestyle of its inhabitants can only be understood on the basis of the close ties that have linked them to the outside world ever since the village was founded. To stress the autonomy of North Subang would also be inaccurate from the administrative viewpoint. Notwithstanding its prominence as a residual nucleus standing alone in the Javanese countryside, the settlement has remained until the present day no more than a *kampung*. Together with two other hamlets, North Subang constitutes a village unit which numbered three thousand nine hundred and ninety-six inhabitants in 1990. The desa office in which the local administration and the government agencies that it represents are established, is located in the largest of the hamlets, about three-quarters of an hours' walk (three-and-half kilometres across open fields) from North Subang. In 1990, when I carried out my field research, this *kampung* consisted of two hundred and sixteen households totalling eight hundred and nine members. Although it is still too small for self-government, the settlement will in due course undoubtedly be elevated to a village in the administrative sense of the word just as, conversely, the *desa* to which the hamlet now belongs was constructed in the not so remote past by splitting-up a number of *kampung* into separate villages. There is ample historical evidence that the majority of localities on Java have been established through management from above, a form of administrative engineering that dates back to colonial policies from the beginning of the nineteenth century onwards (Breman 1978).

Socio-economic configuration

The majority of the population, a hundred and sixty-three of the two hundred and sixteen households or 75%, depend on agriculture for their livelihood. This agrarian majority can be subdivided into two categories of almost equal size: eighty-two peasant households that have some land, whether it is their own or leased, or a combination of the two, and eighty-one households that are landless and entirely or largely dependent on earnings from agricultural labour.

The agrarian hierarchy, however, is far more complex than this basic dichotomy might suggest and has emerged over a long time period. The first settlers started to cultivate the wasteland with their own labour power. Such heavy pioneering work and the still very favourable man-to-land ratio is the cause of the high proportion of farm-owners-cum-cultivators among the offspring of the first generation. Most arable land is still owned by descendants of the original owners. Those who came later found the cultivable acreage already occupied and became dependent on farmer-owners, either as tenants or as agricultural workers. Constant crop failure and other economic adversity during the early 1960s caused a shift in ownership relations. Those peasant households which did not move out then to Banten and who managed in difficult times not only to consolidate their farms but even to enlarge them, later made considerable progress. The man who became a landlord par excellence managed to amass a total of sixty hectares within and outside the *kampung*. His current fortune is based on profiteering practices, through which he ensured that peasant-owners fell in debt to him and became his tenants on their own land. As a result of the contracts he concluded with them, his name replaced theirs in the village record of land rights. Changes in the demand and supply balance of labour caused the value of land to increase. This development was not only influenced by steadily increasing population pressure but also by higher productivity. As mentioned before, the latter trend has not been uninterrupted.

With the completion in 1968 of a new irrigation system, which in effect meant the absorption of the small existing network into the expanded Jatiluhur canal system, it became possible to move from one harvest a year to two. This enormous step forward was given a further boost in the early 1970s with the use of new, higher yield seed varieties. Yields rose from 2.5 tons per hectare in 1969-1971 to almost four tons in 1978-1979 in the rainy season, and from 2.1 to 2.9 tons in the dry season (Hayami and Kikuchi 1981:201). Ten years later the average yield for all farmers had risen above four tons even in the dry season and in the rainy season they were reaching levels of 5.5 tons per hectare (Pincus 1996:155, 132). As the green revolution progressed, the demand for labour substantially exceeded that available in the settlement itself. New households were set up, including a number of families who had fled during the bad times in the early 1960s to Banten, and the population grew rapidly. But a small number of families, who had been living in North Subang from the very beginning, maintained control of the land. Due to the greatly improved value of agrarian property, brought about by the increased productivity, most of the newcomers were unable to buy land of their own. A relatively large minority managed to enter into leasing or sharecropping agreements, but the remainder were forced to spend their lives eking out a meagre existence as landless labourers. They were joined at harvest time, now twice a year, by an army of migrant workers. These nomadic labourers originated from the eastern districts, along the coastal zone to Pemalang and Tegal in Central Java, and have maintained their ties with these areas to this day through bonds of marriage.

The combination of demographic and economic dynamics explains why a fairly egalitarian stratification in the early history of North Subang had made way for increasing differentiation in a manner that has not been accompanied by a proportionate dispersion of agrarian holdings. This may be seen from the large number of households, a hundred and sixty-nine of the total of two hundred and sixteen (78%) that do not own any land. Pincus, who conducted a more detailed survey shortly after my departure from North Subang in 1990, arrived at a slightly lower figure of 72%.[2] A rather small minority of twenty-one households owns 80% of arable land in the locality. By that time the power of the small elite in the locality of our fieldwork seemed as good as unassailable and many from this milieu in particular had become haji. As Pincus had calculated, the 4% of leading households which owned more than two hectares accounted for 70% of all the rice fields. This was in sharp contrast to the three-quarters of all households which were landless. The extremely unequal distribution of the most important form of agricultural capital was compensated to only a limited extent by allowing landless households to cultivate land which they did not own. According to both my own figures and those of Pincus, agricultural producers – consisting of peasant farmers, tenants and sharecroppers – accounted for less than 40% of the total number of households at the time of the study.

In other words, tenancy only very partially neutralizes the gap between the two poles of the agrarian hierarchy. Of the forty-seven farmer-owner households, twenty-one also hold land on a tenancy basis. On the other hand, among the fifty landless households that are tenants, fifteen cultivate so little land, that is, an average of a quarter-hectare, that its yield is less than half their total income, too little for them to be qualified as self-employed agrarian producers. Instead of exploiting their widely scattered estates themselves by waged labour, the landlords parcel off their property under lease arrangements to tenants or sharecroppers, usually for no longer than one or perhaps a few seasons. In this way, they prevent their 'clients' from gradually building up a stronger bargaining position. Why did more landless from the

2 This slight discrepancy is probably partly due to a small difference in the total number of households counted. In mid 1990 we counted two hundred and sixteen households in the village; later in the same year, Pincus arrived at a total of two hundred and ten. The difference might be related to the method of counting households which cultivated land some distance from North Subang and spent a large part of the year away from the village. The determining factor in including these households as part of the village population was the length of time they were away. We may have applied a different period than Pincus.

village not try to secure contracts as tenants or sharecroppers in or around the *kampung* instead of becoming sojourners who have to leave again and again on sorties which are exhaustive and scarcely productive? The simple answer is that, as members of the non-propertied under-class, they lacked the necessary creditworthiness. And most of them did not have the social capital to compensate for this economic shortcoming. To stand any chance at all of benefiting from the benevolence of one of the prominent patrons in the village, it was necessary to have family ties, or to have lived in the village for a long time. Without such credentials to show they belonged, the landless were kept at a distance and condemned to a state of perpetual, circular mobility.

Tenancy arrangements can be one of three types: a. *sewa*, the leasing of land for one or more seasons for an amount of money that is usually paid in advance; b. *gadai*, the temporary ceding of land to a creditor who then has right of usage over that land for the duration of the loan; and c. *maro*, a shareholding agreement under which the land operator receives half the yield in return for his labour, after deduction of 50% or more of the remaining production costs.

Farmers who want to cultivate more fields than they own usually prefer a sewa relationship with a non-working owner. The supply of land for this purpose is so restricted, however, that many interested candidates have to seek another way by which to support themselves as independent agrarian producers. During the 1980s more than thirty such people managed to lease wasteland in the coastal region to the northeast of Jakarta at quite a distance from the village, which they cultivate in the rainy season. The yield is not high, but is nevertheless much more than they would earn as agricultural labourers. Like farming nomads and with or without their families, they travel back and forth between what is still their home in North Subang and the place which has become their worksite.

In the past, *gadai* transactions have been connected to the need of small farmers in particular to convert their agrarian property for a definite period into ready cash with which to meet necessary expenses. They were frequently unable to repay their debts, with the result that land pledged as security was lost for good. Although this has occasionally occurred in North Subang, most cases of *gadai* involve larger landowners who need cash with which to buy more land or to invest in other ways. The yield enables them to repay the amount borrowed, after which the temporarily transferred property is returned to them. The credit taken up is thus used to increase their total capital, as part of an accumulating strategy. Only a small elite with sufficient reserves at their disposal can afford the risks attached to such financial transactions. *Maro* is a tenancy agreement which in effect is advantageous only to marginal landowners or landless workers; in other words, categories that are forced to adopt a survival strategy. The sharecropper is not an independent producer, but is accountable to his employer. Those who, as a favour, are given land to cultivate on a sharecropping basis are recompensed for little more than their labour power. Sometimes *maro* is used as a means of support for a poor relation. More often it is an extra reward that larger families give to their permanent workers or which they hold out as a prospect, that is, a bonus for faithful service rendered or to be rendered by farm servants to their master. In all such cases the amount of land is minimal, amounting to a mere fraction of the total acreage. The first two forms of tenancy mentioned above are more significant, but even agreements entered into under such conditions cause little real change to the distribution of land among the various agrarian classes in the village. Landless and small farmers do not have the necessary cash with which to take over land in *gadai* and *sewa* arrangements mostly involve the renting of land far away from North Subang. There is such a shortage of the principal form of agrarian capital that small owners in the middle social ranks are only able to hold their own by transferring their farming activities elsewhere for part of the year. Their strategy of consolidation forces them to take up the cultivation of land in another region.

Agriculture is the principal but not the only source of livelihood. Quite a large number of inhabitants are also active in other sectors of the economy, a quarter (fifty-three of the two hundred and sixteen) to such a degree that I have classified them as non-agrarian. These people depend for half or more of their total incomes on other earnings and employment. Their role in the non-agricultural economic hierarchy is also determined by the amount of capital at their disposal. At the top are the large traders and shopkeepers. The buying and selling of goods, particularly of paddy, is a profitable source of income but one that is not easily visible to the researcher. Operators in this category customarily combine their transactions with the granting of credit or even act as moneylenders pure and simple, making it even more difficult to establish their degree of prosperity. They charge interest on loans at the rate of 50% per crop cycle, implying on an annual basis a doubling of the original loan. A few act as middlemen in commercial transactions as a sideline. Their task as *calo-calo*, or commission agents, is to bring two sides together in the re-sale of movable property (for example second-hand bicycles or motorbikes), in concluding tenancy agreements, et cetera. It is far more difficult for the outsider to divide traders into large and small than it is to classify shop owners on the basis of their working capital. The two *toko* in the village each have a large assortment of goods for daily consumption and also more durable commodities. There are many more *warung* holders selling the common necessities and prepared foods in the neighbourhood. Permanent employment providing a regular and adequate income can also be considered a form of property. Teachers and civil servants belong to this category, as do the village officials. The head of the *kampung* is a landowner, rice trader and shop owner. His case demonstrates the way in which agrarian and non-agrarian activities are merged almost unnoticeably with one another.

Transport is a service industry practised in and outside the village. Owners of motorbikes carry pillion passengers, a form of transport known as *ojeg*. The only motor van in the village belongs to a subcontractor who also uses the vehicle to carry freight. A number of artisans with a modest supply of tools find work in the vicinity of the village, some on permanent sites and others at varying locations. People who work in factories nearby Jakarta may also have some degree of skill. This brings us gradually to the landless milieu in the non-agrarian sector, in which I include all unskilled workers who earn their livelihood in ways other than agricultural: for example, navvies and road menders, building labourers and transport workers who do not own their own vehicles. The latter include a few men from North Subang who drive motorized three-wheelers (*bajaj*) in Jakarta or a pedicab (*becak*) in smaller towns. The vehicles in which they transport their passengers are hired from the owners in a sort of sharecropping arrangement. Others work away from the village as street hawkers and many more as domestic servants in the city, with one or two even going abroad in that capacity. Domestic servants are almost all women, and a surprising number of those who declare

Boys waiting for passengers on their motorbikes at the entrance to the village

The owner of a flock of ducks selling eggs to a trader

this to be their employment in Jakarta are in reality prostitutes.

All these cases have to do with employment outside the village. There is little opportunity in North Subang to earn a living outside the agricultural sector. Those who are able to do so do not entirely lack their own means of production. For example, they own a mobile market stall, a barrow or a game of chance with which they earn money at festivals and other feasts, either locally or in neighbouring villages. A few shepherds and duck herders are also not entirely without property. The former look after an owner's sheep flock on a sort of sharecropping arrangement under which half the lambs born become the property of the original owner. The men who look after the five flocks of ducks in the village are all in debt to a moneylender to whom they must sell many or all of their eggs for less than the market price. The skills of the masseuse (*tukang pijit*) and of the exorcist can also be regarded as a form of property. A handful of women depend for their living on a few hours' work each day in the houses of the more prosperous, cleaning or doing the laundry. Men without any employment will cycle to the coast to catch crabs or chop wood in state-owned forests. They sell the fruits of their labour at a local market on the way home, but this is nothing more than a modest side business. A number of old men and women who live alone and lack the physical strength needed to work the land, are without any resources whatsoever. They are always active at marriages, circumcisions and other ceremonies or festivities in the village, they glean the fields after harvesting (*ngasak*) and sometimes, but not always, are slipped something by relatives or neighbours on the frequent days when they can earn nothing at all.

This inventory of economic activities causes me to deduce that work and incomes earned away from the village partly determine the position held within it. As I shall discuss later in more detail, this applies to both agrarian and non-agrarian activities. At all events, recent literature has dispelled the impression that the rural population of Java is involved in nothing other than agriculture. An impression that is still quite fashionable, however, is that when people seek employment away from their own village they tend to do so in other sectors of the economy than agriculture. In my further argumentation I shall show that this supposition is incorrect. I also place on record that the social position of the villagers is dependent on the amount of capital at their disposal. Access to land is undoubtedly the most important measurement in this respect; nevertheless, ranking can only be determined if the acquisition of property outside agriculture is simultaneously considered. In effect, these are mutually-reinforcing trends whose inter-connections need also to be studied. Based on a status combination, a stratification consisting of three classes can be constructed:

- upper: owners or cultivators of more than one hectare of land, large traders and shop owners, senior civil servants and teachers;
- middle: owners or leasers of at least a quarter-hectare of land, traders with little business capital, warung holders, owner-operators of motorbikes, artisans with some degree of skill and labourers with permanent jobs, lower-ranking civil servants (for example watchmen and lockkeepers);
- lower: agricultural workers, marginal landowners or tenants, unskilled and casual workers outside agriculture, transport workers without a vehicle of their own, street traders and domestic servants.

Among the economically-active population, slightly less than one-fifth (18%) belong to the upper level, almost one-third (31%) to the middle, while half (51%) belong to the under-class.

Social mobility occurs only to a limited degree, both with regard to size and scale. An exception to this is the large farmer-cum-moneylender who, many years ago, came to the village as a stranger without even owning the flock of ducks that he brought with him. Kinship ties are very significant for providing access to sources of income that otherwise would be denied. For example, a farmer will lease-out a parcel of land to enable his younger brother to buy a motorbike to use as *ojeg*. I also noted various cases of landowners who had divided among their children the larger part of their land, bought with the results of their own labour, at a time when they themselves were still economically active. The majority of marriages are between partners of the same social background, but occasionally the son of an agricultural worker marries into a landowning family. In such a case he may work as a sharecropper on land of his in-laws that will eventually be left to his wife as part of her inheritance.

Capital is mobile not only vertically but also horizontally, from agriculture to trade and vice versa. Mobility is greater at the higher than at the lower social level, while the exact opposite seems to apply to labour. As against the relative few who manage to work their way upwards through their own efforts – whether in or out of agriculture, locally or elsewhere – downward mobility is at least as frequent. Apart from economic adversity which makes eating into one's capital unavoidable, regression on the social ladder is not infrequently caused by a lifestyle that prevents any accumulation or even consolidation of property, for example gambling, divorce, or other behaviour which is strongly consumptive. Notwithstanding such individual movements across class divisions, and however much these may attract the public eye, the existing separation between the rather small top and the broad base of the social system is becoming more acute. This result of my fieldwork refutes an important conclusion drawn by Hayami and Kikuchi on the basis of research undertaken rather more than a decade ago in the same location, namely, that the economic progress enjoyed by the *kampung* during the 1970s had had no effect on relative income differentials between landowners and landless (Hayami and Kikuchi 1981:207). If such a tendency indeed occurred at that time, it has certainly not continued. This rebuttal needs further elucidation, but I shall first discuss the significance of agricultural labour in the local economy.

Work and the nature of agricultural labour

The two hundred and sixteen families that inhabit the *kampung* have a total of five hundred and forty-one economically active members. The remaining two hundred and sixty-eight of the total of eight hundred and nine residents, that is, one-third, are almost all either too young or too old to participate in the labour process. The economically non-active are equally dispersed among the various social classes. Irrespective of whether landowning, landless or non-agrarian households are concerned, the proportion of members who are too young or too old to work fluctuates between 32% and 34% in all groups. However the economic positions may differ, the demographic composition of households is almost equal, as can be seen from the following example. The eighty-two farmer and/or tenant households consist of three hundred and twenty- five members, of which a hundred and eight are children under the age of fifteen; the eighty-one landless households total three hundred and six members with a hundred and one children in the same age bracket: 1.32 and 1.26 respectively per household. Not only does this pattern signify a far lower degree of reproduction than is usually assumed but, I would emphasize, households such as those of the landless who live in poverty-stricken circumstances are neither larger than those of the more fortunate section of the population, nor are they distinguished by a greater number of children. The idea of a higher rate of demographic growth in the socio-economic milieu of those who can at least afford it, suggested in a study by the World Bank (1990:31), is not confirmed by research at the local level such as that which I have undertaken.

The five hundred and forty-one men and women whom I have classified as economically active on the basis of age and physical condition may be divided per occupation as shown in Table 1. This classification confirms yet again the predominantly agrarian character of the local economy. Three-quarters of the men and women are employed principally on the land or depend mainly on its yield.

Agricultural labour is by far the most important source of livelihood. The number of men and women who earn their living in this way not only surpasses the number of farmers, but is even greater than employment in all other agrarian and non-agrarian occupations listed. Agricultural labour, however, is an extremely elastic concept which needs further qualification. The figure of two hundred and forty-nine refers to wage labourers, at least half of whose income derives from work carried out on land that does not belong to them. The majority of these workers belong to completely landless households, and a minority to households of small farmers, owners or tenants. Many but not all – the exact number can only be established on the basis of longer-term research – combine this principal occupation with other activities, whether in waged employment or for their own account. Some of these activities have already been discussed: catching crabs on the beach and chopping wood in the state forests. They also sometimes work as navvies or as unskilled labour on construction sites in the neighbourhood. In the dry season, where there is little demand for their labour power, they grow cucumbers in nearby fields for which permission need not be asked of the owner, or they dig mud with which to make bricks. On the other hand, those whose

Table 1. Occupation of the 541 men and women classified as economically active

Agrarian	agricultural labourers	249
	farmers	82
	duckherders	5
Non-agrarian	shopkeepers (toko, warung)	25
	transport workers (incl. ojeg)	16
	traders (large and small)	14
	prostitutes	14
	civil servants/teachers	11
	construction workers	10
	domestic servants	10
	artisans/factory hands	9
	masseuse, dukun	2
	dock worker	1

Source: Author's village survey North Subang 1990.

incomes derive primarily from other occupations also sometimes work for payment on land belonging to others. This applies both to members of small farmer and tenant households on days when they are not occupied with their own farms, and to unskilled, low-paid casual workers who seek their living outside agriculture for a large part of the year. The secondary movements of labour in both directions, that is, away from and back to agriculture, keep one another roughly in equilibrium. As a result, out of the total number of days worked by the economically-active population on an annual basis, almost half are in waged agricultural work carried out at the command of others.

The above breakdown based on main occupation does not distinguish one segment that I would describe as that of co-workers. This category, amounting to ninety-three out of five hundred and forty-one (17%), consists of men and especially women who, on the basis of age and physical condition, must be counted among the economically active population, but whose labour power is only incidentally utilized. The majority of these co-workers, eighty of the ninety-three, were found among owners of capital, both agricultural and otherwise. They are women members of households of large landowners, traders, *pamong desa* and teachers for whom no outside work is available which is compatible with their higher social status. In this milieu, young people not only stay at school for more years, but are not forced to accept gainful employment after completing their education. They help in the family home or business but are not pressurized to use their labour power externally, let alone to make it as profitable as possible. The landless, on the other hand, do not have the necessary economic basis to allow any of their active members to be exempted in this way. Of the ninety-three whom I have classified as co-workers only thirteen belong to landless households. To be more precise: the eighty-two farming households have two hundred and fifteen members in the economically active age brackets of whom sixty contribute only occasionally; on the other hand, in the eighty-one households of agricultural workers, only seven of the two hundred and eight people capable of working are spared in this manner. These figures show that in the lowest economic ranks it is very difficult to ignore the obligation to earn according to one's ability. At the bottom of the social ladder, poor health is found less acceptable as a reason for not working. Among adults, only the chronically ill, the disabled and women with very young babies or in the last stages of pregnancy are exempted. In this milieu people also enter the labour process at an earlier age and leave it later. This greater economic participation in these households further accentuates the fact that agricultural labour is the main source of livelihood in the village. In my estimation, at least half of all the work that is carried out – but not the income derived from it – is related to waged labour in agriculture. This fact forms the basis for the following discussion which focuses on patterns of agrarian employment.

In view of the nature of the local economy, it is hardly surprising that the rhythm of employment is determined by the agrarian cycle. We have already noted that the switch from one to two harvests per year brought about an important change in the system of production. Until the early 1970s paddy was a wet season crop, but extension of the irrigation canal system made it possible to grow it also in the dry season. The farmers gradually started to do so and, since the early 1980s, it has become general practice. This put a stop to the cultivation of legumes and other *polowijo* (second crops) which were formerly grown after the rainy season. *Rendangan* is the name given to paddy's growing cycle, which finishes early in February when the rains also come to an end. Seedlings are put out in late September or early October and transplanted a few weeks later. The paddy harvested in the dry season is known as *gadu*. Preparatory activities start in March and the crop is taken from the fields at the end of June or early in July. Apart from a few nearby plots which are temporarily used by some agricultural workers for cucumber cultivation, the land is left fallow after the second paddy crop until it is time for the next planting. The alternation of peak and slack periods in agricultural work is made even more marked by the cultivation plan that has been drawn up for the total village acreage. The local authorities say that they took the decision to impose a collective schedule in order to improve the use of irrigation water by a block-by-block method, which would also help in combating plant disease. Their reasoning seems logical, but it is difficult to avoid the impression that the prescribed uniformity in land-use and field operations accords with the desire for order and discipline which Indonesian state personnel at all levels show to such a remarkable degree.

Over time, the paddy crop has remained very labour-intensive, which does not imply that the double harvest has caused an equal increase in employment. For a start, the second crops which also demanded the input of many hands, are no longer grown. Secondly, a number of radical changes introduced into production technology have had a labour-saving effect. For example, the rice knife (*ani-ani*) with which each ear was cut in turn has been replaced by the sickle which, with the use of a sweeping movement close to the ground, is able to cut a number of stalks simultaneously. This innovation has contributed to a drastic reduction in harvest time. Moreover, land preparation now takes place only with the aid of a tractor. There are only a few such machines in the kampung, but many more are stationed in the neighbourhood ready to be hired out to farmers complete with driver. This mechanization has made it unnecessary to keep draught-cattle, with the result that not only has the buffalo disappeared from the landscape, but far fewer workdays are now needed for ploughing and tilling.

Mechanization in North Subang has depleted the paddy fields
of both labour and cattle

The establishment of a village plant schedule to which all farmers must adhere has had the unintended effect that fluctuations in the demand for labour have become more acute. Not only the preliminary work but also all subsequent activities such as transplanting, weeding and harvesting occur almost simultaneously and frequently only last a few days. Older agricultural workers who experienced the earlier unrestricted regime, complain that local harvesting does not extend to more than a couple of days. Although there used to be only one crop per year, the greater spacing over time meant that throughout the growth cycle the workers had access to the fields of many owners and at the end were assured of a larger share in the total yield of the village acreage than is now the case. In the shorter time that employment is currently available in their own locality, they lack the opportunity to profit from it to the greatest degree. As we shall see below, this reduction in employment is only partly compensated by the considerable lengthening of the agrarian cycle. Nowadays, work in the fields is no longer characterized by fairly long alternating periods of activity and non-activity. The peaks and dips in the employment pattern have not disappeared but, due to changes in the organization of production, now alternate far more rapidly with one another. On days when no agricultural work is available, workers try to supplement their incomes with secondary activities of the kind already discussed. It should be noted, however, that in many cases this is only last resort

Agricultural labourer at work

work which yields little income, even less than can be earned from agricultural labour. Moreover, the periods of great activity and of non-activity inside and outside agriculture, now run parallel to one another rather than antithetically. When land under cultivation lies fallow, there is also little to do in other sectors of the local economy. Conversely, the period of feverish activity at harvest time, also extends beyond the fields. The trade in rice and its transport out of the village needs many workers, and petty and temporary traders set up roadside stalls at which they sell refreshments, food and sweets to the multitude of hard-working men, women and children.

In the modality of agricultural employment a distinction should be made between permanent and casual workers. Permanent labourers employed by large farmers are known as *kulikang* or *anak buah.* I counted fourteen such farm servants in the locality – far fewer, according to my informants than there had been in the past. That decline seems to be linked to the far greater ease with which landowners can nowadays meet their labour needs on a short-term basis. They no longer have to employ people permanently in order that their requirements for hired help may be fulfilled during busy periods. By adopting a different strategy, to be explained below, farmers are able to vary their labour input according to the successive highs and lows of field operations. One task formerly entrusted to farmhands, to recruit temporary workers for their employers from their own milieu, has almost or entirely disappeared. Owners of more than one hectare of land still find it worthwhile to employ one of two farmhands, and occasionally one will be shared by two farmers. These are tried and tested workers to whom more responsible jobs can be delegated and who are able to deputize for the master (*juragan*) during the latter's absence. The dispersed location of the fields, which are often worked simultaneously, means that the landowner cannot always be present at the most critical moment, the dividing up of the harvest. The task of operating the scales with which the harvesters' share (*bawon*) is determined has then to be entrusted to the farmhand. The latter also keeps an eye on the threshing, the filling of the sacks, and the transport of the still wet paddy (*gabah*) to the owner's house. It is said that the master relies more on the farmhand who has shown him years of faithful service than on his own children. The *kulikang* works primarily on the land but has to be prepared to work in the master's house when necessary. That obligation also extends to his wife, who does the laundry or cleans house for the employer, while the master may further command the unpaid help of his subordinates on festive occasions. Rich farmers cannot manage without at least one such farm servant. The households of the rural elite which own some dozen of hectares (none of which are found in North Subang) employ a number of such workers. Two landless workers in the *kampung*, together with eight others living elsewhere, form the permanent workforce of a haji who lives near the locality and owns approximately a hundred hectares.

Farmhands work longer hours than casual workers, usually starting earlier and not returning home until six pm, but do not earn a higher wage for this greater effort. In summer 1990 the majority of farmhands had to be satisfied with one thousand five hundred rupiah per day, five hundred less than daily workers were paid. The certainty that this amount will be paid every day or at least with great regularity, however, means that the position of farmhand in permanent employment is much coveted. That attraction is due particularly to the chance that the worker will be given a plot of land on a sharecropping basis as extra remuneration. By no means all farmhands are entitled to such a right; my data show that the custom is restricted primarily to those who are poor relations of the landowner.

The majority of landless earn a living as day workers in agriculture. Although they work for many farmers in a season, it appears that many of the generally short-term agreements that they enter into with employers are not one-off affairs but are usually recurring extensions of a contract made much earlier which has been kept active by at least one of the parties, sometimes after a long interval. In seeking a livelihood, casual workers have to depend on information as to where employment is, or is likely to become available, whether inside or outside agriculture, locally or further afield. Neighbours, relatives and friends keep them informed about different activities, and at the *warung* and other meeting points they learn who might be able to hire them, either immediately or in the near future. The coming together of supply and demand is not unstructured, but follows lines of mediation with which are all familiar. What seems to outsiders a complex and ambiguous or undefined arena of work is a transparent field of operations for those who take part in it.

The work carried out by day labourers is based partly on agreements made earlier. Only if acute scarcity threatens, which now rarely occurs, will employers pay an advance (*gajar*) to casual labourers who, in turn, pledge themselves to report on the agreed day or for the agreed job. A farmer will more frequently ensure the necessary labour force for an operation from beginning to end, particularly for the transplanting of paddy which is done by groups, by concluding a contract earlier with the leader of a planting gang (*kepala rombongan*). The latter is given a sum of money which is then distributed among the women in this gang who, in due course, will do the work that has been sealed with the payment of earnest money. Since tractors became commonly used for preparing the land, work with the hoe (*pacul*), which formerly occupied the men for many days in succession, is far less common.

Harvesting is a field operation accessible to all. The prevailing open field system means that no one who reports to the owner or his foreman to participate in the work may be refused. Workers who do not depend on agriculture for their livelihood and who are absent from the village for most of the year, have just as much right to share in this peak in the agrarian cycle as do the landless who did all the preparatory work. Men and women who have heard that the owner will declare the crop ready for harvesting, gather at the edge of the fields in the early morning. Quite often they start work immediately, without awaiting a sign from the owner or his agent that the operation might begin. Everyone is in a hurry, because anyone who does not work will be left behind in the fight for a share of the crop. As soon as a field is finished, the horde moves on to the next. Single workers are excluded from this finale, not in principle but in practice. Harvesting is a joint activity for a couple from the same household, normally a man and his wife. The latter cuts while the former threshes, fills the sacks and carries them away. This division of labour explains why single women are only able to get access to the harvest if they are helped by a male partner who is not needed for another team. However great the customary supply of labour, demand at certain peaks of the agricultural economic cycle, particularly at harvest time, seems to be so boundless that farmers cannot and will not make do with the local agricultural proletariat. On the other hand, employment in the village fields is insufficient on a yearly basis to meet minimal living costs for the numerous landless households in the locality. The outcome is obvious: a sizeable migration of labour, both to and away from the village.

By devoting considerable attention to these economic links between the *kampung* and the outside world, a completely different view of the nature of the rural economy emerges from my study and that of Pincus to that portrayed by Hayami and Kikuchi. Their point of departure was the colonial stereotype of the unchanging Asian village, structured in a communal framework which had come under increasing pressure in recent times as a result of population growth.[3] The suggestion they gave of long-term continuity based on the agrarian order in which the rising demand for work was constrained in immobility was remarkable in more than one respect. To start with, the view of the 'traditional village community' on which it was based and which was already obsolete when they published their findings. Secondly, one of the four case studies on which the Japanese economists based their argument clearly did not fit into their static model. As they themselves indicated, North Subang was hardly two generations old when they conducted their study

3 One typical example of the way Hayami and Kikuchi presented a distorted picture of the village economy was their division of the one hundred and ninety-one households living in North Subang at the time of their investigations into only two classes: peasants and agricultural labourers. Consequently, their findings acknowledged no other forms of occupation or employment outside agriculture (Hayami and Kikuchi 1981:196).

and the number of inhabitants living in the *kampung* had fluctuated considerably in the preceding years (Hayami and Kikuchi 1981:197-8). They did not consider these facts sufficient reason to reject the myth of the reproduction from generation to generation of the traditional Asian village system.

Extension of the agricultural labour market

The inflow of seasonal migrants occurs primarily at harvest time, but is then so massive that the a density of workers involved in this operation can reach a hundred per hectare. Men and women crowd into the fields, leaving them empty just a few hours later. That such a multitude of workers invade the coastal plain in the search for paddy to cut does not necessarily mean that outflows are occurring elsewhere in the countryside. The greater mobility could be linked to the tendency in various parts of Java to save harvesting work for people who have been involved in earlier field operations, according to the so-called *ceblokan* system. This trend, to which attention has been drawn in a number of recent studies (for example Hart 1986b), can have the effect that regions where the open field system is retained tend to come under extra pressure. Many workers from elsewhere flock to the village, particularly for the harvest at the end of the rainy season. They are so numerous that local workers, also many in number, are in the minority. Most outsiders do not come from far away. It is estimated that 75% travel no more than fifteen kilometres and usually return home at the end of the day. The rest, who make a longer journey, find shelter with relatives or simply spend the night along the roadside. The great inflow which formerly came all year round, not only for harvesting but also for tilling the land and other activities, and which originated in Pemalang and other places along Central Java's northern coast, has now dried up. Familial contacts still continue, however, and recruitment could again take place along the same lines should landowners show sufficient interest. During the last few years this has not occurred, for obvious reasons: no reasonable purpose would be served by encouraging an even greater inflow of temporary labour than is already the case.

The migrants disappear after harvest just as quickly as they came. The land is then deserted and, for the time being at least, offers no work even to the local landless. Indigent widows and other women who are too old to work are then kept busy for a few days with gleaning, gathering the rice stalks and ears that have been left on the fields by the harvesters. The larger landowners in the village are able to relax, but the small farmers, let alone the landless, cannot permit themselves such luxury. Harvesting continues in the vicinity of North Subang, and members of households with little if any land now leave the *kampung* to join the army of workers who descend on neigh-

The importance of the bicycle for the transport of commodities in the rural economy

bouring villages. The workers learn by word-of-mouth where and when operations will start, information that is of strategic importance for all their activities. The harvesting couple leave home early in the morning, on foot or by bicycle with the man pedalling and the woman riding pillion. They return before dark, now using the bicycle to transport their hard-won share of the paddy. The bike facilitates labour mobility in that a greater distance may be covered in less time. Harvest sites located fifteen to twenty kilometres from North Subang are within range for cycle owners, but the added advantage of being able to carry a sack of rice on it means that they are no longer forced to sell the *bawon* immediately to one of the small traders stationed along the roadside. Instead, they can take their harvest share home to keep for their own use or to sell later at a higher price.

The increased return for labour in terms of time and proceeds explains the bicycle's growing popularity in the landless milieu. The cost of a new vehicle far exceeds the household budget. A second-hand bike, in which there is a brisk trade, therefore has top priority among the goods asked by a landless boy from parents or parents-in-law on the occasion of his marriage. When harvesting is farther away, it is impossible for the workers to return in the evening. That particular form of commuting is called *ngadugdag*, a name referring to the beating of the drum near the village mosque to mark the end of the working day. When the workplace cannot be reached on foot or by bicycle, the harvest workers then travel by *colt* (minibus) from the main road which passes close to North Subang. Those with the same destination will join together in small groups. The night away from the village is spent preferably with relatives, and the destination may be chosen on that basis. Comfortless nights spent along the roadside are no exception, however, and form part of the price that many are prepared to pay for extending their share in the harvesting campaign. Pincus estimated that for these labourers, more than half of their income comes from farm work outside the *kampung* and more than a quarter from outside the district (Pincus 1996:105).

Not all those who have been active in the fields of their own village will take part in hunting the harvest elsewhere. Small farmers will pull out as the distance increases. Work connected to their own farm keeps them at home: that is at least the reason they give, but considerations of status are equally important. They find it beneath the dignity of their position to behave in a way that is more typical of a landless existence: roaming about in search of work and an income. Moreover, the harvest share decreases proportionately to the distance from home. Workers living in the near vicinity have the advantage in time and knowledge. They can reach the fields earlier in the morning and work later, while their familiarity with local conditions favourably affects the share that they carry off. The handicap of being an outsider does not deter agricultural workers, but does put off landowners who are accustomed to higher remuneration for their effort. Also, the men who go out in search of work are not always accompanied by their wives or elder daughters. Young mothers and older women in particular will remain at home as harvesting becomes more distant from the village. This is the category that I have described earlier as co-workers who are occasionally rather than constantly active. Obviously, only those households who manage to accumulate an adequate surplus, that is, food supplies or other sources of livelihood that provide an income in slack periods, can permit themselves not to send all able-bodied members as long as rice-cutting continues in the region.

Agricultural labour not only departs en masse at the end of the crop cycle. Transplanting is an early operation which many women participate in. Contrary to harvesting, the work is done by groups, and advance arrangements have to be made with the leader of a gang (*kepala rombongan*). Five men in the locality act as such group leaders. Two accept orders only from neighbouring landowners and, together with their team, return each evening to the *kampung*. Women who are recruited by the other three go farther from home and stay away for days or even weeks at a time. These include far more women from the landless milieu than the two less mobile groups.

We have seen that gang members are bound by the leader by payment of earnest money often obtained from employers even before the seedlings are planted. The ultimate price is not negotiable but is fixed for the coastal plain as a whole: at the time of my fieldwork this was fifty thousand rupiah per hectare. All *kepala rombongan* maintained that they received no extra payment in the form of commission from the farmer and/or a percentage of the gang's wages for their services, that is, arranging the contract and supervision over proper execution of the work. I find this remarkable, but have no evidence to the contrary. The money is paid to gang members immediately after completion of the day's work, after deducting costs for travel and food, rather than waiting until they reach home again. The leader of the biggest gang travels each season with about fifty people, mostly women, to a village twenty-five kilometres away to transplant rice for a *haji* who owns so much land that he employs five other gangs in addition to that from North Subang. The landowner provides sleeping places, but the gang leader has to supply the meals. His wife or daughter prepares all the food in pots and pans that they carry with them. One young worker told me that on his last trip he brought back forty thousand rupiah.

Planting gangs first appeared after the introduction of new methods of rice cultivation which require considerable precision. The women stand in a row and plant the seedlings along a rope whose ends are held by two men. Walking backwards, the planters wait until the rope is pulled taut before them and then repeat their stooping movement. The women work at a great pace under difficult conditions in the wet *sawah*. To have to stand all day ankle-deep in water with a bent back is very strenuous work indeed. It is thus hardly surprising that women belonging to landowning households show little desire to join a planting gang. Females of landless households, on the other hand, are unable to weigh the advantages of good physical health against the need to do work that will vitiate it. To give higher priority to the former assumes a freedom of choice that is incompatible with the survival strategy which forces landless workers to look no further ahead than the following day. They are always in dire need of cash income or advances and this explains why gang leaders have little trouble in disposing of the earnest money. No other than the healthy and sturdy are contracted: experience has taught women to report for such work only if they are capable of doing it.

It might be deduced from the above that the mobility of agricultural labourers is restricted to a radius of a few dozen kilometres from their own village, but this is not so. When rice harvesting is finished in the fields of the *kampung* and after one or two weeks in the entire northern plain of the whole Subang district, agricultural workers belonging to families of landless and marginal landowners prepare to journey towards the west, to regions where the harvest starts later. Krawang, Bekasi and even Banten, beyond the metropolitan area of Jakarta, are their new destinations. We can be brief on this matter since the pattern of these sallies does not differ drastically from their short-distance commuting.

Younger people in particular sometimes leave home without definite plans about their destination or possible length of absence. Based on advance information and on earlier experience, however, they know where and when work is available to outsiders. It is rarely a case of trying one's luck. Everyone has a number of locations that qualify for regular visits. Contacts made in this way are not primarily through employers but stem from relatives or friends living there who belong to the same landless milieu as most of the migrants. The widening of the rural labour market that has come about makes the cultivation of kinship and other primordial ties outside the own locality a valuable element in the survival strategy of the landless under-class. Such networks are for them of no less importance than the bonds connecting members of the landowning classes albeit for other economic reasons.

The absence from home seldom lasts more than a few weeks, nor is there any continual movement during this period. Labour migrants do not travel to Krawang, Bekasi and Banten in sequence; those who go to the latter do so directly without seeking work on the way. The constant alternation of departure and return of labour, so characteristic of the landless existence, occurs far less in the higher echelons of the village economy because big landowners have no need for this type of work migration. The coming and going takes place mostly on an individual basis and is not synchronized. In other words, seasonal migrants do not all leave simultaneously, they have different destinations in mind and, with the exception of women who depart in gangs for rice transplantation, they do not join up into groups. That occurs mostly in the case of women who depart as a team to transplant rice.

It is quite common for workers from the same village to meet in other places. They will have left on different days and travel back home together only if it suits them to do so.

But has the harvesting operation never been carried out on a gang basis? When I persistently queried this, one *kepala rombongan* answered after much thought that in the past, when migration first started to the more distant western plain, he had led a group of mostly younger people who had never before been away from the village. He took them to the fields where work was in progress and saw to it that a bivouac was arranged for the night, but after that everyone went their own way. He was not responsible for contacting the landowner or his agent, and was not involved in payment of the workers. The newcomers showed their thanks for his guidance by selling their share of the harvest to him rather than to one of the many dealers. The total amount of paddy that he collected enabled him to negotiate a somewhat higher price with a wholesaler. After having done this a few times, the landless from the *kampung* went their own way and no longer needed his guidance.

The village landowners are sometimes involved in the deployment of agricultural labourers elsewhere. This applies particularly to households who have leased land in the region northeast of Jakarta. As we have seen, this strategy of consolidation entails transferring their activities there for part of the year. They send to their own village for all extra labour that might be needed, for example for working the soil by hoe or tractor, transplanting, weeding and harvesting. Tractor owners also take on work far from the village, sending their machines together with drivers to the worksite. One machine and its driver, who lives in North Subang, has even been put onto a lorry and taken to Banten to plough the land.

It would be incorrect to suggest that, until a few decades ago, farm labour on Java was confined to the village economy from which it has only recently freed itself. To draw such a simple contrast between past and present, marked not only by a late but also a fairly sudden change, does not do justice to the mobility of landowners and landless in an agrarian society that has been subjected to transformation processes dating back to far before the colonial era. Acknowledging the state of flux as the 'normal' condition of the rural order, however, should not prevent us from establishing that, throughout Java, a definite acceleration has occurred in the pattern of labour migration during the last quarter-century, made possible by the *revolusi colt* (Hugo 1985:62; 1990: 231). The extension of the scale of operations to which this has given rise concerns both the magnitude of the work mobility and the distance covered. The dynamics of more people and longer distances is due mainly to the development of a physical infrastructure that has enabled rapid and cheap movements of the production factor labour. The enormous increase in demand for transport has had to be processed by a road system that was not designed for it. The imbalance causes inconvenience and not inconsiderable health and safety risks, but does not hinder people from periodically seeking other and more distant work locations, whether on foot, by bicycle, or as paying passenger on the motorbike, in colt or bus. Using the village as home base, members of households with little if any land circulate in a greatly enlarged labour market.

Limits of mobility

In the literature on this subject, the increased mobility of labour in rural Java is almost always linked with a shorter or longer stay in the urban arena. In my research village, some of those who depend mostly or even entirely on non-agricultural earnings have indeed found work in the big-city economy, at least temporarily and sometimes more permanently. With the exception of one or two who have found work in Bandung, these people all work in Jakarta or its outskirts. This is the largest growth pole in West Java and is easily accessible from North Subang: first by *ojeg* and *colt* to the market town of Pamanukan on the highway along the northern coast, and then by bus to the capital. Day and night a stream of vehicles is on the road, the distance of a hundred and twenty-five kilometres easily being covered in roughly four hours. Such a short travelling time there and back immediately raises the question of why more villagers do not go to Jakarta to seek an income. It is a widely held belief that this is more easily found in the urban milieu, both in view of the greater demand for labour as compared to the hinterland, and of the higher wages paid. Nevertheless, the number of workers who penetrate into the city is surprisingly low, that is, less than 10% of the working population, or forty out of the total of five hundred and forty-one that I have classified as economically active. Of those, skilled workers in permanent employment or small non-itinerant self-employed businessmen are by far in the minority: two local government officials, a few artisans and small traders, a handful of factory workers, a dock worker, and a driver employed by a multinational enterprise. They have found shelter in what is known as the formal sector of the economy, and spend the greater part of the year away from the village. Their visits home are constant though not frequent, and the money that they bring with them largely supports those who remain behind. Notwithstanding their relatively secure existence, they usually do not earn sufficient to permit the entire family to move to the town.

The ambition to provide shelter to relatives is even farther out of reach of those who find it even more difficult to keep their heads above water. Not only is their income insufficient, but their working conditions are such that living as a family is out of the question. They include house servants, prostitutes, street traders and unskilled construction workers who operate in the so-called informal sector, partly as small self-employed, partly as wage earners. Their stay in the city is not only far more precarious but is also subject to considerable instability. They return to the village more frequently, and lengthen or shorten their stay at home according to conditions in the workplace. Their behaviour seems to be impulsive and arbitrary, but such lack of regularity results from their inadequate grasp on the mode of employment. Their incomes are lower than those of the more skilled and continuously paid labourers in the formal sector, with the exception of prostitutes who earn by far the most of all those who work away from the village.

Employment in the formal sector is scarce and access to it protected, partly but not solely by demands regarding training and experience, so as to resist and in effect to frustrate too great pressure from the lower ranks of the working population. Villagers who have found a safe niche in the urban economy react dissuasively to requests that they should bring others into contact with employers or with personnel recruiters. Such claims for recommendation cause them embarrassment, to such a degree even that they tend to deny that they are ever harassed by requests for mediation. Their caution seems to be due partly to their own vulnerability as migrants.

It is far less difficult, according to common opinion (for example Hugo et al. 1990:233), to find work in the informal sector. The threshold is said to be low or even non-existent, with the consequence that everyone coming from the countryside can work wherever, when and for as long as necessary. This is misleading in more than one respect. Irrespective of whether it concerns servants, building workers, prostitutes, street traders or roadmen, casual and irregular work is bound by all sorts of restrictions which make the alleged free access and exit illusory. Availability at a particular time, intercession by a third party prepared to accept responsibility for the good behaviour of the newcomer, and consent to pay for training or protection, are just a few of the conditions that have to be met by applicants.

Apart from the fact that upward mobility to more highly-respected employment in the formal sector seldom, if ever, occurs there are also horizontal barriers within the informal sector, with the result that there is no question of homogeneous and flexible market for unskilled and low-paid labour. After a boom in the building industry lasting many years, the declining economic situation combined with the increasing capital intensity of this branch of industry has led particularly to a fall in the demand for casual unskilled labour, so that a decreasing number of landless still leave the village in the hope of finding such work in the city. During their stay in Jakarta they have not gained the experience and contacts needed to enable them to diverge vertically or horizontally into other activities.

This applies even more strongly to the *tukang becak*. During the last few years, these operators of pedicabs have been chased out of Jakarta, first from the centre and then increasingly from suburban thoroughfares. Although some managed to prolong their stay by paying fines that usually have the character of hush money, all but one have ultimately returned to North Subang to take up their old work as agricultural labourer. The one exception is a man who has managed to upgrade himself to driving a motorized three-wheeler. The story of his success, which he told me with much satisfaction, shows why others have not followed his example. For a start, he was fortunate enough to have a friend who drove a hired *bajaj*. This friend was willing to teach him how to use the vehicle but could only do so when both had free time and when the bajaj was not hired-out to a second man in a 24-hour period, a combination of circumstances that rarely occurred. He also had to be prepared to pay for the fuel used during the lesson and to provide his friend with refreshments in return for his trouble. The expense involved was a heavy burden on his earnings as *becak* rider, money that was intended for

One of the village women working as prostitute in Jakarta

his family in the village. Even when he had mastered the use of the vehicle, he had to wait a considerable time before being issued with his driving licence. Whenever he was arrested, which happened fairly frequently because chasing workers in the informal sector is a lucrative and popular occupation for the police, he had to pay a 'fine' of a thousand to one thousand five hundred rupiah. After paying rental to the vehicle's owner, he had little if anything left at the end of the day. The financial sacrifices that he had to suffer and the time that it took to overcome all these hurdles, make it understandable why his former colleagues have returned to the country while he now lawfully drives round Jakarta, in a vehicle which earns him more money than he had formerly scraped together.

Commentators who draw attention to the fences put up around urban employment are usually concerned with the effort needed to penetrate them. Sometimes, however, the way out is also guarded and mobility in that direction subject to restrictions. The intimidation of domestic servants, particularly women, is common practice. Restrictions on their freedom of movement include the employer's refusal to terminate the employment and the infliction of punishment if the servant attempts to leave. Debt bondage is also part of the manipulation to which workers in the informal sector are exposed. Women from the village who work as prostitutes in Jakarta have to cope with a cruder show of power, including physical violence. Some of these women regularly come back to North Subang and make considerable contributions to their family's budget. Eventually, however, they stay away and are rarely heard from again.

It is not only employers who set restrictions on the behaviour of labour migrants in the city. Numerous government institutions, especially those charged with the maintenance of law and order, tend to consider the massive army of people who are dependent on casual and often itinerant work as superfluous and troublesome vagrants. Men and women belonging to this under-class have to disappear from the townscape as quickly as possible, or are only tolerated if they make themselves almost invisible. The city centre is more or less forbidden territory to them. The fate of the *becak* riders is no exception. Food vendors are expected to supply their uniformed 'hosts' with free meals, while street traders risk losing their wares when the police hold a razzia. Authorities pursue them and other *kaki lima* as though they were hunting outlaws. Instead of encouraging employment in the informal sector, official policy seems rather to ostracize this segment of the urban economy, which is regarded as parasitic, and to send the people involved back to the countryside.

At the start of the 1990s my fieldwork village was still surprisingly agrarian in character. Little if any change seemed to have occurred in the situation described in an earlier study of the same location, based on data for the period 1972-1981 (White and Wiradi 1989:294). Just as then, agriculture forms the main source of livelihood for the villagers. This is a surprising conclusion because in the intervening years it has become easier to leave the countryside and, measured in time, the urban growth poles have become closer. The fact that only a relative few have managed to shift the base of their economic activities towards those poles is closely connected to the restrictions placed on mobility in the direction of Jakarta.

The 'reserve army' of landless and unskilled men and women is confronted by national and urban policy-makers who tend to seal off cities to an incessant inflow of people whom they cannot and will not assimilate. On the other hand there is the belief that the countryside is an empty space, an arena within which labour can circulate without hindrance. What has been discussed so far could be seen as confirmation of this assumption, which at first seems so plausible. The green revolution that has swept through the villages during the last twenty-five years seems at last to have yielded a credit balance in terms of more employment opportunities. Labour has undoubtedly been pushed out, but the increased crop intensity resulting from expansion of the irrigated area, combined with the slow progress made in mechanizing field operations, explains why agriculture absorbs more labour than ever before.

In this respect, the dynamics in my fieldwork locality are illustrative of a trend that has occurred elsewhere on Java, particularly on the plains. True, the village's own fields do not provide work all year round. In addition, the non-agrarian sectors of the village economy, although they have also experienced modest growth, cannot adequately make up the minimal income needed by the under-class of people with little land or none at all. Nevertheless, households at the base of society are now less dependent on local sources to meet their basic needs. The strong growth of transport means that distances can be covered more easily and more cheaply. The movements of labour follow the spatial variations in the pattern of agrarian employment, as is clearly shown by the pursuit of harvesting operations far from the home village.

The hordes of people who roam the regions where paddy is harvested under the open field system (*bawon*) are perhaps the most convincing proof of the thesis that the balance of supply and demand in the rural economy is conditioned by no other force than that of the free movement of labour. That is to say, in a manner that ensures that the inflow of workers changes to an outflow and vice versa with the alternating peaks and falls in the agrarian production cycle. I consider it misleading to suggest such a perfect operation of the market mechanism. It would again give life to the fiction, now for the rural system, of open ingress and egress which has long and tenaciously, though incorrectly, dominated the image of the urban informal sector (see Breman 1980).

The literature does mention a growth of restrictive practices, particularly the conversion from an open to a closed system of harvesting, that is, from *bawon* to *ceblokan*; nevertheless, a critical appraisal of the structure of the rural labour market has not been forthcoming. My own scepticism regarding the persistently-voiced notion that barriers play no part in this milieu can be substantiated with the aid of a few concrete examples. As we have seen, the landless inhabitants of North Subang make regular sorties to Banten when harvesting begins there. Some people told me, however, that they had stopped making the journey because they were subjected to acts of aggression during their short stay. A few migrant workers have even had their makeshift night shelters, set up in open fields or along the roadside, set on fire. The experience has clearly frightened them. When I enquired into the background of such incidents, I was usually told that the culprits were unknown people who disliked strangers, or that it had been due to a quarrel among the harvesters which had got out of hand. There is little inclination to admit openly that the opposing interests of local and of migrant workers are behind such conflicts. In 1969 the authorities of Krawang prohibited the open field system, fearing the social tension that might arise if the horde of labour migrants should be denied access to seasonal work (Hart 1986b:690). Nevertheless, there are signs of a type of consciousness which suggests a linkage between the right to work and the provenance of labour. The idea that local workers should indeed have priority explains why people feel vulnerable when harvesting paddy away from the village; on the other hand, it is not thought self-evident that outsiders should be given unhindered access to the crop on the village's own fields. If the crop is harvested under the open field system, workers from elsewhere cannot be openly refused, but it happens more covertly. A few seasons ago, a small landowner in the kampung wanted to keep as much as possible of the crop for himself; he was therefore the first to start harvesting and continued working after dark. Resourceful but 'not done', was the general opinion. The *pamong desa* put an end to it, fearing that the village would get a bad reputation.

A person present when I was told of this incident related how another farmer and his sons had gone to his field during the night to harvest his crop, equipped with a torch rather than a petromax in order to attract as little attention as possible. I also heard about the collective closing-off in 1990 of the area to be harvested in a neighbouring settlement, not to all outsiders but specifically to people from the *kampung* of my fieldwork. The site of this prohibition had formerly been part of North Subang but now has its own *desa* administration. I went there in search of further information and the story was confirmed by the local agricultural officer, who added that the initiative had not been taken by the landowners but by the workers. Why? The workers wanted revenge for the refusal by the inhabitants of S to admit them to the harvest in the previous season. Only when I asked my hosts about this did they acknowledge that the story was correct. So they had started it? If I wanted to put it that way, yes. But, they argued, we only did it on that one occasion so that we could pay for two important village festivities. According to them, it does sometimes happen that the harvest is declared closed to outsiders. This is done by marking the blocks of land with flags and stakes. Those who want to harvest the paddy then have to share their *bawon* with the owner of the field who is obliged to hand over the harvest share deducted to the village authorities. To work under these conditions is disadvantageous in that the same effort is required but the result is only half a *bawon*; outsiders therefore avoid such fields and local workers have the harvest to themselves. What started as a one-off exclusion has provoked a counter-move by the neighbours which threatens to be of a more permanent nature and may spread further in the surrounding area. At the time of my fieldwork, that escalation was the subject of discussion at the sub-district office. The landowners had insisted on this, fearing that migrant workers would stay away in future and that their own scope for manoeuvre versus the local landless would weaken as a result. Whether it will be possible to restore the former situation is questionable. In another village in the near vicinity the open *bawon* method of harvesting has been abandoned and replaced by the closed *ceblokan* system. The same transition has been observed in other parts of Java. It would be simplistic to see this trend as indicating concern among powerful villagers for the welfare of their weaker neighbours (Hayami and Kikuchi 1981) or, conversely, as a sign of growing strength in the negotiating position of local agricultural workers. An explanation in such straightforward and mutually exclusive terms does not agree with the more complicated reality (Hart 1986b).

We have seen that access to work is subject to numerous restrictions, in both urban and rural domains. Labour has become mobile, but it does not circulate freely throughout the economy and is confined more or less to particular segments. The customary dividing lines concern employment within or outside agriculture or the contrast between city and countryside. The results of my research, however, show that these are not the divisions that mark the economic conditions of landless households. Seen from the viewpoint of this sizeable under-class in North Subang, the structure of the labour market is determined far more by a different demarcation. More important than the dichotomies mentioned is the distinction between wage labour and work on one's own account and at one's own risk on the one hand, and casual or permanent employment on the other. Put more broadly, it means that a division of the economy into formal and informal sectors cannot support a breakdown into urban and rural labour or industrial versus agrarian employment. This point of view will not be further elaborated upon in this present study. (For further elaboration see Breman 1996).

Quality of working class life

Improvements to the welfare level in Indonesia, based on strong economic growth during the last quarter-century, have been extended to the countryside. This is certainly the case in West Java, which is known as the most prosperous province of the country. That economic dynamics are concentrated in a semi-circle around Jakarta – referred to as Jabotabek, an acronym of the urban nuclei situated within this industrial zone – does not alter the fact that the production and productivity of agrarian regions outside that zone have advanced substantially, especially during the 1980s. What has been the impact of this trend on the lives of the mass of landless labourers?

For a start, there is sufficient evidence of a genuine improvement in real wages. This is the tenor of both commissioned reports and of numerous more independent studies. My own village-level research results enables me to be more specific about this general conclusion and, at the same time, to add a few critical comments.

With regard to the proceeds of employment in agriculture, by far the most important source of income for working households, I distinguish between payment for harvest work and that for pre-harvest field operations. During the last few years, payment for the latter, mainly hoeing, transplanting and weeding, has equalled or even slightly exceeded the rise in the cost of living. A similar trend was observed in this and other locations between 1970-1971 and 1980/1981 (White and Wiradi 1989:Table 13.9). In mid-1990, one thousand five hundred to two thousand rupiah per day were paid for hoeing and one thousand to one thousand five hundred rupiah for weeding. The lower rate applies to the growth cycle in the wet season. The higher tariff paid in the dry season is partly due to a more sluggish supply of labour. Landless households then still have stock available from the earlier season and, moreover, harvesting has already started elsewhere. To ensure sufficient workers, farmers thus have to be prepared to pay a slightly higher wage. As we have seen, transplanting is done by workgangs and paid on a piecework basis. The women who do the work earn around two thousand rupiah or rather more.

Over the last half-century, the *bawon* has been reduced from one-fifth to one-tenth. In the 1940s the harvest share was 20%, and until the late 1970s almost half the *sawah* owners parted with an amount varying between one-seventh and one-ninth of the yield. Nowadays, not a single farmer in the *kampung* will give more than 10%. Before examining the background of this reduction, which has also occurred in other regions of Java, I would first like to draw attention to the important fact that payment is still made in kind. Given the high degree of monetization of transactions within the local economy, this seems a remarkable phenomenon that ought to be the subject of far more discussion in socio-economic literature on the agrarian situation in

Java than at present is the case. In 1990, landowners in my fieldwork locality in fact bought back the rice immediately after harvesting. The reasons that they gave for doing so were, firstly, that the workers had difficulties in drying their share in the wet season and, secondly, that traders (*bakul*) preferred to do business with landowners who could supply them with large quantities rather than to collect individual *bawon* from landless workers. These arguments are valid but by no means new. More convincing, in my opinion, is the workers' version to the effect that the change forced on them was due to an unexpected and temporary rise in the trade price for rice. Now that this has returned to its former level, the workers are again paid in kind.

In the early 1970s a relative of one of my key informants among the landowners was the first to reduce his harvesters' share to one-tenth. The workers did not agree with this reduction and complained to the village authorities. And with success, because the *lurah* determined that settlement must be made on the traditional basis. A year later, however, many more farmers announced that they would reduce the size of the *bawon*. In addition to increased production costs, particularly of artificial fertilizer, they gave as a reason that far too many workers turned up for harvesting and that the reduction would discourage too great an inflow. Landowners who did not wish to conform gradually dwindled in number, and the 10% *bawon* has been universally accepted since the beginning of the 1980s.

Low-class dwelling inhabited by household of agricultural labourers

Landless informants drew my attention to another change to their disadvantage. Until a few years ago the paddy was shared out in the field immediately after threshing, using a litre tin with which the *bawon* was measured. Not to let the tin overflow was considered to be niggardly. The introduction of scales, a sign of the progressive rationalization of farming, put an end to this. The harvesters' share is now measured precisely, in effect rather miserly. The man who started this in 1985 said that the workers at first shunned him. He put up with the inconvenience which, as he had expected, was only temporary because his example was soon followed by other landowners.

That agricultural workers have nevertheless progressed in real terms is due to increased crops and higher yields. Although the transition from one to two crops per year did not bring a doubling of the *bawon*, which had in any case been reduced, the total amount remaining in the hands of workers nevertheless increased considerably. The upward trend in the yearly harvest wage has also been stimulated by increased productivity per unit of land. This change, observed in North Subang at the end of the 1970s (Hayami and Kikuchi 1981:204-5), has since continued. By changing to new cropping techniques, using more artificial fertilizer, and by behaving entirely in a manner expected of green revolution producers, landowners have successfully raised the rice yield per hectare from 2.5 tons in 1971, to 3.8 tons in 1981 and (according to my information) to about 5 tons in 1990. These figures apply to wet season crops. The second harvest in the dry season is smaller but nevertheless shows a similar degree of growth, namely, from about two to almost four tons between 1971 and 1990. The accompanying increase in the share apportioned to workers has to be reduced by the income formerly derived by harvesters from the growth of second crops, not only as wage but also in direct disposition over this *polowijo*. Nowadays, they are obliged to buy this nutritious part of their food packet in the shops for a higher price. But even after taking this effect into account, it is clear that agricultural workers have also profited from the considerable advances made in agrarian production and productivity, to such a degree even that the reduction in their harvest share is a direct consequence. The farmers say they were forced to take this step which has been observed in other parts of Java, namely, that the share of wages in total income realized from paddy cultivation has declined during the last twenty years or so (White and Wiradi 1989:284; Manning 1988:54).

The reduced significance of the labour factor in growing what is practically the only agricultural crop in North Subang is paralleled by a continual growth in the number of people who depend largely on that crop for their livelihood. Without the proceeds of labour migration, the standard of living of landless households would not have improved but declined. In other words, the percentage of income earned away from the village has risen sharply. Agricultural work, particularly harvesting, is the greatest source of that income. In 1981, research in North Subang showed that the most important economic activity for the inhabitants was agriculture (White and Wiradi 1989:294). The results of my own study undertaken in 1990 indicate that this conclusion is still valid although, for a growing part of the population, work on the land and the earnings derived from it are no longer linked exclusively or even primarily to sources of livelihood within the village itself. More detailed and longer-term research is needed to show what quantitative shift has occurred in the relation between local and non-local employment.

Has the strongly increased mobility of labour caused wage standardization, as is suggested by Manning on the basis of Lipton's argumentation (Manning 1988:70)? My data demonstrates that this is only marginally the case. The tendency does occur in pre-harvest operations, but the harvest share shows great variations in different regions. In Banten, for example, migrant workers from my research locality can still count on a one-fifth share. It is interesting that farmers who lease land in the neighbourhood of Jakarta give the harvesters whom they summon from North Subang more than they do at home, namely, a one-seventh share. When asked why this was, they told me that they give migrant workers more because there were no *orang kaya*, that is, large landowners, to force them to follow their example of a lower wage rate. This reply says more about the rancour harboured by these respondents with regard to the elite in the home village than about the authenticity of the implied solidarity with those who are less fortunate than themselves. They give a higher *bawon* simply because it is standard practice in the area. Refusal to do so would undoubtedly cause the workers from North Subang to leave their fields and go to work on those of the local farmers. The standard adhered to by the latter for the harvest share is even slightly higher, amounting to a ratio of 5:1. That a division is used in this part of the coastal plain which has long been superseded elsewhere is, in my opinion, linked to the fact that there is only one harvest per year. The norm for what is due to the labour force is apparently related to agriculture's total annual proceeds. In other words, when production increases, the share that is paid as wages increase absolutely but decrease relatively. The shift is due to the notion that the owners of capital, that is, the landowners, are primarily entitled to the growing surplus. I shall return to this moral aspect of the economy at the end of this chapter.

What remains is the income from work outside agriculture. Data compiled in the early 1980s show that landless households in North Subang derive one-third of their total income from this source, considerably less than in other researched localities on Java (White and Wiradi 1989:Table 13.12). Little if any change seems to have occurred since then. In my opinion, that standstill should not be seen as indicating lack of interest among agricultural workers for employment in other economic sectors. Basically, the larger majority lack access to alternative, more or less continuous sources of livelihood in the countryside or in the urban sector. The modest number of landless who have done so with some degree of permanency earn scarcely more than members of households who still depend largely or entirely on agriculture. I have found no proof of the thesis that, other than formerly was the case, a much higher hourly rate is paid for unskilled and low-paid work outside agriculture than within it (Manning 1988:67). At the time of my fieldwork, the official minimum wage for casual labour employed by industries in Cikareng, an industrial zone on the periphery of Jakarta, was a mere two thousand one hundred rupiah per day. According to reports regularly published in the capital's newspapers, however, many employers refused to pay even that, and government undertook no action whatsoever to force them to do so.

On the basis of information supplied by people who have returned to the village, I conclude that the daily earnings of building workers, *becak* drivers, domestic servants and many others in the informal sector are at the most 30% above the rate earned by agricultural labourers. In mid-1990 they amounted to about three thousand rupiah or slightly less. Against this higher level of earnings, however, the urban worker has to meet extra expenses for transport, housing, food and unforeseen costs such as fines, protection or hush money. In determining the proceeds from labour circulation within the rural milieu, the costs of a household divided between the place of domicile and that of work also have to be taken into account. As a result, any extra money earned outside the village and agriculture hardly compensates for the greater expenses that accompany work outside agriculture. This also explains why those who choose to work away from the village, or have ended up there more or less accidentally, do not give the impression of having made much economic progress.

The obvious target of Indonesian government policy regarding agriculture and industry is to increase production, irrespective of the effect this may have on employment. The creation of more jobs is an incidental bonus, but one that is given high and emphatic priority only on paper. Government agencies make little effort to increase or even to maintain labour's share in the economic process as regards size and price. The high capital intensity inherent to the modern sector is applauded as a sign of modernity, even if it leads to the loss of more traditionally-organized trades and industries that are characterized by greater labour intensity. The substantial growth of factories and workplaces in West Java, first in the cities but spreading from there into the countryside in the form of enclaves, the copious expansion of transport and services facilitated by an enormous increase in communications, a gradual rationalization of farm management, are all parts of an economic transformation which, by and large, has actually provided a powerful incentive to the demand for labour. The manner in which labour is inserted into the production process, however, is defective: as a floating stock of casual workers, unskilled and under-paid. Against the background of these macro-social dynamics, I have focused in the format of a micro-study on the constant mobility of much of the rural population, consisting of marginal landowners and the landless, who are pushed out to work places far distant from their own homes and then pushed back again in a never-ending cycle.

In the analysis of this problem a question that immediately arises concerns the effect of economic growth and extension of scale on relations among the different social classes within the village system. Based on research carried out at the end of the 1970s in the *kampung* that was also the location of my own fieldwork, Hayami and Kikuchi concluded that a structural change had occurred during the previous decade or so. The strongly homogeneous peasant community that had formerly existed in Java – a doctrine that they adhere to despite copious historical evidence to the contrary – had, in their opinion, only fairly recently made way for greater heterogeneity based on landownership. Stratification and not polarization is the way in which they discuss this process of transformation. The interaction between the small elite of large farmer-landowners and the much broader basis of small landowners is analysed by the authors in terms of a patron-client relationship, based on mutual help and advantage and with no place for antagonism (Hayami and Kikuchi 1981:215). They find support for this interpretation in the manner of distribution of agrarian production, which had grown by roughly one-third over the preceding ten years. In the absolute sense, the income of farmers and workers has risen, while the figures presented also show that the relative share of the parties involved in growing paddy have remained unchanged in a ratio of almost 2:1 (Hayami and Kikuchi 1981:207). When proved correct, this result gives reason for satisfaction: general progress without increasing inequality.

I beg to disagree. Certainly, during the 1980s the landless households in the *kampung* undeniably benefited from the increased yield per hectare and, accordingly, the real wage level during this period rose significantly – as it had, incidentally, throughout Java. Pincus charted this upward trend in greater detail and noted that it had already started to level off towards the end of the decade (Pincus 1996:128-31, 198-203). He calculated that, in spite of the falling demand for labour as a result of the new agrarian technology, the per hectare cost of working land increased annually between 1970 and 1989 by a substantial amount. The decreased use of labour at the various stages of rice cultivation in our *kampung* of research was more than compensated for by the switch to two harvests a year once the irrigation capacity had been increased. The real rise in the wages of agricultural labourers in the early 1980s, however, did not detract from the fact that landowners profited much more from the growth in agrarian production. In the total package of costs and benefits, the costs of hired labour decreased, which essentially means that landowners appropriated a disproportionately large part of the surplus for themselves.

My findings, like those of Pincus and other contemporaneous researchers of rural Java (for example Hart 1986a), directly oppose the analysis of the Japanese economists in their interpretation of the nature and dynamics of the interaction between the landowning elite and the far more numerous landless under-class in North Subang. For the locations they studied, Hayami and Kikuchi presented agricultural labourers and peasant farmers as partners in a localized order that had traditionally been structured along communal or cooperative lines. According to them the systematic shift thas has been going on in more recent times is a matter of differentiation rather than of polarization. For them, this trend, which they saw as being accompanied by continued social cohesion and the emergence of a patron-client relationship, is a process which results in what they call increased stratification:

> a multiplication of peasant subclasses in a continuous spectrum ranging from landless labourers to non-cultivating landlords within the social mode of the peasant community in which villagers are tied to one another in multi-stranded personalized relations in contrast to the impersonal market relations which accompany polarization (Hayami and Kikuchi 1981:214).

My criticism of this interpretation is not so much aimed at the absence of any discussion of an enormous quantity of anthropological literature on the social structure and culture of peasant societies in past as well as present. What is particularly striking about their revisionist standpoint is that they describe the changes in the Asian village at the end of the 1970s as a transition from homogeneity to differentiation, and the replacement of reciprocity with patronage as a principle of social organization. Such a reduction of the complexity and diversity of the rural economy to a simple dichotomy in the agricultural sector was not only naive but also misleading.

I have taken a different view of the character of the 'traditional village on Java to Hayami and Kikuchi, an interpretation for which I have marshalled evidence in a number of publications (Breman 1978, 1983; see also Boomgaard 1991). Moreover, I disagree fundamentally with their account of the recent dynamics within the locality which is our common research subject. My opinion is based not only on my own data but also on other macro- and micro-studies pertaining to rural Java that show a more critical understanding of the processes of change that have occurred in the last few decades.[4]

[4] Hugo 1985, 1990; Hart 1986a, 1986b; Manning 1988; Hüsken 1988, 1989; White and Wiradi 1989; Pincus 1996.

Most, if not all, of these authors pay a great deal of attention to incomes and employment outside agriculture and away from the village, aspects that Hayami and Kikuchi have consistently not considered. That was a significant omission even at the time that they completed their study; now, ten years later, it is even greater.

My conclusion is, firstly, that the modernization of agriculture has further increased income inequalities between landowning and landless households in North Subang because the rationalization of farm management practices has produced a greater yield for capital than for labour. Secondly, the diversification and scale-enlargement of the economy, and the mobilization of the production factors of capital and labour for activities outside agriculture and the village, have articulated rather than compensated the growing intra-village inequality. I shall explain these conclusions briefly, on the basis of my earlier distinction in social strategies that I have attributed to the three classes into which the village population can be divided.

House of agricultural labourer

Dynamics of welfare and poverty

Accumulation is the key to analysing the economic behaviour of the upper class. The small group of landowners, among whom a disproportionately large part of the total agrarian capital is concentrated, are seldom if ever found in the fields. They leave the cultivation of their land to tenants and agricultural labourers, but exercise supervision to ensure that their affairs are efficiently managed. For many of them trade is a secondary source of income, for example the buying-up of newly harvested paddy, its resale after polishing, the provision of cash loans, land transactions in their own village or elsewhere. Some landowners join the village administration, not because of the money involved but to promote their own business interests up to the district level. A number are *haji*, and it has become increasingly customary for the men in this milieu to make the pilgrimage to Mecca accompanied by their wives.

Attained prosperity has to be displayed, and even in the *kampung* where I stayed – which is the least prosperous of the village – the first modern bungalows have appeared, constructed of decorative stone, with glass windows and tiled floors. Even more opulent houses have been built in the wealthier centre of the village. A garden planted with flowers and shrubs and comfort within the house, including ample settees covered in velvet or artificial leather, a dining area, large cupboards filled with glassware and crockery to be used on special occasions, all kinds of bric-a-brac, pictures, et cetera, all indicate a lifestyle that has much in common with that of the better situated townspeople.

That orientation is strengthened by ownership of a refrigerator, TV (in North Subang still run on batteries because there is no electricity), and by the family's style of dressing. The children go to school, and although continued education after primary school has become more customary in recent years, none have yet gone to university. Parents do not force their children to start work immediately after finished school. Boys drive an *ojeg*, but more as a sideline; girls are expected to help in the housekeeping. These *orang kaya* will spend a million rupiah or even more on major festivities such as a wedding or circumcision.

The strategy by which small landowners and tenants are guided I have called consolidation. The members of households belonging to this middle level of society are actively involved in farming and help in the work on the land that they own or rent. This class has little visibility in the village economy, although it includes roughly one-third of the inhabitants. By utilizing their women and older children they have only incidental need for the labour power of landless people. On the other hand, they will work for money on other people's land if they have no alternative source of income. Their side-

House of small farmer

House of a wealthy landowner-cum-trader

lines include the retail trade, commission for mediating in commercial transactions, driving an *ojeg* or keeping a neighbourhood shop. These *warung* are mostly run by women who often buy their own supplies in the market of the neighbouring town. Small landowners and tenants prefer to work for themselves and at their own risk. This does not apply to employment in the formal sector of industry away from the village and agriculture, but access to such work is restricted owing to insufficient education and lack of contacts.

In their own *kampung* the pressure of living is so great that slipping down can only be avoided by leasing land elsewhere when the local harvest is over. The example was given in 1983 when a resident of North Subang was given permission to cultivate waste municipal land close to the coast, in return for his promise that he would cease the hiring-out of his five *becaks* in this small town situated northeast of Jakarta. He managed to interest six more people from the *kampung* who rented land through his mediation. Since then, seasonal migrant farmers from my research location in Subang district, at a distance of more than a hundred kilometres, have further increased in number. In the summer of 1990 the settlement (there are two smaller ones nearby) included twenty-three farmers from North Subang, five of whom were renting land there for the first time. Together, they cultivated about twenty-five hectares. The land yields less than that of the *kampung* but this is compensated by the far lower rent. And – as one of them put it – it is better than to have to earn a living as an agricultural labourer.

The temporary settlement can be reached only by wading through the fields, and the loosely-grouped collection of primitive shelters makes a wretched impression. The nearest supply of drinking water is two kilometres away; for other daily necessities the migrant residents have to travel four kilometres. Nevertheless, most of these seasonal farmers are accompanied, for some time at least, by their families. There is no school in the direct vicinity, so that children who come with their parents are deprived of education for the duration of their stay. There is no prospect of permanent settlement. The land was sold a few years ago to a private enterprise and will eventually be used for industrial purposes.

At the end of the season, the harvested paddy is bought by the *kepala kampung* from North Subang and transported back there to be polished and then sold. What benefit does this type of migration have for those who take part in it? It has turned out to be a sufficiently attractive proposition, in the sense that it prolongs their autonomy as producers in the part of the year when there is little to do at home. Together with secondary activities, they earn just enough to keep going economically. Not so much, however, as to enable them to buy land in their own village. The price of that land has risen to twelve million rupiah per hectare, a gigantic increase in comparison with the inconsiderable amounts for which land changed hands in the early 1960s.

Cukup, sufficient, is nevertheless how my informants described the way in which such households live. At this middle level, progress is also expressed in improvements to the house and its furnishings, the possession of more consumption articles, slightly greater reserves and creditworthiness with which crises can be overcome. Amounts of five hundred thousand rupiah or more are spent on family festivities.

How to survive, that is the question directing the economic behaviour of the rural proletariat made up of people who are almost or entirely landless. A few authors have expressed doubt about the proletarian character of this broad under-class to which at least half the population of Javanese villages generally belongs. Their reason for doing so is that landless households, although they often earn their living with the aid of wage labour, do not do so exclusively or continually. Local research carried out by Hüsken between 1976 and 1978 in the northern coastal plain of Central Java, brought to light the fact that half the village acreage was issued on a sharecropping basis. The author argues that although participation in agriculture under such conditions makes for a relationship of dependency, a considerable percentage of the landless nevertheless manage to maintain access to the means of production in this way. Hüsken concludes from this that the proletarianization process is not yet complete (1988: 250; 1989:323).

Hüsken's prediction that, for the time being, sharecropping relations will not decline in significance is belied by micro-studies carried out in the early 1980s in various regions of Java. In their report on this research, White and Wiradi mention a reduced frequency of sharecropping in various villages, while in many others landless people said that it became more and more difficult to find a landowner willing to enter with them into such a relationship. The *kampung* where I stayed is a clear example of this trend which, in my opinion, is due to the increasing capital intensity of agriculture. Only a small minority among agricultural workers, usually those employed as farmhands by a landowner, are eligible for a plot of land to cultivate as sharecropper. Nevertheless, White and Wiradi also reject the term 'proletarians' for the landless of rural Java. They argue that the livelihood of these households is determined by a great variety of occupations, agrarian and non-agrarian, inside and outside the village. The incomes earned in this way are partly, though not always entirely, derived from wage labour. In view of the diversity of sources of livelihood, they prefer to speak of a semi-proletariat (White and Wiradi 1989:296; see Hugo 1985:73).

I am inclined to use the term 'proletariat' with less reservation and to rid it of such additions as 'semi' or 'pseudo', for two reasons. Firstly, the large landless class in my research locality quite definitely depends for its livelihood largely or even entirely on waged work. For the majority of them, income from retail trade or other forms of self-employment is fairly insignificant. Further research is needed to show whether this is an exceptional situation which seldom occurs outside my research village, or whether wage labour also increasingly determines the existence of the under-class elsewhere in rural Java. I would add, perhaps superfluously, that the persistent imagery of the urban informal sector as being dominated by self-employment, is a complete fallacy (Hugo 1985:74).

The second consideration is more fundamental in character and amounts to reappraisal of the notion that the admissibility of the term 'proletariat' is dependent on the degree to which wage payment has become the dominant or even sole modality for the remuneration of labour performance. To maintain that this quality is the outstanding defining characteristic would not do justice to the particular road to capitalism followed by Asiatic societies, nor would it adequately portray the emergence of what was said to be the classical proletariat in industrializing Europe. In any event, the unique course taken by the transformation process in Europe during an earlier period, whether actual or assumed, is no reason why, at the end of the twentieth century, the working masses on Java should not be qualified primarily as genuinely proletarian in character. In the landless milieu, the term 'property' has a significance which even extends to reasonably secure conditions of living. Seen from this point of view, stable employment and all that it entails – an assured income that is not subject to constant fluctuations, regularly recurring pursuits, standard hours of work and a fixed workplace – is a form of property which the majority have just as little chance of acquiring as a plot of land. To be forced to earn a living on the basis of casual labour of diverse nature and variable pay, causes a worker to take a very short-term view of the future and makes great demands on his or her manoeuvrability. The daily rhythm is determined by temporary input at rapidly changing sites. The search for and/or acceptance of work, the rejection or even refusal of a job, has to be based on nothing more than a rough estimate of what might be gained from other options. Finally, the use of the word proletariat, with no further elaboration, to describe the quality of the work and lives of the landless under-class in North Subang, does not in my opinion mean to say that the situation of the poor in the village can be characterized in terms of progressive poverty. In my view, however, the already existing divide between the top and bottom of the agrarian hierarchy has further widened and I tend to disagree with the observation that patronage somewhat helps to mitigate class differences. What nevertheless helps to prevent or moderate acute misery at the bottom end of the village economy is the possibility of escape by seeking work elsewhere, either within or outside the agricultural sector. The way in which this mobility of labour, both geographically and between sectors, gathers momentum and how it affects the local distribution of income has been at the core of my fieldwork in the early 1990s.

Mobility rather than containment in agriculture and the village typifies labour in rural Java, that is the essence of my argumentation. It is a fairly commonly held opinion that poverty makes people immobile. Following in Lipton's footsteps (Lipton 1980, cited in Manning 1988), Hugo marshals empirical evidence in defence of the thesis of the immobility of those who live and work at the bottom of rural Javanese society. According to Hugo, agricultural labourers lack the necessary reserves to accept the risk of leaving home. They have no choice other than to foster their ties with landowners in order at least to satisfy their minimum needs (Hugo et al. 1990:228). The results of my research contradict that opinion. Similarly to various other authors, Hugo bases his report too much on a patron-client relationship within the village sphere which has long ceased to exist in rural Java. An abundance of labour, which is the usual state of affairs, combined with sharp fluctuations on the demand side due to rationalization of farm management, have put an end to accommodation of the landless multitude in patronage relationships. Mutual assistance (*gotong royong*) and other communal support mechanisms mentioned by Hugo (Hugo et al. 1990:233) have also disappeared or lost much of their effectiveness. I further disagree with Hugo regarding the alleged complementarity in labour flows between countryside and town according to a rhythm determined by the agricultural cycle of production. The following quotation is given as an example of his strong functionalist-tinted explanation of the behaviour of labour migrants.

> Circular migration or commuting provided a means whereby they could maximise their incomes by encouraging some members of the household to work in the village at times of peak labour-demand, such as planting or harvesting, but to seek work in the city or elsewhere between such times while other members of the household remained to cope with limited village based labour demands. In addition, by leaving dependents at home in the village, the movers (mostly men) effectively reduce the costs of subsistence in the city or other destination – not only because the costs of accommodation, food and transport are usually greater at the destination (especially in the city), but also because the solitary mover can put up with cheaper and less comfortable conditions than his family would require, and thus cut personal costs to a bare minimum. (Hugo et al. 1990:232.)

The labour migrant is portrayed here as someone who not only understands but controls the situation of the moment, and who makes a well-considered decision on that basis: where and when to go and in due course when to return, who should be left behind and why, and how to save as much as possible by cutting costs. The nature of labour migration as a survival strategy is not sufficiently emphasized. To describe the restless circulation between city and village within the rural system as a question of free and controlled choice shows an unrealistic view of the economic compulsion that is the essence of the urge towards continual movement, and of the costs connected with a shorter or longer stay away from home. Amongst the latter I include the prolongation of the working day, a shelter that does not meet minimum requirements, health hazards, and other elementary deficiencies in day-to-day life, but above all, a constant uncertainty about what tomorrow may bring.

The working life of the landless masses is subjected to strong seasonal influence. Inclusion in the local production process is of limited duration and ends irrevocably in expulsion, a consequence that can only be avoided by moving away and back. Hunting the harvest typifies the worker's loss of security in his home environment. I perceived among my informants a downright reluctance to have to leave home yet again. One old woman ended a conversation about her neighbour's regular absence by jokingly exclaiming that he much preferred to jump at night on his wife's soft belly than to lie miserably on his own in an open field. The ties that bind migrant workers to their homes have loosened, but indefinite settlement elsewhere does not occur.

The impact of enforced mobility on relationships between members of working households is a problem that requires further study. Circulation as an important dimension of employment modalities seems to have strengthened the position of men as against that of women. The latter are tied more to their homes in caring for family dependents, especially young children. Apart from that, there is reason to believe that more preference than formerly is given to men when allocating work. On the other hand, the economic consequences of growing gender differentiation in the use of labour can only be overcome through the involvement of as many household members as possible at times when employment opportunities are at their maximum. That necessity causes pressure on the economically active population in this milieu to start work at an early age and to retire later in life. In other words, old people have to work longer while children are begrudged anything more than a short and often interrupted schooling.

The widening of the labour market has undoubtedly improved the material situation of the landless under-class to some extent, as evinced by the increased durability of their housing. In the sections of the village where they live, bricks are increasingly used as building material, and in the houses themselves more consumption articles are now to be found, for example furniture and a transistor radio. It is doubtful, however, whether the labour circulation strategy will enable the landless masses of rural Java to escape from the plight of poverty which still conditions their life (Hugo 1985:83-4): Upward mobility assumes access to permanent and better-paid work. Lacking the education and contacts necessary to gain that access, however, the chances of making such a leap forwards are extremely small. Those who are living on the wrong side of the poverty-line have little opportunity to create any reserves with which to cope with small or major household crises, let alone to invest in the future. The budget for important family occasions is very modest but the amount involved, often less than three hundred thousand rupiah, swallows up so many day's income that payment of the costs can only be made after the celebration with the help of gifts of cash or rice brought by the guests. *Kurang*, or the lack of what is minimally necessary, is how the landless and those who, as marginal landowners, are slightly better off describe the deficiency of their material existence. Their deprivation is not only absolute but is growing in the relative sense because the socio-economic gap is increasing between them and those who belong to the higher social strata in the countryside. In accordance with almost all the micro-studies referred to above, I conclude that inequality in welfare at the village level has become greater in recent years. In notable contradiction to this opinion is the recent World Bank study on the poverty theme. The macro-data it presents in support of the thesis that income inequality has decreased are not very convincing (World Bank 1990:9).

The inability of landless households to create any reserves with which to cope with adversity, let alone to invest in the future, is an important reason why their livelihood should be described in terms of poverty. For a few categories, in fact, material need is not only acute but also permanent, that is, those households whose principal workers are chronically ill, invalid or aged, and single women (widows, divorcees) with growing children. Support provided from their own milieu is insufficient to counteract the miserable conditions in which they live. Under-consumption is the strategy with which these ill-fated people, roughly 10 to 15% of the under-class, survive as best they can. The collection of *zakat*, a village levy for support to the needy of the community, did not amount to more than 350,000 rupiah in the year preceding my fieldwork. It is distributed during the *paceklik*, the slack period during the rainy season, to all inhabitants who qualify in the eyes of the village authorities. I have been assured, however, that this allowance to the ultra-poor is adequate only for a short period of time.

Lastly, on the basis of my North Subang fieldwork I would like to challenge the benign view of the dynamics of poverty and prosperity in rural Java which was such a pervasive feature of policy reports disseminated in the early 1990s. Both at the time of my village study and in the years that followed, according to official statistics, the proportion of the urban and rural population living below the poverty line in Indonesia had fallen drastically. While recognizing that this statement was correct in general terms, I expressed doubts about claims made by both the Indonesian government and transnational agencies about the speed and scale with which the standard of living of the landless class had improved. In support of this contention, I pointed to the low level of wages and the absence of any opportunity to back up the extremely vulnerable bargaining position of rural labour through collective action. Conclusions of micro-studies like mine sharply contrasted with those of the World Bank, insisting that income distribution tended to become more rather than less equal. It was clear that the type of macro-studies promoted by the World Bank and other donor agencies served a political purpose and that the statistics had been manipulated (for more detail, see Pincus 1996:14, 18, 21).

Contrary to what was suggested by World Bank documents, the economic policies of the Indonesian government did not give high priority to poverty alleviation. The emphasis was on what one author called an 'avowedly productionist strategy' (Manning 1988:50). The argument that material deprivation could best be reduced in degree and intensity by strategies aiming at growth, made insufficient allowance for the counterproductive consequences of a process of social change in which the interests of labour are systematically subordinated to those of capital. This, in my view, was the essence of the official economic agenda. Landless households in rural Java lack resources of their own that could be increased in value and productivity by subsidy or credit. Capital goods granted to them on loan – such as land, a means of transport, commodities for sale, et cetera – were burdened with such outrageously high rates of interest that beneficiaries sometimes did not even retain the price of their labour from the business risks that they incurred.

To raise the wage level was, in my opinion, the only way by which to ensure a better existence for the landless workforce in the countryside. Under the New Order regime the political will to do this had fallen into abeyance. Government and employers were in agreement that saving on labour costs had to remain an integral part of the growth strategy that was followed with so much 'success' close to the end of the twentieth century. The failure to introduce a minimum wage for agricultural labour must be seen against this background. Where such a rate had been introduced, in particular for formal sector employment in the urban-industrial milieu, practice showed a consistent lack of any control over compliance with the legal regulations. It would be a misconception, however, to ascribe the anti-labour policy solely to economic motives.

Political considerations were equally important, an aspect to which Hart (1986a) gave extensive attention (see also Hüsken and White 1989:947-54). Fearing a shift in the social equilibrium in favour of the huge under-class, the power elite tried to keep the working masses invisible and fragmented. Opposition and suppression rather than protection became the fate of those who, in or out of the agricultural sector, in town or countryside, were brave enough to exert themselves to improve labour's bargaining power in the market place.

CHAPTER III

The impact of krismon

Introductory note

Social science research at the grassroots of Indonesian society was not something that the New Order authorities were keen to encourage. Obtaining a permit was a tiresome and time-consuming exercise. You could not reach 'the field' until your documents had been registered and approved at district and sub-district level. And even then you were not able to go about your research business unimpeded. Especially during the first phase of the study one of the *pamong desa*, the village officials, used to accompany us wherever we went. The reason given for this guidance was to properly introduce us to the heads of households, but the constant presence of a representative of the powers that be, complete with the official safari dress, naturally inhibited the spontaneity of the people we spoke to. The file of basic data that we gathered from our conversations in the various households differed very little from the statistics used by the government to maintain its surveillance over the people. Official government records were far from accurate, but this did not change the fact that, given the prescribed behaviour towards those who were considered to represent the state, even independent researchers could easily find themselves in a position in which their efforts to investigate more in-depth were seen as a covert intelligence operation. The 'command style' in which political power was exercised meant that a non-response was not tolerated. In such a situation, it was understandable that respondents tried to keep a low profile. They therefore tended to fob off researchers armed with pen and paper with vague, evasive and contradictory answers. This experience led Pincus, for example, to adopt a more informal approach:

> questionnaires were not used after the completion of the first round of interviews, since it was apparent that the presence of the questionnaire itself was a major obstacle to frank and informal discussion. Instead, interviews were more loosely structured around a list of questions compiled for each household. Because of the sheer quantity of information involved, it was unavoidable that notes be taken during the interviews; however, there was in fact a noticeable difference in the tone of discussions after the questionnaires were no longer used. (Pincus 1996:27.)

This was also the methodology that we followed. Apart from obtaining a few basic details for each household, we tried to steer conversations with our respondents to their specific work and life situations. Like Pincus, we were prone to receive widely varying answers to questions about income, employment and prices. We tried to correct factual biases, which often could be traced back to differences in social class, by subjecting the data obtained to close scrutiny and discussing the reactions to our queries with other actors than those directly involved. A clear indication of the eclipse of the New Order was the gradual relaxation in the official surveillance over our rural research. Naturally, when accompanied on our rounds by local officials, we restricted ourselves to gathering the most elementary statistical data and waited until the opportunity arose for more intimate conversations to probe a little more deeply. Increasingly, however, the *pamong desa* had other worries than keeping a close check on our whereabouts. Even the *babinsa*, the extension agent of the military authorities in the district who had earlier made incidental efforts to accompany us in our local rounds had faded away towards the end of our stay in the village.

Socio-economic change 1990-1998

In 1990 North Subang was accessible from the main centre of the village only by means of a country road. On foot this journey would take three-quarters of an hour. The road was so bad, in both wet and dry weather, that the only way to speed up the journey somewhat was by bicycle or *becak*, the three-wheeled pedicab. No other motorized traffic could negotiate the route than the *ojeg*, the two-wheeled taxi. Fortunately, heavier vehicles rarely needed to use the road. The settlement consisted of little more than a collection of houses and a few shops with a limited assortment of goods. With the exception of a mosque and a primary school, there were no public amenities. The *aparat desa* was represented by a *kepala kampung*, the head of the locality, who conducted his business from home and maintained contact with his superiors by visiting them at the village office in the centre. The fact that North Subang was not connected to the telephone or electricity network only added to the impression of backwardness. The image that this calls up of a relatively isolated, introspective and small-scale community, a persistent stereotype of rural Java dating back to the colonial era, was already difficult to sustain ten years ago. Contrary to Hayami and Kikuchi, who still adhered to the conventional view of the Asian village as a closed economic circuit characterized by a high degree of stability and homogeneity, both Breman and Pincus commented in their reports on the close integration of the North Subang economy in terms of labour and capital with the outside world.

One pleasant surprise on our return to the *kampung* in July 1998 was the improved access. The asphalting work on the rough country road from the main village centre to North Subang had been started shortly after our first visit. The work was not completed all at once, but a stretch at a time. The *lurah*, the village head, told us that the World Bank had already long ago provided funds as part of a programme to improve the rural infrastructure. Much of the money for this *proyek* found itself into the wrong pockets, so the work had to be contracted out several times before it was eventually finished. Under the New Order regime, from the commanding heights of the government in Jakarta right down to the local *aparat desa*, the term *proyek* came to represent an extra source of income to supplement the civil servant's salary. The eagerness to acquire as many 'development projects' as possible and the half-hearted implementation must be seen against this background. What had become standard practice at the time of Suharto, addressed as Bapak Pembangunan (Father of Development) in the sycophantic style of politics which was then in vogue, occurred again at the beginning of 1999 when a large part of the limited funds supplied under the emergency programme to alleviate the impact of *krismon* disappeared into the pockets of the village officials instead of being used for public works in North Subang.

During our first tour of the *kampung* on our return, we were immediately struck by the improved quality of the housing. It was a clear indication of improved living standards between 1990 and 1998. The best and most expensive houses still stood in their relatively large compounds in the village centre. They were owned by the descendants of the peasant pioneers, who had settled in the area in the early twentieth century. But the contrast with the outlying hamlets was less marked. More and more landpoor and landless families had replaced their hut-like constructions of bamboo walls and thatched roofs with more durable houses. The buildings may have been smaller and simpler than those of the more prosperous villagers, but they were still made of cement and bricks and had tiled roofs. A relatively large proportion of these households were even connected to the electricity network, although many of them had not as yet been able to enjoy the luxury of the various coveted consumer durables, such as a TV set, a ventilation fan or a refrigerator. Such modern conveniences not only make life more pleasant but also play a role in the determining the status of the more and less prosperous among the village inhabitants.

The *kepala kampung* still officiates from his own house but, since the campaign for the 1996 elections, he operates a radio set which allows him to have instant communication with the administrative headquarters in the village centre. Such technological equipment enabled the civil and military authorities to consolidate their control over rural communities right up to the final days of the New Order. To make himself more mobile, the *kepala kampung* bought a car, claiming it to be indispensable to the performance of his public and private affairs throughout the sub-district.

While ten years ago North Subang appeared to be a backward and inaccessible settlement, it nowadays no longer gives an immediate impression of deprivation and isolation. Shortly after the village was connected to the electricity grid the number of TV sets, not longer battery-powered, rapidly increased. This medium, much more popular than newspapers or magazines have ever been, has helped to promote an urbanized lifestyle in a rural milieu. Another sign of connecting up with the outside world is the establishment of a *wartel* (*warung telpon*). This facility, in the centre of the village, makes it possible for inhabitants employed outside the village or even abroad to remain in touch with their families at home To the casual visitor, North Subang seems little different in terms of prosperity and accessibility to other neighbouring localities. It has apparently been successful in catching up where it previously lagged behind by accelerating the process of development. What was the main factor driving these dynamics? Before looking in more detail at economic growth and distribution we will first examine population increase and, in view of agriculture as the dominant sector, changes in access to land available for production.

Population: size and growth

The village records are insufficiently reliable to be used for an analysis of population trends. Various counts based on surveys – first by Hayami and Kikuchi (1981) and then during Breman's initial fieldwork in 1990, outcomes which were backed up by the subsequent findings of Breman and Wiradi in 1998 – show that increase in the number of inhabitants over the past twenty years has never risen above 1%. This average says very little, however,

Table 1. Population growth in North Subang, 1979-1998

Census year	Number of inhabitants	Annual growth	Households	Annual growth
1979[1]	774		191	
		0.5%		1.25%
1990[2]	809		216	
		1.2%[4]		2.1 %
1998[3]	891		261	

1 Hayami and Kikuchi 1981:197-8.

2 Breman 1995:2.

3 Breman and Wiradi: fieldwork data.

4 The number of inhabitants of the village of M. grew from 3,996 in 1990 to 4,423 in 1998, also an average growth of 1.2% per year.

because the statistics on population growth in North Subang have been subject to considerable fluctuations.

There is solid evidence that the demographic transition in rural Java was already leaving its mark towards the end of the 1970s and that the village of our fieldwork was no exception to this generally observable trend. Hayami and Kikuchi attribute the rapid, even startling growth that they reported in the four decades prior to their investigations not to a higher birth rate but to an influx of migrants to this sparsely populated area. The immigration must have been even more substantial than they assumed because many of the new settlers left again when the economic climate took a turn for the worse. A prolonged drought in the early 1960s led to such a dramatic exodus that, according to Pincus, there were no more than twenty households left in the *kampung* (Pincus 1996:22; see also Breman 1995:2). That was about half the number that existed just before the outbreak of the Second World War (Hayami and Kikuchi 1981:197-8). Some of those who fled the area returned later, after the rehabilitation and expansion of the system of canal irrigation.

Behind the strongly fluctuating inflow and outflow of migrants up to the end of the 1960s lies another demographic shift, the steady fall in the household size, from four members in 1979, through 3.7 in 1990 to 3.4 in 1998. A significant parallel development was that the number of households rose much quicker than the number of inhabitants as a whole. The fall in average household size in the last thirty years can largely be attributed to a marked preference for the nuclear family as the basic residential unit. It is rare to find three generations living together under one roof. Comparison between the results of our fieldwork show that in 1990 two hundred and sixteen households inhabited two hundred and twelve houses, while in 1998 two hundred and sixty-one households were distributed among two hundred and fifty-four houses. Young people prefer to set up their own household when they marry, while also older inhabitants told us that, although they like to have their adult children close by, they prefer to live independently. The progressive separation of generations is, however, not the only factor that has contributed to the fall in the number of people per household. Women of child-bearing age tend to have fewer children than in the past. This finding contradicts Hayami and Kikuchi's view that family size has remained stable over a sustained period (Hayami and Kikuchi 1981:198).

A large number of studies show that the slowing down of population growth in the 1970s and 1980s was caused by a fall in the birth rate, resulting in a demographic increase of not more than 0.6% in rural West Java. The speed with which this trend took hold is generally attributed to the successful policy of the New Order regime. Showing great resolution, the government finally took steps to restrict the number of children. Although the poor especially were inclined to see children as a material asset, their unbridled multiplication had become a severe burden on the Indonesian economy in general and on that of the already densely populated Java in particular. Completely in character with the authoritarian nature of the New Order, the policy-makers did not confine themselves to promoting the conventional techniques of birth control. Women were obliged to refrain from reproduction 'voluntarily' and targets were imposed on village officials regarding the number of 'acceptors' (note: of various methods of birth control) they should recruit. I decided to make these practices, which were based on scarcely concealed coercion, public during my stay in North Subang in 1990. An article in a Third World magazine published in The Netherlands while my fieldwork was still in progress provoked a fierce response (Breman 1990; see also Breman and White 1995 for a review of the exchange of arguments). The heated debate that followed – this was incidentally shortly after Suharto had been presented with the UN Population Award – drew the attention of the then Minister for Development Cooperation in The Hague, causing him to cancel the grant to the Indonesian National Family Planning Board. This decision was one of the reasons why the Indonesian government shortly afterwards terminated the aid relationship with the Netherlands. The change of policy from encouraging voluntary birth control to the imposition of rigid restrictions on women's reproductive behaviour failed to recognize that, as White and others correctly observed, people had already chosen to improve the quality of their lives now and in the future by having fewer children (White 1993). Several factors lay behind this choice: better access to health care, increasing participation in education (with girls gradually catching up, particularly where attendance at primary school was concerned) and, lastly, the raising of the age at which marriages were arranged. White pointed out once again, after Hugo and others, the fallacy of the assumption, particularly popular among policy-makers, that poor households in particular tended to have a large number of children (Hugo et al. 1987:156-7 and Breman 1995:9).

Migration has played a decisive role in the demographic history of North Subang. The turbulence of settlement and departure that was typical in previous generations has made way for a greater degree of stability. Out-migration still occurs but no longer involves tens of households at the same time. One thing in particular that appears largely to have come to an end is the seasonal migration of peasant cultivators back and forth between North Subang and a location to the northeast of Jakarta to lease fallow and relatively infertile land for at least a part of the year on which to grow rice (Breman 1995:37-8; Pincus 1996:33). Most of these households decided to settle in this area for good, even though it meant breaking the economic ties that required they return to North Subang for several months each year. Others were forced to give up this 'distance farming' because the corporate owner wanted to use the land for non-agricultural purposes and terminated the leasing contract, which was always agreed for one harvest only. The twenty-three households which shuttled back and forth in this way in 1990 had shrunk to only nine by 1998. Lastly, a handful of villagers had qualified for a permanent job in the urban economy of Jabotabek and had left North Subang, together with all other members of their households. As far as in-migration is concerned, outsiders still settle in the village but their arrival is mainly the result of marriage. The time is long over when this part of the northern plain, opened up not yet a century ago, was known far and wide as a catchment basin, an empty space with an unlimited capacity to absorb superfluous labour from other parts of coastal Java.

Agriculture and land occupancy

For the great majority of the people, agriculture – in practice, growing rice – has remained the main means of subsistence.

Of the heads of the households, three were not economically active in 1990 and seven in 1998. They were mainly single old people, and in one case, a mentally disturbed woman who had no occupation or independent source of income. These people depended on relations or neighbours for their basic needs. There were of course many more aged and handicapped people, but they either tended for themselves or were part of households in which the head and other members were economically active. Table 2 also shows that agriculture has remained the primary source of economic activity, albeit for a decreasing percentage of heads of households. The proportion of people who earn more than half of their income outside agriculture increased from 26% in 1990 to 37% in 1998.

In 1990 the village economy was characterized by a highly skewed pattern of land holdings. The very large proportion of the population that owned or operated no land corresponded to the tenaciously held view of rural Java as a culture of shared poverty, of a peasant economy with little differentiation in socio-economic status. The great contrasts between ecological zones and variations in population density should be reason enough to resist such generalizations. North Subang was one of the settlements on Java on which the

Table 2. Employment of heads of households in and outside agriculture, 1990-1998

Year	Heads of households	Economic		Agriculture	
		non-active	active	inside	outside
1990	216	3	213	160	53
1998	261	7	254	161	93

Source: Village survey Breman 1990 and Breman and Wiradi 1998.

Table 3. Land ownership of heads of households, 1990-1998

Year	Heads of households	Owning land	Landless
1990	216	47	169
1998	261	45	216

Source: Village survey Breman 1990 and Breman and Wiradi 1998.

Agro Economic Survey had based its report on continuity and change in the modes of agrarian production. A recent study comparing these villages and others in which rural research had been carried out (the results of which Pincus had conveniently condensed in table form) showed that, of the total of seventeen, North Subang did indeed have the highest percentage of landlessness. On the other hand, the unequal distribution of the most significant agrarian capital was not particularly abnormal. Pincus' table shows that half or more of the people in twelve of the seventeen villages (that is, two-thirds of all cases) owned no land (Pincus 1996:208). Nothing changed in this misdistribution of agrarian resources in the final decade of the twentieth century. While the number of heads of households owning land in North Subang remained constant (forty-seven in 1990 versus forty-five in 1998), the fact that 83% of households belonged to the landless class in the latter year indicates that the trend towards social concentration of this primary means of production continues.

Lastly, this high level of exclusion from land ownership is remarkable given the relatively favourable man:land ratio in the village of our fieldwork. According to the land register, North Subang covers an area of sixty-five hectares. Hayami and Kikuchi calculated that this produced an agrarian density – the number of inhabitants per hectare of rice-growing land – of no more than twelve (Hayami and Kikuchi 1981:197). Although this figure has now increased to nearly fourteen, as a result of population growth, it represents a strikingly low pressure on available agrarian resources compared to other parts of Java. But this suggestion is a distortion or reality in more than one respect. First of all, the Japanese economists incorrectly assumed that land ownership remained confined to the territory of their research. Inhabitants of the *kampung*, however, own rice fields in other parts of the village or elsewhere in the sub-district and, conversely, outsiders own land in North Subang. Secondly, this fluidity is even more marked in the case of landless labourers. As with landowners, density should not be measured on the basis of their residence in the *kampung*. They travel far from home to hunt the harvest and, when it comes to North Subang itself, an enormous army of migrant workers descends on the village at the peak of the agricultural cycle. These empirical observations, already referred to above, deny the premise of

Table 4. Distribution of the working population within and outside agriculture, 1990-1998

	In agriculture			Total
	Peasant cultivators	Other agrarian producers	Labourers	
1990	82	5	249	336
1998	73	9	229	311

	Outside agriculture				Other		Total
	Trade	Transport	Services	Govermental	Permanent	Casual	
1990	39	16	26	11		20[1]	112
1998	80	29	69	11	8	30	227

1 This category had not yet been divided into permanent and casual employees in 1990

a closed economic arena, on which Hayami and Kikuchi based their argument about the low land:man ratio.

Employment

We determined the size of the working population on the basis of an elementary survey of all households. The results are shown in Table 4. The two hundred and fifty-four economically active households have six hundred and eighteen members, an average of 2.4 men and women per household, who constitute the workforce residing in the *kampung*.

To facilitate comparison, the same categories were used as in the survey conducted in 1990. This means that, as in the initial round of fieldwork, the aged and those with chronic illnesses or disablement (leprosy) as well as schoolchildren were counted as non-working (that is, as having made little or at the most a marginal contribution to the generation of income). These groups accounted for a little more than 30% of total household members.

Employment within agriculture

The number of working members of households active in agriculture has fallen even more than the number of heads of households working in the sector, from 62% in 1990 to 50% in 1998. This fall would have been even greater if the outbreak of *krismon* in the autumn of 1997 had not led to a decrease in jobs in the non-agricultural sectors of the economy. North Subang is becoming less and less a rural settlement dominated by agriculture. This trend has accelerated to such an extent over the past twenty years, despite the recent interruption due to *krismon*, that even Hayami and Kikuchi would not be able to ignore the phenomenon in an eventual restudy of the locality.

Those who work in the agricultural sector are divided into peasant-cultivators and agricultural labourers. The first category includes not only forty-five who own at least part of the land they hold, but also twenty-eight who do not own land but who cultivate fields of a quarter hectare or more as tenants or sharecroppers. The latter constitute a slight correction to the very unequal distribution of agrarian capital. The figures show, however, that the opportunities for the landless villagers at least to operate land, if not to own it, have not increased. The number of households that do not own *sawahs* (irrigated rice fields) or which do not cultivate them as tenants or sharecroppers for one or more seasons increased between 1990 and 1998 from one hundred and thirty-four to one hundred and eighty-eight (that is, from 62% to 72%). The increase reflects the fact that the several dozen landpoor and landless households that used to make a living from farming by leasing fallow and infertile land at some great distance from North Subang, in the northeast of Java, now have almost no opportunity to do so. This is one reason why the percentage of peasant farmers in the working population fell from 15% in 1990 to 12% in 1998. Our finding was corroborated by informants who stated that land ownership is concentrated among some twenty heads of households. Only their holdings are sufficiently large to yield enough to live on without other sources of income. In August 2000 the cost of one hectare of land had risen to seventy million rupiah.

One finding of our follow-up study in 1998 was that the estates amassed by the previous generation of large landowners in the sub-district had not survived. Even before he died, *haji* S., who in his lifetime was the outstanding magnate in North Subang, had started to divide his property among his nine children. Through a twist of demographic fate, he had more children than any other household and this meant that, although some of his heirs could still count themselves among the big landowners, none were able to take over the hegemonic position of their reputed ancestor. In fact most of his children came to a sticky end, a fate that the villagers were only too pleased to attribute to the unfair way in which their father had accumulated his wealth. The lack of entrepreneurial spirit of the new generation played an important role in the downward mobility of the entire family. Instead of trying to consolidate their capital, the *haji's* children used their inherited wealth to live in grand style. Pincus observed the same tendency, expressed through the more widespread sale than purchase of rice fields within the *kampung*, and suggested that a process of disaccumulation had been set in motion (Pincus 1996:165). It would be premature to explain this trend as indicative of a levelling down of land ownership. As remarked earlier, there has been no question of increased access to agrarian means of subsistence for landless households after 1990. Although the monopoly position of not more than a handful of leading landowners may have been broken, at least half of all cultivable land is still in the hands of a relatively small elite, most of whom are the descendants of the first generation of settlers. Between these two extremes in the agrarian hierarchy the middle class of peasant farmers seems to have acquired greater significance. The eclipse of the largest landlord in North Subang has also meant a decrease in the former volume of leasing and sharecropping contracts. *Krismon* has made it rather unattractive for the larger landowners to have their fields cultivated by sharecroppers who lack the capital for hiring a tractor for land preparation or buying fertilizers and pesticides. Instead of giving loans for such expenditure to their needy clients, these patrons prefer to hand over their land to tenants with greater solvency. Unlike the rural magnates, not only in North Subang but also throughout the sub-district, the middle-sized peasant-cultivators prefer to operate their own farms. This way they do not have to share their yields by leasing their fields out to landless households. In August 2000 the payment required for leasing one bahu (0.7 hectare) of land for one year amounted to four million rupiah.

It would be incorrect to deduce from the shift in control over the agricultural land that the process of accumulation ceased in North Subang between 1990 and 1998. A more accurate observation is that capital owners during this period had become less prepared to invest in land. This reluctance is a direct consequence of the relatively low profit from renting out land. The absence of a new breakthrough in agrarian production had much to do with this. In comparison to the tripling of the yield per hectare between 1970 and 1990, the almost constant level of the harvest over the past decade is an indication of stagnating productivity. Average harvest results in 2000 were six tons per hectare in the wet season and 4.5 to 5 tons in the dry season. On top of this, prices have not developed very favourably for producers. According to our calculations, in the years 1999 and 2000 one hectare yielded the owner an average net income of four million rupiah for the wet season and roughly two-thirds of this amount when selling the dry season crop. In the preceding years, the government's main concern was to provide cheap food – and rice in particular – for the urban consumer. This policy, designed to support the regime's aim of keeping wages down, shows that towards the end of the Orde Baru regime the balance between the agrarian and the non-agrarian economy had shifted rapidly in favour of the latter. It is still too early to say that this pro-urban bias has come to a halt. Although farmers are paid higher procurement prices now for their rice, all monetary advantage is outweighed by the rising cost of fertilizers and other inputs. According to one of our informants in the farming business, before *krismon* the selling price of one quintal of *padi* was enough for buying two quintals of fertilizer. Nowadays, it is the reverse: the cash received for two quintals of *padi* is hardly enough for the purchase of one quintal of fertilizer.

Lastly, we identified a small group (2%) of self-employed producers in the prime sector of the economy who keep ducks, geese, goats or sheep. The animals are the main means of subsistence for these seven households. Two others also made a living, one growing bananas and the other cucumbers, on a small patch of ground. Including these nine petty entrepreneurs in our category of peasant-cultivators the proportion of owners of agrarian capital in the workforce of North Subang up to 13%.

How has the landless under-class fared in recent years, in comparison to the landlords and self-cultivating farmers? As in the past, agricultural labourers form the largest economic segment in the village. The fall from two hundred and forty-nine to two hundred and twenty-nine indicates a downward trend (from 46% in 1990 to 37% in 1998). The decrease would have been even more marked if our survey had been held prior to mid-1998. By then *krismon* had caused many non-agrarian workers to return to the village. Faced with no other source of employment many of them called themselves agricultural labourers again, because this was how they were forced to make their frugal living. The figure stated was based on responses to the question we asked about the most important source of income. The answers were somewhat subjective but most respondents immediately mentioned agricultural labour even though they did not only seek work only in the prime sector of the economy. Furthermore, the size of the entire workforce fluctuated considerably. The records do not include all those who work as agricultural labourers no more than occasionally. During the harvest, many small peasants grasp the opportunity to supplement their income from self-employment. Marginal cultivators – those who own less than a quarter of a hectare or who are sharecroppers – do this even outside the peak season. The distinction between full-time and part-time agricultural labourers is not always clear and we drew attention in our earlier fieldwork to the great elasticity in what exactly constitutes the main source of subsistence. The figures in Table 4 show that the two main classes into which the agrarian workforce can be divided in North Subang have remained constant, with three agricultural labourers to one farmer.

As we shall see, the decrease in the number of agricultural labourers in North Subang reflects the fact that more and more men from landless households were absorbed into employment outside agriculture, and almost always outside the village. This shift is the consequence of a combination of factors on both the supply and demand side. As far as the first is concerned, the magnetic effect of the metropolitan economy of Jabotabek has been felt deep in the rural hinterland of Java. The incentive for labour to flow in that direction received an added impulse from the more severe fluctuations in employment in the agricultural sector resulting from the technology introduced by the green revolution. Draught animals were replaced by tractors and the use of pesticides and insecticides increased dramatically. The labour-intensive nature of the harvest means that it requires an enormous number of hands for as long as it lasts, even to such an extent that the local pool is insufficient and migrant labourers converge on the village from far and wide. In and immediately around North Subang harvesting lasts for about one month at the end of the wet season and for one week less than that in the dry season. This means that for the large majority of landless inhabitants, there is inadequate employment in agriculture outside the peak period in the rice growing cycle and they can only find work in the sector by hunting for the harvest elsewhere. Twice a year, the sudden influx is followed by a just as sudden exodus. Although a mobile army of harvesters has long been a feature of rural Java, the current large-scale nomadism would have been unthinkable without the ease with which distances can now be covered, in terms of time and money.

The mode of employment has changed substantially. A small category among the landless has become skilled at working the land with tractors. They receive as payment for their labour 30% of the rate that the farmers have to shell out per land unit. In the summer of 1998 this was one hundred thousand rupiah per bahu. With a well-maintained tractor and an assistant paid by him, a driver usually manages to operate about one hectare a day. It is lucrative work and, in the spring of 1999, one of these skilled labourers had taken out a loan to buy a second-hand tractor, with which he was able to make a living. He was the only owner-driver in North Subang. All the other machinery used to prepare the land in the *kampung* for the new growing cycle was owned by outsiders, mostly big farmers who trade in rice and who often have their own hulling mill. The labourers who work for them throughout the whole region are paid per job, without any entitlement to work outside the season or on days when there is nothing to do. The agreement they have with their bosses is a kind of piecework (*borongan*) contract, which is similar to that of a sharecropping arrangement: they split the costs and benefits, with clearly demarcated responsibilities for both parties, the providers of capital and labour.

The larger farmers contract their work out mostly or even exclusively to casual labourers. This includes not only the maintenance work required before the crops are planted, such as fencing the farmyard, repairing the dykes around the fields, and irrigating and fertilizing the land, but also spraying the crops with insecticides and pesticides. Casual workers are normally paid a daily wage (*harian*). Only the large landowners still have farm servants in permanent employ – many of whom also receive a piece of land on a sharecropping basis – and their numbers are falling. There were fourteen in North Subang in 1990, and only eight in 1998. The progressive replacement of attached workers by casual labourers is a reflection of the surplus of available labour outside the harvest period. The same applies to the practice of farmers giving labourers advances on work expected to be performed during the busy season, which was already becoming unusual during our earlier research in the locality and which had fallen even more into disuse by the time we returned in 1998. The only exception is the advance agreement on the transplantation of rice, sealed with an upfront payment of cash to a *kepala rombongan*, a man who recruits a team of women to do this work at the stipulated moment in or outside the village.

Apart from the harvest, this is about the only possibility for women to find work any longer within the agricultural sector and so contribute to the household income. With the increased use of herbicides, weeding is now almost completely unnecessary. Second crops (*polowijo*) have not been grown in North Subang for many years. The employment of women at the beginning and end of the rice growth cycle means for them the interruption of a long period in which there is little or no work for them. An indication of the marginalization of female employment in agriculture is the increasing difference between them and men; both in terms of days worked and wage levels (see also Pincus 1996:130). Women take part in the harvest as fully-fledged team members, usually together with their husband or another male from the household. Their involvement at this crucial stage continues to be indispensable. But women who have no male partner to thresh the rice, cram it into bags and carry it from the field to the road are excluded from participation at this most productive moment in the agricultural labourers' annual cycle; they have to work as quickly as possible to accumulate as much rice as they can to tide them over the coming slack season. This is the direct cause of the vulnerable position in which many female heads of households find themselves – widows, divorced women, or those whose husbands have another partner living elsewhere on whom they spend part or all of their income. To benefit in some small way from their labour power, these women join the old or otherwise non-productive villagers in combing the freshly harvested fields to gather husks that have not been completely emptied by the hasty threshing. Instead of seeing this gleaning (*p'rik*) as a marginal activity, we are inclined to consider those who are forced to ensure their survival in this impoverished manner to be fully-fledged agricultural workers.

The daily wage for agricultural labourers, which was five thousand rupiah in the first half of 1998, had risen to seven thousand rupiah shortly before our arrival in the summer of that year. The farmers blamed the economic crisis. *Krismon* had made everything more expensive, including the cost of labour. As the cost of living continued to increase, the daily wage went up again in early 1999, to ten thousand rupiah. The immediate impact at village level of price changes that were the result of disastrous macro-financial management by the Indonesian government is an indication of the high degree of monetization of the social production relations in the agricultural sector. The rapid decline in the value of money underlines the importance of the traditional habit of paying for a proportion of the work in kind. This consists of a meal sometimes in the morning, but more usually in the middle and at the end of the day for all workers paid by the day. It is expressly not intended for the most labour-intensive activities, such as transplanting, harvesting and now also ploughing – which are performed on a piecework basis (*borongan*). Among the main body of agricultural labourers, there is a small group of foremen, employed by the big landowners and agrarian contractors (*penebas*) to oversee the harvesting and other large-scale field operations. They not only have a more regular employment relationship with their employers but they are also much better paid, receiving double or more than that of daily wage labourers. Like tractor drivers and foremen, they are better trained and possess the skills to supervise the work of others. The open field system, which gives workers the right to participate in the harvest irrespective of where they come from or whether they know the landowner, is still in force. The share that they receive for cutting, threshing, bundling and carrying the still wet and unhusked rice (*gabah*) from the field to the roadside or the farmer's house has also stayed the same since the last time it was lowered at the start of the 1980s – one-tenth of the yield. This proportion may slightly go up in the case of harvesters who are related to the field owner or if they are asked to carry the bags to the house of the farmer.

Nor has there been any change in the influx of large numbers of migrants during this high point in the agrarian cycle. And in turn, those from the land-poor and landless households, especially the young men, leave North Subang as soon as the rice has disappeared from the fields in and around the village. In the slack season that follows they go – as they have done for many years – in search of the harvest elsewhere in the district and further afield. It is a pattern of seasonal circulation over long and short distances that has continued unabated to the present day. The conditions under which these migrant labourers are employed are not the same throughout the whole coastal plain. Daily wages vary and the percentage of the harvest that they may keep differs from place to place. The determining factor appears to be supply and demand. The greater the distance the smaller the chance that harvest labourers will bring their earnings back home in kind. But where the fields can still be reached by bicycle, it is not necessary to sell the *bawon* to the farmer or another buyer for cash at the end of the day. For the landless, the bicycle not only increases the radius for employment outside the village, but it can also be used to carry the *bawon* home. The fact that agricultural labourers also go to the hulling mill these days to have the *padi* (rice sheaves) that have earned polished in exchange for a tenth of the weight is an indication of how the options of the landless have somewhat improved. The stock of rice they build up is intended for their own use in the lean months to come or is sold later at a much higher price than they would have got if they had sold it immediately.

In the report on his initial fieldwork Breman drew attention to the large gap between landowners and the landless in North Subang. While the first group came to the *kampung* as colonist farmers, the latter came as migrant workers, too late to be admitted to the circle of original landowners. The majority of these latecomers also failed to enter into leasing or sharecropping agreements. This privilege was reserved for the creditworthiest among them or for the rare cases of young men from landless families who married a farmer's daughter. Marriages have always been, and continue to be, overwhelmingly limited to one's own circle. Hayami and Kikuchi already noted that the village was not any longer a community based on reciprocity in which the inhabitants supported or were concerned with each other. Loans were granted at an interest rate of 50% per planting season. They concluded from this that:

> the community in the North Subang Village has not yet been sufficiently solidified to establish such mutual help and insurance systems because of its recent settlement and large inflow of migrants. Early settlers were mainly Sundanese who moved into this village from the surrounding districts. Many recent migrants were the Javanese from the eastern edges of West Java or even from Central Java. The village's ethnic heterogeneity seems to be one of the reasons why the community has been loosely structured. (Hayami and Kikuchi 1981:200.)

This statement was difficult to reconcile with their claim that farmers and agricultural labourers were each others patrons and clients and that the additional yield from the sudden leap forward in agrarian production that occurred at the time of their study had been distributed fairly. Breman reached the opposite conclusion during his own research in North Subang ten years later. A trend towards an increase in disparity between landowners and landless was also one of the main findings reported by Pincus in his study (Breman 1995:33-6; Pincus 1996:108). The quotation above suggests that for Hayami and Kikuchi the contrast between the landowning elite and the much more numerous under-class had its origins in their different ethnic backgrounds, and that the polarity would gradually disappear in time. This prediction, however, did not materialize. Our return study in North Subang in 1998-1999 produced not a shred of evidence to support such a levelling down at the base of the agrarian hierarchy. There was no question of increased access to land among the lower echelons, not even in the sense of an increase in leasing and sharecropping agreements. If at all, the trend appeared to be in the opposite direction: no patronage but contractual and impersonal relations. The scarcely concealed hostility among the landless to the member of the village administration who accompanied us on our first tour of the village on our return in 1998 was indicative. It is, however, also possible that in the final days of the New Order such resentment could be expressed more openly than before. The persistent refusal of the landowners in North Subang to protect and favour the landless in their own village has resulted in the refusal of the landless to behave as loyal subordinates. They came to the *kampung* as migrant workers. The fact that they have settled in the village did not really change what has always been a characteristic feature of their nomadic livelihood: a perpetual state of mobility. The landless go where they please, when they please. A large part of the year they are outside the village and, as we shall see, they are increasingly escaping – at least for some of the time – from the straitjacket of the agricultural sector. An old woman explained this behaviour to us as *ilmu burung*, augury, literally the wisdom of birds: to know where to find food and to accept the continual movement from place to place that this entails as part of the deal.

Employment outside agriculture

Table 4 shows that, in 1998, two hundred and twenty-seven of the six hundred and eighteen labourers earned a living outside agriculture. This figure almost doubled in number in 1990, an increase in percentage terms over this period from 21% tot 37%. A year earlier, before the outbreak of *krismon*, the rise in the number of non-agrarian labourers would have been even more marked. As noted above, many of those who returned to the village called themselves agricultural labourers although they had not earned their living this way for many years. The effect of this mass return notwithstanding, the proportion of the working population active outside agriculture is now higher than it was in 1990. At that time, North Subang was still predominantly agrarian, more so than many other parts of rural Java. Many village studies in the 1970s and 1980s showed that more than half of the incomes of the majority of households came from work outside the agricultural sector, but North Subang was way behind in this growing diversification. In 1990, only a third of all households had one or more members working exclusively or predominantly outside agriculture (Pincus 1996:67). By 1998, however, our survey found that this had risen to 65% (one hundred and sixty-seven households). This doubling meant that North Subang had as good as caught up in the process of economic diversification. How can we explain this striking change in the pattern of employment?

Toko with tv performance at night

Non-agrarian work within the village economy

Employment outside the agricultural sector within the village has stagnated at a low level. Very few people are engaged in trade, transport, services and skilled crafts. In 1998, the total was eighty, that is, 13% of the working population. In 1990, the percentage had been the same, with sixty-nine of the working population of 541 working outside agriculture.

For their more important purchases, the villagers can visit the two *toko* (large shops) in the village centre. The largest of these also serves as a café where young people in particular gather in the evenings to watch television. The seats are free but they have to pay for the soft drinks. The nine *warung* (smaller shops) distributed throughout the four neighbourhoods stock only the absolute necessities and then by no means a complete assortment. The smallest of these retail outlets, which open and close as the owners see fit, consist of little more than a table or a few shelves offering a limited range of wares – some pans of ready-made food, a pot of sweets, matches, a few packets of *kretek* (clove-spiced cigarettes), et cetera. These simple *warung* are run by single women who are the heads of households and who often have no other source of income. Three people make a living selling bamboo and wood, ice blocks, and petroleum. Lastly there are six perambulant vendors based in North Subang who peddle their wares (sweets, fruit, brushes or clothes) on foot or by bicycle in the vicinity. During the harvest, they are joined by others who sell food and tasty titbits to the workers in the fields. Some of these seasonal traders buy up the *bawon*, the rice paid to the harvesters in kind. The large dealers who purchase the rice directly from the farmers also buy from these petty traders. One of them also sells all kinds of agricultural inputs. In addition to the head of the *kampung* and his staff, who are paid employees of the *aparat desa*, there are a number of other people in government service including an official who has a job in the sub-district office, four teachers, an irrigation supervisor and a retired civil servant. While their numbers have stayed the same since 1990, more people have found employment in the transport sector. These are the owners of a *becak*, a motorcycle or, in one case, a delivery van, who earn a living carrying goods and passengers. The village also has a handful of women who do domestic work (cleaning, washing) in the better-off households a few hours a day or a few days a week and who are paid in the form of meals or a small amount of money. They are included as part of the working population as these activities, no matter how badly paid, provide the largest part of their income. The only male servant is permanently employed in the household of the *kepala dusun* (the head of the hamlet) who also utilizes him as a messenger. Among those who work outside the agricultural sector in the village there are a number of craftsmen, including a carpenter, a bricklayer, two mechanics (a father and son) who repair tractors, cycles and motorcycles, an electrical repair man and a welder. They all operate from their homes, but can also be called outside the *kampung* if necessary. The daily rate for a carpenter which was fifteen thousand rupiah plus meals in 1999, had risen to twenty thousand rupiah one year later. Their unskilled helper (*kenek*) did not get more than half of the daily wages for artisans. All of these craftsmen cater to village customers on a regular or incidental basis. A few manufacturers occasionally earn additional income by moulding and baking bricks. Their production, however, never exceeds some two hundred bricks a day. None of these industrial activities aim wider than the local market.

Non-agrarian work outside the village economy

The volume of work performed outside the agricultural sector and outside the village has expanded substantially: from forty people in 1990 to eighty-two in 1998. In percentage terms, this represents a doubling, from just over 7% to 13%. The activities involved fall into three categories: a. those in permanent or regular employment; b. those who are more or less self-employed and c. those who work as casual labourers drifting around a wide variety of work-sites. In the first category there are three factory workers, two shop assistants, a taxi driver, a truck driver, and two others employed by a private company and a government agency. This group – seven men and two women – constitute a privileged minority of relatively well-trained and well-paid employees, who have managed to penetrate the lower echelons of the formal sector economy in the Jabotabek metropolis. The man employed by the electricity company in Jakarta is the best paid, with a monthly salary of eight hundred thousand rupiah while a factory worker earns five hundred thousand rupiah per month. A butcher has his business in the market of Bekasi town. He told us that after *krismon* his daily trade had decreased by 40% because many of his customers could no longer afford to buy meat regularly. What prevents this minute vanguard from settling permanently with their families in the city is the high cost of living. The supply of low-priced housing in Jabotabek lags way behind demand. A few building projects have been realized for income classes at the bottom of the urban economy. These very simple dwellings, known as Rumah Sangat Sederhana, are referred to by the people as *RSS SS SS* (too small even for sexual intercourse). The short distance to the urbanized zone around Jakarta allows these workers to spend their free days (paid weekly or monthly leave is part of the job) in the village.

The second category are self-employed workers in the metropolitan conurbation. There are fifteen men and four women in this group. The men are petty traders, who roam around the streets of Jakarta selling their wares. Nine of them work together making and selling *singkong* (fried cassava). They fetch the ingredients from a wholesaler late in the morning and prepare the food in a place that they have rented together. Four are employed by the same boss who allows them to sleep in a shed from whom they rent their *pikolan* at a daily cost of two thousand five hundred rupiah. They go out onto the streets in various residential areas of the city to sell their snacks during the late afternoon and evening. The other men sell cigarettes, newspapers and other items in buses, on markets and street corners. The four women all work as prostitutes in the north of Jakarta.

The last category includes all those who move around in Jabotabek engaged for casual and low-paid work. Most of the forty-five unskilled men in this group are earth-movers or navvies (*kenek*) in the building sector, regularly changing their work sites. They are taken on by foremen and jobbers. The nine women either work as housemaids or on street stalls. All of those in this category are commuters, circulating between the village and the city and between jobs. For this group, more than for the other two categories, it is extremely difficult to distinguish between their main occupation and other sources of income. This was apparent in our fieldwork in 1990 and the same problem of classification arose in the course of our investigations from 1998 to 2000. As researchers, we took some solace from the fact that many respondents themselves seemed unsure about what their main occupations were and the extent to which the various activities they had performed, either in sequence or simultaneously, had contributed to their income.

These three categories have different social identities. The lucky few who have qualified for permanent employment in the formal sector of the urban economy must usually attribute their good fortune to family or friends, who have preceded them and have put in a good word for them with employers, and to the fact that they have an education. A secondary education is indispensable for those who wish to do simple administrative work. These qualifications equip them to conduct themselves as expected of all those seeking access to more or less permanent and well-paid work. Only the truck driver is a self-made man who got his job more through luck than any special training. When they return to the village for a visit, they bring with them elements of an urban lifestyle associated with middle class status and which they are able to afford because of having landed regular and better paid jobs. Their families belong to the property-owning class in the village and provided the funds required for them to leave the village in the first place. Once they have become firmly established in the formal sector, all contact with their former agriculture-based life is severed. They do come for visits to their relatives in the village but they have severed their ties with the agricultural economy. The price they have to pay for their success is to act as bridgeheads for many others in the village who aspire to follow in their footsteps. Inability or unwillingness to meet up to these expectations can lead to jealousy and friction both within and between families. Some of the men have a second wife in Jakarta. This means that they return to the village less often and spend a large part of their income in the city. Their village wives are just as vulnerable as single women who have lost their husbands through death or divorce.

The majority of those in the other two categories come from the landpoor and landless classes in North Subang. The street vendors who peddle their wares in Jabotabek may have put some distance between themselves and a life based on agriculture, but generally speaking they maintain the links with the rural milieu in which they have their roots. It is this environment of self-employed peasants that provided the physical and social capital indispensable to obtain a foothold in the informal sector of the urban economy: a little money to set yourself up and an entrepreneurial zeal that expresses itself in the determination to remain independent mixed with a shrewd business acumen. These are the same traits of character that enable the small agrarian producers to survive. One striking finding reported by Breman in the outcome of his first round of fieldwork in 1990 was that, although many labourers from the landless under-class often found work outside the *kampung*, this work was more often than not in the agricultural economy. Non-agrarian work outside the village accounted for only a third of the income of the households concerned, a much lower percentage than that found by many contemporary studies in other parts of rural Java. Unfamiliarity with other forms of employment and the low incomes associated with unskilled work in other sectors were important reasons for their agrarian mode of existence (Breman 1995:33-4). Pincus gave a similar explanation for this phenomenon:

> Temporary migration to urban centres is not a realistic option for these workers, who lack the personal contacts in cities, skills and the resources needed to support an extended period of unemployment during the job search (Pincus 1996:62).

These arguments proved inconclusive when, in mid-1998, our survey revealed that in the intervening years, the share of income from work outside the agricultural sector had risen to a half or more of the total income of landless households. What factors were responsible for this shift in the employment pattern? Firstly, as Jabotabek continued to expand, the travelling time to this enormous reservoir of non-agrarian work from North Subang grew shorter. The rapidly growing main town of Bekasi can be reached within two or three hours. Secondly, there is an extensive and sustained demand for the sort of work agricultural labourers are familiar with: earth-moving involving heavy manual labour, preparing land for building, digging drainage canals and sewage trenches, constructing roads and fetching and carrying raw materials for these infrastructural works. The wages for such unskilled and irregular work are low and, after the costs of accommodation and travel have been deducted, they are little more than those of agricultural labourers. Non-agricultural work is not attractive because it pays well, but because it significantly cuts back the number of days when there is no work. The option of working outside the village has helped these workers escape the underemployment of their landless existence, or at least made it considerably less restrictive. Jobbers and foremen facilitate access to this work outside the village. Although they take a large cut from the wages earned by the migrants for whom they find jobs, they also ensure that there is sufficient work, they find new contracts as soon as possible after existing ones expire, and ensure that the labour gangs they recruit have accommodation for the duration of the job. It is not a question of whether work within or outside agriculture provides a better living for the great mass of landpoor and landless households. It is the combination of the two that has increased living standards at the lower end of the village economy. We did, however, note that the trend towards employment and income outside agriculture, which has been gathering momentum over the past ten years, has accelerated across all social classes. We shall return to this observation later when discussing the dynamics of the distribution of prosperity and poverty in North Subang.

What is particularly striking in the picture sketched so far of the employment situation in North Subang is the marginal position of women both within and outside agriculture. In the past, when the fields were used to grow a second crop after the rice harvest, the wives of the farmers and the labourers took an active part in the work. The almost complete disappearance of *polowijo* (secondary crops cultivated after the main rice harvest) after the doubling of the rice harvest and the switch to new agrarian technology during the green revolution has put a stop to the use of draught animals, which were often tended by the women, and made redundant activities like weeding, which were also traditionally left to the women. Their role is now limited to the transplanting of the young crop – in gangs and under male supervision – and cutting the rice during the harvest. Men without a partner can take part in this crucial stage of the agrarian cycle, but single women may not. They have little to do at this time than to glean the fields after the harvest, and this they do only in the close vicinity of their own homes. And the last traditional task of the women during the final processing phase of production – to pound the rice in the farmyard – is also a thing of the past as the *padi* is now taken to the hulling mill.

The trend towards male gendering of most agricultural work has not been compensated for by increased local employment for women in other areas outside the prime sector of the economy. Women are relatively active within the village in trade and the provision of services. The fact that they are less mobile than men, whose involvement in the preservation and reproduction of the family and the household is minimal or non-existent, appears to explain why women largely run the smaller *warung*. But, as mentioned above, the total number of jobs outside agriculture in the *kampung* is too small to carry much weight. There is only one woman working as a civil servant, while in the transport and craft sectors, there are none at all. The management of capital and the gains made from education and training are seen as primarily a male prerogative, while women play a supporting role. Education generally used to enjoy a very low priority among the people of North Subang, resulting in a high level of illiteracy (including more than half of the older generation of adults). Later, it was considered more important for boys to go to school than for girls. Pincus' data from 1990 shows that, among the villagers older than ten, a quarter of the men had completed primary school, while this was true of only 11% of the women (Pincus 1996:218). The persistent low level of education is undoubtedly one of the reasons why so few of the young people from North Subang manage to find jobs in the higher echelons of the non-agrarian economy. But even in the much larger informal circuit, dominated by vaguely described occupations requiring little or no certificated training or education, there are far fewer women than men. Of the eighty-two people who shuttle between North Subang and Jabotabek to work, sixty-six are men and only sixteen women, a ratio of almost 4:1.

The exclusion of women from paid work both within and outside agriculture was an issue which Breman drew attention to in the report of his fieldwork in 1990. Many women whom we questioned on this issue explained the under-utilization of their labour power in the urban economy of Jabotabek in terms of a lack of dignified work. Pincus summarized this barrier to women finding employment in the city as follows:

> the demand for non-farm wage employment far exceeded the supply of suitable jobs: as in other regions, the limited variety of non-farm jobs open to women, constraints on unsupervised female migration and the low wages paid for factory and domestic work all represented formidable obstacles to off-farm employment (Pincus 1996:68).

The distances to be travelled presented a much greater obstacle for women than for men, both for practical reasons and because of a cultural code which imposed more restrictions on women. In this sense, the increasing pressure towards horizontal mobility appeared to contribute to a shift in the balance of gender power in favour of men (Breman 1995:41).

Internationalization of women's labour

The forcing out of women from paid work described above needs to be modified in the light of a new development. Table 2 shows that the number of people working in the service sector almost tripled between 1990 and 1998. This increase can almost entirely be attributed to young women who are sent abroad as TKW (Tenaga Kerja Wanita), by a state directed female employment agency. They commit themselves to work as domestic servants (*pembantu*) for two years in another country. This form of labour migration has increased spectacularly since the end of the 1970s. At the time of Breman's first fieldwork, recruitment of these young women was much more advanced in neighbouring villages (see Pincus 1996:70), while only one woman from North Subang had left for Saudi Arabia. This changed very quickly in the years that followed, however, and by mid-1998, fifty-seven women from the *kampung* were abroad. The majority of them were still going overseas as domestic servants, but the range of destinations had since expanded to include other countries in East Asia, particularly Malaysia. Candidates have to be at least eighteen years old and, if married, have no children below twelve months. These conditions are, however, easily circumvented. For divorced women who have to fend for themselves, working abroad is an attractive option. Many single women who have to fend for themselves would previously have become prostitutes in Jakarta, and the numbers choosing this solution have fallen drastically. In the past, overseas recruitment agencies in the city would send agents to the villages to seek candidates, but this is no longer necessary. The village to which North Subang belongs has several local brokers or *sponsor*. Outside their houses hangs a sign declaring which agency they represent. In 1998 three of them vied for

Bungalow of one of the local *sponsors* recruiting young females for employment as domestic servants abroad

clients in North Subang but *haji* Rahmat is the most outstanding in this business. He used to work before as a farmer and salesman of duck feed. His new professional life started when his own wife left for Saudi-Arabia to work as a housemaid six years ago. In order to save on the amount that has to be paid for getting an overseas work permit Rahmat got in touch with the urban recruitment office himself and took care of all formalities. From that personal experience he learnt that a lot of money could be earned from mediation. The firm which contracted his wife gave him a letter authorizing *haji* Rahmat to act as their sponsor and this is now his full-time profession. In the last four years he has prepared contracts for some one hundred and fifty to two hundred women from North Subang and the surrounding villages. His modest claim is to have done this just in order to be helpful to his customers who come to bother him with all their problems. Looking at his newly-built house – which is the most opulent and expensive bungalow in the *kampung* – it is quite clear that the business of recruitment has been most profitable for *haji* Rahmat in the very first place. His anxiety now is that, pressurized by media reports about the maltreatment and sexual abuse of many Indonesian women working overseas, the government may now prohibit young females from going abroad. *Haji* Rahmat emphasizes that not only do these maid servants contribute substantially to the income of their households in these bad times of *krismon*, but also that the government is more than ever before in need of the foreign currency which they bring into the country.

Women who come to register have first of all to produce a whole pile of documents: birth certificate, primary school diploma, identity card, passport photographs, medical certificate, certificate of good conduct, written permission from their husband (if they are married) or from their parents, and a licence issued by the village administration that it has no objection to the woman concerned going abroad to work. The candidate herself must, of course, pay for all these documents, and for the medical examination that has to determine whether she is pregnant, or suffering from tuberculosis or AIDS. Until mid-1997, the local brokers charged on average an initial sum of between five hundred thousand seven hundred thousand rupiah for their mediation. The candidates themselves mostly had no idea what this money was for, but understood that more or less legal taxes had to be paid to all kinds of official authorities at district and sub-district level before their departure could be arranged. The relationship between the *sponsor* and the recruitment agency in Jakarta or Bandung also remains a mystery to the candidates and they are as ignorant of the financial transactions between the local broker and the state agency which have to be cleared before permission for departure is given. Until a few years previously, the recruitment offices used to pay commission for every woman sent abroad, but stopped doing so as supply started to grow faster than demand. The agents are now dependent for their profit on the fee they themselves charge candidates over and above the actual costs, a round sum presented as *ongkos* ('expenses'). After the first selection round, the approved women are summoned to take part in a course lasting several weeks to prepare them for their assignments. Candidates from North Subang to be sent to countries in the Persian Gulf are lodged in a hostel (*asrama*) nearby in Bekasi, while women nominated for countries in East Asia generally go to Bandung. During the course, they receive some elementary instruction in a relevant language (Arabic, Chinese and/or English), lessons in cooking, housework and child care, a general introduction to the country and its culture and, lastly, how to behave towards their new employers. The agency pays for their food and lodging, but all other expenses have to be met from the pocket money they take with them from the village. Members of the family who come and see them at weekends have to pay for extra for accommodation. After the course, the women usually leave for their overseas destinations almost immediately, but occasionally they have to return home and wait until they get the green light.

By that time, the women have already invested quite a large sum of money in the job and the income they hope to enjoy for the coming two years (the standard duration of a contract). The families of some of the women are able to pay these preparatory costs themselves, from their savings or by renting out or selling possessions. These households, which already have a reasonable surplus, choose this strategy in the knowledge that it will eventually bring in a much larger net return. Women from households with no such accumulated means, or who are for other reasons unable to pay these initial expenses themselves have no other choice than to take out a loan to pay the *sponsor* and cover the other costs. They can obtain a loan from the local broker himself or from one of the moneylenders in the village against the standard interest rate of 50% per season. This means that after a year they have to pay double the amount received. And this is not the only form of exploitation to which these women are exposed. Their foreign employers also have to pay a hefty sum to their recruitment agency for a residence/work permit and for the flight tickets, no to mention the commission fee. And all of these costs are in the end of course passed on to the women themselves. On their arrival one of the first things the new boss tells them is that they will have to work the first three, four, or sometimes even five months without pay. So these long-distance migrants end up paying for everything themselves: the preparatory course, the selection process, official permits in their own country and in the country in which they are going to work, premiums for compulsory insurance against which they can never make a claim, departure tax, plane ticket both ways and, on top of all this, the not insubstantial profits of the intermediaries on both sides.

The working conditions are onerous, with extremely long working hours. They must be ready to do as commanded by all the members of the household, young and old, at all times. The work consists of taking care of the children, helping to prepare meals, cleaning and doing the laundry as well as well as other chores in and around the house. They have to perform all these duties from early in the morning to late at night, sometimes into the early hours. Time off is a favour rather than a right to which they are entitled on a regular basis – a day a week or a month. Most of the women are allowed only to leave the house in the company of the family for whom they work. Some have made the pilgrimage to Mecca or accompanied the family on holiday (in one case, to Paris), but always on the understanding that they continue to perform their duties. Unfamiliar with the environment in which they find themselves, the women become very isolated. In Saudi Arabia, this is reinforced by a culture that forbids women to appear in public places unaccompanied. Contact with others from their own country is rare. If they are lucky they may be permitted to visit or receive a visit from a compatriot in the same situation who they may have met by coincidence. Such opportunities are very few and far between and are grasped with both hands as a chance to break through the relentless routine and to cook together and eat familiar

Young children of mothers working in the Gulf countries are left behind in the care of grandparents

food again. We listened to stories, however, of women being beaten by their employers for having spoken to a compatriot whilst shopping at the market. And there were two sisters in North Subang who worked in the same city and never saw or spoke to each other. Letters home, which we were given to read, reveal great loneliness and homesickness. For most women, this is the first time, if they are able to do so, that they have expressed themselves in this way. They say little of their experiences or how it makes them feel and usually offer superficial information of the 'how are you, I'm fine' variety. Yet the few sentences about the children they have left behind ('Take good care of...') and about how long it is before they will see everyone again speak volumes. The reason for the first letter is often to give instructions about what to do with the money remittances, usually accompanied by a reminder to save it and not spend it all. These letters are rarely answered, while regular correspondence almost never develops. This is not to say that the desire to see the women again is any less strong at home. Young children never stop asking for their mothers and newly married young men can tell you exactly how many days are left before their brides return. Some of the husbands continue to live on their own, perhaps trusting the care of their children to their wife's

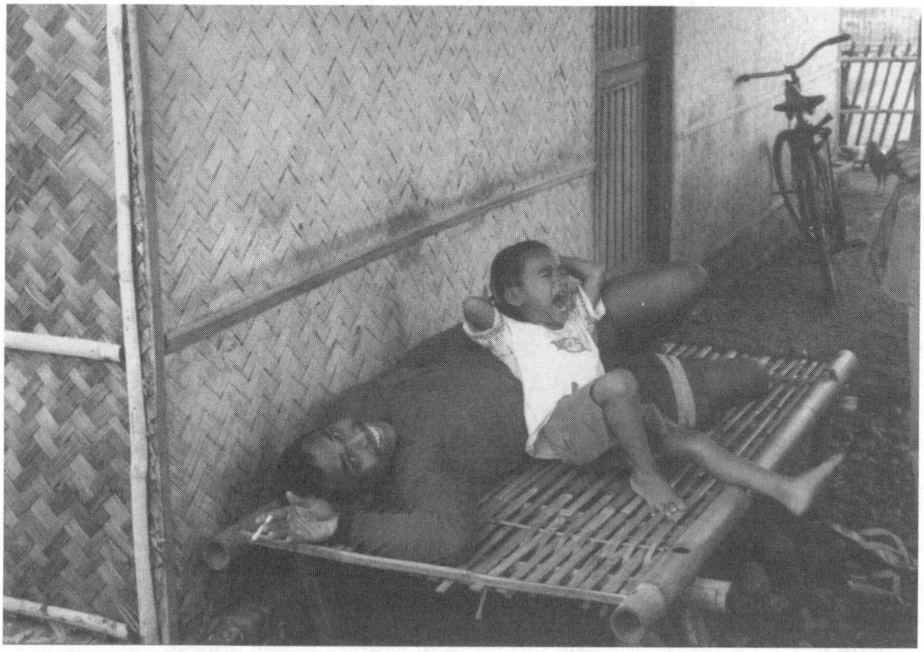

Young father looking after his son while his wife has gone abroad for two years

parents. Others just move back to their parental home until she returns. The telephone represents a modern form of communication which can bridge the distance between the women and their families for a few short moments. Until our final visit in August 2000, the inhabitants of North Subang had to go to a *war(ung)tel(pon)* along the national highway close to Pamanukan but now this facility has become available within the village itself. Nevertheless, to make or receive calls from abroad is very rare and remains restricted to cases of sudden and serious illness or a death in the family. After all, the cost of a call to for example Malaysia is thirty-five thousand rupiah for not more than a few minutes. Apart from the high expenditure, many people are simply not used to talking to each other across great distances unless it is about serious matters and then in formal fashion. Just as with the *haj*, the pilgrimage to Mecca, it is customary to give the women a good send off before they go and a hearty welcome when they return. These are festive occasions, when a whole crowd of relations gather at the airport in Jakarta.

What do these foreign-employed housemaids earn? In mid-1998, those working in Saudi Arabia received six hundred real a month on top of bed and board. This 'allowance', which the women understandably see as their only income for the work they perform, has been the same since the early 1990s.

Maids in Malaysia received three hundred and fifty ringgit a month in 1998. The usual practice is to send this money home every three or four months, but this is only possible with the consent and collaboration of the employer. In some cases, he will suggest that he takes care of the money until the time of departure. This will save her commission expenses and will ensure that the money does not go astray en route. Although this offer may be made with the best of intentions, some women have found themselves on the plane home without their savings. And, as the victim knows better than anyone, appeal against such fraud has little chance of success. Since the women have little understanding of how their income is made up and how much is deducted for all the above-mentioned expenses, they do not know exactly when they actually start building up credit on their wages. Additional deductions are made, which far exceed the 'pocket money' paid out to the women every month. This in itself, if only because of the limited scope for spending it, is only a small proportion of the monthly 'allowance'. Extra deductions include loss of income owing to illness and medical treatment, the cost of replacing household articles that have supposedly been broken or gone missing and for which they are held responsible, and penalties imposed by the employer for not adequately performing their duties. Those back in North Subang who receive the money sent home have even less idea than the women themselves how it is calculated and what periods it covers. We received vague replies to our questions, and not always because of reluctance to answer. This induced us to make further enquiries. Why had no money been received even several months after the woman concerned had gone abroad to start her job? Why did the wages of women working in the same country vary so much that one was able to save quite a lot and the other almost nothing? Yet even in these latter cases the supposition is that the trip was worthwhile, to the extent that the money left over still exceeded the costs. The fact that this was generally true explains the unfailing enthusiasm for sending women to work abroad, but there were nevertheless a number of cases in which it clearly was not. The women are basically helpless against malpractices. Some only realize after several months that their employer has no intention to pay them at all. Running off to another boss is in Malaysia at least a possibility to terminate the contract, but in Saudi-Arabia even that option does not exist.

Failures can have a number of causes, and they occur frequently enough to give the women a sense of insecurity. First of all there are those who suffer considerable financial loss because they have not been paid the full amount to which they are entitled. Others do not complete their contracts because of a conflict with their employer, illness or homesickness. A perhaps even larger group are those who have completed their two-year contract, but who have paid a high cost in terms of their own well-being. They may have been treated badly or sexually abused, unable to escape by returning home because of the isolated situation in which they found themselves. It is not considered decent to talk about such experiences, but the fact that three women have been sent home pregnant shows that it is not a exception. In North Subang there are two babies who came to the village from abroad with their unmarried mothers. The already great vulnerability of young women who have to survive far from home is reinforced by the fact that the relative confidence and openness with which they are accustomed to approach the opposite sex at home is interpreted, particularly in the Gulf States, as licentiousness. Housemaids everywhere have little more than physical resistance with which to repel the unwelcome advances of their employers or of his sons. With a little luck, these confrontations will lead to an early return home, attributed euphemistically to cruelty on the part of the employer. However, a woman from one of the other *kampung* of the village tried to commit suicide as a result of such treatment. It very rarely happens that a woman who has gone abroad to work for two years stays away for good. There is one case of a woman from North Subang who left to work in Malaysia eight years ago. Nothing has been heard of her since. Her mother is bringing up her small son, who was two when the woman left. She told us that she hopes that her daughter is still alive and has found a new life, but showed little confidence in either. Similarly, *pak Muk'min* has no idea of the whereabouts of his son who left for Malaysia three years ago. There is no end to the rumours that have reached him, of people who claim to have seen him walking around an urban market, but he has not been able to check the veracity of such stories.

We found that the best time to determine the net profit of the time spent abroad is at the end of the two-year period, when the contract expires. The calculations, based on the total amount transferred and any money brought home in cash, confirm that earnings vary widely, even when the promised wage is fully paid out. These differences are in the first place related to the variable circumstances under which the women go to work abroad. Those who have incurred substantial debts before their departure, or who are going for the first time and have no idea what to expect, have much lower savings, often less than half, than women who have paid for themselves or who have worked abroad before. Wages also vary considerably from country to country. Coincidence plays a major role in where the women are sent and their plight when they get there. The third – and now major – cause of these differences is the year in which the women have gone abroad. Housemaids who worked in Saudi Arabia up to mid-1997 could, depending on their own contribution to the recruitment and other expenses, have saved between three and ten million rupiah by the end of their two-year contract. Those whose contract started after mid-1997 could earn three or four times as much. In one case, the most lucrative so far, the woman accumulated a veritable fortune of thirty million rupiah. This sudden rise had nothing to do with a sudden leap in the real value of their labour, but was the consequence of the fall in value of the Indonesian rupiah against harder currencies like the real. *Krismon,* which had such a disastrous impact on the great mass of the working population in Indonesia, had exactly the opposite effect on this group of overseas workers. For reasons which were beyond the comprehension of the people of the village, the exchange rate of the money sent or brought home from abroad shot up to unknown heights. They were even more mystified to discover that not all the women working abroad benefited equally from these unexpected windfalls. Those working in Malaysia and other Asian countries, which were also suffering from the crisis – albeit to a lesser extent than Indonesia – received scarcely more rupiah than before. But now, more than ever, working abroad was clearly worthwhile, despite the fraudulent practices of the recruitment agencies, the minimal opportunity to have a say in which country you were to work in, uncertainty about how you would be treated once you got there and about how much you would be able to save from your earnings, which all added to the risks involved.

How is the money spent? That varies, depending on the women's own background and circumstances. Golden ornaments are, however, a popular choice across the board. For women from landpoor and landless households,

Woman returned from abroad back in the village

paying off the debt incurred to be allowed to go abroad at all is a high priority. Recruitment agents and other moneylenders naturally keep a very close eye on the repayments. The money remitted or brought back home by the women is also used to cover basic living expenses. Purchases are made more easily, even when they are not a basic need. The sometimes extravagant behaviour is described as *foya* – 'leading the good life'. The rest is used to buy bricks or other materials to gradually improve the house. Women who have paid their own way and who therefore have more income left to spend tend to use the surplus to pay off their household's debts, and thereby to increase their creditworthiness. In mid-1998 the price of a new house could be as much as fifteen million rupiah or more. The more expensive of these, built in the style of city houses, are still primarily found in the centre of the *kampung*, where the local elite lives, but these outward displays of prosperity can now be found in other neighbourhoods of the locality as well. The most luxurious bungalow was still under construction during our last field visit. The leading recruitment boss in the area, *haji* Rahmat, was building it for one of his wives. According to his neighbours in the kampung, his frequent visits to her also allow him to maintain regular contact with his extensive circle of clients in the locality.

After the debts have been paid off, are the remainder of the earnings of these women used only for making consumption-oriented purchases? If this is so, then it is mainly because of the lack of opportunities in the village and outside the agricultural sector to make investments that would increase productivity. The purchase of a motorcycle for a brother may add to his income by enabling him to operate for *ojeg* but the return on this sort of investment is low. Expanding the stock of a *warung* run by the mother would probably be more profitable. We recorded several cases of savings being used to finance the cultivation of rice or to lease a field for one or more seasons. We found that the actual purchase of farmland was much less common. This may have been because of the greater investment required, but could be a reflection of the falling value of agriculture as a target for investment in recent years, in both economic and social terms.

As can be seen from the above account, the opportunity to work abroad has led to a considerable upgrading of the significance of women as breadwinners. Working as a maid, which requires almost no training, brings in more than the majority of men earn in or outside the village. This explains why even young women from the landowning upper class, single and married, are tempted to register for jobs abroad. From the conversations we had with villagers on this matter, we got the impression that many of the leading citizens in North Subang still consider it beneath their dignity to hire out their daughters as *pembantu*. In spite of the not inconsiderable risks involved, working abroad has proved so lucrative – especially since *krismon* – that the well-to-do are now prepared to send their daughters or even wives abroad for factory employment. In comparison to domestic service such jobs are more prestigious and also result in higher earnings. This shows that the tendency in the past to exempt women from paid work after they were no longer employable in agriculture, had nothing to do with status considerations but was much more inspired by a lack of possibilities to find suitable work in or outside the village. Lastly, to suggest that the women who decide to go and work abroad do so purely or even largely because they have been put under pressure by the men in the household would not do justice to the choices that they increasingly tend to make in their own right. In fact our impression was that their fathers and husbands sometimes seemed more reluctant than the women themselves. This also applies to how they spend the money they have saved. The male recipients of the money sent home by no means have the last word. Even young unmarried women often give clear instructions in the few letters they write home about what should happen with the savings. The parents are not forgotten, but a large part is put in the bank for later, for the wedding or for the 'bottom drawer'.

Women are acting more and more as a vanguard, showing men the way to foreign destinations. In mid-1998, fifty-seven women and eight men from North Subang were working abroad: forty-one of them in Saudi Arabia or one of the smaller Gulf States, twelve in Malaysia, two in Singapore, one in Taiwan and one in Korea. With a few exceptions, all were contracted as housemaids. In the past, a small number of the women were accompanied by their husbands, who worked for the same employer as drivers or gardeners. Unmarried men are now also eligible for other jobs, such as waiters, building labourers or factory workers. In 1998, five of the eight men were in Malaysia, one was in Korea, one in Taiwan and one in Brunei. The preparations for men to go abroad to work are more time consuming. While the procedures for women often require no more than two months, those for men take eight. The reasons for this difference are unclear, but our informants told us that it had something to do with the fact that men are recruited for more skilled work and are also better paid. In exchange for the higher overhead costs, the men of course have to pay more for the services of the intermediaries. The more experienced brokers as well as individual migrants avoid all this by making use of illegal routes which are cheaper and quicker. Malaysia can actually be reached without the prescribed documents quite easily via Riau. The major deterrent for those who are tempted to seek this solution is, more even than the fear of getting caught and deported, that they have to settle for a lower wage and will generally find themselves forced to pay bribes – not once but repeatedly – to the jobber or the police.

During our fieldwork in 1998, these overseas workers, all but a small minority legal, already accounted for 10% of the economically active popula-

Young mother soon going abroad again

tion in North Subang in the final round of our research. The expectation, or at least the hope, was that this percentage would continue to increase. The *sponsor* had an abundant supply of candidates, but were not at all convinced that demand would be sustained, given the impact of the crisis in the wider region of Asia.

What happens to the *pembantu* after they return from working abroad? They are generally unable to find the same work in the village and difference in pay in Indonesia is so huge that there is little incentive. They spend the first few months after their return taking what they rightly consider to be a well-earned rest after two years of hard work. 'Tired, mister, tired', we were told by a woman in July 1998 who had recently returned after working for a Chinese boss in Malaysia. But when we returned to North Subang in the spring of 1999, she had just been accepted for a preparatory course for a new assignment in Hong Kong. There were many like this young woman in the *kampung* who were prepared to return abroad for a second or a third two-year period. Even the woman who had returned from Saudi Arabia after trying to commit suicide had left again for Brunei. Once again, it would be misleading to suggest that these women had been put under pressure by the men in their households. Yet to say that they did it of their own free will would also be untrue. The realization that in the village there is no gainful employment for them, while they can earn good money abroad makes the decision easier. Their sacrifice is being away from home for another two years, with the chance that their marriage may collapse, that they will be caring for someone else's children rather than their own, and in the knowledge that, at best, they can look forward to a long period of hard work and loneliness. Their previous experience helps them to make the decision. They try to have more of a say in which country they are assigned to, preferring Malaysia or other destinations in Southeast Asia to Saudi Arabia or the Golf countries, despite the better pay in the latter. Those returning for a second or third assignment also avoid, if they can, accruing large debts to ensure that a disproportionate part of their future earnings is not owed to others in advance. Our impression is that men find it more difficult to deal with the brutal work regime that overseas migrants often have to face. Two men from North Subang, who came back from Saudi Arabia before their contract had expired, complained profusely about the long and irregular hours they were forced to remain at the beck and call of their boss. Although for their job as private car drivers they were paid double the going wage for housemaids, this was poor compensation for the brutal work regime to which they found themselves exposed. Both cut short their stay, whereas women do not only have to tolerate much worse treatment but would also meet with less sympathy in case of their untimely return home.

If we interpret the earlier tendency in North Subang for women to be excluded from the labour process as indicating a shift in the balance of power in the household in favour of men, the newly rediscovered economic value of the former could lead a drastic restoration of that balance. But such a shift takes time and further research will be needed in the years to come to confirm it.

Work and unemployment at the time of krismon

A sliding scale

The two hundred and fifty-four of the two hundred and sixty-one households in North Subang that we counted in 1998 as part of the active population had a total of six hundred and eighteen members in gainful employment, in the sense that they were supposed to contribute to the maintenance of the household to which they belonged. Of these six hundred and eighteen men and women however, eighty do not fit into any of the employment categories. So what is the nature of their employment status?

This category of people in employment but who do not fit into any occupational category were designated as 'co-workers' in the report on our find-

Table 5. The employment status of men and women within and outside agriculture in mid-1998.

	In agriculture	Outside agriculture	Total	Reserve	Total
Men	180	123	311	11	322
Women	131	104	227	69	296
Total	311	227	538	80	618

Source: Village survey Breman and Wiradi 1998.

ings in 1990, that is, men and women who do not have permanent or even regular employment, but who work on an occasional basis. In 1990 they accounted for 17% of the working population (Breman 1995:11), while in 1998 this had fallen slightly to 13%. The drop reflected the improved employment rate of women, who however still constitute the largest part of what should be seen as the local pool of reserve labour.

The off-and-on members of the workforce, consisting of those whose age and physical condition render them fit for work, is mobilized when the demand for labour is at its maximum, such as during the rice harvest, but then returns to its normal state of rest when the peak is past. Is the choice not to go in search of work restlessly a matter of free will? One observation that supports our contention is the fact that nearly all of the people in this reserve category belong to households in which other members already earn sufficient income to guarantee a reasonable standard of living, certainly above the poverty line. Young adolescents from slightly or much better families are in no hurry to start their working lives after finishing their schooling, while elderly men from this milieu can afford to give up work earlier than their propertyless counterparts. The same applies to the girls and women, but to an even greater extent. It is not only the women from the households of the *pamong desa* (village officials) who are exempt from gainful employment, but also those of teachers, traders and landowners – all professions associated with the upper class. In conversations with the members of these households, the emphasis was on the caring and reproductive tasks of the women, which would be in conflict with their working outside the home. Yet, as observed above, the financial benefits also play a major role in the decision. If they are considered to be too low, the women concerned can just as well continue to 'do nothing'. But this abstinence will soon change if the rewards for working increase, as can be seen from the increased interest among women even from the propertied classes in going abroad as *pembantu*. Even the mothers of small children, from whom it would be almost taken for granted that they would not work within or outside agriculture or the village, do not hesitate – if they get a chance – to leave their families to spend two years working overseas.

Cutting wood as a source of income

Classifying a man or woman as generally unemployed remains an arbitrary matter. Older men who occasionally gather wood, catch fish, cut grass for goats to graze, keep sheep on a sharecropping basis, make a few bricks outside the rainy season (and bake them much later when they are dry), or plant cucumbers on a piece of fallow land, fall into the category of casual workers because they do not perform these activities for a large part of the year or in combination with one or more other occupations. The same applies to women who sell drinks or snacks during the harvest, help prepare the food at parties or distribute wedding invitations, do the washing for another household a few hours a week, et cetera. Their income is so low and the time involved so short that it would be an exaggeration to classify them as workers. Payment in kind, whether in exchange for work carried out or not, is usually not included in survey data. The relevance of this omission can be illustrated with the case of a woman, the single head of her household, who gives shelter to a flock of ducks in her roadside yard at night. For this she receives two eggs a day as 'rent'. The sale of these eggs accounts for a substantial part of the small income on which her livelihood depends. Yet this is not sufficient to classify her among the working population.

We did, however count the women who glean the fields immediately after the harvest (*ngasak* or *p'rik*) as part of the workforce. They can collect between five and ten kilograms of rice stalks per day. In this way, by staying active in and around the village for several weeks a year they can earn enough to ensure their basic subsistence. We also included under the category of petty vendors, the women who sell prepared food, fruit or snacks from a table or a few shelves in front of their houses. Their sales are so extremely modest and their businesses so irregular that they would be better described as occasional workers than as *warung* owners. Other examples of marginal cases among the working population are the few young men who have been bought a motorcycle with money given to them by their parents or a sister who has worked abroad and who offer themselves together with their vehicle every now and on rent to cover the cost of maintenance. They do not do this on a daily basis, like the more professional *ojeg* drivers.

In the same way that occupational multiplicity makes it difficult to draw a sharp line between a jack of all trades and an agricultural labourer, the transition from occasional to more regular work is very difficult to quantify. The number of days worked per year could be a useful way of distinguishing between employment and unemployment, but this would require long-term observation (covering several seasons) from close range. In our experience, basing calculations on the recall of informants leads to conflicting accounts and a distorted view of reality, even for the previous week. The figures in Table 5 on the size and gender composition of the pool of reserve labour must be seen as reflecting a complex and ambiguous problem (the shortage of paid work) and not just as a collection of individuals whose employment position can be clearly and accurately defined on the basis of a survey. One of the decisive criteria for including someone in this last column is whether, if the opportunity were to arise, they would enter into more permanent employment to ensure that they could meet their basic needs or to improve the quality of their lives. But we admit immediately that even the most decisive of answers to this question must remain hypothetical, given the lack of unambiguous evidence.

The impact of krismon on employment

When we came to North Subang for a brief visit in the spring of 1998 in preparation of our subsequent longer stay, we could already see that the turbulence that held sway in Jabotabek had not left the rural hinterland untouched. In the previous month, more than twenty Chinese shops in the market town of Pamanukan, some twelve kilometres from the village, had been set on fire and looted. The graffiti on the walls of buildings near to the charred remains of the shops sent out a clear message: *Muslim asli* (authentic Muslims). What had caused the riots? Several stories circulated. Some informants linked the unrest to the massive price rises that sometimes followed each other within days, or even hours. Enraged buyers who felt cheated had attacked shopkeepers, and the crowds that rapidly gathered soon followed their example. But another rumour said that it had been the work of *agents provocateurs*. Early on the day of the riots, before the morning call to prayer, two trucks full with athletically built young men with close-cropped hair had driven into the centre of the town. They were not in uniform but looked and acted like soldiers. They split up into small groups and started smashing things up, calling on passers by to join them and set fire to the shops. Were the villagers involved in the riots? A boy who had been in the

Slogans were also painted on village shops to pre-empt attacks on Chinese-held property

market square by coincidence was arrested but released shortly after. The events left a deep impression on our informants, who saw them as a sign that bad times were on the way. In the village the same comments could be heard as in Jakarta: that the people's anger should be directed vertically and not horizontally, that is, at the political leaders rather than at other segments of the community. Such remarks were a sign that the power and authority of the New Order was starting to fail. By the time we returned in July 1998 the instability had accelerated. The urban-based protagonists of the *reformasi* campaign who had succeeded in forcing Suharto to resign two months earlier were also calling for the lower echelons of the government apparatus to be purged. In a nearby village, a group of youngsters had carried a *lurah* known as being excessively corrupt around on their shoulders, shouting slogans that expressed the scorn and derision of the local people. In North Subang there were no such public expressions of dissatisfaction. We could see no signs, for the time being anyway, of a political revitalization at the grassroots in response to the new from the cities. There was, however, a growing feeling of insecurity, which manifested itself as a threat to community by ill-defined outside forces. As a defence against this eventuality, the *kepala kampung* started nightly patrols to ensure that robbers and other 'bad people' had no opportunity to disturb the peace. Local officials now found good use for the walkie-talkie sets they had been equipped with during the 1996 elections. Our host in North Subang used them to maintain contact with the patrols on their rounds after nightfall. With this permanent surveillance he wanted to demonstrate that the security of the village was in good hands. The sarcastic responses that this invoked among the inhabitants were soon silenced when some of them were robbed on the provincial highway and, in a nearby *kampung*, a thief killed his victim when he was caught red-handed. All of these bad tidings confirmed that the end of the New Order was in sight without anyone having the faintest idea of what would replace it. For the time being at least, it seemed, nothing but political turmoil and administrative paralysis. But what was the economic impact of *krismon*?

Agriculture seemed unaffected at first. As a result of the rising price of fertilizer (urea and phosphate more than doubled in price) and pesticides (which went up six-fold), many farmers did reduce their purchases of these inputs, leading to lower harvests in 1998 (4 to 4.5 tons per hectare). It is impossible to say to what extent the harvest was also affected by other factors, such as too little rainfall or too many rats in the fields. The lower production was by and large offset by the increased profits from the sale of the product. In the spring of 1999, with widespread rumours of severe food shortages across the country, traders in the village happily paid between one hundred thousand and one hundred twenty thousand rupiah per quintal, a hundred kilogram bag. This was a little more than twice the price of a quintal the previous year during the rainy season. Fearing crop thefts at the time of harvest, we were told that more farmers than in the past had sold the rice to *penebas* just before the harvest. These contractors use their own harvesting gangs which are paid in money rather than in kind. They employ foremen who keep a sharp eye on the field operations. Other informants, however, denied that the advance selling of paddy occurred more than in previous years. As already earlier mentioned, sharecropping arrangements have become less popular. Non-cultivating owners prefer to lease out their land on a money rent and candidates for such contracts have to bear the risks themselves including all financial outlay during the cultivation cycle.

Prior to our return to North Subang in July 1998 the daily wage for agricultural labourers had gone up to seven thousand rupiah plus the usual two or three meals a day. In the early spring of 1999 the rate rose again, to ten thousand rupiah a day. How did these revisions come about? A number of employers told us that the wage hikes were to help compensate for the rapidly increasing cost of living. In our own opinion, however, it was related to a link between the wages paid in kind during harvest time and other farm work paid in cash. There was no change in the actual share of the harvest for

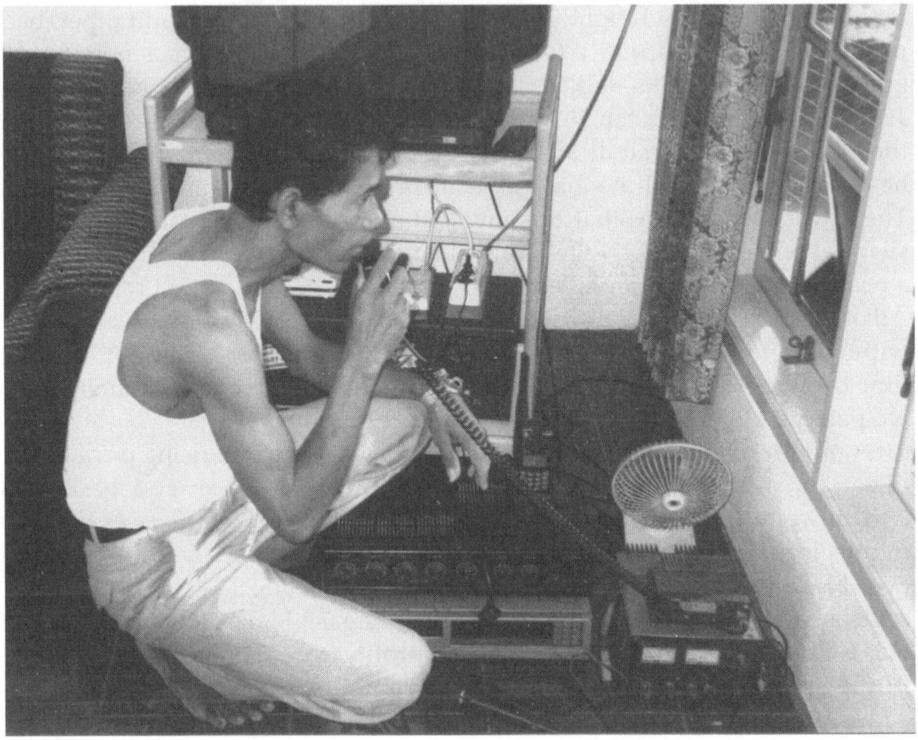

Walkie-talkie set used by *kampung* head for communication

the labourers and the fact that the *bawon* could be sold for a higher price made a rise in the daily cash wage for other activities as good as inevitable. The other costs of working the land had increased, too. Tractor owners pushed up rental rates to compensate for the enormous price rise of spare parts. Sometimes the parts were not even available and the tractors had to be taken out of operation.

Return from Jabotabek

The impact of *krismon* on non-agricultural employment was much more far-reaching and this would have been even greater but for the large number of women working abroad as housemaids. As mentioned above, when the exchange rate of the rupiah started to fall in late 1997, two thirds of all households had one or more working members whose main or only source of income was outside agriculture. Once the full force of the crisis hit, this percentage fell to 40% as waged labourers and self-employed workers in the informal sector came back to the *kampung*. Their escape from the village economy was interrupted, at least for the time being. The most heavily affected were those few who had qualified for a permanent job and who had been with their employers for a relatively long time. Their dismissal came at a time when there was no alternative available and they had no choice but to return to the village where they were used to spending only their spare time. This group of workers included a headloader who had worked in the docks in Jakarta for many years, an offshore worker employed by a construction company who had been all over the archipelago, a taxi driver, a female shop assistant, one of the factory workers (the other two managed to keep their jobs, but with shorter working hours and the loss of all extras, such as travelling expenses and clothing allowances). A man who collected instalments on goods bought on hire purchase told us that he lost his job when the showroom of his Chinese employer's showroom in Glodok had been set on fire. The boss survived but fled with his family to Hong Kong. A number of petty traders stopped operating in Jabotabek to wait for better times. This decision was made largely in response to continual price rises, which reduced their turnover substantially. Another factor were the riots, which constantly broke out and prevented them from selling their wares. The same fate befell those working in the transport sector, the drivers of the *bajaj* (three-wheeled motorized taxis) and the drivers and conductors of the *angkot* (minibuses). The reasons why two of the women who tried to make a living as prostitutes in Jakarta returned to North Subang for good are less clear. We understood from their comments that their business, too, suffered from a loss of customers. Other self-employed workers try to keep their heads above water in the urban environment by settling for a lower turnover and a smaller margin between costs and benefits. This group includes the *singkong* sellers, who purchase fewer ingredients and sell half portions for the same price they used to charge for a full one. Most of those who came back said that their daily, weekly or monthly income had fallen below the level required to enable them to live in the city. With their limited reserves they were able to survive without income for a short time, but when demand for their services in the sector in which they were accustomed to operate fell beyond a critical level they had little choice but to make a rapid exit from the metropolitan economy. As we shall see they did not return to the village expecting to find a niche to replace the one that they have lost, at least provisionally, in the city. As far as they are concerned it is a temporary stay until the urban economy recovers from what has developed into *kristal*, total crisis. Why do they not seek employment in agriculture? The more the work they performed outside the village was removed from farm labour, the less they were prepared to go back to the latter. Their higher income implied that they had opted out of agriculture (see also Pincus 1996:59).

Those who, driven by need, might want to get involved in agricultural work are rarely given the opportunity to do so because farmers prefer to employ real agricultural labourers, that is, men who have continued cultivating the land. The small traders and craftsmen who have been forced to leave the city try to earn a living in their own occupations closer to home. The limited size of the non-agricultural sectors in the village economy make this an almost hopeless exercise before they even start. No new activities have emerged that might provide income for those who have returned. On the contrary, the trade and services that were already present in North Subang have suffered from the loss of non-agricultural earnings in many households. Clear evidence of this has been closure of four of six of the smaller *warung* out of a total of sixteen, owing to a fall in turnover and the reduced creditworthiness of their customers.

As to how long the workers who have returned from Jabotabek will remain out of work, no one can say with any certainty. Previous prognoses, based on little more than wishful thinking, to the effect that the collapse of the non-agricultural economy was a consequence of overheating and that, with a resolute policy, it would soon be brought under control again, soon proved unfounded. The victims, too, have lost their initial optimism. One man who had lost his job as a factory worker told us in a resigned fashion at the end of our conversation that even those with higher education had become unemployed. A number of others listening to our conversation just nodded their heads in agreement.

The majority of those who found work outside the village were unskilled, low-paid circulatory labourers who worked mostly in the building sector, moving from job to job. All but a few of them are now back in North Subang. Their mobility was not only rural-urban, but they also moved back and forth between agricultural work and similar work outside the prime sector of the economy. They did not experience the inter-sectoral mobility as an abrupt shift as is apparent from the terminology to which they refer, *kuli* for short, while describing their daily routine and the wages earned with these wide-ranging activities. Yet they still tend to present themselves generally as agricultural labourers. This is not merely consequence of the fact that their employment niches outside the agricultural sector have largely or completely disappeared. The resulting reduction in their work profile does not mean that they can devote the extra time that they now have to earning more in what has now become again their main source of income. The fact that they retreated from the rice fields to do other casual work, especially in the building industry, was due above all to their steadily growing redundancy in agriculture. In this sector nothing has changed in the intervening years that would enable this surplus to be reabsorbed. On the contrary, price developments under *krismon* against falling real wages for unskilled work seem to have killed any chance they earlier may have had of a future as self-cultivating farmers. In mid-2000, a one-year *sewa* contract (mortgaging of land for a loan) cost 4.5 million rupiah per bahu; the price of a *gadai* transaction for a piece of land of the same area – a rental contract which has actually been forbidden since the mid-1960s – would be twenty million rupiah. The downright purchase of land was, of course, much more expensive: not less than seventy million rupiah per hectare.

The only glimmer of hope is that *krismon* resulted in an increase in the earnings of the women who went abroad to work. This particularly affected those who went to Saudi Arabia and the other Gulf States. Because of the oil-based hard currencies of these countries, the women were able to send higher remittances and also bring home more in cash at the end of their contracts. Their substantial savings had a particularly great impact because it came at a time when the earnings of most male workers were falling considerably. As already mentioned, this unexpected windfall did not affect all the overseas workers equally. The fall in value of the ringgit, although less dramatic than that of the rupiah, meant that the women and men from the kampung who had worked in Malaysia did not benefit as much from their stay. But on the other hand, the greater affinity with the language, culture and social climate of Malaysia made it more attractive for young women to contract themselves for works as maid servants in this country. The disincentive is, of course, the much lower wages they are paid, three hundred and fifty to four hundred ringgit a month. This amounts to roughly eighty US dollars, half of what a domestic servant in Saudi-Arabia is able to earn. Besides, employers in Malaysia tend to deduct all expenses they have incurred to the workers contracted by them. At the start of krismon it looked as though the Malaysian government might send all foreign workers home. When police efforts to clamp down on illegal aliens were stepped up, a large number of Indonesians who had crossed into the neighbouring country illegally could not avoid being deported. Because of the economic recovery in Malaysia, however, the demand for foreign labour soon returned to its earlier level. This favourable trend is expected to breathe new life into the overseas migration of labour both to this country and to others in East Asia. Those who want to qualify for a factory job in Korea or Taiwan need a secondary school certificate and the cost for processing their applications are also much higher, up to twelve to eighteen million rupiah. But for this investment their income is much higher. Haji Rahmat's stepdaughter is employed in a garment factory in Korea for two years for three million rupiah per month, nearly as much as the salary of the lurah, the highest ranking official in the village.

The rapidly expanding popularity of working abroad has led to the status of *pembantu* being upgraded. Women from the middle classes in North Subang who would never have worked as domestic servants to home no longer hesitate to apply for a contract for overseas employment. In their view, spending two years in a subordinated position by far outweighs the monetary loss suffered by males in their households who have forfeited their non-farm and non-local jobs.

Open unemployment

What was the net impact of krismon on employment in North Subang? The main effect has been a significant decrease in the number of days spent in gainful work. A sample survey which we conducted in July 1998 of one hundred and twenty-one heads of households (40% of the total; seventy-eight of whom worked in the agricultural sector and forty-three outside), revealed that forty-five (37%) had not worked on that day and forty (33%) had not worked on the previous day. The concept of gainful employment is applied in the broadest sense, and also includes activities that resulted in income in kind such as gathering wood, fishing, gathering weeds for use as vegetables, doing small chores in exchange for a meal, et cetera. The way the people of North Subang responded to the economic crisis depended on the social class to which they belonged. Pincus observed in his study that landpoor and landless households tended to react to the fall in income by searching for other work, within or outside agriculture (Pincus 1996:176). The problem that confronted many households was that from the start of krismon this solution was no longer open to them. The escape route out of both the agrarian and the rural economy was temporarily blocked. Open unemployment seems to be a new phenomenon in Village Java. Yet this state of affairs has become normal, particularly for those men and women who until recently were thoroughly embedded in the metropolitan economy of Jabotabek. Return to the village does not mean for them the first step in falling back on work in the agriculture, if for no other reason than that the sector already has a surplus of labour. These slightly better educated and better paid migrant workers never succeeded in completely breaking away from their roots in the village and establishing a solid foothold in the urban environment. They find it difficult to accept that they have been pushed out again. The most determined victims in this massive army of the instantly dismissed (phk), continue to make expensive sorties to the city to meet former bosses and one-time workmates who might be able to help them find a job, no matter how temporary or badly paid. These expeditions, even with such humble expectations, generally lead to nothing. Unlike the labour nomads who camped out semi-permanently in the Jabotabek zone, most of the workers from landpoor and landless households always spent at least a part of the year working in agriculture. When they were deprived from access to employment outside the sector and outside the village, which had yielded an increasingly significant part of their total income, they reverted to their former identities as agricultural labourers. However, their familiarity with this kind of work did not prevent them from being exposed once again to the strong fluctuations in demand between the peaks and slacks in the agricultural milieu.

In several branches of economic activity signs of a slight recovery was noticeable by mid-2000. Several *warung* in the village which had closed down in the preceding years were back in business, although their female owners told us that the turnover was much lower than before *krismon*. It is like *paceklik* (the period of no work and no income between harvests) in former times, one of them complained. The vendors of *singkong* and other edible goods from North Subang have also gone back to the streets of Jakarta. They still commute in cycles of three to four weeks, but the earnings they bring back to the village are much lower than they used to be. There are no signs, as far as yet, of a return to normality in the building industry. Skilled craftsmen have to survive with maintenance and repair work but they get few orders lasting more than a couple of days. So far there is hardly any demand for the labour of navvies and other unskilled workers, which means that life remains extremely difficult for the landless who are and always have been the most vulnerable as well as the most invisible in the rural economy.

Changes in social distribution

The situation on the outset

Breman's fieldwork in 1990 led him to conclude that, on the basis of the distribution of income from property and employment, the inhabitants of North Subang could be divided into three social classes: an upper class consisting of 18%, a middle class accounting for 31% and a lower class comprising the remaining 51% at the lower end of the socio-economic spectrum (Breman 1995:8). His findings were, with marginal differences, identical to those reached by Pincus during a study of the same *kampung* at practically the same time. Pincus conducted a detailed survey of the ownership of consumer durables, the quality of the dwelling and the possession of small and large means of production (other than land), which included a total list of twenty-four items. The survey revealed that, with an average score of 6.4, the poorest quarter of the population owned no more than three of the items on the list, and that 51.5% of all households owned no more than five. Above these poor households was a class consisting of under a third of all households which owned between six and ten of the items. This was what we referred to as the middle class. The elite class, 17% of all households, owned eleven or more of the items on Pincus' list (Pincus 1996:27-30). The picture that emerged from both these studies was one of great and increasing inequality. These conclusions contradicted those of Hayami and Kikuchi, who claimed that the growth of the agricultural sector in the late 1960s and 1970s, which resulted in a dramatic increase in yields per hectare, benefited the landowners and the landless in North Subang equally. Without probing deeper they concluded that both farmers and labourers recorded significant gains in absolute income, while their relative shares remained largely unchanged (Hayami and Kikuchi 1981:207). Breman and Pincus acknowledged that the real wages of agricultural labourers did increase during this period. The agrarian lower class had undeniably benefited from the breakthrough generated by the green revolution, but relatively speaking to a far lesser extent than the large farmers. They both saw the same trend as continuing in the 1980s (Breman 1995:35; Pincus 1996:135). In presenting the results of their fieldwork, both Breman and Pincus pointed out the growing significance of work and income outside the agricultural sector. This argument also contradicted the analysis of Hayami and Kikuchi who, assuming the closed nature of the village economy, asserted that the owners of capital had no other choice in their quest for accumulation than to invest in land (Hayami and Kikuchi 1981:221). Pincus refuted this by focusing on what he called the tendency to disaccumulation, that is, disposing of land to buyers and tenants from outside the *kampung*. He attributed this major fall in capital concentration to specific circumstances related to the collapse of the enormous estate built up by the biggest landlord in North Subang. On inheriting their father's property, his children showed none of his enthusiasm for progressive accumulation and sold off – or more frequently leased out – a large part of the family land, so as to live a comfortable life from the proceeds. On the basis of this salient example, Pincus points out the ease with which a number of prominent households acquired their wealth. In the early 1970s, the introduction of new agricultural technology led to a sudden rise in the value of farmland, most of which was already in the hands of a small elite. Pincus believes that this windfall created a lifestyle which gave little incentive to strengthening entrepreneurial capability (Pincus 1996:170).

Progressive accumulation

Breman came to a different conclusion. The successful magnate from the previous generation in North Subang was actually much more of a money-lending capitalist than a genuine agrarian industrialist striving to maximize productivity on the vast domain he had built up. He made his profits by renting out his estate through endless and continually rotating leasing and sharecropping arrangements. Our point of departure is that, after the dramatic increase in rice production caused by the green revolution, there were no further breakthroughs in the agricultural economy. Under the New Order regime, the emphasis shifted to the urban based sectors, especially trade and services. This shift was accompanied by a sharp fall in the value of capital invested in agrarian property. It is by no means certain that the motivation to invest among the *kampung* elite was as weak as Pincus believed at the time of his fieldwork. Rather than speaking of disaccumulation, we would suggest that the better-off households in North Subang had adapted their economic strategy, shifting the balance in favour of investment outside agriculture. Pincus actually examined this aspect in considerable detail. His figures show that the profits earned by the largest landowners from their non-agrarian activities were five times higher than the average of all the other households in North Subang. This finding seems to confirm the observation made by Breman of a congruence between agrarian and non-agrarian incomes in a way that reinforced the already existent inequality in the village economy (Pincus:1996:72; Breman 1995:35).

But what are the new investment options that the diversification of the rural economy give rise to? The problem in answering this question is that the village elite is extremely reluctant to talk about it. Their transactions seem to bear little relation to typical industrial activity. We had the impression that the mobility of capital has undergone the same scale-enlargement in recent years as that of labour. The members of the propertied class in North Subang have extended their field of financial operations outside the sub-district. They have started investing their money in commercial enterprises, real estate and building projects in the urban economy. They do, however, continue to extend credit to the people of the village for a variety of expenses, such as circumcision or wedding festivities, the purchase of building materials or household goods, clothing, a bicycle, or simply for daily necessities at the usual interest of 50% per season. The extent to which they do this is difficult to estimate. The loans are paid off in instalments, when a household member returns with pay earned while working elsewhere, or after the sale of harvested rice. The better-off borrow money to pay for the *haj*, while all classes are allowed to borrow to bear the initial cost for sending of a wife or daughter abroad. This is very profitable business indeed and the high interest can even be charged to close relatives. If it is difficult to obtain a clear picture of such financial practices and more so when it comes to transactions that have no legal standing. Corruption, collusion and nepotism, abbreviated to *KKN*, are terms supposed to express disapproval of such shady dealings. The actors directly involved, however, are prone to judge them primarily on the basis of their profitability. *Ersatz* capitalism is grounded in a mode of political economy said to be typical of the authoritarian regimes found in Southeast Asia, with Indonesia as a prime example. Kunio, who introduced the term, defined the corresponding rent-seeking behaviour as the provision of a wide range of monopolistic 'favours', including permits, contracts, protection and other forms of official authorization. They are issued by or on behalf of a person or government agency to recipients, who pay a rent or commission that is much lower than the legal rate or the market price (Kunio 1988:68). The literature on this phenomenon almost exclusively focuses on the higher echelons of government and the circle of cronies around the head of state. This preoccupation with the prominent clique that makes up the President's entourage means that insufficient attention is given to the extent to which corruption extends right down to the lowest levels of the state apparatus in the era of the Orde Baru. The absence of any countervailing power among the population at large has reinforced the monolithic nature of the village administration, inherent since colonial rule. The authoritarian climate allowed village capitalists to thrive who acted as petty cronies and established links with the authorities from the local level right up to the district headquarters. Being a member of the *aparat desa*, or being a part of the social circuit around it, ensures having access to financial gains that are difficult for the researcher to follow up. The hidden incomes are much higher than the formal salaries of the village officials, which in 2000 amounted in North Subang to four million rupiah per annum for the *lurah* (village head), three million rupiah for the *sekdes* (village secretary) and 1.5 million rupiah for the *kepala kampung* (head of hamlet). Under the heading of political accumulation, Pincus gave examples of blatant embezzlement on a large scale by a prominent member of the community in North Subang. In 1986 this man disappeared with an exorbitant amount of money that belonged to the department of the Koperasi Unit Desa (KUD), the village cooperative unit of which he held charge. There have been other similar cases of rent-seeking since. The Bulog (Badan urusan logistik), the food procurement agency set up by the government to which farmers were forced to sell their rice, was renowned for being a hotbed of corruption and fraud. Rice traders in the village became embroiled in a chain of illegal transactions that reached as far as the Dolog (Depot logistik) in the district capital of Subang. We had the very strong impression that the share of the leading households in the gross village product had further increased in the final years of the New Order, but we lack the hard evidence with which to back up our suspicions. We have already described the machinations around the asphalting of the road, firstly to the centre of the village and then to the *kampung*. Another example was the grant programme for the purchase of goats and sheep, which was especially aimed at small farmers. The annual reports of the government agency concerned show that a large sum of money was spent on the programme in North Subang without anyone whom we spoke to pretending to know where it had gone. It was the same story with countless other *proyek* funded by the government under the label of development. It was quite clear that the capitalists and local officials had colluded to ensure that a large part of the money was never spent as originally intended and later on dutifully registered in the village accounts. Describing the situation in this way might still create the impression that poverty reduction or the provision of credit to micro-entrepreneurs was the actual, genuine intention of those who provided the funds. That is in itself very doubtful; it is more likely that these funds served to increase the legitimacy of the New Order by buying the collaboration of the local elites. Given the space for building up collective action and sustained protest at grassroots level against the intimidation and terror exercised by Suharto's regime right up to the end, it is difficult to deny that this political strategy was very successful for a long time. The increased wealth of the local elite could be seen in the opulence of their lifestyles. In contrast to Pincus and in agreement with Antlöv we believe that state patronage played a very prominent role in the marked improvement in the prosperity of the village capitalists (Pincus 1996:191; Antlöv 1999).

The non-agrarian strategy of accumulation included investment in the secondary education of the new generation in the hope that they would qualify for a position in the formal sector of the economy, preferably by finding a job in the government apparatus or with a large company. The realization is gradually gaining ground that to satisfy aspirations of upward mobility outside the village and outside agriculture requires more and different knowledge and training than can be acquired purely through experience. As mentioned before, in North Subang even primary school attendance was comparatively late in developing, especially for children from landpoor and landless households, but the decision by a growing percentage of parents, particularly in the better-off households, to at least ensure that their children got a secondary school diploma was driven by the conviction that this would guarantee them a job in the formal sector. However, as Pincus noted earlier (Pincus 1996:173), more advanced education than just elementary school might be a necessary condition for finding permanent and better paid work, but it was by no means a sufficient one. In the intervening years, the problem of young people who are too well-educated for the low-skilled work they have to do for want of anything better has only worsened. It looks as though the poorer households in particular are losing their recently awakened interest in this costly investment, which certainly in their case promises to reap insufficient benefits.

Persistent poverty

The difference in participation in secondary education is an outstanding feature of the greater gap between rich and poor in the village. We by no means wish to claim that the deprivation of half of the inhabitants of North Subang who lived in poverty in 1990 has since steadily and uniformly deteriorated. In fact, at least for a very sizable segment of them the state of acute insecurity diminished, a hopeful trend that that started in the early 1970s. The initial improvement in the standard of living of the mass of landpoor and landless households was the result of the rise in real wages in the agricultural sector and mainly resulted from the leap forward in agrarian production and productivity. The impact of this change lasted until the 1980s and then there were no further improvements for the price of labour in this sector. The fact that the households hovering around the lower echelons of the *kampung* economy nevertheless managed to alleviate somewhat the situation of persistent poverty was related to the growing availability of work outside agriculture. As circulatory migrants they increasingly alternated their jobs as agricultural labourers with unskilled work in the building industry. The metropolitan zone around Jakarta, which until the outbreak of *krismon* had been expanding rapidly, became an important, albeit intermittent, source of employment. It was unskilled, low-paid work that did not earn them much more than they were used to in the fields, but it did allow them to work for many more days of the year. In other words, they were able to realize the earning potential of their labour power to a higher degree. In addition to the actual increase in income, their occupational multiplicity also added to their credit rating in the eyes of the moneylenders. They could afford more consumer goods, daily necessities as well as durables, in the relative certainty that the debts they incurred could be paid off in instalments. Even though most landless households succeeded in subsisting at a higher level than before, their margins remained small and they were still unable to build up reserves to protect themselves against eventual setbacks, such as an inability to work because of illness or old age. In this social milieu, it was only under optimal circumstances – namely when most or even all the members of the household managed to contribute to the shared income – that the combined revenue from work within and outside agriculture was sufficient for a standard of living slightly above the poverty level. Demographic dynamics alone – the birth of a child, health failure or a household member reaching an age at which he or she was no longer fit to work – could put an end to the optimal life-cycle phase. Upward social mobility was even more uncommon, given the obstacles that prevented these households from tilling the land as self-employed cultivators and in view of their lack of social capital necessary for access to more highly skilled and better paid work outside the agricultural sector. The wide gap in the kampung between the majority belonging to the bottom class and the more prosperous households at the top, who had extended their strategy of accumulation, grew even larger between 1990 and 1998.

Our conclusions contradict the view that, until the outbreak of *krismon*, poverty was increasingly rare, eventually becoming little more than a residual phenomenon, primarily related to backwardness and to be found only in so-called minus regions on Java, of which the Subang district was certainly not one. World Bank reports suggested that this falling trend had reached such a point in the final decade of the twentieth century that, in early 1997, only 11% of the population could still be classified as poor. The empirical evidence presented to support this was extremely weak and, as had already happened before, the national and international bearers of the good news resorted to the large-scale manipulation of quantitative data and refused to take account of the critical results of more qualitative case studies conducted at the grassroots. While wishful thinking lay behind the desire to conceal the continued survival threat at the lower end of both urban and rural economy, the elite enrichment remained underexposed partly through a lack of transparency and partly due to an equally great need on the part of the policy makers to keep the increasing disparity hidden from the public eye. As a result of this incomplete representation of the trends at both ends of the social spectrum, the myth evolved that, despite all the criticism of the authoritarianism of the New Order regime, it had succeeded not only in as good as eradicating poverty but also in establishing a social order based on greater rather than less equality (Manning 1998:278). This view is in sharp contrast with the situation in North Subang, which – until the outbreak of the Asian crisis – could be typified by sustained poverty at the bottom and enrichment at the top. How had this situation changed in North Subang since mid-1997 on our return for a new round of fieldwork a year later?

Consolidation versus regression

The loss of income, either from self-employment or waged labour led to an undeniable fall in the standard of living. This effect was felt across the board by all social classes, but with different degrees of intensity. We found no evidence of dramatic cases of downward mobility among the well-to-do households in the village. Yet a number of informants who, on the basis of our survey findings, were included in the upper class insisted that they now belong to the middle class. Actually, the net incomes of the large landowners appeared to have gone up, while the businesses of the leading traders and shopkeepers also did not seem to have suffered much. We were unable to find out whether their non-agricultural investments have decreased in value. Once again, our informants tended to give vague and elusive responses to our questions. Any losses they may have incurred through the non-repayment of credit, particularly by clients from the landpoor and landless class, are probably compensated by the gains to be made from providing advances to pay for the recruitment costs of the larger number of women who have gone overseas. The *orang kaya*, the rich people, complained about the steep increase in price for the *haj*, which nowadays can be as much as nineteen million rupiah for a couple. The higher cost of living has not of course gone unnoticed in the elite households, but there have been no noticeable cutbacks in daily spending. A large farmer-cum-rice trader spent more than twelve million rupiah on his daughter's wedding. The three-day celebration in the

Marriage party for the daughter of one of the local influentials

spring of 1999, to which many hundreds of guests from the village and further afield were invited, including the *camat*, the official in charge of the sub-district, was marked by the slaughter of a cow, a *jaipong* (a Sundanese song and dance group) and the consumption of large quantities of strong liquor, especially by the younger guests.

The loss of income suffered by a large majority of the landpoor and landless had serious consequences for the well-being of these households. Many of them have great difficulty in meeting their daily needs and their consumption levels are far below those to which they had grown accustomed during the 'good times'. All kinds of goods bought on credit cannot be paid off and the shopkeeper or moneylender often demands them back. In order to get the badly needed cash, emergency sales of radios, bicycles, household goods, clothing and other items of any value are a regular occurrence. This reinforces people's suspicions that misery has once again returned to their lives. To describe this behaviour as disaccumulation would create an exaggerated view of the surplus that has been built up. Costs are cut on everything that is not considered essential for survival. Although younger children still attend primary school – conversations with teachers confirmed what parents have told us in this respect – secondary school and, later, higher pro-

A Sundanese song and dance group performing to celebrate a marriage party in the household of a wealthy inhabitant

fessional training has become virtually inaccessible for children from the lower social classes. Their parents simply cannot afford the recurrent costs involved, which largely consist of illegally imposed donations and collections. This means that the new generation is doomed to earn a living performing the same unskilled and low-paid work as the current generation. The reduced budget also no longer extends to medical expenses. Good health has become a valuable asset because there is no money to combat ailments and disease with patented medicines. Officially, visits to the doctor or paramedical staff at the *puskesmas*, the primary health care centre located at some distance from North Subang, cost little or nothing. But, as everyone knows, services provided by government agencies are never free or cheap, so visits to these educated professionals have fallen sharply.

The issue of land to households which are accustomed to earn their living as self-cultivating producers (as tenants or sharecroppers) but which have insufficient capital to demonstrate their viability as small farmers could offer some solace. As stated earlier, however, the trend is against widening access to land resources and there is nothing to suggest as yet that the economic crisis has changed this. The introduction in the 1960 Agricultural Act of a ceiling on private landholding, which was meant to put an end to the maldistribution of agricultural property, became one of the main factors leading up to the coup d'etat in 1965. In Suharto's Indonesia, land reform has remained a taboo issue from the beginning until the end. It is too early to say whether the fall of the New Order will lead to the agrarian restructuring of the early 1960s being implemented after all these years. The shift in the highly skewed balance of rural power this would require is completely unimaginable so far.

Differential impact

This is not the first time in its short history that North Subang has faced an economic crisis. In the early 1960s sustained drought caused a series of failed harvests. The way in which the people of the village respond to crisis follows a standard pattern, as Pincus has already observed. Apart from cutting down on consumption and 'solutions' described above, there is presently one great difference. One of the first lines of defence which farmers fall back on is to seek non-farm work outside the village (Pincus 1996:176). By its very nature *krismon* excluded that particular option, because the roots of the crisis lay outside the village and outside the agricultural sector.

Yet, in a different way, it could be said that salvation came from outside. With more and more men becoming unemployed, the recruitment of women going abroad as housemaids expanded dramatically. The disdain with which the better-off looked down at this form of employment was soon replaced by a growing interest when it became clear that the fall in value of the rupiah significantly increased the earnings of women overseas on a two-year contract. Working so far away from home helps to conceal, for the men left behind in particular, the full extent of female subjugation to foreign bosses. Talk of the abuse to which daughters and wives are often exposed is avoided. In August 2000, at the time of our last visit to North Subang, the *kepala kampung* was busy preparing for the departure of his own daughter. The girl, barely seventeen years old, has a secondary school certificate and has been promised a contract for a factory job in Taiwan. Her mother's sister is already there and the payment of eighteen million rupiah for all costs, including travel, is no problem. Her aunt's husband, who has recently returned from Taiwan because of an employment problem, will soon be leaving again for Korea. Their four-year-old daughter will be taken care of by the woman's sister, the wife of the kepala kampung, in exchange for a monthly allowance. The man has happily given up his job as a sports teacher at several schools in the sub-district. His salary as a government employee has lost much of its purchasing power and he is confident that his savings from abroad will enable him to make a new start on his return. This young couple represent the aspirations of many of the younger members of the village elite. Perhaps the most striking illustration of the lure of a job overseas is that the *sekdes*, the village secretary – one of the most prominent members of the village administration – resigned to go as a contract labourer to Brunei. His trip was a total failure because shortly after his arrival, his employer's business went bankrupt and, having forfeited his work licence, he had to come back to North Subang without a penny. Still, he is unflinching in his desire to make good money abroad and is now in search of somebody willing to pay for his departure. Even the wife of the village head has signed a contract to go to Japan where she will work as a performer of Sundanese dances in a hotel. A decent job, her husband has been reassured by the recruitment office, but not everybody in the village is willing to believe this. Any reservations the couple may have had themselves seem to have faded away because of the incredibly high wage the woman is going to earn.

Our impression is that the upsurge of interest among young women belonging to well-to-do households in working abroad has been accompanied by a fall in the number of successful candidates from the landless class. This reverse in supply has been influenced by two factors. With the expansion in the number of interested candidates, the admission criteria have been tightened up. We encountered a young woman who wanted to go, but was refused because she did not have a primary school diploma. This formal requirement already existed before but the hurdle of not having a school leaving certificate could easily be waved with the payment of some extra money. Secondly, and more importantly, *krismon* has reduced the credit rating of the propertyless classes at the lower end of the village economy. With no work or income, these households are in a precarious position and moneylenders hesitate to extend them loans that they are less able to repay than before. Several informants told us that the credit amount is linked to the price of gold. With this rising threefold – the initial price of. twenty-five thousand rupiah per gram had gone up to seventy thousand rupiah by mid-1998 – meant that, for a loan of five hundred thousand rupiah a sum of one million and five hundred thousand rupiah had to be repaid within the same period stipulated in advance. This increase effectively priced women from poor households out of an attractive niche in the labour market which might have compensated for the sudden rise in unemployment among the men in their households. For the latter, one of the few escapes left to them is illegal emigration to Malaysia. Once there, they manage to earn about thirty ringgit per day (in August 2000 one ringgit was equal to two thousand three hundred rupiah) as unskilled labourers in agriculture or construction, a wage which was many times higher than they were ever paid in Jabotabek. The problem is the sum they need, six to seven million rupiah, in order to pass the border illegally or with false papers (work permit and passport). They do not have that sort of money themselves and even if they qualified for a loan from a moneylender, the interest rate would be excessively high. In addition to this, there is always the risk of being deported and in that process losing all their savings to corrupt police or other officials. During our final stay in North Subang we met a young man who had paid 5,5 million rupiah to a labour broker who had guaranteed safe passage and employment immediately on arrival. He got stuck, however, in Medan and after having waited for several months in vain, decided to go back home. Four of his work mates had similar stories to tell.

Table 6. Membership of social class and share in wealth of households in 1990 and 2000 (in %)

Social class	Share of households		Share in wealth	
	1990	1998/2000	1990	1998/2000
upper	18	15	55	60
middle	31	25	25	20
lower	51	60	20	15
of which				
poor	36-41	35	15	10
ultra-poor	10-15	25	5	5

Source: Fieldwork data Breman 1990 and Breman and Wiradi 1998-2000.

In conclusion we can say that the economic forces unleashed by *krismon* brought about a dramatic social redistribution in North Subang. These changes, presented in Table 6, include the findings of the fieldwork performed during our repeat visits to the *kampung* between 1998 and 2000. In a certain sense it is easier to gather data on poverty than on prosperity. Notwithstanding the opulent lifestyle of the prominent households, we were unable to obtain a full picture of how they acquired the surplus that allowed them to live in this way. In attempting to do this we have estimated their share in agrarian and non-agrarian sources of wealth.

A first qualification to be made concerning this conclusion is that the situation described cannot be considered the final outcome of *krismon*. The crisis started as an economic recession and then expanded to become a much more widespread form of malaise which continues to make itself felt. This means that the socio-economic dynamics have not yet fully run their course and further research will be required to determine their ongoing impact. Secondly the fall in standards of living is such across the board that it has led to a realignment of the social classes, with a resultant increase in the gap between prosperity and poverty. The new configuration is expressed in a decrease in the relative significance of intermediate households that were accustomed to a certain amount of accumulation, or at least were able to ensure their survival from one generation to the next at a level considered by local standards as *cukup*, sufficient to lead a decent life. Our findings showed that the share of households in which the members live in acute poverty – that is, are unable to meet their minimum subsistence requirements on a regular basis – has increased from around half in 1990 to 60% of the inhabitants of North Subang in 1998-1999. The final part of our study looks at the situation in which this expanded lower class now finds itself.

Mechanisms of exclusion

Poverty and pauperisation

The poor in North Subang do not form an undifferentiated class. Such uniformity is also not to be expected from a mass of people embracing nearly two-thirds of the *kampung* population. A little over one third of the households has insufficient income to guarantee a decent standard of living. Not only because their labour power is not used to its full potential through lack of demand, but also because what little they do earn buys less than it did before the outbreak of *krismon*. The reason for this is the enormous rise in the prices of all daily necessities, particularly rice, which is the main item on the budget of all of these households. Our findings once again underline the significance of the still customary practice of remunerating labour at harvest time at least partly in kind and also to provide one or two meals for other field operations. Yet the need to make all kinds of cash payments, including debt redemption, demands the immediate sale of the harvest share. Consequently, this staple food has often to be bought again later from the shop, at a much higher rate. The difference between the purchasing and selling price of rice has increased dramatically in recent years, the result of the recent withdrawal of the state subsidy aimed at keeping down the cost of living, particularly for urban consumers, to allow the government to maintain its low-wage policy. The subsidies were finally withdrawn only after repeated threats from the IMF and the World Bank that, if they were not, Indonesia would no longer receive the credit on which the New Order depended for its survival. The food riots that broke out in many parts of Java, including the nearby town of Pamanukan, immediately after the sudden increase in the price of daily necessities led to the fall first of the President and then, shortly afterwards, of other leading figures in the authoritarian state system. The collapse led to social turmoil that had not been foreseen by the international financial institutions when they forced the Indonesian government to accept their monetary dictate. This disregard bears witness not only to their lack of political alertness but also to the indifference of these agencies for the life-threatening circumstances into which their policies had plunged the majority of the population.

The combination of lower income and higher prices ensured the increase of poverty in North Subang. Most households are doing their best to cope with this reversal of fortune, but it is no easy task and demands the sacrifice of goods and provisions that contributed to the earlier rise in their standard of living. The search for casual labour is usually futile, but is nonetheless pursued relentlessly. The inability to even approach the previous income level has made drastic cutbacks inevitable. First of all, in the quality of food and then in the quantity also. Little remained for expenses other than food when the crisis was at its worst. Since then, the retail price for rice has fallen again, in August 2000 to two thousand one hundred rupiah per kilo. Although at least one thousand rupiah lower compared to one year before, it remains minimally twice as high as before the start of krismon. Sheer survival is still characteristic for day-to-day existence. There is no scope for financial considerations that might lead to structural improvements in the longer term. Expenses aimed at preserving or restoring health are postponed as long as possible. Children can no longer go to secondary school after completing their primary education. This is a conscious choice to abandon aspirations for better life prospects for the next generation. Children at primary school are already aware of the severity of the situation. They no longer receive the pocket money with which they used to buy sweets or snacks from the stall that used to stand outside the school during the break. The vendor running this micro-business has gone bankrupt because her little customers have not paid off their debts. Consumer durables are either sold off or, if payments of the monthly instalments have not been kept up, claimed back by the original seller or the moneylender. Lastly, there is a sharp fall in spending referred to as social costs. This is intended to distinguish them from economic costs and to imply that they can be reduced without causing too many problems. However, festivities on the occasion of weddings or circumcision ceremonies (or attending them, which is by no means always free of expense) are investments which allow households to maintain their ties with family members and neighbours, and to consolidate their social standing in the locality. Even a low-cost wedding can add up to two to three million rupiah, which often means taking out a loan. If households are forced by economic circumstances to cut such expenses dramatically, or even to refrain them entirely, the result is a disaccumulation in a social network that will, in the last instance, result in growing exclusion.

This is the situation in which the ultra-poor find themselves in. Although this category existed already in 1990, it was much smaller than it is now (Breman 1995:42-3). Then it used to consist of propertyless households which, through a shortage of labour power, did not have the means to provide for their minimal daily subsistence requirements. These were single women with young children, old people who were no longer productive and the long-term sick or disabled. These people still fall into the group of ultra-

The vulnerability of the old aged increases if they have no children to support them

poor, but they are now joined by those members of the working population who have the ability to work but who do not succeed in finding gainful employment on a regular basis. They are often unemployed and appear to have joined the ranks of the rapidly growing pool of reserve and destitute labour. When asked what he did all day, one of our informants said: 'Eat and sleep'. He then corrected himself: 'I eat a little and sleep a lot.' These people seem to have lost the resilience they need to fight their way back to a working existence, and no longer go actively in search of odd jobs which, even though they may be few and far between, at least keep them busy. Any consumer durables they may have had are already gone. Their economic and social existence is characterized by vacuity. They are distinguished from the greater mass of the poor by a more intense misery marked by malnutrition and bad health. The support they receive from family and neighbours, which is occasional and marginal rather than permanent and significant, cannot fundamentally alter their state of exclusion. After all, those who do try and alleviate their misery belong almost without exception themselves to the poorer segments of the population and cannot afford to give much to those who have even less.

Do the better-off households not feel a moral duty to help the growing numbers of poor in the village? It was in the belief of the surviving tradition of harmony and incorporation uniting all members in the small-scale localities that the national and urban-based policy-makers placed their hopes when they insisted that the large mass of circulatory migrants return to their rural homes after the outbreak of *krismon*. They based their wishful thinking on the myth of a village community in which surpluses and shortages were evened out through a system of distributive exchange. But the lack of social cohesion in North Subang had already been pointed out by Hayami and Kikuchi when they referred in their study to the extremely unequal distribution of land ownership in the village. The situation encountered by these Japanese economists at the end of the 1970s contradicted the patron-client relationship which they wanted to see as the organizing principle in the social relations of production in the Asian peasant order. Breman expressed criticism of this assumption at an earlier date, on the basis of his fieldwork in 1990, and described the polarity in the *kampung* as a more typical than exceptional reflection of the social order in many rural areas on Java. Although Pincus took a slightly more nuanced view of the rural class structure around the same time – stating that local conditions were of decisive importance in the variety of bargaining position – he also strongly emphasized the inaccuracy of interpreting the socio-economic configuration in the *kampung* in terms of a closed economic circuit completely dominated by agriculture.

The changes that have occurred since then fit in with the same pattern of limited mutual concern and involvement between rich and poor in North Subang. The hunt in preceding years by an increasingly large proportion of the working population for work outside the agricultural sector has contributed to further loosening of the ties between employers and employees in the village. Many only have brief and contractual encounters with each other, such as during the rice harvest, and even that has become much less common since employment outside the village took on a more structural character. Symptomatic of the lack of moral cohesion that accompanies a sense of community is that members of the under-class in the village have little or no access to facilities that should be available to everyone, such as health care. When we returned to North Subang at the start of 1999, the *kepala kampung* was not at home. Suffering from typhoid, he had been rushed to hospital in Pamanukan. He and his family told us how quickly his situation had deteriorated but that, thanks to the first-class medical help he had received, he would soon be on the road to recovery. And, sure enough, several days later he was back at home with a course of medicine and orders to take it easy for some time. While he was recuperating, we came across another case of typhoid in the *kampung*. The man was a small sharecropper who occasionally found work in Jabotabek. He had just returned from the hospital, where he had spent the night. They had sent him off because the money he had taken with him was just enough for a day's treatment (eighty-one thousand rupiah) and because he had no proof to show that he was entitled to free medicine. He had been told that he could get the required forms from the *puskesmas* if he had a letter from the village office confirming that his state of poverty gave him access to medicine without cost. The man was clearly in a bad condition and his wife was at her wits' end. Firstly because of her husband's state of health, secondly because it would cost time, money and effort to obtain the entitlement to free medicine, and thirdly because the harvest was about to start and he would not be able to work. She had no idea to whom to turn for help to solve this problem. The well-to-do among our informants showed little interest in the fate of their fellow villagers who had lost their income from outside employment. There was nothing they could do about it, was their comment, and why should they feel a responsibility to help alleviate the suffering of these low-quality people? That was the government's job. The *orang kaya* consider their comfortable lifestyle as a mark of distinction by which the distance separating them from the less well-off in the community is underlined. Writing about elite perceptions of the poor, Antlöv commented:

> the rights they talk about – to live in privacy; to spend money as they want – have certain limits and are only for the rich and the powerful. Ordinary people, the *massa bodoh*, are seen by the new rich as having different rights: to support the present path of development, to be loyal citizens and to accept the new ways of living. (Antlöv 1999:198.)

This recent description of the changing attitude of the nouveau riche in a West Javanese village seems to have achieved general applicability under the New Order.

A social safety net?

Collective social security arrangements to cover setbacks such as illness or unemployment have made their appearance with any degree of efficiency only in the upper echelons of the formal sector economy. The myth remains intact that people living in the rural hinterland are protected from such risks by traditional, communal and kin-based social support mechanisms. The only evidence for such an expression self-practiced charity in the *kampung* was when the mosque distributed seven kilograms of rice to mark the occasion of Idul Fitri, the festive closure of the Ramadan. This one-off donation, collected shortly beforehand from households which are prepared to donate two kilos per person, is part of the *zakat*, the religious duty to support those in need.

The assumed solidarity within the village community as a fall-back mechanism in times of adversity has also been used as an excuse not to introduce social insurance provisions for the large masses of circular migrants who work as casual wage earners or self-employed workers in the informal sector of the urban economy. And although those in regular employ at the lower end of the formal sector are obliged to pay contributions for private company or state-run sickness and unemployment benefits schemes, actual payment of entitlements are more the exception than the rule. The small number of men and women from North Subang who had semi-permanent jobs in Jabotabek, and therefore some form of social insurance, returned to the village without receiving even a single allowance after being dismissed at the outbreak of *krismon*. This also applies to women who return home early from jobs abroad, for example because of illness. The contract they sign before they leave contains a compulsory insurance with PT Jamsostek, a semi-public corporation. The price of the policy is charged to the women as part of the costs of sending them off. We only heard of one case in which a factory worker received six months' salary as redundancy pay. He did not know whether this was a token of his employer's gratitude or a benefit for which he had paid contributions. One thing is certain, a large part of the funds collected disappeared into the pockets of the PT Jamsostek board and their political patrons. Particularly in the lower strata of the formal sector, there was little awareness that employees could derive any rights from the dues they were forced to pay. The employees themselves thought the contributions had to be paid to be eligible for continuation of the employment contract. The initial response of the government to the outbreak of the economic crisis was limited to the occasional distribution of food here and there, particularly in the cities. Faced with a shortage of funds, the government 'encouraged' (with the intimidating support of the local military) large companies to provide packages of basic necessities free of charge or at greatly reduced prices. This did not occur systematically, but erratically without announcing the time or place for public distribution When the crisis persisted and national and international policymakers began to realize its true extent, preparations were made from the summer of 1998 on to launch a social safety net programme known as Jaring Pengaman Sosial (JPS). The implementation of this programme, driven by fear of a recurrence of food riots, started in the autumn of the same year and was intended to restore lost confidence in the government and the apparatus of the state. A striking component in the measures introduced was replacement of the customary top-down model with an approach that allowed more scope for popular participation. This reversal of the style of public administration at the local level was intended to help increase transparency in the expenditure of the funds provided and guarantee efficacy and efficiency in achieving set targets. Minor differences in shaping the design of the Regional Empowerment Programme to Overcome Economic Crisis (Program Pemberdayaan Daerah dalam Mengatasi Dampak Krisis Ekonomi, or, for short, PDM-DKE) were more the result of local circumstances and of coincidence than due to any deliberate strategy. The IMF in particular provided the necessary funds, while Bappenas, the Central Planning Bureau, was responsible for overall coordination. The decision to place day-to-day implementation in the hands of the authorities in the sub-districts reflected the desire to delegate the facilities close as possible to the rural population. Acting President Habibie used dramatic language (terms like mission, vision, action) to outline the aims of his new development model with its strong local focus (Program Pengembangan Kecamatan or Sub-district Development Programme). The total package included the restoration of public confidence, the alleviation of acute distress and the encouragement of initiatives aimed at increasing small-scale production.

Impact of state-provided social care

The fieldwork that we carried out in North Subang in March and April 1999 had a twofold purpose: first of all, to determine how the working population of the village responded to the further impact of *krismon* after the initial phase. Secondly, we wanted to ascertain what form the social safety net, introduced by the government with such a flurry of pomp and publicity, had taken at the local level and what effects it had had. The first question has been covered in the foregoing pages. The remainder of this argument will examine the results of the support policy pursued by the authorities. That means that we have to include the state of affairs in and around the government apparatus in the sub-district of Binong, under which North Subang falls, in our study. This office was instructed to keep the records for PDM-DKE activities in the eighteen villages in the sub-district. Almost all of this information was readily made available to us (one cupboard stayed shut because the official concerned was on leave for an unspecified time), and we used it to provide a statistical underpinning for the impressions we got during our investigations in North Subang.

One of the staff members at the sub-district office had been released from his other duties to oversee the village-level activities. In addition to this field coordinator, there was a new figure, the *fasilitator kecematan*, supposed to represent non-governmental organizations. This man, selected by the *camat* because he had studied social work, only showed up at the office to collect his salary. He gave the impression of representing no one but himself. We never managed to arrange a meeting with him and his official counterpart told us that he had no idea what we should discuss with him. They were both members of the Executive Team for Village Activity (Tim Pelaksana Kegiatan Desa, TKPD), which also comprised a field agent from the department of the

Office of the sub-district agency in charge of crisis relief

National Family Coordinating Planning Board (BKKBN) that maintained contacts with the sub-district office and a local-level *fasilitator*. The latter was chairman of the youth club and head of the social affairs section at the village administration office. The nominal leader of this team was the chairman of the LKMD. The members of this reconstituted council, the Village Community Resilience Board, all happened to belong to the local elite.

The monthly accounts kept in the village and sub-district offices for the implementation of the social safety net scheme provide the following picture of what we call the dynamics of poverty statistics (Table 7).

In the newspeak jargon typical of the New Order, the degree of poverty was described in terms of the extent to which the households lacked prosperity, *sejahtera*. The first two categories, Pra-KS and KS-1, represent that proportion of the population that falls under the official poverty line. The first category comprises those who, in these Orwellian terms, have not yet made progress on the road to prosperity. These are classified in our own analysis as the ultra-poor. It is interesting to note that, until the start of the JPS programme, the percentage of inhabitants of the sub-district and the village of our fieldwork that lived in a state of abject poverty, was at the same low level as that calculated for the country as a whole by the Badan Pusat Statistik (Central Statistics Agency), that is somewhere around 10%. North Subang village was

Table 7. The dynamics of poverty statistics in a village and sub-district of Subang

North Subang									
Date		Total number of households	Distribution of households according to 'prosperity' level						
			Pra-KS	KS-1	KS-2	KS3	KS-3+	Pra-KS & KS-1	
Month	Year							abs	%
March	1998	647	44	177	287	129	10	221	34
April	1998	647	44	177	287	129	10	221	34
July	1998	647	44	177	287	129	10	221	34
Aug	1998	647	44	177	287	129	10	221	34
Sep	1998	647	131	178	200	133	5	309	48
Oct	1998	647	370	177	65	33	2	547	84.5
Nov	1998	647	370	177	65	33	2	547	84.5
Dec	1998	647	370	177	65	33	2	547	84.5
Jan	1998	647	370	177	65	33	2	547	84.5
Feb	1998	647	370	177	65	33	2	547	84.5

Binong sub-district									
Date		Total number of households	Distribution of households according to 'prosperity' level						
			Pra-KS	KS-1	KS-2	KS3	KS-3+	Pra-KS & KS-1	
Month	Year							abs	%
March	1998	16771	2236	3892	6482	3879	282	6128	36.5
April	1998	16771	2236	3892	6482	3879	282	6128	36.5
July	1998	16771	2234	3894	6482	3879	282	6128	36.5
Aug	1998	16771	2236 (!)	3894	6482	3879	282	6128	36.5
Sep	1998	16771	4270	4272	5726	2221	282	8542	51
Oct	1998	16862 (!)	6471	4154	4320	1744	172	10625	63
Nov	1998	16771	6339	4206	n.a.	n.a.	n.a.	10625	63
Dec	1998	16771	6471	4154	n.a.	n.a.	n.a.	10625	63
Jan	1998	16771	6471	4154	4123	1841	184	10625	63
Feb	1998	16771	6472	4153	4173	1789	184	10625	63

Source: Fieldwork data Breman and Wiradi, March-April 1999.

just under this average, with 7% Pra-KS, while 13% of the population of Binong sub-district fell into this category. It should be clear that, in the light of the findings of our fieldwork in mid-1998, that these figures give a distorted view of reality. The sudden increase in the size of the lower class from August 1998 on to 57% in North Subang village and 38% in the sub-district could be taken as an indication that the earlier underestimation of the level of deprivation had now been rectified. This conclusion cannot be taken seriously, since it would assume that the new official statistics were valid. In fact, the 'updated' figures are just as unreliable as those they replaced. This new distortion of what was going on in real life simply served different motives. Where the central government had earlier been concerned with providing quantitative evidence for a rapid decrease in poverty, the desire for large-scale international assistance after the outbreak of *krismon* now made it imperative for the government to produce statistics showing that the large majority of the population were fighting to survive. This sudden jump in the poverty figures in the autumn of 1998 was therefore not a coincidence but was closely linked to the urgent need for statistical evidence to prove that two-thirds to four-fifths of the people were under threat of pauperization.

Determining the scale and identity of the target group in North Subang was the task of the field coordinator at the sub-district office, the man who worked for the regional department of the National Family Planning Coordinating Board (BKKBN). For this purpose, he called in the help of 'volunteers' whose job it was to acquire a clear picture of the extent of poverty and prosperity in the various hamlets into which the village was divided. To help them in this endeavour, a manual had been prepared, explaining how to classify the people they interviewed according to a number of criteria relating to their material condition. The volunteers were not fully paid for this work, but received pocket money of two hundred rupiah for each interview. It later became clear that they also made the interviewed households pay one hundred rupiah each, promising them that they would then become eligible for financial support from the government. Their efforts produced the information required, a sudden increase in poverty statistics, which helped in exercising pressure on the IMF and the World Bank to grant funding for the JPS programme. When the emergency aid programme was ready for implementation, however, these statistics had become irrelevant. We were told that the exercise was conducted by order of higher authorities and, as laid down in instructions received from them, reports had to be submitted to them. But the government officials in the village and the sub-district all claimed that the information gathered by the volunteers was unsuitable for their purposes. They preferred to trust the figures provided by the *kampung* heads. Verification of these lists, however, also called this method of registration into doubt. In the same month, the hamlet officials submitted different figures for the number of people falling into the Pra-KS category, depending on the nature of the support on offer. In the *kampung* in which we conducted our fieldwork, the total fluctuated between seventy-four and ninety-six households (30% and 37% respectively), for reasons which remained unclear even after we asked for an explanation.

Provisions for support and recovery

The PDM-DKE programme comprised a combination of social support and economic recovery. These objectives were subdivided into four components: food security, employment, promoting small-scale business and, lastly, crisis aid for health care and education. We shall examine each of these components in turn.

Food security

The first round of public rice distribution was at the end of August 1998. A consignment of 6.5 tons reached North Subang at this time and around the same amount was received during a further nine deliveries in the months that followed. With the one hundred kilogram bags divided into rations of twenty kilograms each, nearly all of the households falling into the Pra-KS

Still in the style of the New Order regime slogans were raised inviting the local inhabitants to overcome the crisis

category could have received a share. This rarely happened, however, for a wide variety of reasons. First, the quality of the first consignment was so bad – rumour had it that it had been supplied free of charge by Japan and had already gone bad by the time it arrived – that many people refused to accept the ration to which they were entitled. The village head told us that the poor preferred to buy the cheap broken rice from the hulling mills, which was actually intended for use as chicken feed. Since he had to pay for the consignment anyway, at a rate of one thousand rupiah per kilogram, he sold it to a chicken farm outside the village. But later deliveries, the quality of which gave no cause for complaint, did not reach those for whom they were intended. Our *kepala kampung* told us that the areas closest to the village centre were the first to benefit and that those further afield, like the one he lived in, only got what was left. Another time, the rice arrived while the harvest was under way. The poor people, who were also involved in the harvest operation, did not need the extra supplies at that time and preferred to use whatever earnings they made for more urgent expenses. The cash needed to buy the emergency rice supplies, although it was half that of the price in the shops, was far and above the main reason why people did not get the rations to which they were entitled. They simply did not have the money, even to pay the reduced rate. All of these factors explain why, according to the estimates of the people we spoke to in the *kampung*, that not much more than a third of the emergency rice actually reached the households that needed it most. The demand for the cheap rice was, however, so great that the village administration decided to reduce the monthly ration, firstly from twenty to ten kilograms and then to five kilograms. But, even at this low level, many Pra-KS had to forego their ration due to lack of cash to pay for it. This meant that other, better-off households could benefit in their place. They did not, however, benefit as much as it would appear on paper. The rice was sold not per kilogram but per litre (= 0.7 kilogram), but at the same price, allowing the local officials in charge of distribution to earn a little extra on the side.

The Special Market Operation (Operasi Pasar Khusus, OPK) was the most extensive but not the only food distribution programme in North Subang. The Jarum cigarette company also provided rice for alleviating the misery of the poor: one hundred bags in February 1999 and another hundred the following month. Kodamil, the military organization in the Subang district, had arranged for monthly rice deliveries to thirteen needy households in the village. Lastly, it is worth mentioning that the district administration made a one-off delivery of cheap rice to households in the KS-1 category, under its own anti-poverty programme. These households may be better off than the Pra-KS, but had also slipped under the poverty line and certainly qualified for support to mitigate the impact of the crisis. But for this increasingly large proportion of the village population, too, a more forceful and sustained effort would be required to achieve a more lasting effect. We conclude from all this that the food security promised under the JPS programme was not properly targeted and did not benefit many of those who were most vulnerable.

Public works

The intention of this part of the programme was to provide gainful employment for men – women were excluded in advance – from low-income classes who had been made redundant. Not only does paid labour ensure that people do not remain idle and help to increase purchasing power, but public work schemes can also provide a stimulus for economic growth. In North Subang a number of these *proyek* were contracted out and completed, including the construction and repair of sewage and water pipes. However, the records which we consulted show that material costs accounted for the lion's share of the budget for these projects, while labour costs were just a small fraction of the total. The only activity that falls under this heading in the kampung of our fieldwork was the surfacing of the roads. The small roads joining the different hamlets have been surfaced with gravel, for which the contractor was paid two thousand rupiah per square metre. Labour costs were non-existent because the work was performed on the basis of mutual assistance (*gotong royong*). The men called upon to do the work therefore were made to work for nothing.

Promoting small-scale business

Only households which possessed some capital in the form of means of production and could increase the return on it with the aid of cheap credit were eligible for this part of the programme. They received an interest-free loan, paid out in instalments. The Executive Team for Village Activity (TKPD) decided what activities qualified for funding from the limited budget. On the basis of their occupation, the selected producers formed groups (*kelompok*) and chose a leader from their number, who was responsible for distributing the credit and collecting the repayments. The members of the group are expected to work together but why, how and for what purpose is unclear. They live in different parts of the village and share only their common interest in the same economic activity. The initial discussions led to the setting up of four groups: the first for small livestock holders, the second for farmers, and the other two for *warung* owners and street vendors. The first group never got off the ground. The idea was to use the credit to buy ducks but the sharp rise in the price of feed torpedoed that plan. The next proposal was to buy cows but the loan was too small for that. The second group was also a failure because farmers could get credit from another programme at the same soft terms. To prevent overlapping, it was decided that this initiative should be scrapped. The two groups for *warung* holders and street vendors did become active, but the number of people who benefited was limited because of the small budget. We spoke to a few people in the kampung who had received a tiny loan but many others were either unaware of the programme or told us eligibility for credit depended on being close to a member of the village administration. They accepted their exclusion as a matter of fact, since this was how things always had been arranged.

Extra support for health care and education

According to the figures supplied to us, one hundred and forty-six people in the whole village received an authorization entitling them to free medical assistance at the *puskesmas*, the primary health care clinic located at some distance from North Subang. A closer look revealed that the list consisted almost entirely of old people. one hundred and thirty-three of them were older than fifty, and most of this group were over sixty. And rightly so, because the dire situation in which the men and women in this no longer productive age group find themselves is largely the result of their failing state of health. Having said that, it should be added that by no means all old people were aware of this free facility and would have been pleased to make use of it had they known how to obtain the authorization. We recall a conversation with a couple in this predicament. The wife told us that her husband had a terrible pain in his arm, but was afraid to go to the *puskesmas* because they had no money and the *mantri*, the clerk in charge, might ask him to pay for the treatment. As we have pointed out before, Pra-KS in younger age groups may also suffer from diseases or ailments which require medical treatment that they cannot afford. There appears to be no solution for these cases, most of them acute, where treatment is necessary but is usually not sought through an inability to pay.

Lastly there is the funding provided to prevent children from leaving school prematurely. Instead of being used for study grants and other allowances, such as for clothing or transport, this budget of one hundred and one million rupiah was earmarked to finance urgent repairs to the primary school in the *kampung*. But at the last moment, there was also insufficient support for this plan. It was therefore decided to use the money to renovate the religious school in the centre of the village. This is indeed what happened, although the decision was not motivated by educational considerations but eagerness to favour the contractor who got the job. We would like to add that, of the total sum spent on the project according to the village administration, labour costs accounted for only 10%.

When we left in the spring of 1999, it was by no means certain that the JPS programme would be continued. The results were anything but encouraging when compared with the original objectives of the programme (see Sumodiningrat 1999). But this did not appear to be the main concern. An evaluation report drafted in March 1999 on the activities undertaken within the framework of the PDM-DKE programme for Binong sub-district in 1998-1999 was mildly critical. The main complaints made concerned the organizational complexity in implementing the programme and the delays and unexplained 'deductions' in the funding. Nothing was said of the disappointing outcome for the target group itself. We estimate that around a third of the total budget destined for North Subang was absorbed by the apparatus implementing the programme, while an equally large proportion leaked away to other categories than those that were entitled to the support. What remained was too limited to alleviate the dire situation of the target group, which we calculated had grown to include a half to two-thirds of the population of the village. The provisional character of the support confirmed the impression that the beneficiaries were being granted a favour, from which they could derive no rights. The poverty alleviation provided by the JPS programme was a form of inefficient and ineffective charity that was unable to turn the tide of social and economic exclusion. The way in which this policy was implemented confirmed more than denied the lack of interest among policy makers at all levels in the plight of the landpoor and landless masses at the broadened bottom of rural society. In North Subang, in the short time that it was used, the term Pra-KS took on a denigrating significance. On our return in August 2000 the social safety net facilities earlier provided by the local government had dried up. Public work projects were not any longer executed, stipends for attending school had been dispensed with, because of paucity of funds no further business loans could be extended for small-scale production. The few occupational groups that had been constituted, were disbanded and, as everybody had known beforehand, none among the selected beneficiaries had repaid even a single instalment of the credit amount received. Cheap rice was still being distributed, although only occasionally and in rations of not more than five kilograms per household. No official in the village or at the sub-district was able to tell us whether in the near future the JPS, in the same or a new shape, would be continued or not.

Reformasi in the village

Social security does not exist for those who need it most. *Krismon* has increased the severity of the disparities between rich and poor in the village. The history of this *kampung* is primarily one of a process of inclusion and exclusion, in which the first wave of settlers took possession of the cultivable and, while the migrants who came later remained landpoor or landless. North Subang has never been a 'traditional' community, with a homogeneous peasantry working together on the basis of communal reciprocity. The villagers therefore did not respond to the crisis that threatened their survival in the early 1960s with collective action based on feelings of joint solidarity. The most vulnerable households had little other choice than to leave the village, and their departure only contributed to the concentration of land ownership in the hands of a small elite. It was not a sudden crisis caused by failed harvests that in later years led mainly those from landpoor and landless households to seek work outside the village and outside the primary economic sector, but more long-term hardship caused by increasing pressure on the agricultural means of production as a result of demographic growth and technological change. The rapidly rising demand from the mid-1970s on for cheap, low or unskilled labour in the metropolitan zone around Jakarta provided the opportunity for this exodus. Those who left the village did not depart for good, but went for casual employment. Circular migration was a logical response to push and pull on both sides, the lack of sufficient economic and social security in the village as well as the absence of opportunities to establish a more permanent foothold in the city. After almost a quarter of a century, *krismon* closed this escape route, at least temporarily, and put a stop to the increased socio-economic security it provided. The labour nomads were forced en masse to return to their villages. During our successive visits to North Subang, the first in the spring of 1998 and the last in the summer of 2000, we tried to find out about collective strategies aimed at increasing the resilience of the vulnerable classes at the bottom of the village economy. We found, however, no evidence of such strategies, either in a vertical or in a horizontal direction, that is, between or within the different classes. So was Antlöv mistaken when he recently suggested that, in spite of the tendency among the rural elite to distinguish itself from the common people through ostentatious consumption patterns, an ideology of redistribution had been preserved? In his view, elaborated upon in his follow-up study to his earlier West Javanese village monograph, this was expressed in the moral duty of the rich to offer the poor political protection and economic security. We tend more to agree with Hart in her observation that such demonstrations of patronage as compensation for social inequality are notably absent in Java. The rapid increase in labour migration is according to us a central factor in this phenomenon. In villages like North Subang – and there are very many of them – the interdependence between employers and employees in a localized system of economic production dominated by agriculture is increasingly a thing of the past. Consequently, it is very rare for the better-off households to make all kinds of transfers to their less fortunate neighbours. And the opportunities for the returning circular migrants from the city to find work in the agricultural sector are equally rare. The landowners keep access from below to the agrarian capital which they control firmly closed.

Can the increase in harvest theft since the outbreak of *krismon* be understood as signalling an attitude of resistance among the landless class against exclusion? Farmers complain that not all the rice cut in the fields is delivered at their house and refer to such instances of pilferage to explain why they are keen to sell the crop to contractors while it is still standing in the fields. The overseers engaged by these *penebas* keep a close check over the fixed harvesting gangs recruited by them. In order to reduce theft at work, the authorities of the sub-district in which North Subang is located have prohibited the sale of *bawon*, harvest shares, along the roadside. The growth in petty crime in general is indicative of the waning power of government which in the Orde Baru era did not tolerate any disturbance to the public peace. The behaviour of village officials has become less authoritarian and they make muted complaints about an increase in disrespect and disobedience towards them. Among the young male adolescents in the village many have taken to drinking hard liquor and arrange parties for each other to show the porno videos which are on hire in Pamanukan town. Along the highway they stop vehicles to collect money and valuables from drivers as well as passengers. Thefts are also reported from houses and compounds in the village. In reaction to such individual or gang raids but also as a result of the more general sphere of insecurity, the village inhabitants feel threatened and do not shy back from resorting to physical violence once they feel provoked. A bus driver who collided with a motorbike on the nearby provincial road was beaten up so badly that he did not survive the accident. Such minor or major cases of aggression demonstrate that the state has lost legitimacy. Some of our informants vented their unease by wondering aloud if the ancient times of *perang desa*, the village at war, would come back.

Economists and anthropologists who have investigated the situation in North Subang in the final quarter of the twentieth century are in agreement about socio-economic polarization being a striking feature of this village on the coastal plain of West Java. Hayami and Kikuchi argued in their study that a patron-client between the landowning elite and the majority of the land-poor and landless was in the best interest of both these segments at the polar ends of the rural hierarchy. Although suggesting that such a configuration was typical of rural Java in general, they were forced to conclude that the situation in North Subang did not fit this harmonious model of communal exchange working to the mutual benefit of all. In summing up the lesson which the Japanese economists drew from their findings they stated that 'there is a threshold of inequality in wealth and power distribution beyond which polarization will begin' (Hayami and Kikuchi 1981:220). Twenty years later the threshold which, according to both authors at least, helped to defuse the disparities between rich and poor in the locality of our common research is nowhere in sight. Given the trend towards the further acceleration of inequality, the burning question is what policy can best be followed to end, or at least alleviate, the severe vulnerability to which the under-class in particular became exposed once *krismon* made its impact felt in the rural hinterland. The Asian crisis, expressed in the combination of unemployment and the rising price of daily necessities, has convincingly illustrated the urgent need for public intervention to keep the free and harsh interplay of market forces in check. The provisions made available under the JPS programme have proved totally inadequate to alleviate the misery. It would be incorrect to attribute the disappointing results solely to the improvident schemes and their poor funding. The underlying notion in the design of the security policy is the enduring myth of a village community in which the composite segments, if not involved in reciprocal exchange with each other, are at least united in collective action to confront the crisis. The realization, after the fall of Suharto, that his autocratic style of government was counterproductive in achieving the stated national objectives – such as democracy, equity and the rule of law – led to a reappraisal in the previous policy of intolerance towards non-governmental organizations. Their agents were expressly invited to participate, a turnaround that was intended to demonstrate that the command model had been replaced by a bottom-up approach. People were urged to insist on their participation in the decision-making process and, in addition to that, constant and fair representation in the execution of development projects. Yet, neither the interests nor the voice of the poor masses carried much weight in the efforts to deal with the effects of the economic crisis of which they were the primary victims. The exclusion of this vast majority of the population must be seen against the background of the policy of demobilization and depoliticization of the 'floating masses' pursued under the New Order. After the coup of 1965, every hint of subaltern protest was seen as a form of subversive activity. The banning and physical destruction of organizations that defended the interests of the landpoor and landless classes put an end to any countervailing power against the alliance between the local elite and those wielding power at supra-local level. Displays of assertiveness and feelings of resentment against exclusion, only recently seen as expressions of disloyalty to the authorities incited by forces skulking in the darkness, are now again seen as a form of spontaneity and welcomed as reflecting the common desire for *reformasi*. Militancy is permissible, as long as it is not antagonistic and stays within the limits designated by the government. Concepts like community and collectivity are at the forefront. The emergency programme for economic reconstruction is full of terms like cooperative village development, community self-reliance and village resilience. The government seems to want the village to be reconstructed along the lines envisaged by Boeke, a late-colonial policy-maker who pleaded for the revitalization of the 'traditional' village community (Boeke 1952). It is an idée fixe that is far removed from social reality and its dynamics. The *fasilitator* is seen as a kind of magical figure who can mobilize the members of the target group like a herd of sheep without losing his grip on them. It is his task to activate his 'clientele', by organizing public meetings, spreading the information about what the government has in mind for them, to invite all and sundry to become enthusiastic recipients of state benevolence, and to encourage this mass, previously coerced into silence, to participate with fervour in whatever is going on. The meetings of course never take place, or only on paper. The same applies to the *kelompok masyarakat (pokmas)*, the groups formed as an expression of the cooperative spirit to pursue the common goal: the restoration of economic growth. It is a façade that conceals a different reality; a local regime that is structured along corporative instead of co-operative lines. In that framework, the power is still in the hands of a small elitist clique, just as it has been in past decades. Pincus had the following to say about this local elite of North Subang:

> selection of village heads is screened by district officials, and previously elected village administrations have been replaced by 'village community security bodies' (LKMD) appointed by the village heads. The centralization of local power in the hands of village, sub-district and district heads, in tandem with the suppression of autonomous political activity, has deprived the rural labouring classes of protection from illegal levies and other abuses of power on the part of village and supra-village elites. The absence of social control on the behaviour of village elites has naturally widened the scope for various forms of political accumulation. (Pincus 1996:7.)

His observations, describing the situation at the beginning of the 1990s, are as acute nowadays as they were in the dark years of the New Order. Corruption, collusion and nepotism, known by the abbreviation KKN, are the order of the day at the centre of the Indonesian state – but not only there. They also colour the distribution of favours and prerogatives at the local level. This has to do with what Antlöv called 'the disciplinary powers of registration' (Antlöv 1999:193). If the villagers ever did present a homogeneous front against external, higher authorities it is now certainly a thing of the past. The local elite is not only an instrument for preserving law and order at the lower end of society, it also uses its elevated rank to turn the impositions, monetary and otherwise, on the most vulnerable groups at the bottom to its own advantage. Our final conclusion is that the urgently felt need for basic social security among the great mass of the population will not be met unless there is a far more dramatic shift in the balance of political power than has occurred until now. And this shift cannot be based on a preconceived belief in some natural sense of shared destiny between classes in very unequal positions, a belief that is heralded as the organizing principle for social action. The turnaround from exclusion to inclusion, what we understand as *reformasi*, is not a moment but a process. The evolution of this process, in good times and bad, requires continued monitoring, in North Subang and elsewhere.

SECTION 2

East Cirebon

CHAPTER IV

Diversification of the rural economy

Introductory note

The fieldwork location which is designated East Cirebon in this study is a village situated in the district of Cirebon bordering on Central Java. This region became the focus of a historical study in which Breman investigated the character of the agrarian economy in the late colonial period and the effects of a colonial land reform at the beginning of the twentieth century (Breman 1983). This earlier research was based on archive material preserved in Jakarta and The Hague, but also discussed the consequences of the pressure exerted on agrarian resources in the early stage of the post-colonial era. Major factors affecting this situation were both the consistent population growth and the compulsory cession of land to the sugar mills, the oldest of which dated from the beginning of the nineteenth century. The concluding part of the study, dealing with the post-colonial sequence of agro-industrial production in the coastal plain, drew attention to the phenomenon of labour circulation which was triggered off by the increasingly adverse man:land ratio in the densely populated district. Summing up the argument, Breman commented that:

> Only sporadic and fragmented information is available on even the most important aspects – e.g. the duration of the absence, the distance travelled, the mechanisms of departure and employment elsewhere (whether organized or not, individual or collective), the sort of employment and the working conditions, the necessity and/or possibility to return eventually to the home village. It has been established that labour has become mobile to a degree and in a fashion which indicates drastic changes in the social organization of the structure of agrarian production. (Breman 1983:126.)

Several years later the opportunity to explore this theme in greater detail presented itself in the framework of a research programme which focused on the extent and dynamics of non-farm employment in the Javanese countryside (White 1986). A village was selected for more intensive fieldwork in the eastern part of Cirebon district about which several reports had already been published in previous years by the Survey Agro Ekonomi. This was a research agency sponsored by the Indonesian Ministry of Agriculture and affiliated to the Agricultural University of Bogor. One of these reports, authored by G. Wiradi, examined the way in which the agro-industry in the area made use of the farmland for the cultivation of sugarcane (Wiradi 1991). During his fieldwork conducted in 1989 Breman was assisted by Agrar Sudrajat. The first part of Section 2 relates to his findings in that year which have not been published before.

Village in an urbanized landscape

The village which we have called East Cirebon lies on the coastal plan of West Java, twenty-eight kilometres southeast of the capital of the district of Cirebon and close to the border with Central Java. The history of this area is inextricably intertwined with the cultivation and processing of sugarcane. On the way to East Cirebon the visitor passes two sugar mills, those of Sindanglaut and Karangsuwung, which have occupied a large area of the land of the farmers in the surrounding area. In this region sugarcane, not rice, is the dominant crop. The extremely high population density is another factor which is immediately conspicuous. The sub-district of Karangsembung of which East Cirebon is a part had a total population of sixty-two thousand and six hundred spread over twenty-two villages in 1989, which is the equivalent to a density of one thousand forty-one per square kilometre. At that moment East Cirebon had a population of twenty-three hundred and eleven and with an area of slightly more than one square kilometre, the density there rose as high as two thousand seventy-five. Despite the enormously high pressure placed on the local means of subsistence, there had been no diminution in the demographic growth as a consequence of the government-promoted transmigration to areas which had been set up for new colonists outside Java. Continued population growth at an unbridled high rate nevertheless seemed less likely because of the stringent government demographic policy. Presented as voluntary but in reality virtually compulsory participation in birth control – 89% of married couples of a fertile age were registered in the administration of the sub-district as *akseptor* (receiver) of the propagated techniques – had to ensure that the number of children born in a marriage dropped in the near future. The three hundred and thirty-six houses in the nucleus of the village offered shelter to four hundred and ninety-five households, an average of seven people per house and approximately 4.7 members per household. These figures are thrown into sharper relief by observing that nearly one-third of the households lived with somebody else and had neither a house nor a piece of land to call their own.

Only a small area of the village territory – seventeen of the total of one hundred and eleven hectares – was taken up by houses, public works and other facilities (roads, irrigation canals, the *balai desa* (village office), mosque, school, and cemetery), which reinforced the compact character of the settlement even more. East Cirebon did not correspond to the classic image of the average Javanese *desa*: a village surrounded by cultivated fields and a group of farm houses separated from each other by larger or smaller yards. Even at the time of this first period of research, our research location more closely resembled an urban *kampung*, characterized by dwellings which were built close together without any real space between them planted with typically home garden crops. To the extent there was any vacant land at all, its use was already planned out: the building of a house for children of marriageable age or for the children of the owners of the houses round about who were already married. The land which was being used for agricultural purposes also did not encircle the village in an unbroken belt of green. The cultivated area of nearly ninety-four hectares was divided up into five large blocks spread in various directions, some of them close to, other further away from East Cirebon. This parcelling out of land was inexorably linked to the rotating claim laid on the cultivated land of the peasant population by the agro-industry. The urban aspect of the residential nucleus was strengthened by the building materials which had been used. Of the three hundred and thirty-six dwellings, two hundred and thirty-five were built entirely of bricks, seventy-four were half brick, and only twenty-seven fell into the category of houses made of bamboo (*bilik*) and with a thatched roof. The houses merged imperceptibly with those of a neighbouring village, East Cirebon Wetan. As the name already hints, both of them were originally parts of the same village community. The splitting up into two separate administrative units was carried out in 1984 and was the result of a government ordinance which had been around since early colonial state formation for conveniently arranged, small-scale locations as the lowest administrative unit.

East Cirebon consisted of two halves located on the left and right sides of the road which led on to the next village. Each of the two *dusun* was divided up into two parts (*rukun wilayah*), which in their turn were split up even further into two neighbourhoods (*rukun tetangga*). Since 1979 a little more than a quarter of the houses (eighty-eight of the three hundred and thirty-six) had been connected with the electricity grid. However, by means of self-improvised tapping into the house next-door, a service for which something had to be paid to the neighbour but much less than the official tariff, the majority of the households had electricity, whether legally or illegally. The sixteen neighbourhoods and the four living areas were linked to each other by small, unpaved paths. The main street, which had a length of one kilometres, was the only asphalted thoroughfare. This improvement was made in 1974 and was paid for by those people in the village who were somewhat well-to-do.

This made road was also the link to the main town of the sub-district of Karangsembung which was three kilometres away. The way there was an almost unbroken ribbon of residential area which also contributed to the urban character of the densely populated landscape.

How did the people earn their living in 1989? A prior distinction has to be made between local and non-local forms of employment and earning an income. The first category included agriculture, rural industry, and a mixture of trade, transport, services, and trades. The second covered the money earned by labour migration to Jabotabek, an acronym for the metropolis of Jakarta and the urban-industrial nuclei of Bogor, Tangerang, and Bekasi clustered around it. In my discussion of the pattern of economic activity observable during the first round of fieldwork reported in this study, I shall also look into the shift which had become visible in the relative significance of these sources of income.

Marginalization of peasant agriculture

The agricultural land in East Cirebon covered an area of 93.5 hectares and consisted almost exclusively of *sawah*, irrigated fields. This meant an agrarian density of almost twenty-five inhabitants per hectare The skewed distribution of the agrarian capital was one of the most conspicuous characteristics. This began with the fact that the peasant owners had access to only seventy of this area. The other 30% – a good twenty-eight hectares – was laid claim to by the members of the village administration. The money earned from these plots represented the salaries of the village head and his staff, the payment for their work as local officials. This was particularly true of the *bengkok*, the 'salary fields', which covered a good twenty hectares The head of the village himself had the right to 7.5 hectares of these, 2.5 more than the permitted legal maximum; the remainder was assigned to his closest associates according to a fixed scheme of distribution. Apart from this *bengkok*, there were another seven hectares set aside as *titisara*. Although on paper the yield from these fields was destined for the financing of all sorts of expenditure from the village funds, in practice the proceeds from the produce of these fields also found their way into the pockets of the village office staff. It was the same story in other villages in the Cirebon district, with the benefits accruing to the *pamong desa* (White and Wiradi 1981:24) and it represented a continuation of the abuse of power and the lining of one's own pockets through a system sanctioned by the higher authorities which had begun in early colonial times (Breman 1983).

The land which then remained over in the hands of the farmers, called *kasikepan*, amounted to almost sixty-five hectares The rights to this land were held by the *sikep*, those inhabitants of the village who according to tradition were descendants from the founders of the village. In the colonial period they formed a farmers' collective under whose aegis the annual distribution of the communal land took place. Only those who belonged to this privileged agrarian category were eligible for the allocation of a *patok*, share. One *patok* was the equivalent to three hundred *bata* or 0.42 hectare. In earlier generations the size of this allotment must have been bigger. When the circle of those who had right to an apportionment grew as a result of the population growth, it was only possible to keep the then existing system of allocation running by the periodical revision of the allotments, reducing them in size. In neighbouring villages the allotments could be as large as four hundred or even five hundred *bata*, which I take to be an indication of a steeply increased pressure on the agrarian resources of East Cirebon. But, even the allocation of smaller portions could not prevent a large proportion of the inhabitants being excluded from a share in the communal land. The maldistribution was exacerbated by the colonial administration which introduced an experiment in land reform in eastern Cirebon at the beginning of the twentieth century, under which small landowners were deprived of their land rights. In the area in which East Cirebon is located more than one-fifth of all farmers – five thousand out of a total of twenty-four thousand – lost their land as the result of this measure. The well-prepared and executed operation has been the subject of a historical study in which the background, planning and execution of this early reorganization of the farming community is discussed in detail (Breman 1983). The most important motivation was to rid agriculture of an impoverished substratum of small landholders who, in the official mind, had too few means of production at their disposal to produce a surplus or even to grow enough for them to keep body and soul alive. Instead of acquiescing in this structural deficiency, the colonial policy-makers opted for a radical solution to the agrarian problem in Cirebon which was already an overpopulated province. The land which was released came into the possession of the large- to middle-scale farmers, who were given the opportunity to show their potential as modern agrarian entrepreneurs with the additional capital which then came their way. According to this school of thought, the lower layers of the society would also be better off. Once deprived of their minuscule piece of land, which was too small to cultivate properly, they would form a rural proletariat for whom there was plenty of work outside their peasant mode of agriculture: as seasonal workers in the agro-industry in the sugarcane fields and sugar mills, and as stevedores in the harbour of Cirebon. There was also employment to be found as casual labourers in all sorts of activities, not further specified, in town and countryside.

The colonial land reform which was carried out around 1920, roughly three generations ago, most certainly contributed to the high degree of landlessness in East Cirebon. With the exception of one hundred and fifty-seven households (32%) that lived on someone else's land, another hundred and eighty-nine (38%) owned no more than a house and the yard around it. This meant that a total of three hundred and forty-six of the four hundred and ninety-five households (70%) had no land in an agrarian sense, and even for Java that was an exceptionally high proportion of the village population.

The 1960 Agrarian Law did away with the communal system of land-ownership which had survived up to then. Even in East Cirebon, the *sikep* then received their share in perpetuity and as their own property, as *milik*. The new regulation allowed the land to be sold and this has been freely made use of since. The one hundred and forty-nine *patok* which were entered in the village register in 1989 were in the hands of only eighty-four *sikep*. This indicates that a number of owners had managed to gain possession of more than one allotment. The declining importance of the pursuit of agriculture, now in the wake of the free market effect of supply and demand, is underlined by the latest round of this long drawn out trend towards concentration of landownership. Now numbering no more than seventy households – a small 14% of the total – landed proprietors among the farmers are a very small minority in the village population. Quite apart from this far from all the areas of land are in the hands of the inhabitants of East Cirebon. To some extent compensating the sale of a portion of the arable land to outsiders, is the purchase of land from neighbouring villages by farmers from East Cirebon. The upshot of this two-way change of ownership has been a marked fragmentation of the fields which makes their cultivation a very unwieldy process. Only a handful of the owner-farmers have more than half a hectare of land (Ernaini 1991:6).

Possession of a deed to the land did not mean that the holders were free to use their land as they wanted. Each year the sugar mills in the area sequestered a large proportion of the arable land, an arrangement which had begun quite early in the nineteenth century. Until the abolition of the Cultivation System in 1871, this periodic transfer was a legal obligation. After then, up to the end of the colonial period, the increasingly powerful agro-industry organized the temporary dispossession of a considerable and continuously changing section of the property of the farmers through the village administrations. This practice did not change after Independence. Just as it always had been, official pressure continued to be the foundation for the cultivation of this crop in Java (Breman 1983:124). A 1960 Land Ordinance, which was followed by a Presidential Instruction enforced under the Orde Baru in 1975, dealt with the leasing of land to the sugar industry. This latest directive ordered the farmers to surrender their land – to a maximum of half the arable land of the village – and contained stipulations about the time at which this had to be made available, the amount of the rent to be paid and so forth.

In 1989, the Karangsuwung and Sindanglaut sugar mills had managed to secure almost two-thirds – namely eighty-five hectares– of the arable land of East Cirebon, considerably more than the maximum allowed by law. Nearly half of this consisted of the salary lands allocated to the members of the village administration. Following a long-standing local tradition, the village head and his subordinates did not cultivate the land to which they had a right. In order to emerge as winners in the election campaign for the local administrative posts, these officials, above all the village head, had had to go into debt. This was not just to buy votes from the electors, but also to pay the sum expected at the sub-district office which was claimed by the members of the higher-ranking bureaucrats as a compulsory contribution. The prospective village head could only get around to paying back the loan he had taken out by leasing out the salary fields which were allotted not only to him but also to the subordinates he had selected to fulfil the other functions.

The farmers who actually owned their land had just as little freedom in making any decisions about how the land was to be used. The mill issued a directive indicating which fields belonging to the farmers were designated to be joined together in blocks for the planting of sugarcane for the coming season and, if farmers proved recalcitrant, the help of the village administration was called in. In 1989 this was still taking place according to the so-called *tris (tebu rakyat intensifikasi)* which had been introduced into East Cirebon in 1980 (see Wiradi 1991). This form of management claimed that the cultivation of sugarcane was being carried out on a co-operative basis. This fiction pretended that the mill allotted the fields it had leased to the original owners who combined into groups (*kelompok*) were entrusted with the planting and other activities until the beginning of the harvest season, an operation for which the mill recruited the labour needed. Each farmers' group was supposed to cultivate ten to twenty hectares and consisted of forty to fifty members, each of whom had not contributed much more than 0.3 hectare Depending on the size of their input, they received an advance which was made up of the production costs and a supplement for their living costs during the growing season. As has just been said, this was no more than a fiction because in the *kelompok* in East Cirebon to which the farmers were attached in 1989, there was not one single one of which the members were actually themselves engaged in the cultivation of sugarcane. In a few cases they left the running of the operation to an appointed group leader (*ketua kelompok*) who acted as contractor in dealings with the mill. He claimed the sum which has been paid in the form of an advance on the production costs, supervised the work in the fields of the workers whom he had hired, and he was the one with whom the factory settled up at the end of the harvest season. A fairly frequent occurrence was that, well before the beginning of the new planting season, sometimes as long as one or two years earlier, the farmers leased their land to rural magnates/big businessmen (*cukong*). These figures operated as large-scale entrepreneurs who took over the usufruct of the land from the owner for an agreed period. The scale on which they were able to operate made the cultivation of sugarcane a lucrative affair for these agrarian capitalists. Among the *cukong* who did business in the area of East Cirebon and its environs were those who had leased more than a hundred hectares for this purpose. Of the acreage of the village which was planted with sugarcane, more than 40% was in the hands of the *cukong*. The management of the sugar mills in the region, the *pamong desa* and the rural magnates had interests which ran parallel with each other and formed a close alliance, which set further limitations on the limited room to manoeuvre still available to the farmers who worked for themselves. There is not a shadow of doubt that, had it been a matter of free choice, the crop pattern of East Cirebon would have looked very different.

On that land which was not taken up with sugarcane, the owners grew rice in two successive crops and after these, secondary crops (*polowijo*) like lentils, peanuts, Bombay onions and *kedeleh* (soy beans). This secondary cultivation after the rice could only succeed if there was sufficient water available. The management of the mills made sure than when it came to using the irrigation capacity of the area, the sugar fields were given top priority.

To the same small extent that owners of the land worked the sugar fields themselves, there were those among them who left the cultivation of the remaining fields with rice and other crops to tenants. There were two forms of tenancy. *Maparo* was an arrangement under which the yield was divided equally but the input required (especially the seed, artificial fertilizers, and pesticides) was paid for by the owner. Under the *mertelo* agreement the tenant took two-thirds of the yield but also assumed all the costs related to the cultivation. In all these cases the owners of the land preferred to seek work outside the agricultural sector, either in the village itself or elsewhere.

What has just been described shows that peasant agriculture counted for very little in the economy of East Cirebon. The small amount of land owned, the way in which the plots were scattered, the continual claim laid on what land there was by the agro-industry all meant that farming had lost its attraction, even for those households in the village which were owners of agrarian capital. The low returns made on investments in this sector explain why the number of peasant enterprises has shrunk drastically in the course of the years. Their lack of prominence was very conspicuous in the village in 1989. Yards in front of houses with tethered animals or agricultural implements were the exception which confirmed this. There was not a single tractor or any other mechanized agricultural implement in East Cirebon.

Work in the agricultural sector was of course not confined to those who owned land. Alongside them there was a category which earned their living from working on the land. It might have seemed very obvious that they would have turned to working in the sugarcane cultivation, the labour-intensive crop which dominated the landscape of East Cirebon, to find employment. But this was hardly ever the case. Only a few of the women from farm labourers' households said that they sometimes did make themselves available for the planting of the cane or for any other jobs like weeding which cropped up in the course of its growth cycle. As far as their husbands were concerned, any participation in the heavy preparatory work which had to be undertaken before the planting could take place was far more exceptional and when it came to the harvest, they were completely out of the picture. The neglect of the opportunities offered for work in the cane fields by these labourers, even though there were so many of them ready at hand, was related to their own decisions as well as to supply and demand. The labourers themselves cited the low pay offered and the frequently long distances to the cane fields as the main reasons for their lack of interest. The daily wage was no more than one thousand five hundred rupiah for a working day which lasted from six o'clock in the morning until three in the afternoon. It is true that this is the same sum which the farmers paid, but for a much shorter work day, with the additional extra of some form of food, at least one meal. The tariff for women was even lower, 750 rupiah, only half of what the men received. Another reason was that work in the cane fields had the reputation of being extremely arduous, which was part of the reason it was held in such low esteem. Almost any other form of physical labour was considered to be more worthwhile than undertaking coolie work for the agro-industry. We think that the fact that farmers and landless peasants both went out of their way to avoid sugarcane cultivation is partly due to the bad odour which had clung to the agro-industry as early as the colonial.

It also has to be said that on the side of demand, there was limited interest in employing the local landless people and this had to do with the organization of the businesses. Both the *cukong* and the *ketua kelompok*, who were the pivotal figures in the cultivation of sugarcane, used the services of a *mandur*, who kept an eye on what was going on in the fields – working the soil, planting, irrigating, weeding – for their boss and it was up to them to recruit the people who were needed for these operations. By preference they sought these people in the most easterly of the villages, virtually as far as the border with Central Java, where wages were generally at a lower level than were those in East Cirebon. Even taking the extra transport costs into account, it was cheaper to employ these short-distance migrants than to look for volunteers among the landless peasants closer to home. The agro-industry never let the actual harvesting work out of its own hands. Agents from the mill – they were also *mandur* – led campaigns to recruit the labour they needed, also searching far and wide for what they needed. The army of cane-cutters – large numbers of men and of women – were signed on by contractors at the behest of the mills, by offering advances paid beforehand, for the duration of the cutting season. They were divided up into teams over the whole area which was ready to be harvested. Trucks fetched the teams from the villages early in the morning and took them home again in the evening. Migratory workers who lived too far away, in Brebes or Kuningan, did not travel on a daily basis but were allotted temporary accommodation close to the mill. Along the road leading to East Cirebon there were sheds where, during the 1989 season, approximately one hundred and fifty male and female cane-cutters were put up. The preference shown by the agro-industry for this external labour force was related to two factors, the method of payment – payment by piecework and not by the length of the day worked – and the fact that the migrants were easier to control. Why did this army of migrant labourers, like the many land-poor and landless peasants in East Cirebon, not seek work outside the agricultural sector in and around Jakarta which would have paid them much more? The main explanation is the lack of a bridgehead into the urban economy. As later became clear, the emigration out of East Cirebon had begun quite some time ago. The next generation was able to use the contacts established by earlier migrants and could profit from the experience in work outside the agricultural sector which had been gained by brothers, fathers, and even grandfathers.

The farmers in East Cirebon did use agricultural workers from the village for the cultivation of rice and other food crops, as has been said, to the degree in which they were able to do this. Landowners had to hand over their fields to the sugar mills for a period of two years and therefore only had control of their own property every three years. In earlier times this proportion in use was the precise opposite, but because of pressure exerted at a higher level, stemming from the growing domestic demand for the product, the sugar mills had stepped up their production capacity and with this their need for more land for expansion of planting increased strongly.

In the course of the year in which the farmers could till their own soil, they made regular calls upon the labour of the local landless peasants, especially for all stages of the cultivation of rice: preparation of the ground, sowing the seed, transplanting, weeding (now not as essential as it once was because of the heavy increase in the use of insecticides and pesticides), and finally harvesting. There were two three-monthly rice plantings a year: from the onset of the rainy season in December-January until the harvest in March-April and the following cycle began directly after this as the season became drier up to the harvest in June. Generally speaking a working day consisted of five hours, from seven in the morning to noon. For this men were paid one thousand five hundred rupiah and women seven hundred and fifty, and both were entitled to one meal. The standard answer the men gave to the question of why there was such a great difference in the respective wages between the sexes was that women's work required less physical input, leaving their bodies less exhausted than did the tasks which the men were expected to perform. With the exception of the meal which was served as part payment, the day wages were not paid in kind. A daily wage of one thousand five hundred rupiah was sufficient to purchase a quantity of rice which was estimated to be sufficient for an average household (four to five people).

However, the most usual way of setting people to work was not on a daily basis, but under an arrangement which is known in the literature as the closed field system, *ceblokan*. The terms of this agreement were that a couple, consisting of a man and his wife, assumed the responsibility to undertake various operations at the beginning of the growing cycle – above all the transplanting of the rice – in exchange for a portion of the harvest in kind, which would be equivalent to one-fifth of the yield. The key figure in the agreement undertaken by the owner was the *tukang pacul* who prepared the ground for sowing. It was up to him whom he chose as partner to help him, usually his own wife. The transplanting was her work and they tackled the harvest together. On occasions a woman could help with the harvest without a male partner – whom she either did not have or who was living outside the village as a labour migrant – and in such a case she had to content herself with the half of the share in the harvest, one-tenth of the yield. The choice the farmer made about who was to work on his land was regarded as the granting of a favour which mostly fell to the lot of his own family relatives, neighbours, and other good acquaintances. A landless household tried its best to make as many *ceblokan* agreements as possible so that its members could see themselves safely through the months after the harvest with what they had collected. The work of an agricultural labourer was a series of marked ups and downs, a short period of maximum effort, preceded and followed by much longer periods in which the farmers had little or no use for their presence in their fields. As time went by, conditions for the landless peasants deteriorated. A fair time earlier, the landowners had once paid the women separately for the transplanting, but later this was regarded as being inclusive in the payment of the share in the crop. This was tempered by the fact that the fight for harvest contracts was no longer as fierce as it had once been according to informants. It might then happen that agricultural labourers were already at work in the fields at three or four in the morning to ensure that they brought in the highest possible return. There can be no shadow of doubt that this change had been induced by the expansion of the labour market outside agriculture and far beyond the villages themselves. Just as the position of farmer had changed significantly in meaning over the years, the job of agricultural labourer had changed as well. According to our database for 1989, based on a random sample of one hundred and six households and verified in interviews with members of the village administration and other local notables, work in agriculture was then confined to no more than one-quarter of all households in East Cirebon. Moreover, this percentage did not remain constant throughout the whole year, but fluctuated according to the peaks and slacks of work available on the net area of arable land available. The slack was much more marked and prolonged than was the short peak above the average. The progressive trend towards the marginalization in agriculture has been affected by both push and pull factors. The latter is what will form the theme of the next chapter. One telling indication of the former was the extremely high agricultural density which characterized East Cirebon in 1989. This figure – the number of inhabitants in comparison to the area of arable land – amounted to almost twenty-five people per hectare a good three times higher than that which was the figure for the Cirebon district as a whole. It was against this background that the at that moment already intense interest in seeking work and an income outside agriculture and, to a very large extent indeed, outside the village, that our research findings should be understood.

Labour migration to Jabotabek

The redundancy of labour in the agricultural sector and the exodus from the village has been a long-term process and it was strongly affected by the colonial land reform implemented in the 1920s. One old man narrated how he regularly went to what was then Batavia as a navvy as early as 1938. He covered most of the distance by public transport. He began by walking from the village to Karangtengah, which took him a couple of hours. From there he took the tram to Krawang, where he arrived around nine o'clock at night and from there he went straight on, arriving in Batavia the following morning. His wages consisted of four picis, that was forty cents per day. His story made it clear that his was no exceptional case. He estimated that at that time one out of the ten men left the village, compared to one in three men at the time when I interviewed him, that was in 1989. The marked increase indicates the enormous demand for this type of seasonal worker, especially during the last thirty years. Once the New Order was firmly installed, the process of urbanization in the zone around Jakarta went ahead like wildfire. This area, known as Jabotabek, consists of a semi-circle which is steadily increasing in size around the capital in a southerly, easterly and westerly direction. This growth vortex is characterized by an unceasing wave of frenetic construction activity which is part and parcel of urban expansion on a large scale, the building of factories and smaller workplaces, warehouses and offices, residential areas and road-construction. East Cirebon is one of the many catchment reservoirs in the hinterland of Java which answered the virtually insatiable demand for building workers for all these infra-structural projects. The out-migration, which has been shown had been going on for some time, moved more and more in the direction of Jakarta. Some of the workers who left the village in an earlier phase probably did not venture as far and also sought work in the rural sector, not necessarily in agriculture, in search of temporary employment. In rounding off a historical study about the agrarian question in the late colonial period and the after-effects which this has had since that time, on the grounds of information obtained during a short fieldwork visit to the area of eastern Cirebon, I ventured to conclude that both the intra-rural and rural-urban labour migration, caused by the high density on agrarian resources, were important topics for further investigations. This observation became the point of departure for two new empirical case studies which I conducted in the coastal plain of West Java in 1989 and 1990. While my report on East Cirebon dating back to local fieldwork in 1989 has remained unpublished until now, I did manage to write up the outcome of my research a year later in a second village, situated in Subang district (Breman 1995).

In the case of East Cirebon it is clear that the acceleration in the migration of landless and virtually landless peasants for most of the year to Jabotabek was the logical consequence of a longer standing migratory tradition. One factor which has contributed greatly to the increase in volume is the modernization of the transport system, which has meant that it is now much easier to cover the distance than it ever was before. The travelling time from East Cirebon to the capital Jakarta, which still took a day and a night at the end of the thirties, has been cut down to no more than six hours now, half a century later. Deservedly, in the study of migration in Java, attention is paid to what has been called the *revolusi colt* (Hugo 1985:62; 1990:231), the transportation of people in mini-buses which penetrate even to the most isolated villages to bring their passengers to the bigger transport interchanges from where they can continue their journey by long-distance bus or by train.

The work for which by far the majority of migrants from East Cirebon came was in the building industry. The bosses were big contractors who handed over the execution of the orders they received – preparing land for building, the construction of buildings, shopping and residential complexes, the construction of roads, bridges, laying on sewerage, mains water, electricity, telephone connections and other infra-structural provisions – to a long chain of contractors, sub-contractors, and their agents. The higher echelons of this complex business hierarchy remained well out of sight of the ordinary workers. They only came into contact with the lower ranks of sub-contractors, gang bosses and foremen who recruited the numbers and sorts of workers needed for the project and were present on the work floor to supervise the daily running of things. The hired workers were employed on a temporary basis and for short duration, no longer than the project lasted. This could be a matter of several days, weeks, or months. Any agreements that were valid for longer than the current season were very rare indeed. The demarcation between the seasons was not so much the change from the dry and the wet monsoons but the annual cycle of feast days which punctuated ordinary life, especially *lebaran*.

In most cases the actual employer was the gang boss who hired the workers and then dismissed them after a longer or shorter period. He maintained relations which the contractor who did bother to note down the details of his agent in his business administration, but went no further than noting the number of workers the former contracted without adding any further particulars. The labourers dealt wholly and solely with the gang boss. He gave orders about the daily tasks, inspected the work in progress, organized the conditions under which the work was carried out and took care of the payment of the wages. In his turn, the gang boss was held responsible for the achievements of his temporary employees.

The division of labour in the building industry depended on the nature and scale of the project which was being worked on. By far the majority of the labourers were divided up into teams which were led either by the gang boss himself or, in really large ventures, a foreman whom he had appointed. Any further differentiation between the members of the team depended on the nature of the work to be undertaken. In the case of craftsmen – including carpenters, masons, plasterers, tilers, fitters and turners, and steel benders – the differences in training were far more apparent than when the work was limited to earth-moving. But even then it was usual to make a distinction between more experienced workers, who needed very little direction in the carrying out of their daily tasks, and newcomers who were able to wield a shovel at the very least, but were still ignorant of the demands which teamwork required.

A first glance at the building sites or workplaces showed that this was very obviously a man's world, from which women were almost completely absent. The gang was not simply a work unit, it was also a living unit as well which offered its members a certain degree of shelter and protection so far away from home. As the evidence showed, in that respect the gang bosses also played an important role. Not all the labour migrants from East Cirebon made up gangs put together by jobbers. Some of them operated on an individual basis. They preferred to find their own way in the urban agglomeration, shunning the help of agents, and they sought work through a network of contacts which had been built up over the years either by themselves or by close family members. The more highly skilled the occupation the labour migrant from the village commanded, the greater the chance that the individual work contract he entered into outside the village would bear a more individual character. All categories of migrants as they left East Cirebon were determined to return to their homes at some later stage, every fortnight or so or at the most every couple of months. The migration bore a circulatory character and it very seldom ended up with permanent settlement in an urban environment. Having given a more general introduction to the labour migration outside the village, the time has come to turn to a more detailed discussion of a number of facets.

Recruitment

Recruitment for work in Jabotabek sometimes began in East Cirebon itself, undertaken by one of the gang bosses who lived there or in one of the neighbouring villages. In other cases one of the migrants had permission from the jobber or had even been expressly asked to bring a new member for the gang with him from his next trip home. Many of the men ventured forth for the first time under the guidance of their father, brother, or uncle who literally showed them the way. Another recruitment place was Jakarta itself, to which many migrants made their way trusting that upon their arrival they would find work in the city. It was their custom to choose a *warung* in Tebet, run by a fellow villager from East Cirebon, as their contact point. They would leave their few belongings and any tools they might have with them while they made the rounds of the building sites and the addresses they knew in their attempts to get themselves hired. Also when they had no luck the first day or when they were out of work during the lay-off time between the one job and the beginning of the next, they could come to the *warung* owner for shelter, food, and even some pocket money. Their faces were known and as good customers they could have credit. Likewise, sub-contractors and gang bosses from the surrounding area came to these sorts of lodging places knowing that they would find workmen there whom they needed to set to work immediately. The migrants led the life of nomads without a fixed abode or permanent place of work. Their current project determined where they stayed and when that was finished they left in search of further work or, laid off, they made their way back to East Cirebon. Their contact with the urban milieu was superficial and was characterized by a high degree of transience. This was another good reason why it was important to maintain good contacts with the gang boss. His deep knowledge of this alien area transformed him into the prop and stay for the members of his team. The *mandur* recognized no obligation to extend the oral contracts but during the course of the project sacked all the members of his team who were superfluous, whose work was not up to scratch, or as the result of any conflict. Nobody had any right to decent treatment or even to demand conditions for pay or work which could be applied as standards. However, a jobber-cum-supervisor who treated his men badly in this respect would find difficulty in keeping his gang together or in recruiting new members for the next project. It was certainly in the *mandur*'s own interest to surround himself with a fixed nucleus of trusted workers on whom he could rely as a work force in his search for new contracts, people he had learned to know over the years as skilled, loyal team members. It was through them he could adjust the size of his gang, either cutting it back or expanding as the moment required. Some gang bosses who were prepared to pay a bit more for this loyalty or to grant incidental favours had more success at this than did others. There were migrants from East Cirebon who had followed their leader for years, not just to different locations in Jabotabek, but also in his peregrinations through the archipelago. These journeys had taken them criss-cross through Sumatra, Timur, Kalimantan, Riau, and Sulawesi, without them really being aware of the geographical location of these destinations or even being able to remember with any accuracy in which precise sequence or when exactly they had visited them. Just as little as the migrants from East Cirebon necessarily attached themselves to a jobber from their own village, did the latter feel obliged to give preference to inhabitants of East Cirebon when they were composing their gang. When they were recruiting the first thing they looked for was the proven quality and trustworthiness of those who put themselves forward, in which his satisfactory experiences with employees who had worked for him before was the deciding factor. When it came to hiring new people he allowed himself to be guided by the opinions of others, colleagues or subordinates, on whose judgement he made his choice. The migrants from East Cirebon whom we went to visit at various places in Jabotabek were members of gangs which consisted in part of fellow villagers but which could also included labourers from other parts of Java, recruited at the work site. According to information acquired in 1989 from five *mandur* who were domiciled in East Cirebon, at that moment they headed work gangs which consisted of three hundred people in total. Fewer than half of them came from the village in which we were doing fieldwork or from its direct environs.

Circulation

The journey to Jakarta took about six hours. So to make sure of not missing a workday, the departure usually took place in the late evening or at the beginning of the night. Where the access road into East Cirebon met the main road from Karangsembung to Ciledug, three kilometres outside the village, was the Karangsuwung sugar mill. This was the place from where the bus which made this trip daily departed, but it was certainly not the only possibility. Day and night buses following a route from other places around eastern Cirebon to the capital stopped there too, so that the opportunities to make the journey direct or to change buses at the bus station just outside Cirebon were legion. The fare differed according to the destination, just before or past Jakarta, and fluctuated between three thousand to four thousand rupiah, which was the equivalent to a day's wages. The sum also included some refreshments. The way in which the migrants made the trip differed greatly. Some of them travelled together, in the company of other members of the same household or of friends. This did not necessarily mean that the travelling companions were all headed for the same work site and the same boss. Others preferred to undertake the journey alone and also returned unaccompanied. It was very seldom indeed that a whole gang made both journeys together. The coming and going did not follow any regular rhythm but was much more a matter of chance circumstances. The migrant himself decided how long his visit to the village would last and the breathing space varied from a few days to not more than a week. Only exceptional circumstances – prolonged rains, the change over to a new boss, health problems, or special occasions, both festive and sad, in the household – seemed to justify a prolongation in the break in the commuting circuit. How long did the migrants stay away? The average length of absence was about six weeks, but variations at each end – shortening or extending the trip – were high. It was only to a certain degree that migrants had any control over the decision. The work went on as usual during their absence and the jobber was very keen to ensure that not too many members of his gang went on leave simultaneously. The women at home had no idea when they would see their husbands again and often did not know where they were staying. Communication between them was very scanty to say the least. No news was good news was the attitude displayed by both sides. When the opportunity arose friends or kinsmen who had just arrived from the village or were returning there brought messages, but this was not a common occurrence. Illness was a reason for a premature return, and so was the end, whether premature or not, of the current project. The way of life of a migrant worker was a skill which had to be mastered and not every newcomer to the job managed to adjust to the absence of interaction with those members of the household who stayed behind or to the inconveniences of the footloose life. It was seldom indeed that migrants who were employed in the construction industry were successful in qualifying for a permanent job in the urban economy. The majority of them did not have the requisite skills: a fair degree of schooling, payment at a fairly high and constant level, and, last but not least, a network of contacts in order to achieve greater security to the environment to which they had come.

Construction labourer recuperating for a few days with his family in the village

Conditions of employment

Work began early in the morning and continued on into the afternoon with an hour's break in the middle of the day. The length of the working day fluctuated between eight and ten hours, but there could also be peaks when there was strong pressure to finish a project. Everything that had to do with earth-moving – transporting and dumping of soil on the building site being prepared, the digging of trenches for the laying of mains for electricity and water and sewerage pipes, the levelling of the terrain before the foundations could

Construction workers discussing terms of employment in Jabotabek

be dug, the constructing of roads and the asphalting them – were all carried out as teamwork by pretty unskilled labourers who had very little time to do anything other than what they had come for: work. Most migrants had no days off during their time in Jabotabek. From the moment they arrived until they left again they worked seven days a week. Only the most skilled craftsmen – an electrician, a welder, or a plumber – enjoyed a work rhythm which resembled that of workers whose roots were in the city: the standard was an eight-hour day and Sundays off. The few migrants who managed to break away from the continuous journeying back and forth and to settle for good in the city came from this more highly skilled and better paid category.

Wages varied with the nature of the work performed and experience. The least was earned by the youngest, navvies who were just beginning: three thousand five hundred rupiah per day. Older men who had worked for a longer time were usually paid four thousand rupiah. Among the more highly skilled jobs which required a greater degree of training – carpenters and masons were the most numerous – there was a distinction between apprentices and properly trained workers. The former worked as assistants, *kenek*, for the latter with a daily wage of between three thousand five hundred and four thousand rupiah, whereas skilled workers could count on five thousand or at most six thousand rupiah per day. A few technical specialists such as an electrician were not paid by the day but by the week and earned twenty-four thousand rupiah for a six-day working week of eight hours, with a supplement of two thousand five hundred for every day worked. These sorts of exceptional payments were not regulated by the gang boss but took the form of a transaction between the worker concerned and the contractor. The other migrants also received a daily allowance of two thousand to two thousand five hundred rupiah, and apprentices no more than one thousand five hundred rupiah, but in all these cases this money was deducted from the daily wage. This was the first portion in the periodical wage calculation and had to be paid for living costs, which consisted principally of food, drinks and cigarettes. Sometimes a *mandur* made an agreement with the owner of a nearby *warung* to provide the members of his team daily with food and drink. He made a commission on this arrangement and he fobbed off his workers with a much lower sum under the guise of daily pocket money.

As has already been mentioned, the team boss managed the financial administration. He received the earnings of his team and settled up with each of them individually. The amount the gang boss retained for himself was a well kept secret. Asked about this straight from the shoulder, he had the tendency to claim that he did not receive any more than any other member of his team. In reality the *mandur* made considerably more. The workers estimated that he pocketed at least double the total amount which he paid them. It is difficult to say precisely how much this was. The agreement he reached with the works foreman or sub-contractor was not based on an hourly rate but on piecework: per truckload of sand delivered, amount of soil moved per cubic metre, bricklaying per linear metre, a price for each dozen door or window frames delivered, street laying per square metre and so forth. In agreement with the gang which he brought with him he usually transformed this piecework into a daily wage or, when he had to deal with more skilled workers, he also employed a job wage but once again for a sum which was much lower than that which he earned himself. The transposition of a piecework tariff into a time-rate brought with it the risk that the gang boss was acting as a work contractor. His profit rose to the degree that he was successful in encouraging his gang to raise its daily levels of work. If this remained below a reasonable level he suffered a loss, sometimes to the extent that he actually went bankrupt and this finished his career as a *mandur*. According to our information, he retained between 40 and 50% of the budget set aside for the work. The jobber-cum-supervisor only guaranteed payment for the actual carrying out of the work and accepted no responsibility for his gang during the period preparatory to or just after the completion of a project. There was no reason to tie the workers to him by paying them an advance. It was not difficulty for the *mandur* to enlarge their gangs, according to the requirements of the moment, or then to reduce them in size again. In the rural hinterland of Java there was a virtually inexhaustible reservoir of workers available and by intensive circuits of the villages, mobilization of this reserve took no more than a few days. This explains why the gang bosses refused to pay the travelling costs of the migrants out of their own pockets, or indeed even to give an advance on them. They pretended that they did not have enough funds to advance such credit. It is possible that they made an exception for permanent members of their gang. The latter were able to ask for small loans occasionally or a little extra in the way of favours in order to retain their loyalty. These sorts of splurges were well hidden from the other workers and they took good care not to mention them to one another.

The calculation of wages took place at fixed times, depending on the gang boss's superior: at the end of every week, every fortnight, or when the project was of very short duration straight after it was finished. Naturally the gang boss was in a very vulnerable position when the wage settlements agreed were not honoured by the contractor. This could occur as the result of dissatisfaction with the quality of the work performed or if the work tempo tended to lag. It was not unheard of for the patron to be defaulted on by his contractor or for the former to act in bad faith in the payment of the sums of money he owed. In his turn, the gang boss usually passed on these blows to his team who were simply not paid their wages. If there was insufficient reason to doubt the explanation or the *mandur* that the contractor had defaulted, there was little else that the workers could do but to foot the bill themselves. But any gang boss to whom this happened more than once found his good name threatened from two sides, in his retinue of migrants and among the contractors and builders of Jabotabek, and only succeeded in finding enough labourers for the next project with a great deal of difficulty.

Accommodation

The most salient characteristic of the nomadic existence was the multiple changes of the locations where the migrants put up in the course of a year. Most of these were situated in the steadily encroaching belt of Jabotabek, but they could easily end up in destinations much further afield. For instance, a dozen or so men from East Cirebon were part of the gang of a local *mandur* who worked on contract for a builder who specialized in the construction of petrol stations. He had work throughout the whole archipelago, which meant that these workers spent a short time in places where they had never been before, and where they would almost certainly never come again. The trips were so brief and the destinations were so different that most of the migrants did not even bother to leave their address behind when they left the village. Quite often they did not even know this themselves and the gang boss himself was unable to give any guarantee of certainty about lodgings. It was a regular occurrence that the temporary lodgings were organized only after they had arrived. Buildings in a fairly advanced stage of construction offered a poor excuse for a roof over their heads, and sometimes literally not even that. This was the fate which most often befell those migrants whose job was to put the finishing touches to a building like carpenters, tilers, painters or plasterers. For the navvies especially this was out of the question. The gang bosses of these sort of workers did their best to find lodgings as close as possible to the site. Sometimes they would rent a shed for the estimated length of the project in which the whole gang of thirty, fifty or more men could be housed or else they resorted to renting rooms for the night in one or more houses. Migrants who came to Jabotabek under their own steam had also to find their own accommodation. Either individually or in groups of fellow workers they would sign a contract with landlords who specialized in renting to these birds of passage or they went to a *pondok* where the owner also provided food for his guests. If this was not the case, they could always find their way to a *warung* close by. In a few cases it might happen that the *mandur* or one of the other members of his gang would sometimes be accompanied by his wife or daughter, who was paid to prepare a number of meals. Their presence immediately created a different atmosphere in a situation which was heavily male oriented. The owner of a *pondok* in Tebet, who was a native of East Cirebon, had built a sort of dormitory above the shop which offered shelter to some twenty migrants from the village. It consisted on one large room which was used during the day as a place to store clothes and other bits and pieces, packed in a bag or a tin, which the men had brought with them from the village. Late in the evening, they laid themselves down to spend the night like sardines in a tin. The house rules of these tightly packed dens required that the old hands could claim the best places, close to the window, and the newcomers had to make the best of it in the worst section, close to the door. The migrants spent what little free time remained to them at the end of the long day in this place in each other's company. The continual proximity of the companions in adversity meant that there was a strict social control, which facilitated the supervisory task of the *mandur*. In such a situation it was difficult to behave in any fashion other than that which was considered seemly, in other words, going to work every day, behaving oneself tractably, and not squandering hard earned money in too spectacular a manner. These restrictions were balanced out by the material and emotional support when they were ill or found themselves in other sorts of difficulties. All this goes to show that, in almost all the cases, the life of a migrant – not just the short excursions to the city but more than anything else being closed up in a living and working environment that was cut off from the people settled about them – did not mark the initial phase of a more definitive arrival but actually stood in the way of this. The way in which the migrants set out and their roamings around the urban outskirts transformed them into modern hunters and gatherers.

Training and job mobility

By far the greatest majority of migrants from East Cirebon belonged to the category of unskilled or low skilled labourers. The need for precisely this sort of worker was connected to the low degree of mechanization in the building industry. Gradually changes did begin to make their way in, but labour was so cheap and so easy to hire and fire that a switch to a more capital-intensive organization of production did not seem very attractive to the lords of the construction industry. The heavy road and house construction equipment which was introduced was expensive and was only profitable when it was put to a fairly continuous use. When not in use these high-grade machines did not give a return on the money spent on them, whereas payment of labour ended the day that the project was completed. Even the gang bosses made no claim to any sort of bridging allowance and were sent away the moment that their services were no longer needed.

The human labour force remained the primary factor of production and in any decision about the usefulness of a migrant his physical condition played a decisive role. This was also expressed in the preponderance of younger labourers among the workforce. Recruitment began at puberty when the boys were not much older than fifteen and reached a peak among the young adults. Once thirty had been passed interest waned. The trips were then less frequent and lasted only a short time. The aging men said that they were sick and tired of the constant travelling back and forth. Because of the lack of any other sort of employment in the village they felt themselves obliged to persist in their commuting but their personal preference was to remain at home more frequently for longer periods of time. This was not just their own choice it was also that of the gang bosses. The older workers and men who had passed the ages of thirty and thirty-five became worn out. The advantage of their experience could no longer offset their failing capacity for work.

The working life of a migrant in the building industry was twenty years at the most and training, to the extent that there was any question of skill formation, occurred at the beginning of this cycle. Traditionally this was a practical training in which a son learned from his father or a younger brother from an older by working alongside them on the job. As early as 1989, there were some younger men who had attended the lower technical school after finishing primary school in order to acquire formal qualifications for a technical skill, but in most cases the old ways still prevailed and training was on site. The apprentice, *kenek*, was helper to the carpenter, mason, tiler or the like, and after an apprenticeship of an indeterminate length went further on his way as a craftsman. One important factor which played a role in this alongside the learning process, was the necessity to provide himself with the tools of his trade most commonly used. For a navvy this was limited to not much more than a shovel, but a carpenter needed more. An informant from the latter trade category estimated the value of the simple contents of a toolbox at least one hundred fifty thousand rupiah, a sum which was the equivalent to roughly one month's work. If he did not have this equipment, no *mandur* would be prepared to employ him.

As far as training was concerned, the working landscape in which the migrants moved around was fairly flat. Apprentices who had made their way into the realms of craftsmen had reached the limits of the heights they could reach in their occupation. The one figure who stood head and shoulders above them was the gang boss. What qualities did he need to reach this position? First and foremost he needed a reasonable knowledge of the technical sides of the work which was being carried out. Chief among these was a fair competence in reading, writing, and arithmetic. One gang boss explained how he used to go to the site hut in the lunch break so that he could see what the technical supervisors were doing with their paper designs and drawings. The *mandur* carried out his work in tandem with the sub-contractor or contractor but, if he was going to do this properly, he needed to be able to do some simple administration himself, as well as taking measurements and doing calculations, plan the work for his gang, supervise the day-to-day progress, and anticipate what would be required to be done for the following day. He also needed to be able to get on with his superiors by acting towards them in an exemplary manner, a combination of skill and submissiveness. In his contacts with the members of his team, it was important to convince them that he was looking after their interests properly, and conversely to discipline them into delivering an adequate work output and to be responsible for a good atmosphere within the gang. Work on site was also the best schooling for such an intermediary. For those gang bosses who had trouble fulfilling one of these qualifications, there was little choice but to return to the large mass of migrants and instead of recruiting, being himself recruited. At the beginning of his career, he was dependent on the intercession and support of other labour brokers who set him on the way to the higher bosses. Not one single *mandur* from East Cirebon had ever been able to progress any further than *pemborong*, works foreman or sub-contractor. This was not so much because their knowledge of things was insufficient, but more because they just did not possess enough working capital or the network of contacts which were essential to the awarding of contracts. The working capital was needed to register for projects which were put out for tender and to pay 'commission' to civil servants and others who had granted favours. Generally speaking, building up a network of contacts in the higher echelons of the construction industry only succeeded by moving to Jabotabek for good. From the village itself, or commuting back and forth between the village and the city, it was fairly impossible to exert a steady influence on those who awarded contracts and to begin once again on a search for new projects.

Identity of the migrants

As has already been mentioned, the migrants working in the construction industry were exclusively males in a relatively young age group. In nearly all instances their formal education has never progressed beyond the end of primary school. This limited training immediately precluded them from gaining entry into any of the better paying occupations and more permanent forms of employment. Other characteristics were inextricably linked to the social background of the labour migrants. The large majority of them originated from the ranks of peasants who were either landless or owned only a minuscule field, categories to which around three-quarters of the population of East Cirebon belonged. Notably, any mutual differences between the migrants, for as far as these existed, could be traced back to the various positions which they held in the village economy. Migrants who owned some land were at least more successful in obtaining a practical training in a skill than most of their companions in adversity. On patches of ground which had not been laid claim to by the sugar mill, they stubbornly continued to cultivate rice and they keep as much of the harvest as they could for themselves. This slightly better off category of people was able to regulate their nomadic existence by undertaking the journey to Jabotabek in a more regular rhythm and not varying their place of destination as much. This sort of migrant tried to find his own way as much as possible and did his best to find work without the mediation of a gang boss. These were the ones who either lodged with the owner of the *warung* who himself was a native of East Cirebon or found their own place to stay by renting temporary accommodation with a few mates. It was also their strategy to try to find work on projects which would be worked on for some time. But the guarantee of continuous employment did not stop them from returning to their village following a more or less regular schedule for brief visits to the household they had left behind. They nonetheless also allowed their coming and going to be influenced primarily by the wages they could earn. Instead of using the number of days or weeks outside East Cirebon as the yardstick for calculating when they would take a few days' break, the overriding factor in their case was the amount of money they had saved. After all, the patterns of expenditure of the households dependent on them was calculated on the basis of the supplementation by a minimum amount of cash. For all those concerned, the premature return of a father or husband was perhaps emotionally very welcome but financially unattractive. Pondering the question we had posed him, one of the migrants answered that the stimulus to remain away longer lay in the possibility of returning home with a larger amount of money saved. What helped him in his resolve was the self-discipline which he had learned from mates which ensured that he spent as little money as possible in Jakarta.

Those men who came from family with no land had no training when they left and usually had to spend their existence as a migrant working as a navvy, the work ranked as the lowest paid category in the building industry. Often it was not they themselves who took the initiative to undertake the journey, they just bided their time until a gang boss summoned them. Their migrations lacked regularity both in destination and in length of time. Those who did not belong to a permanent gang found their lives characterized by an unsettling pattern of coming and going, now leaving to go to somewhere close by, now to somewhere much further away. Their absence could last just a couple of weeks or it might last a period of longer than two to three months or even more, and they had just as little to say about the place to which they would be sent. This highly unsettled pattern was expressed in the greatly fluctuating returns which they made on their excursions out of the village. These men were extremely vulnerable to the ever-present risk of unexpected unemployment. In the event of illness, the sudden termination of a contract, or being thrown out of the team they had little or no time over in which to look for another job. Among these migrants we were told the story more than once of how the shovel – the only means of production which they owned – had to be sold to find enough money to pay for their trip back to the village. Conversely, these landless people were now so far removed from agriculture that the beginning of the rice harvest was no longer a reason to return to East Cirebon precisely at that moment.

All this had very little connection with a feeling for enterprise or perseverance. The labour migration had its roots in a particular situation of inequality and the outcome of this led to an accentuation of the contrasts, even though these were not greatly marked, which were already present in the initiative. Those households which owned some land had some reserves at least and these allowed them to build up some surpluses and, for instance, to invest in the education of the next generation. This possibility was simply not open to the landless households. Any money which did come in went immediately to the local shops in East Cirebon to pay off the debts which the women had had to run up in the absence of the men. When, in spite of everything, these households did decide to buy some more durable consumer articles – a transistor radio for instance – it was quite a common occurrence that not long afterwards it was given to the pawnbroker as security for a loan which was needed to buy food during a spell of unemployment. After their return, nearly all the migrants would have preferred to remain longer in their villages or even not to have had to leave again at all. This aversion was caused by the arduousness of work and life as labour nomads. But their first venture and then the other departures which had to be faced repeatedly were in most instances inevitable, being purely and simply a matter of economic necessity. The men who had the least were also obliged to continue to go away until they were fairly old. It was only after their physical strength had been totally burned up that they returned to East Cirebon for good, unproductive and in fact just as poverty-stricken as they were at the beginning of their working life, which had now drawn to its close.

Apart from the men who worked in the building industry which, as was shown, was by far the majority, the road to Jabotabek was taken by a small number of other sorts of migrants. There were, for instance, some six men who plied their trade as sellers of cigarettes and tobacco, combs, and scissors. They formed one large family of peddlers in which the members from East Cirebon who came from various households were split up by shared quarters which they had rented in the centre of the city which served as a gathering place and lodgings. Carrying a box on which their wares were displayed, they left to do their rounds in the morning and returned to their joint base in the late afternoon. These itinerant small traders procured their supplies from the same purveyor, who also lent them their boxes, and acted as guarantor for each other for any eventual debts which they might run up with him. The men seemed to alternate with one another in a pattern of coming and going and this regular circulation strengthened the close contact with the home front. They earned somewhat more than did workers in the building industry and as small independent entrepreneurs clearly thought themselves a cut above the navvies and other unskilled migrants in social status. As was the case with many *kaki lima*, they did not escape regular or incidental depredations on their daily earnings by the security guards of building complexes and policemen.

Apart from these men, there were a few individuals who had found work through the intervention of kinsmen or friends who had settled in the urban agglomeration: as a private chauffeur, as a vendor of drinking water in the street, as assistant in a repairs business, as a garbage collector, and finally there were three young women, of whom two worked as maids and one was employed in a bakery. All these examples show that we are talking about work in the informal sector of the economy. Entry into formal sector employment – a steady job at a reasonable wage and to some extent protected conditions of employment – was restricted to a few of the younger people from households which were counted among the village elite. Faced with the absence of the requisite school diplomas and perhaps even more because of the lack of strategic contacts with the higher economic circuit which offered a reasonably safe existence, the average labour migrant had no chance to penetrate to this level.

In the discussion of the results of the 1989 research, the rare cases which related to the international labour migration circuit should be mentioned. This concerned four men who had been sent to Saudi Arabia as building labourers for a period of two years by a commercial employment agency in Cirebon. Abroad the day began at six in the morning and ended at half-past six in the evening, interspersed with a longish break between half-past eleven and half-past three. They were housed in barracks and the work regime was based on a semi-military model, with roll call in the morning and again in the evening and a marching to and from the work site under the leadership of the gang boss. These had been arduous years, and despite the high return – the monthly wage that was made over to home by these labourers was six hundred real (the value of the real then stood at one hundred and twenty rupiah) – none of them had accepted the offer of a second work period. After their return, three of the four had again joined the army of labour migrants to Jabotabek. Only one man had saved so much of his earnings that he was able to open a shop in East Cirebon. When the employment agency closed down a little while later, the opportunity to be sent to the Gulf States came to an end. In 1989 it seemed that this long-distance migration would not be continued.

Rural industry

Labour migration to far away destinations was however not the only alternative on offer for the rapidly diminishing significance of agriculture in the economy of East Cirebon as a long-term process. There was yet another source of income taking off in which a considerable number of the local population had already found work in 1989. This was the manufacture of bricks in the fields on the eastern side of the village. Little is known about the history of this rural industry but its presence can be traced at least as far back as the nineteenth century. The *lurah* of East Cirebon recounted that his grandfather was involved in supplying the bricks for the Karangsuwung sugar mill which, it would appear from the date which is set into the chimney, was built in 1896. Until deep into the twentieth century the demand for bricks was very limited. Government offices and bridges were built of this material but as far as houses were concerned building with bricks was mainly confined to the towns and cities. In the countryside, bamboo poles and walls of woven bamboo slats were the building materials from which by far the most people in the village built their *bilik* dwellings. Since the 1960s, in East Cirebon the replacement of *bilik* by brick had been rapidly gaining ground. At the beginning of this monograph, it has already been pointed out that in 1989 70% of the houses were constructed solely of brick. This change meant an enormous expansion in the market for this product. An additional stimulus for this was the rapid increase in the mechanization of transportation which also occurred in this period. This meant that distances could be covered more easily. Therefore sales were no longer governed by local demand. Building sites within a radius of thirty to fifty kilometres were now within the reach of producers who were set up in East Cirebon. Since the 1970s these changes have given a tremendous stimulus to the local industry.

Location and management of the industry

Almost all the brickworks, locally known as *pengobongan* or *pabrik bata,* are located on land which forms part of the territory of the neighbouring village. These fields consist of the proper sort of ground – the correct proportion of sand to clay – which was the very best for the moulding and baking of the bricks. These enterprises were readily recognizable in the landscape because of the open sheds in which the baking process took place. The excavation of the land round about indicated the source of the material used, and the brickmakers ply their craft closer to the open shed on levelled pieces of ground. In 1989 there were some thirty brickworks in operation. The number of sheds

Pabrik bata, the brick kilns occupying cultivable land at the outskirts of the village

did not provide the yardstick as various entrepreneurs, known as *bandar*, worked with more than one shed. There was also the matter of the large variation in the size of the businesses. The smallest made no more than a thousand bricks a day, whereas the very largest easily topped ten thousand. The moulding took place in the open air and was therefore extremely susceptible to changes in the weather. In the top months of the year – the dry season – the daily volume fluctuated between one hundred thousand and one hundred fifty thousand bricks but dropped to far below the half of this in the wet season. The three wealthiest *bandar* controlled nearly half the total production. The owners of the brickworks were not all natives of East Cirebon nor were the workers in their employ. Nevertheless, this does not mean to imply that the brick-making industry did not occupy an important niche in the economy of East Cirebon.

The opening of a brickworks required a fairly sizeable amount of working capital, not far short of two million rupiah. Among the initial costs were the renting of a piece of land which could be excavated from the top down. In 1989 the owner of such a piece of land asked a sum of one thousand four hundred rupiah per cubic metre and a reasonably sized business needed to rent an area of five hundred square metres. A shed consisting of a thatched roof borne on bamboo poles was erected as close as possible to this site. The

The sheds for burning are surrounded by the brickfields

building of this simple structure cost around two hundred thousand rupiah. Before the production process could begin, the labour force had to be recruited. This involved spending an advance of fifty thousand to one hundred thousand rupiah on a couple formed by a husband and wife. The smallest brickworks made do with a single couple, but the sheds of a substantial enterprise with a large daily production might need up to ten work teams. Added to this was the prepayment to the *tukang obong*, the man in charge of the baking process. Expenditure in the initial phase finally included the buying up of a supply of rice chaff which would be used as fuel to bake the bricks.

The production process consisted of a number of components. At the beginning of this was the couple, usually a married one, whose task it was to mould the bricks and place them in the shed. The working day began at five o'clock in the morning for the men, the women and children usually arriving an hour later. The work continued into the afternoon. The total length of ten to twelve hours was interrupted in the middle of the day by a break lasting two to three hours. The task of the man was to dig the ground and to carry this close to the moulding place where it was kneaded to a moist consistency. The woman was supplied with small lumps of the prepared material which she formed into bricks in a wooden mould. She did this by continually mov-

Brick kilns in North Subang spread in the *sawah* fields

ing across an empty space that by the end of the morning was filled with the bricks which she had made. The couple were assisted by one or more of their children who worked with them, starting from the age of about six, who, for instance, helped with the scraping clean of the bricks and carrying them to the shed. In the afternoon, from about two or three o'clock to around five or six, the working place was cleared ready for the next day's production. A cubic metre of land yielded eight hundred to nine hundred bricks and in the dry season a work team produced six hundred to eight hundred bricks per day, much fewer in the rainy season. In the late afternoon, the bricks which had been moulded in the morning were placed in rows ready for the further completion of the drying process and scraped smooth before being taken to the kilns a few days later by the brick-makers. The beginning and end of this phase required several days, the length being determined by how long was needed for the drying process (two to three days outside the rainy season but much longer when the weather was damp) and the storage capacity in the sheds for newly moulded bricks. In order to accommodate the next consignment of bricks, it was necessary to clear the bricks which had been baked out of the sheds as soon as possible. Once the bricks had been delivered to the shed, the work of the brick-makers was finished and was then in the hands of the kiln-worker. He was responsible for stacking the bricks in the shed into

Stacking the moulded bricks for drying

a heap for burning. The layers of bricks were interspaced with rice chaff which was burned during the firing process. Twenty to twenty-five sacks of this fuel were required for every thousand bricks at the cost of three hundred rupiah per sack. The firing process took about a week. Depending on the size of the enterprise, this occurred on one or more occasions in a month, and the volume of bricks baked varied from ten thousand to thirty thousand bricks at a time. Supervised by the firer, the cooled bricks were taken outside by day labourers and piled up in rows near the shed waiting to be sold, or were loaded directly onto trucks at the roadside to be delivered to customers who had placed advance orders.

Using these data it is possible to calculate the production costs, the proportion which was spent on labour, and the profit margin of the entrepreneur. The sales price in 1989 was twenty thousand rupiah per one thousand bricks. For this sum, the bricks were delivered to the customer who came to the brickworks. In that case the purchaser paid for the transportation costs which rose according the distance to be covered. The manufacture involved a sum of a round fifteen thousand rupiah per thousand bricks: the renting of the land for this, the rice chaff, the depreciation costs of the shed (which had to be replaced every two years), payment of the brick-makers, the firer, and the loaders in a proportion of a little more than 60% for material and a little less than 40% for labour charges. The difference between the cost of production and the sales price, which was five thousand rupiah at a minimum, was the profit for the owner of the brickworks. But, if he had had to borrow some or all of the capital which he needed to open his business from a moneylender then this profit dropped to not much more than three to four rupiah per brick. Come what may, at an average production rate of only ten thousand bricks per week this was still considerably more than earned by someone working on a daily wage either inside or outside the village. The wages of the actual brick-makers trailed far behind even what was earned by a small-scale *bandar*.

Conditions of employment

Right at the outset it is essential to stress the labour-intensive nature of the production process. The manufacturing of bricks took place literally by hand and from a technological point of view in the simplest possible way. The only tools which were used were a hoe (*pacul*) for digging out the ground by the man and a wooden mould which the woman used to form the bricks. In 1986 the wages of the brick-makers were raised from 3.5 rupiah to 4 per piece, but the actual payment for their labour took place on the basis of the payment of advances. After the first instalment which marked the beginning of the agreement with the patron, their outstanding debt was calculated with the number of bricks which they produced daily. The debt was never fully paid off because long before the time for this came up, they asked for and were given a new advance. The amount of this fluctuated with the erratic nature of their cash requirements. Alongside the recurring amounts of the cost of living were those originating from the more unexpected expenditure in the cycle of the household such as sickness, repairs to the house, or the reception of guests on joyful or sad occasions. Given this, in the course of time the initial debt had the tendency to expand to an even larger sum. This was the inevitable consequence of the very poor remuneration for the work produced.

The payment for the work was so low that other members of the household had to be roped in to ensure that the needs of everyday life were provided for. Payment in the form of piece-rated wages put a premium on the employment of both adults and children. A work team consisting of 2.5 members was paid no more than two thousand eight hundred rupiah for the production of seven hundred bricks a day. Divided up this meant around one thousand two hundred rupiah for an adult and less than half of this amount for a child. Even an agricultural labourer earned more per day for fewer hours work. The plus side was that work in the brickworks was characterized by a higher degree of regularity. Nevertheless, the manufacturing process was strewn with all sorts of hitches and the production for a week of a couple hardly ever topped four thousand bricks. Too many moulded bricks sent to the shed or a delay in the transportation of the baked bricks away from it could mean that there was no more open terrain available for the manufacturing of a new quantity by the woman. It might happen that a couple moved away to another shed or another owner in order to continue production. By offering a *kontrak*, which invariably meant the payment of an advance, the owners of the brickworks tried to tie a number of work teams to them, two to three per shed on average. This strategy complemented the *bandar*'s image of himself as a benevolent master. He affected to behave towards his employees like a father who offered his children care and protection. The gift of clothing on the occasion of *lebaran* expressed this patron-client relationship. But brick-makers who were deeply in debt to their employer had great difficulty in persuading them to pay even more new advances. A stubborn refusal could only be interpreted as a sign that the *bandar* wanted to replace a working couple by a new team. Conversely, the insistent urging for another payment in advance was a polite way by which the brick-makers could show that they were looking for a contract with a new *bandar*. Settlement of the current contract was a condition for the transfer to another patron. The latter lured skilled workers to himself not by offering them a higher wage but by giving them the promise of more generous credit.

The collective nature of the work process to be undertaken rendered production vulnerable. The illness of the man or the pregnancy of the woman could lead to the temporary suspension of the whole team. Some of the brick-makers tried to insure themselves against this risk by hiring an extra worker and making a proportional deal to pay them for their services. A woman on her own said that she helped a couple, consisting of her brother and his wife, three times in the week. But, if she arrived too late in the morning, her place had already been taken by someone else who also did not have a husband. This is an indication of the limited amount of work available to widows or divorcees who, in their struggle to survive at the bottom of the village economy, often found themselves competing with each other. The steep decline in activity during the rainy season was the result both of technical problems – the much longer time taken by the drying process meant that the brickmakers found themselves with too little open area to pursue their production – and of the heavy fall in sales because all building activities were also cut back during this period. During this recess, the employees in the brickworks were obliged to make a living by involving themselves in agricultural operations. By entering into harvest contracts with owners of arable land during the previous months – sometimes this was the *bandar* by whom they were already employed – they managed to ensure that they had enough to eat for the near future.

Marketing

Many customers found their own way to East Cirebon. Regular clients like building suppliers or big contractors had permanent contracts with the owners of the large brickworks. The purchaser paid the amount which was calculated from the roadside, twenty thousand rupiah per thousand bricks. The loading up of the trucks and the journey to the destinations were for their own account. The profits the *bandar* made they ploughed back into expanding their businesses by constructing more sheds. But the highest priority in their efforts to strengthen their market position was the purchase of vehicles, trucks to transport the bricks and pick-ups for bringing in the huge quantities of rice chaff so essential to the daily process of production. Their main marketing area for bricks was the immediate surroundings and the transportation seldom went any further than Cirebon, Kuningan, and a few nearby coastal towns like Tegal in Central Java. When long distances had to be covered the transportation costs rose so high that buying in East Cirebon became unprofitable. All that went to Jakarta was the refuse which was left at the end of the manufacturing process, the ashes of the burned rice chaff that was in demand in the capital as a scouring agent. The sale of this was a little extra on the side for the *tukang obong*, who received fifty rupiah per bag for it.

As was the case in other sectors of the economy, an agent, the *calo*, had set himself up as a middleman in brokering supply and demand. These men hung around along the entrance roads leading to the villages and the brick-

Construction workers from East Cirebon building a new pasar in Bekasi town in late 2001

works. They had a keen eye for potential clients and approached them with the offer of being able to fix up the most favourable transaction for them. Usually they worked on the basis of a commission which was paid to them by the *bandar*. However, it did happen that they sometimes bought a consignment of bricks themselves for a sum a little lower than the going rate for the day. When owners of the smaller brickworks had difficulty in getting rid of their stock on time, the agent made his appearance on the scene to make a good deal for himself for which he then went off in search of a buyer in the vicinity. A few of the larger entrepreneurs in the area operated in this way though more systematically. They lent the starting *bandar* the working capital which they needed and in exchange for this made a claim on all or a considerable portion of the production for one or two rupiah less per brick than what was being paid on the open market. Instead of changing over to more advanced technology which would have resulted in a rise in production and productivity, the entrepreneurs preferred a lengthening in the chain of their control over their line of business. They did this on the one hand by extending control down and binding smaller brickworks to them and on the other hand by making investments in the marketing of the commodity by buying means of transport.

Identity and mobility

The brick-makers invariably came from the lowest level of the population. The neighbourhoods in which they lived stood out as the concentrations of the direst poverty in East Cirebon. The extreme form of lack of property which characterized their households made upwards mobility virtually impossible. The many years of experience which quite a few of them had built up in the manufacture of bricks was not limited simply to the technical mastery of the work, but often extended to other facets of the business. Nevertheless, only an exception ever managed to work himself up to be the owner of a brickworks because they were not regarded as good credit risks for the loans which moneylenders were prepared to make only if there was enough collateral security. It was regarded as a risky business to supply them with working capital because it was assumed that they would probably have to spend it all or at least a major part of it on consumption. What happened much more often was that a supervisor was employed by a large entrepreneur to keep an eye on the work in the sheds. Or a *tukang obong* might decide to strike out on his own. He played an important part in the production process by assuming responsibility for the regular delivery of moulded bricks to the shed and then for taking them away after the completion of the firing process. He received a piece wage of one thousand two hundred and fifty to one thousand five hundred rupiah for every thousand bricks. For that sum he had to pile up the moulded bricks stored in the shed in a kiln, supervise the firing process, and when this was completed unpack the bricks from the kiln. In this work, he was helped by one or two boys to whom the heavy labour, especially the carrying of the bricks, was delegated. Having achieved these positions, as foreman or as firer, it was easier to open one's own small kiln. The threshold was even lower if these novice *bandar* had some capital themselves from which they could draw in the teething period for the rent of the land needed for excavation and for the construction of a shed. They saved on labour costs by forming a couple with their wives for making the bricks, and they kept the firing process under their own control. In fact, these self-employed brick-makers-cum-*bandar* formed an intermediate category which was separate from the hired labour on the one hand and on the other from the large-scale entrepreneurs who no longer actually worked in their enterprises and claimed the production of the smaller kilns. A good yardstick by which to measure the size of the enterprise was the number of work teams: there were eight businesses employing more than five couples (three of which employed more than ten couples); twenty units with fewer than five but at least one contracted couple, and ten enterprises run by small self-employed manufacturers who only hired extra labour incidentally. Developing from a small-scale to a large-scale *bandar* was a far less frequent occurrence than mobility in the reverse direction and in a few instances the failed entrepreneur had no other choice than to return to the ranks of the workers who had no property. Our conclusion at the end of this survey is that the distinction between worker and entrepreneur could not be traced back to a simple dichotomy but that the commercial organization of this rural industry was characterized by a greater complexity.

Trade and transport

The most obvious division between those who found employment in these branches of work was between large and small-scale traders. The first were indubitably the most important but were simultaneously the least visible in the daily round of work. Their transactions linked the local economy with that of the area around it and therefore affected the working life and its returns for the other inhabitants of East Cirebon, but they were rarely expressly conspicuous in the public intercourse. To this category belonged the *cukong* who played a central role in the cultivation of sugarcane, the rice merchants who not only did business with the farmers but also gathered up the harvest portions of the agricultural workers via agents, and the money-lenders who provided loans. Finally there were the *calo*, agents who mediated in the buying and selling of all sorts of goods (bicycles, motor-scooters, a piece of land, a load of bricks, gold jewellery, chickens, radios) and who undertook to make a deal on behalf of one of the parties but at that person's risk and expense. The largest capital owners of the village pertained to this circuit. In a certain sense the *pamong desa*, the members of the village administration, could also be counted among them. There are two reasons for this, namely: various of them indulged in money-lending in order to supplement their regular salary, and it was to them the wives of the Jakarta migrants applied for financial support in the form of a loan which they needed to purchase more durable consumer goods or to cover the costs of medical treatment, and because they used their position as local authorities to claim payment for all sorts or services, solicited and unsolicited. They (mis)used their office as a branch of trade from which they derived a lucrative but illegal income.

The petty traders had a far higher public visibility, but also among those who exercised these occupations, tradesmen and hawkers, there were still great differences. Besides three large shops, *toko*, East Cirebon had no less than fifteen *warung*. The assortment which was for sale in the first sort of shop covered a wide range of daily and semi-durable consumer goods and they had a daily turnover of at least fifty thousand rupiah. The middle-sized *warung*, of which there were five, sold goods from a much more limited stock and which were confined to the necessities of daily life, and their turnover fluctuated at around at least twenty-five thousand rupiah per day. The ten smallest *warung* were tiny stalls in front of or next to the house of the owner, sometimes consisting of no more than a small table or a few boards laid on two trestles, on which was displayed a modest collection of articles – cigarettes, sweets, and home-made snacks – worth never more than ten thousand rupiah. Sales could bring in far below this amount and the intervals between restocking were much longer. The owners of the *toko* were men, but all of the *warung* were run by women. It was a constant complaint of the shopkeepers that for between one-quarter and one-third of all their sales they were not paid in cash. Those households which depended on the fruits of the labour migration for their incomes could only settle the account when the men returned home to East Cirebon with the wages they had earned over the past few weeks. The households of the brick-makers also chalked up on the slate until the *bandar* honoured their request for a new advance. The smaller the trade was, the larger the amount of unpaid credit with which it was saddled. It was especially during the rainy season that the lack of ready money was so pressing, so much so that various of the smaller *warung* had to close down until their customers experienced better times.

There were also two sorts of hawkers, those who sold their wares to people at fixed points and itinerant peddlers. Those in the first category included the coconut seller at the *pasar* at Sindanglaut. The small traders who hawked their wares – snacks like *baso*, *bubur*, *gado-gado*, *rujak*, and confections

Small stall along the main village road selling ready-made food

such as *es campur* or fruits – did this in the village and its immediate surroundings on a bicycle or with a handcart. They bought their ingredients at the market and sold these, whether they had prepared them or not, for a slightly higher sum. Hawkers, both men and women, earned not only the most minimal but also the most fluctuating income among all those who earned their living by trading. On good days they might retain two thousand to two thousand rupiah, but on bad this would amount to no more than five hundred rupiah.

In the transport sector the diversity among the businessmen involved was just as great, in this case possession of capital being the decisive factor behind this heterogeneity. A costly and profitable means of production in this branch was the ownership of a truck or pickup for transporting sugarcane, bricks, rice chaff and sand. To move the sugarcane which was taken by road to the mills during the cutting season, trucks were hired for the duration of the campaign from private owners of whom there were two in East Cirebon. When the cutting season was over, they used the vehicles to carry loads of bricks or sand, delved out of the bed of the neighbouring river, and to deliver these materials to those who had ordered them. Pickups were used by their owners for transporting the huge quantities of rice chaff needed to fuel the brick kilns from out the wider surroundings, up to a distance of thirty to forty kilometres. There was not one single owner in East Cirebon who had bought his vehicle new. Of course, the actual value decreased with age but in each case a very high sum of money, to the tune of many millions of rupiah, was involved. Usually the owner only used his vehicle as an investment and hardly ever drove it himself. He left this sort of work to a specially hired employee.

Six motorbikes were used to transport people, with the passenger sitting pillion behind the driver. These were usually owned by young men who ran their business (*ojeg*) from home or waited along the sides of the road for customers who wanted to go to the neighbouring market or the capital of the sub-district. Operating these two-wheel taxis was not very profitable. After the costs of the petrol and maintenance had been deducted, the owner rarely made more than two thousand rupiah per day. There was one owner of a *dilman*, a horse and cart, with which he transported passengers along a fixed route, back and forth between a neighbouring village via East Cirebon to the capital of the sub-district. He made a little, but not much more than the owners of *becak*. There were three of these three-wheel taxis plying their trade in East Cirebon. The owners themselves transported their customers but were prepared to hire out their vehicle for a part of the day for three hundred to five hundred rupiah to riders who were unable to raise the purchase price of one hundred fifty thousand rupiah. Short trips interspersed with long waits in between yielded a sum of between one thousand five hundred and two thousand rupiah at the end of the day, with highs and lows on either side.

As has just been mentioned some owners hired out their vehicles to other users. This practice was especially common with trucks and panel vans. The chauffeur of a truck received 20% of the total sum of the loads he had transported during the day. Under another arrangement, he was paid a flat rate of twenty thousand rupiah per day but out of this had to pay the costs of the petrol, small running repairs, and 'fines' paid to the army and police. He was also expected to pay his co-driver. When it was all said and done the chauffeurs pocketed between seven thousand and ten thousand rupiah per day. They were the most skilled of the transport workers and had to pay a far higher sum for the issue and prolongation of their driving licence than was required in the official regulations. A co-driver, *kenek*, accompanied them wherever they went and by so doing gained experience in the job of chauffeur. The drivers of pickups paid a fixed daily amount and they bought chaff from the owners of rice mills for sixty rupiah per bag and they sold this on to the owners of brickworks in East Cirebon for many times this amount. Depending on the distance to be covered they and their co-drivers made four to six trips a day, from which they were able to take home between twelve thousand to fifteen thousand rupiah net between them, which they split up on a two-thirds to one-third basis. One driver rented a truck in which he transported sand with the assistance of a team which he assembled on a daily basis. While a few helpers delivered orders to clients, the others transported the sand from the river bed to the road in baskets slung on poles carried on their shoulders. The driver no longer concerned himself personally with loading and unloading but it was he who divided up the takings at the end of the day, after reserving a large proportion for himself. The profit from the motorbike and bicycle taxis was so low – five thousand to two thousand rupiah per day – that there was little interest in renting these vehicles.

Most of the men who belonged to the category of transport workers owned nothing and moreover had never had the opportunity to acquire some sort of training in a skill. They included the carriers of bricks and the loaders who rode along on the trucks. They did not work as a permanent team but found jobs as individual workers and were paid a piece wage which seldom exceeded three thousand rupiah a day, often remaining at a lower level. All that they needed was their physical strength and stamina, the upshot being that by the time they were thirty to thirty-five, the more they found it difficult to keep up with the job.

Services and crafts

The provision of administrative services was held in very high regard. In the foremost representatives were the members of the *pamong desa* who embodied the power and authority of the government. The primary school teachers, two men and a woman, also enjoyed a great deal of prestige, not just because of their profession but also because of the reasonable degree of prosperity in which they lived. A woman teacher with nine years service had a monthly salary of one hundred twelve thousand and four hundred rupiah plus thirty-six kilograms of rice. A retired soldier also belonged to this same category. Even at a lower level, work which brought in a fixed income contributed to a greater security of livelihood. The few who were in possession of such a job could obtain credit more easily than the great mass of people who were dependent on casual earnings. In this category fell the seven workers employed in the Karangsuwung sugar mill. One of them was a welder who earned a monthly salary of one hundred thousand rupiah as a skilled tradesman and who also did shift work. The second, who was a member of the technical staff, worked as an analyst in the section in which the sugar content in the milling process was determined and he had a monthly salary of one hundred twenty thousand rupiah. Whereas this technician was paid throughout the year, two others were employed only during the cutting season which lasted from May to September. In that period, for a working day of nine hours, for seven days a week, they were paid one thousand nine hundred and twenty-five rupiah per day, with a chance of paid overtime in the evenings. They were the *tukang rel*, the workers who laid the rails along which the lorries ran which carried the cut cane to the mill from the fields and moved them as required. Once the harvest was over, they joined up with the army of labour migrants who moved off to Jakarta. One man was a school caretaker in a neighbouring village for which he earned eighty thousand rupiah per month and a quantity of rice worth twenty thousand rupiah.

The barber and masseuse, *ibu pijit*, who had set themselves up in East Cirebon did not work fixed hours. The payment they received from clients depended on the extent of their treatment. Their earnings were both low and variable. This was also the case of the woman who provided all the trimmings for weddings, including the make-up and clothing of the bridal couple. The fee she asked varied according to the financial circumstances of her clients and the celebratory package they had ordered. There were few craftsmen who practised their skills in the village. One tailor went to an employer in Sindanglaut every day by bike. He earned two thousand rupiah a day. He wanted desperately to buy a sewing machine of his own so that he could accept work at home but the purchase price, two hundred thousand rupiah, far exceeded his budget. A few men found work as carpenters or bricklayers on building sites in the vicinity of East Cirebon. As skilled craftsmen they earned four thousand rupiah a day, a quarter to a third less than employers in Jabotabek were prepared to pay. The plus side was that they could go home in the evenings and also had far lower travel expenses. Finally, there were a few old men who were not longer able to make a strenuous physical effort but who made their time productive by manufacturing *welitan*, mats of cane leaves woven through a bamboo framework, which were used as roofing materials for the sheds of the brickworks. They did not need to pay for the leaves, anybody who wanted could take these from the fields after the harvest, but they did need to find the money for the other materials they required such as string and bamboo, expenditure which amounted to about thirty rupiah per mat. The *bandar* bought these mats for one hundred rupiah per piece and with a daily production rate of ten to fifteen mats, these elderly men could manage to keep themselves.

Profile of working population and class differentiation

On the basis of the foregoing discussion of employment pattern in the various sectors of the economy in East Cirebon, it is possible to determine their

The Karangsuwung sugar mill near North Cirebon is already in operation since the introduction of the cultivation system in the early 1830s

relative significance in 1989. The unit of calculation is the household. This does not mean that all members of the household performed the same sort of work. There were instances in which older members still engaged in agriculture, whereas younger members joined the labour migration to Jakarta or worked at the brickworks. Acknowledging this variation it should be stressed that the occupational classification of each household presented few problems. There was a good chance that if the father were a small-scale trader, his sons would also try to follow in his footsteps, men who worked outside the village in the building industry showed the next generation the way and in the brick-makers' families there was again a tendency to recruit new workers through the family.

The upshot of the persistent marginalization of agriculture, which had shown itself to be in a process of long-term decline, was that this branch of the economy was the source of livelihood for at most a fifth to a quarter of the working population drawn from nearly five hundred households. This fact underlines the statement made earlier that East Cirebon cannot be regarded as a typical Javanese agricultural village. The money earned from the labour migration to Jabotabek, which largely involved employment in the building industry, was the largest source of sustenance for more than a quarter of the households. The brickworks provided income for another quarter of the households and the workers in the rest of the households, which we estimated fluctuated between one-fifth to less than one-third of the total, worked at a number of different jobs – commerce, transport, service industries and trades – for the most part within the framework of the village economy.

Looking at the picture from a socio-demographic viewpoint, the first thing that strikes the eye is the fairly limited participation of women in the workforce outside the home. To deduce from this that their under-representation stems from a cultural code which prescribed that earning the cash income needed for basic daily needs was primarily men's work would be premature. In agricultural work they way it was pursued in the past, women managed to play a very important role indeed. The encroaching demands made on the agricultural land by the agro-industry and the eviction of the small landowners earlier this century has driven the women from the fields more than it has affected the men. This observation has to be modified by the fact that the local mills at Karangsuwung and Sindanglaut also continued to employ women on a large scale during the planting and harvesting seasons. However, this was almost exclusively labour from elsewhere which was hired specifically for these activities. On the limited cultivable area which remained for the growing of food crops, above all rice, women were indispensable. Compared to the men, sooner rather than later it was they who comprised the labour force needed for this type of agriculture. There was not one single woman among the migrants who set off to look for work in the building industry in Jabotabek. While the men were away, their work consisted of taking care of the members of the family who remained behind, children and perhaps elderly parents. One remarkable fact was that unmarried women without children who had failed to find employment in East Cirebon remained at home unemployed and had not left the village to seek for an income outside. In contrast to this, the division of labour in the brickworks was very much based on the involvement of women. Even the productive efforts of children, despite their limitations, could not be missed in this branch of employment for garnering a wage which was enough to provide a minimal living for the household concerned. Men preponderated in the great diversity of jobs which were pursued among the remaining section of the working population, but women were certainly also present as well. To a large extent they dominated petty trading, but they were non-starters in the important transport sector.

A second outstanding socio-demographic fact which emerged was the youthful composition of the working population. With the exception of the call made on children by parents who were attached to brick-manufacturers, first work experience in a paid job began not earlier than the age of about fifteen. Girls especially were put to work earlier in household tasks, but the attitude to adolescent boys was remarkably tolerant. Even when they had followed no sort of training after leaving primary school, it was still a number of years before they were expected to make themselves gainfully employed. And when this did happen they were not expected to contribute to the family income, at least not to the cost of their own upkeep. Very gradually, often only from the moment they married, did they learn to stand on their own two feet. At the other end of the spectrum there was no unexpected or abrupt end to enrolment in the work process. Retirement was not a question of a sudden and complete break but of a decreasing suitability. To the degree that the sort of work allowed it, the most appropriate form was the gradual switching over to lighter work which required less physical strength and stamina. The age at which this occurred was earlier for the sort of work that was acknowledged to be arduous. Not only the person concerned but also his employer or teammates showed their dissatisfaction with the decline in his achievement, and inexorably external pressure was exerted to make way for fresh, younger workers. Whereas the market for unskilled work was largely dominated by adolescents and young adults and did not extend much beyond the age of thirty-five, in those sorts of employment which were in part based on possession of capital and a reasonable degree of training, older people continued to be active. Until they, around about the age of fifty, were also set aside as a spent force.

There was a close correlation between schooling and the technological level of economic production. In all sectors employment still bore a largely manual character. The sort of work to which the inhabitants of East Cirebon had access, both inside and outside the village, was conspicuous because of the extremely limited use of capital. The leap up to the formal sector of the economy required such a lengthy and costly training with support from the network of contacts which were fine-tuned to it that most of the younger generation, when it is all said and done living in a rural backwater, never dreamed of attempting to achieve it. To the extent that there was any question of professional training, this was instilled at the practical level by the expedient of trained workers passing on their knowledge to newcomers. This was as true of tradesmen in the building industry as it was for truck drivers, brickmakers, itinerant salesmen and *warung*-keepers. Learning on the job was made much easier because of the limited quantity of modest equipment which was sufficient for the needs of most of the workers. For the navvies this was a shovel, for the agricultural workers a *pacul*, for the female brickmakers a wooden mould and for the harvesters in the cane fields wielding a cutting knife. When workers did not own these simple means of production themselves, the employer covered the eventuality by lending them the equipment for the period of work. For instance, the sugar mills made a number of machetes available to the *mandur* of the teams recruited for the season and these were collected when the work was finished. If they were not handed in, the team boss was given a penalty in the form of a reduction which was equivalent to the purchase price of the number of tools which were missing. The low capital intensity was associated with the low grade of the division of labour, just as conversely the superabundant supply of labour and the payment of low wages appeared to be obstacles to the undertaking of any technical innovation.

Usually work was not paid by the hour but as piecework, which was called *borongan*: the amount of earth moved per cubic metre, bricklaying per linear metre, a fixed price for the quantity of moulded and fired bricks, a load (of people or goods) with a tariff per distance, the cutting of sugarcane per field and the harvesting of rice with a pre-determined share of the yield. The most common form of payment transformed the relationship between employer and employed into a contracting out which created the impression of working at one's own risk. Alongside direct payment for what had been achieved at the end of the working day or at the completion of a task, there were instances when the two parties entered into their agreement on the basis of an advance (the brick-makers' contracts) or conversely of payment upon completion (agricultural workers in rice cultivation, labour migrants in the building industry). The intervention of agents in production (contractors and foremen in both the building industry and rice cultivation) and distribution (the *calo* in the brick-making) swallowed up a great deal of the value added in the labour process. When seeking work the most important thing was to come as close as possible to an acquaintanceship with the boss (*juragan*) or agents who were close to him or her. Recommendations from family, friends or neighbours and the request for a good word to be put in by another patron imbued employment with the character of a personal favour which was either graciously granted or withheld. A factor which heavily reinforced these elements was the loose character and brevity of the contract entered into – for a day, for a project, or for the harvest season. Permanent appointments with some degree of conditions of security attached to them, like for instance those held by civil servants and teachers with a government appointment or the core staff of the sugar mill, were highly exceptional. Alongside the security which the privileged position gave them, the recurring regularity of the working day, plus its interspersion with free time, invested the rare possessors of these functions in the formal sector of the economy with respectability. The transference of knowledge and capital from the older to the younger generation reinforced the tendency of households to concentrate on a particular occupation.

In order to give an impression of their familiarity with their particular occupation, the informants used the term *jodoh*, which indicated that such work was what they were fated to do. However, it would be jumping to conclusions to assume from this that the working population of East Cirebon was split up into a number of various clusters which were separate from one another. The segmentation of employment was valid only to a certain degree. Opposing it was a converse trend which exerted just as strong an influence, namely multiple employment. The changing of the seasons and the zeniths and nadirs in the rhythm of production made it necessary to look for other work in another period of the year. The decline in business in both the construction industry in Jabotabek and in brick-making in the village itself meant a loss of income which both the labour migrants and the brick-makers tried to compensate for by work in the agricultural sector. It would be incorrect to describe this change as effortless and smooth. The stereotypical image presented in the migration literature of agricultural work with one foot still in the sawah and the other foot in an urban factory did not apply to East Cirebon and had probably never applied there. Longer or shorter periods of enforced idleness were certainly not exceptional. But, given the low wages for unskilled work in particular, it was out of the question for agricultural workers, navvies, brick-makers, and porters to retain enough of their usual income in any one of these occupations to cover their living expenses during days or weeks without work. Being burdened with a heavy credit risk meant that they had no other choice than to seek the same sort of work in another branch of employment.

This occupational multiplicity was, on the other hand, not a phenomenon which was confined to the lower echelons of the economy. For very different reasons, above all extending their profits, to just as little extent did the owners of capital restrict themselves to their main job. The owner of a number of brick-works did not just buy a number of trucks to transport what he produced, but he also purchased a bus to transport people on the route from Ciledug to Cirebon; *cukong* who delivered huge quantities of sugarcane to the mills also appeared in the guise of rice wholesalers; members of the village administration had income on the side as money-lenders and so forth and so on.

Far more important than the vertical compartmentalization which divided up the various occupations in the different sections of the economy was the social differentiation in the horizontal sense for which the possession, or alternatively the lack of capital was the most important yardstick. At the beginning of the twentieth century East Cirebon had three social classes, referred to respectively as *sikep*, *tangkung* and *penumpang*. The *sikep* were acknowledged to be the descendants of the founders of the village and as a group had a grasp on all the communal land. The village administration was drawn from their ranks. The *tangkung* were second-category farmers who certainly could make no claim to any share of the communal fields but were registered as prospective candidates. Should a place fall vacant as the result of a death or the moving away of remaining descendants of one of those with such a right, it was assigned to them. The third category was composed of landless agricultural labourers who in the past had been counted as members of farmers' households and had performed the corvée services, which the colonial government imposed on the propertied classes, in their master's name. More particulars about this stratum of agricultural society in East Cirebon can be found in Breman's historical study (1983). In this agrarian regime, land was obviously the most pre-eminent form of capital. The changes in the economic pattern of East Cirebon which have set in at an accelerated pace in the second half of the twentieth century have not left the social hierarchy unscathed. At the time the 1989 research was carried out, capital was still the most important key in allotting social positions but the unrelenting marginalization of agriculture had meant that forms of ownership other than that of land had begun to tip the scales. The new division of the four hundred and ninety-five households of which the village consisted in that year was based on a splitting up into three social classes: high, middle, and low. The answers to our questions about the numerical size of each of these categories, put to a limited number of random respondents, did diverge from each other by any significant margins. The classification produced the following result: the prominent upper layer consisted of about 17% of the households which could lay claim to more than four-tenths of the total income generated; the middle class was composed of 33% of the households, the bulk of which was in receipt of a third of the receipts derived from the economy; the bottom layer comprised 50% but could be subdivided into two, the poor who made up 35% and the extremely poor who consisted of 15% of the households who had to make do together with one-fifth of the village income split up into a proportion of roughly 4:1. This inequity in the access to the sources of livelihood inside and outside East Cirebon must be examined in more detail. To begin with there are a few details about the prominent upper stratum. Just as in the past village leadership was in the hands of the *pamong desa* who were recruited from a limited number of families. By allowing them the profits of a disproportionate part of the privately owned agricultural land, they were turned into cheap figureheads for the government. These representatives of the state at the lowest administrative level were granted competences and sanctions by which they could derive extra income which was never noted in the official bookkeeping. This explains why those who aspired to the position were willing to pay for their entry into the village administration. The election campaigns were costly affairs, requiring high payments both front and back stage of the political scene. The *kuwu* who emerged victorious from this fray had in fact already bought their voice in local affairs as moneylenders and during their term of office acted as executors of their own directives. The village head and his immediate associates maintained close ties with the bureaucratic and military authorities who formed the hub of the power network of the sub-district and district of which East Cirebon was part. The exposure of these links in this configuration was taboo as a subject for public discussion.

The farmers who owned the most land, the traders who acted as producers and suppliers of sugar cane to the mills, the wholesale buyers of rice, two brothers who owned a rice mill, large shopkeepers who offered all sorts of urban consumer goods to the village population, the *bandar* of the larger brickworks and the owners of the trucks and vans also formed part of this coterie of prominent people who managed village affairs between themselves. The sort of house in which they lived was valued between five and fifteen million rupiah and would have fetched many times that price in a town. In many other respects their way of life bore testimony to a level of prosperity which left the other inhabitants of the village for dead. In this milieu their children enjoyed a full-fledged schooling and with this in their pockets the younger generation were able to penetrate the formal sector of the economy in a few instances. This was equally true of the three primary school teachers and a few civil servants who were employed in the sub-district office. This elite had abandoned any form of personal physical labour.

The middle class consisted of small-scale traders and businessmen who still did not scorn physical work but did this on their own account and at their own risk as well as having greater skills in their chosen occupations. These were the small shopkeepers and small-scale traders, including the *calo*, the owners of small brickworks who worked there themselves, the more skilled among the construction workers and tradesmen, the drivers of the delivery trucks and vans, the young men who transported passengers on their motorbikes, a few low-ranking employees with a permanent job at the sugar mill, and finally the gang bosses who also acted as leaders of the work teams in Jabotabek. Their lifestyle was simpler than that of the elite with houses which were less elaborate but still had brick walls and glass in the windows, children who were able to attend secondary school but could not go on to higher education, more modest furnishings but still with a level of consumption which gave a strong impression of an urban life-style and could certainly be qualified as presentable. Contributing to their comfort was the (small) buffer they had built up which offered them the opportunity to square up to unexpected reverses. This on its own was enough for them to be considered creditworthy.

The rural proletariat was made up of tenant farmers with a small piece of land of their own, itinerant peddlers, agricultural workers, and navvies, brick-makers, and porters, builder's mates in the construction industry, driver's mates, the men who loaded and unloaded the trucks, the drivers of bike-taxis. Apart from a few exceptions like the owners of *becak*, none of these workers possessed their own means of production unless this was something in the order of a shovel, a hoe, a sickle, a *pikul* or a brick-maker's mould. In other words they lived from the proceeds of their physical labour and referred to themselves as *kuli, buruh liar, pekerja tidak tetap, buruh macul* or *pacul*. These terms were a ready reference to the sort of work they were able to tackle and also served to express their lack of specialization in training in their necessity to look for an income every day afresh, inside or outside agriculture, in the village itself or elsewhere, but firmly stuck at the bottom of the economy. Their houses were more poverty-stricken, even though they were already being built of brick. Around their houses were strewn building materials, bought in small lots to improve the quality of their dwellings. Children did attend school but mostly did not go on to any secondary level. Furnishings were sparse because these households possessed only few durable or high-quality commodities. The possibility to save for a rainy day – illness or longer periods of forced idleness – was virtually out of the question. The earnings from the labour migration to Jabotabek could not be used to invest in the future. The first task facing the men on their periodical returns to East Cirebon was to pay off the debts incurred with moneylenders and *warung* keepers. It was only by taking recourse to these sources of credit that non-working members of households who remained behind in the village could provide for their cost of living. The providers of credit were prepared to throw out a lifeline as long as repayment with a reasonable degree of certainty was a real prospect. Conversely brick-makers could apply for an advance for work which still had to be done, providing that their efforts in the past indicated that they would deliver the goods. These practices of paying in advance or settling of wages in retrospect simultaneously serve to illustrate the precariousness of the lives of the bottom layer of the village. Loss of their ability to produce spelled not just a structural decline in their income, it was accompanied by the drying up of sources of credit to which recourse could be made in cases of dire necessity.

The poorest segment, to which we estimated one-fifth of the village belonged, had to live under these circumstances. They simply did not possess the wherewithal to provide a tolerable income for themselves independently. In other instances, it comprised people whose capacity to work could not be fully utilized as the result of some other call which was placed on their availability. These included the elderly who were steadily having to withdraw from the work process, as well as the chronically ill or handicapped who were able to contribute little or nothing and often could not afford the medical care which they needed, and finally women on their own – widows or divorcees – especially when they had to carry the extra burden of caring for small children. This dependent category tried to seek safety by attaching themselves to a household with working members. In many cases theirs was a forlorn hope and unproductive villagers or those who could produce very little but still had to maintain their own households lived in great and visible poverty. Their houses were extremely small and ramshackle, and the same applied to their furnishings. They could barely afford any durable consumer goods, even the simplest. The incidental help offered by neighbours and children or other family members who lived independently was indispensable in keeping their heads above water. But this did not absolve them for the necessity to seek work, even though this was highly irregular and brought in a mere pittance: the gleaning of the rice harvest in the fields; all sorts of services at *slametan* and other feasts in the area; the making of *welitan*, the woven reed mats which were used for the roofing of the brick sheds; helping a couple in the brickworks with the moulding of a extra quantity of bricks; preparing of food which would they then take around and sell themselves or to *warung* keepers, and so forth.

The class differences were more fluid than rigid and instead of solidifying into closed segments, there were instances of mobility in both directions, upwards and downwards, not just in the case of father and son but also over a shorter period and within the same generation. The circumstances under which this happened were in part structural and in part of a much more fortuitous nature. A favourable balance between working and non-working members over a series of years stimulated accumulation of means and after that, if this was invested soundly, could lead to the socio-economic rise of the household in question. A builder's helper in construction or a co-driver on a truck hoped that by training on the job they would qualify for work which paid considerably better and was also associated with a higher social status. Men who were thoroughly acquainted with the brick-maker's trade were seized with the ambition to begin their own small brickworks. But the climb was generally limited and seldom led to anything more elevated than a rise to the next highest class. A case like that of a labour migrant who opened a shop with his earnings after he returned from abroad, which grew to be one of the biggest in East Cirebon, was simply a matter of luck according to local opinion. Conversely, several gang bosses complained of having had bad luck, in the sense that they had missed the support of the contractors at an opportune moment which would have meant they could have worked their way up to being sub-contractors. Downward mobility was also associated with factors which had effects which were virtually impossible to avoid, like the end of a working life with increasing age. In contrast to those who had capital who usually succeeded in saving themselves before any irrevocable damage had been done, those who had no property had much less chance of offering resistance to their inexorable decline. Economic regression could also be an effect of more chance circumstances: exclusion from production as the result of illness, the collapse of a marriage, a family quarrel, men who gambled away their possessions and the like.

Alongside the division into social classes and the limited degree of movement within the local hierarchy, one aspect to which we paid attention was the improvement in prosperity which had occurred in the recent past. Before launching into this it should be noted that the growth in production has effected no changes in the prevailing inequality. In fact, the old stratification was the point of departure for the specification of the new economic order. Broadly speaking the social placements in this new order bore witness to a continuation of the dividing lines which had earlier settled into place between the landowners and the landless. Nevertheless, the inhabitants of East Cirebon were unanimous in their judgement that, in 1989, the standard of living for all of them was higher than it had been in the preceding generation. This generally held evaluation should be seen against the background of a continuous growth in population, not solved by departing for some other place, in combination with the stagnation, even the decline in employment opportunities in agriculture. The fact that the ever-increasing pressure on the agrarian means of subsistence was not translated into a massive impoverishment of the landless strata has to be ascribed to the expansion of both the local and non-local market for labour in a more diversified economy. In a nutshell, what this means is that more work became available, both in the village and outside it. It was no longer necessary to go to the fields at two or three in the morning in order to beat other competitors to take part in the rice harvest. The virtually offhand remark by an informant from among the landless was testimony to a battle for existence which had been part and parcel of life less than a quarter of a century earlier.

The rise in the demand for labour reflected both the shift in the pattern of employment in East Cirebon itself – the result of the development of the brick industry – and the strong reinforcement of the earlier link with the metropolitan economy of Jabotabek. The poverty in which the landless lowest class in the countryside of East Cirebon had to live was the outcome of low wages and insufficient sources of income for a large part of the year. In the latter regard, a tremendous improvement was set in motion with the expansion of employment in the non-agrarian sectors of the economy but without this effecting any fundamental change in the paltry daily earnings of the poorly skilled and unskilled labour.

One yardstick of the degree of progress achieved was the improved quality of the housing for all levels of the population. However, the price which had to be paid above all by those among the landless was also plain. The brick-makers could only make ends meet by bringing other members of the household, wife and children, into the production process. Without this additional labour the income remained below the minimal expenditure for daily necessities. The up side of this was that at least they could live together as a family. This comfort was denied the families of the labour migrants. Admittedly the road to Jabotabek guaranteed employment for a greater number of days per year than had ever been offered in the earlier rural economy. But none of the migrants said that they preferred this restless existence to remaining put in the village. As travellers in an economic landscape which was alien to them, they missed the contact with East Cirebon in general and naturally with the members of their own households above all else. Both the time spent on the building site in the zone around the capital and the return there was unattractive but ineluctable. The fact that so many men from the village made the choice was born of pure economic necessity.

CHAPTER V

The impact of krismon

Introductory note

The initial reports on *krismon* suggested that the effects of the crisis were mainly felt in the urban economy. After all, the large-scale industry and other formal sector enterprises which laid off part or all of their workforce were located in the cities. Little attention was paid to the situation in the countryside, where most of Java's working population lived, as the financial crisis blew up into a full-scale economic malaise. To capture the impact of the crisis on employment and prosperity in rural Java, we decided to return to the villages along the north coast of West Java in which research had been carried out before. Both of us already had been, not together but separately, involved in fieldwork in East Cirebon at the end of the 1980s. We decided to team up in our efforts to investigate the impact of *krismon* and return to some of the fieldwork sites with which we had become familiar ten or more years ago.

During a first exploratory visit to the village in March andApril 1998 we were informed that the circular labour migration of a large segment of the male workforce to Jabotabek had come to an abrupt end. With no work or income, most of these labouring nomads just hung around the house, stunned by their sudden dismissal and hoping that the building projects on which they had been working until recently would soon resume. The impact of the crisis was not, however, restricted to those who depended on income from work outside the village. At the start of the 1998, after subsidies on basic necessities had been scrapped, prices had risen sharply, resulting in a dramatic fall in the standard of living of the majority of households. There were incidents of looting and arson in the nearby market towns of Ciledug and Sindanglaut. As elsewhere, Chinese traders and shopkeepers bore the brunt of the violence. Our second round of fieldwork took place in July and August 1998, several months after the fall of Suharto. The crisis had acquired a political dimension, a broadening of the process of disintegration that was reflected in a change in the term popularly used to describe it. *Krismon* had become *kristal*. The unrest before and during the change of power at the end of May provoked a new exodus of migrant labour from the cities. Many who had, until then, succeeded with great difficulty in surviving in Jabotabek fled the conurbation to wait for better and – just as important – less turbulent times. Their exodus was a symptom not only of the chaos reigning in the urban labour market, but also expressed the feeling of insecurity that had gripped this mass of casual workers, who lacked any deeply rooted ties with the metropolitan milieu in which they struggled to make a living. The forced optimism that we had encountered in East Cirebon in March and April – the resolute assertions that the recession would not last – had been replaced by a more realistic awareness that economic recovery would be a long process, and would require far-reaching political reform.

During the third round of our study, in March and April 1999, the main issue on which we focused was how the people of the village had adapted to the change in their livelihood since the outbreak of the crisis. We concentrated on the action taken by the state to alleviate widespread distress. A short final round of our investigations in East Cirebon in August 2000 allowed us to test the accuracy of reports that there had been a clear improvement in the economic situation since the beginning of that year. Was *krismon* a thing of the past and had employment in the leading sectors of industry experienced a strong recovery? And was this recovery really accompanied by a substantial improvement in the purchasing power of the people which had fallen so sharply in the last two years?

Our account is based on the information gathered during the various stages of our study. In addition to qualitative observations, recorded in interviews and diaries, our analysis is backed up by quantified data which we collected during the second and third rounds of our stay. An initial survey which we conducted in July 1998 covered nearly a third of the village population. The sample consisted of one hundred and forty-eight houses, inhabited by one hundred and seventy-nine households and consisting of eight hundred and seventy-three men, women and children. The selection was representative of the four hamlets which comprised East Cirebon. The decision to include or exclude households was random, but ensured a reasonable spread across the area covered by each hamlet. The basic data obtained from the survey recorded the age and gender of the household members, their status in respect of the head of the household, whether they were workers or non-workers, the occupations of the working members (both within and outside the village), whether they were working at the time of the survey, the quality of the dwelling and its fittings and furnishings; the education the respondents had completed (or were still engaged in) and their state of health. In August of the same year we arranged for a group of three students from the Institut Pertanian Bogor to conduct a follow-up survey for which they gathered the same information from the remaining households in the village. Their data was a welcome supplement to our own statistics. We concluded the final round of the study in March and April 1999 with a repeat of the earlier survey, but this time restricted to half of the respondents (randomly selected) who had been interviewed nine months previously.

Socio-economic change in East Cirebon 1989-1998

Mid-1998, East Cirebon had a population of two thousand seven hundred and nine (one thousand three hundred and twenty-eight men and one thousand three hundred and eighty-one women), an increase of 1.8% per year since 1989. This meant that, in the intervening years, the already very high population density had intensified further, rising from two thousand and forty-nine to two thousand and seventy-five per square kilometre. In this respect, the village was no exception; throughout the entire eastern part of Cirebon district, the figure was roughly the same. In mid-1998, East Cirebon had four hundred and sixty dwellings containing five hundred and eighty-two households. This represented a fall in the number of households per dwelling with respect to 1989 from 1.47 to 1.21. A trend that we had observed a decade earlier also appeared to have continued: a shift from the multi-generational household to the nuclear family as the basic unit for cohabitation. A decrease in the average number of residents per dwelling from seven to six is a logical result of this development. Average household size had stayed reasonably constant, at 4.7 members.

To provide a general impression of economic life in East Cirebon at the start of our fieldwork, all heads of households were classified according to occupation. Of the total of five hundred and eighty-two, thirty-five (6%) were not economically active. The majority were old people, living alone or as couples, or men and women with long-term disabilities but still managing

Table 1. Occupations of economically active heads of households in mid-1998

Sector	Number	Percentage
Agriculture	97	18
Building	122	22
Brickworks	151	28
Transport	40	7
Trade	32	6
Other crafts and services	39	7
Government service	17	3
Casual and unskilled labour	49	9
Total	547	100

Source: basic household survey Breman and Wiradi, July-August 1998.

their own household. Table 1 shows the five hundred and forty-seven economically active heads of households, categorized according to the sector of the economy in which they themselves claimed to work.

The distribution over the various sectors can be subdivided further:

a according to gender: of the total of five hundred and eighty-two heads of households, forty-one were women (including widows and eight who had never married). A substantial number of these were economically non-active; those who were have been included in the sectors in which they earn their living (agriculture, trade, other crafts and services);

b on the basis of capital ownership and education.

This more detailed classification produces the categorization shown in Table 2.

Table 2. Occupations of economically active heads of households, sub-classified according to capital ownership and education/training

Sector	Capital owners and/or with vocational training		Propertyless/no education	
Agriculture	peasant farmers/tenants	46	farm labourers	51
Building	foremen and skilled labs.	33	casual and unskilled	89
Brickworks	owners	22	brickmakers	129
Transport	owners	17	drivers/helpers	23
Trade	traders, shopkeepers	10	street vendors	22
Other crafts and services	small producers	12	unskilled workers	27
Government service	civil servants	16	guard/messenger	1
Other casual workers	other casual workers	–		49
Total		391		156

Source: Basic household survey Breman and Wiradi, July-August 1998.

Before elaborating on the pattern of employment and income in the different economic sectors, we want to make some preliminary comments on the elementary dichotomy in having or not having means of production and occupational skills. In agriculture, ownership of capital generally means land or, in the case of tenants, disposal over farming tools and funds (cash or access to credit) necessary to work the land. Business capital can be substantial, but may also consist of little more than, for example, the modest equipment required by a tailor (in the 'other crafts' category). A good illustration of the relative nature of this distinction can be found in the widely varying value of property in the transport sector. Trucks, delivery vans or minibuses are very expensive but also give a much higher return to their owners than enjoyed by buyers of motorcycles that are used to carry passengers (*ojeg*) or of the three-wheeled pedicabs (*becak*). Traders include not only large shopkeepers, moneylenders, dealers in rice and other agrarian produce, and brokers (*calo*) who act as commission agents in commercial transactions, but also those who run the small food stalls (*warung*) or vendors of wares (prepared food, fruit, ice, pieces of cloth, crockery, and the like) walking in and around the village with shoulder baskets (*pikul*), a bicycle or handcart (*grobak*). In the strict sense of the word, the latter two categories also have a small amount of business capital, but this is so negligible that we clubbed the holders of the smallest *warung* and the perambulatory vendors (*pedagang keliling*) among the propertyless.

In the same way, the distinction between educated/trained and uneducated/untrained needs some qualification. The heads of households who are employed as government officials have all had at least a secondary education. This is in stark contrast to those who earn a living in the building industry as carpenters, bricklayers, plumbers, tilers, and the like. Almost none of these have had a formal schooling but have learned their trades gradually while working. Their acquired skills enable them to earn considerably more than the countless unskilled labourers working in the same industry. Gang bosses, foremen and subcontractors, too, have worked their way up to these managerial positions. Their added value in respect of the labourers whom they supervise is also reflected in higher earnings. As these examples show, not all unskilled labourers are doomed to end their working lives that way. The *kenek* assisting a skilled worker – often his father or brother – will learn the tricks of the trade from them and is eventually allowed to call himself a craftsman, too. This is also how drivers' mates learn how to drive trucks and other motor vehicles, by watching and practising. The fact that we have put experienced drivers, who – as holders of a licence – could qualify as skilled hands, in the final category of Table 2, shows once again that our classification is not entirely consistent. We have classified drivers as unskilled because the difference in economic status between them and the drivers' mates is far less than that between them and the owners of the vehicles. Apart from a few exceptions of this nature, there is a reasonably close connection between capital ownership and a higher form of education or training. The majority of owners of means of production also have more in-depth knowledge of their profession, while lack of property and of formal education also tend to coincide. Only a little over a quarter of the heads of households (28.5%) fall into the first category. This disproportionate distribution of both factors of production shown in Table 2 is also expressed, as we shall see later, in the significant differences in prosperity levels among the people of East Cirebon.

Secondly, we would like to emphasize that the classification in Table 2 is based on the forms of employment that provide the main source of income. In many cases, the occupation mentioned first is practised together with other forms of work. This multiplicity can sometimes take the shape of activities practised simultaneously, but is often – as in the case of agricultural work – seasonal in nature. During the peaks in the agrarian cycle, the heads of households who refer to cultivation as their main source of livelihood are joined by many others, including brick-makers and earth-movers from the building sector. Conversely, many farm labourers seek work in other sectors when there is nothing for them to do in the fields. It is not only unskilled labourers who have multiple occupations. While, for the majority of the working population, this a way of keeping their heads above water, for those with capital it is a way of increasing their surplus. Local government officials, for example, supplement their salaries by lending money, while the brickworks owners buy not only delivery vans but also minibuses (*angkot*), which they then rent out for use as passenger transport.

Our impression is that this occupational variability received a strong boost with the outbreak of the economic crisis. The recession hit some sectors so hard that many of those who earned their living working in them can no longer do so on a full-time basis. Heads of households who until recently worked in the building sector in Jabotabek have been hit particularly hard. The major part of this army of labour migrants from East Cirebon has since returned to the village. Although many have not yet given up hope of economic recovery in the near future, for the time being they are compelled to seek work elsewhere. Some of them seem to have made a definite break with the kind of work they did previously. This shift in the pattern of employment as a result of the crisis will be considered in greater detail later. First, however, we want to examine the dynamics of the village economy, taking as a starting point the sectoral distribution as it existed roughly ten years ago.

Agriculture

Agriculture accounted for a limited percentage of the economic activity in 1990 and had declined even more in importance a decade later. In 1989, 14% of households owned land, while in 1998 this had fallen to 10%. The change cannot be attributed solely to demographic growth with a constant area of cultivable land. Land has been sold off and consequently become concentrated in the hands of a smaller number of landowners. Several of those who sold their agrarian property used the proceeds to set up a brickworks, an indication of the low returns from cultivation. The agro-industry still takes up a large share of the land in the village, but this now occurs in a different way. The seven state-owned sugar mills in the district of Cirebon have become privatized. This change, which took place some years ago, coincided with the abolition of the tri (*tebu rakyat intensifikasi*) system, under which owner-cultivators had to surrender part of their land to the mills. *Tri* has been replaced by the free renting of fields. By increasing the price for using farm land on a rotational basis, the sugar industry has so far succeeded in preserving the acreage planted with sugar cane at the previous level of 60% of all cultivable land belonging to East Cirebon. *Bengkok*, salary lands which are given to senior members of the village administration, still form the backbone of the agro-industrial power complex in the region. There are, however, signs that this may change in the near future. The cultivation of rice yields a far higher profit for landowners. Farmers only agree to surrender their fields to the sugar mills temporarily because they are pressurized to do so by the village administration. But there are those who pertinently refuse to sign a rental contract at all and the management of the sugar companies are worried that the total acreage available for the cultivation of sugar cane may fall below the minimum level for viable continuation of their industry. The smallest landowners – with less than 0.2 hectares of cultivable land – are not counted as such in our calculations. The yield from their land is so low that they cannot depend on it for their livelihood. They are therefore classified as farm labourers, small traders, brick-makers or casual labourers. Farm labourers having no agrarian means of production outnumber by far those who work the land as owners or sharecroppers. Taking all those who are dependent on agricultural production in one way or the other together, we see that the already limited extent of employment in the sector – estimated at a quarter of all households in 1989 – has decreased further to a fifth. The fact that nearly all newcomers to the workforce of East Cirebon had to be absorbed in other branches of economic activity signals that, with the available technology and current land use, the agrarian resource base could not tolerate any additional manpower. In the period from 1989 to mid-1998 the agrarian density, the ratio of number of inhabitants to hectare of cultivable land rose from almost twenty-five to twenty-nine. There have been no notable changes in agricultural methods. As we have seen, most of the land that could be cultivated by farmers is being used for sugar cane. The remaining fields are planted with the same crops as before – mainly rice – and are worked by the owner or by sharecroppers. The terms of leasing or sharecropping agreements have not changed, and also farm labourers are employed in the same way as they used to be.

Farm labourers are among the lowest paid members of the workforce. In 1998, their daily wage was more than three times what it had been ten years previously: five thousand rupiah for men and between two thousand and a maximum of three thousand rupiah for women. They receive a meal during the working day, which lasts from seven in the morning to twelve noon, and some snacks at the end. The sugar mills employ people on a piecework basis (*borongan*), the men for digging and the women to do the weeding. Here, too, the men earn twice as much as the women (six thousand rupiah). Both have to work longer hours than when they are employed by farmers and receive no food as part of the payment. Almost none of them are willing to cut cane in the milling season. This has not changed during the period under study. The sugar mills pay five hundred rupiah per quintal. At three quintals (0.3 tons) a day, the production of the local cutters is way behind that of the seasonal migrants from Central Java, who harvest eight quintals a day. This earns them less than an acceptable minimum daily wage. For the rice harvest, the *ceblokan* system (in which farmers agree to pay labourers a share of the harvest in kind) is still in use and the conditions of this agreement, which is for the whole growing cycle, remain unchanged. Although we were told that farmers were formerly prepared to pay a little extra for transplanting the rice and other operations preceding the harvest, farm labourers can no longer count on this welcome addition to their abysmally low income. All they receive now for the field operations during the growth cycle is a share of the harvest – a fifth of the total yield. Working together with their wives they can earn a payment in kind of twenty to forty – sometimes even sixty – kilograms of *gabah* (wet and unhusked rice) per day. The larger farmers tend to demand more work for the same share, or to pay out a smaller share of the harvest. In addition to the farm labourers who work on the land throughout the year, many other members of the landless under-class, including brick-makers, carriers and earth-movers, try to acquire *ceblokan* contracts in an effort to build up food reserves for their households. Often, however, they have to sell at least part of their income in kind in order to take care of other cash needs.

What has been the impact of the economic crisis on agriculture? The abolition of subsidies on artificial fertilizer, insecticide and pesticide led to price rises, causing farmers with insufficient capital to buy less of these inputs. The average yield in 2000 is 3.5 tons per hectare in the dry season and 2 tons per hectare in the rainy season. Traders are willing to pay one hundred twenty thousand rupiah per quintal. Although this is far higher than in previous years, the low productivity means that the farming business is not very profitable.

The daily wage for farm labourers has increased to ten thousand rupiah. There seems to be a rather close relationship between the return to their labour and the cost of their food requirements on a day-to-day basis. But consumers have to pay two or three times more for their rice rations than before the outbreak of the crisis. Although the largest part of the price increase does not find its way back to the farmers, they have benefited from the increased value of their produce. Generally speaking agriculture has not done so badly in comparison to the other branches of economic activity. If the cultivation of food crops were to generate higher profits than before, a growing number of landowners would cease renting their fields out to the agro-industry. This shift towards self-cultivation could lead to a slight and possibly temporary growth in the size of the agrarian workforce of East Cirebon. With population pressure having increased to such a high figure and land ownership concentrated in the hands of a small number of households, we consider the chances of a return to a situation in which village economy would be once again dominated by agriculture, as very slight. A certain recovery is certainly feasible but it is easy to exaggerate the scale it may take, given the relatively sombre prospects in other sectors of the economy which are faced with falling employment and income.

The agro-industry appears to face a difficult future and the closure of one or more of the sugar mills in the area – including the one at Karangsuwung – is a real possibility. The plant is in a thoroughly run-down state and many years of fraudulent management have pushed the cost price way above that on the global market. Payment to the farmers of the land rent is far too late, which eventually leads to a decrease in the area of land available for cane. This trend is reinforced by the inability of the regional authorities to make it compulsory for owners to hand over their fields to the mills.[1]

Building industry

In 1989, the building sector was the main provider of income for East Cirebon's workforce. The rapid expansion of the industry was closely related to the almost insatiable demand for workers in the satellite zone around Jakarta for the construction of factories and commercial premises, residential quarters and the concomitant infrastructure such as roads, bridges, sewers, mains water pipes, electricity and telephone cables which together give this national growth pole its metropolitan allure. The labour power for this turbulent growth, which continued unabated until the mid-1990s, came from the hinterland of Java, in the form of an army of migrant labourers who were kept in a permanent state of flux. They were recruited by a jobber-cum-foreman, who contracted them for not longer than the duration of a project. This meant that they drifted from job to job, an existence that most of them kept up for many years. This routine was interrupted only by the irregular and always short visits that they would make every few weeks or months to their households back in the village. These visits illustrate that the push of these migrant workers from their rural homes was more economic than social. In 1989, we estimated that as many as a quarter of the households in East Cirebon depended on the incomes earned by this workforce of circular migrants. In the years that followed, however, this percentage rose even further. Our

1 Shortly before sending this manuscript to press news has reached us that all mills in the vicinity of East Cirebon might be closed down in future. Under strong pressure from abroad to open up the market for the import of sugar produced elsewhere much more cheaply than in Indonesia, sugar cane now could disappear from a landscape in which it has been the dominant crop for nearly two hundred years.

estimate is that in mid-1997, just before the crisis broke out, around 30% of heads of households were working in the building sector and, with a very few exceptions, they commuted to Jabotabek.

The division between skilled and unskilled workers remained constant over this period, with the former (for example carpenters, bricklayers, plasterers, electricians) outnumbered the latter (which included apart from youngsters working as apprentices, also older labourers more permanently without skills) by almost three to one. There were six *mandur* (gang bosses) living in East Cirebon. With the exception of one who had succeeded in becoming a subcontractor, they all earned a living recruiting and supervising gangs of labourers for Jabotabek.

In the decade since the earlier fieldwork, wage levels more or less kept abreast of the rising cost of living. In mid-1997, unskilled building labourers could expect a daily wage of between ten thousand and fifteen thousand rupiah, with skilled workers earning at least five thousand rupiah more. There were a few technicians who were more regularly employed by contractors, such as an installation engineer, who was paid seven hundred thousand rupiah a month. These were gross amounts, from which a number of costs had to be deducted, such as meals, cigarettes and the like, and sometimes rent for a roof over their heads. This means that skilled workers would have some eight thousand rupiah left from their daily wage, while skilled workers would retain as little as four thousand to five thousand rupiah. If the work stopped for any reason, the migrants would have to eat into their savings. In addition to normal days off, this could be caused by delayed deliveries of building materials or just bad co-ordination between the contractor and the site managers. Sometimes they would be unable to work because of illness. There had been no change in the habit of returning to East Cirebon every six weeks or two months. The costs of the return journey were twenty thousand rupiah. On their regular visits home they would bring with them the money they had saved for the maintenance of their households. This would vary between one hundred fifty thousand and two hundred fifty thousand rupiah, depending on their earnings and the length of time they had been away. A large part of the money would mostly immediately spent on repayments to shopkeepers or moneylenders.

None of the sectors of the village economy suffered as much from the crisis as the building sector. As mentioned in the introduction, this was actually the reason to renew our fieldwork in East Cirebon. A large majority of the building workers who worked in Jabotabek returned to the village for an unknown period between mid-1997 and July 1998. The projects on which they were working often stopped from one day to the next. The *mandur* was told that he and his crew could leave and that they should not count on work being resumed in the near future. Many of those sacked on the spot (known as *phk*) also received no wages for the last few days' or weeks' work. The enforced return of this army of migrant workers led to a significant change in the employment pattern. When asked about their main source of income, a large number of heads of households no longer referred to their former jobs in Jabotabek. This explains the fall in the proportion of heads of households working in the building sector from around 30% just prior to the outbreak of the crisis in mid-1997 to 22% a year later. Nevertheless, quite a large majority of these erstwhile labour nomads were quite eager not to dissociate themselves from the occupational identity built up in the urban conglomeration over many years.

This group falls into two categories. Firstly, there are those who continue to search for work in the building sector in and around East Cirebon with a reasonable degree of success. Although the implementation of public works in the countryside has as good as come to a halt, house construction and renovation in the village seems to have suffered less from the crisis. Skilled workers in particular – for example carpenters, bricklayers – manage to find work in the close vicinity of the village for at least a few days a week. They earn less than they did in Jabotabek – from twelve thousand to a maximum of fifteen thousand rupiah per day – but do receive a midday meal, as is the custom in rural Java. Their travel costs, which can vary from two thousand to five thousand rupiah depending on the distance from East Cirebon, have to be deducted from this daily wage. It is more difficult for unskilled labourers to find employment on these local building projects. There are generally enough family members and neighbours around who are prepared to do the digging and carrying work in exchange for free meals.

The second category who still consider themselves to be building workers are those who have not given up hope of a speedy end to the recession. Many still go hunting for jobs in Jabotabek where they meet former workmates and visit familiar construction sites in the hope that projects may have continued or even have restarted. Most gave up making these sorties after the first few months, but a reasonably large number still keep it up for as long as a year after their return. They are prepared to use the last of their money, or to borrow some more, for such desperate expeditions. What makes them keep trying is the hope that, although the jobber or contractor for whom they worked may have no need for them, others might. They spare no effort in trying to find new avenues of employment, but usually with little or no success. It is then not long before they once again have to make the difficult journey home. With no income, their stay in Jabotabek is short. The stories that do the rounds in the village about these sorry adventurers do not seem to deter others, especially the young men, from trying their luck over and over again. The tenacity with which they continue to make the trip to the city, sometimes

Construction workers returned from Jabotabek in search of local employment

against their own better judgement, shows how difficult it is for them to reintegrate into the village economy. In August 2000 a navvy (*kuli gali*) told us that he had returned the day before from three weeks in Bekasi. He had been to see the owner of a *warung* who he used to know. The man had fed him and given him a place to sleep free of charge. After three days he had found three weeks' work digging trenches for a water main. For a day's work, from 7.30 in the morning to 4 in the afternoon, he was paid seventeen thousand rupiah. This was more than he used to earn but, because of the higher price of food, he was able to save less. When the job was finished he waited for other work for four days, but then returned to East Cirebon. He told us that, since his net earnings of eighty thousand rupiah on this three-week trip were totally inadequate to maintain his family, he would be leaving for the city again the next day.

Brick-making

According to our survey this rural industry had become the largest branch of employment in East Cirebon in 1998. In 1989, there were more than thirty small-scale brickworks in operation, and since then fifteen more have been opened, many of which are in the hands of the same group of owners. Since all available land is already being used to the full, some of the works have to get the earth to make the bricks from elsewhere. The production process remains unchanged, labour-intensive and providing work for men, women and children. We did not count the children, who help their parents from an early age, as part of the workforce. They are not full-time workers, as – from the age of six – they combine their work in the brick fields with attending school. But even if we do exclude these youngsters, brick-making has become the leading economic sector, providing 28% of total employment opportunities.

As already mentioned, as a result of the crisis, the production of bricks fell from late 1997 onwards. The fall would have been even more severe if it were not for the continued construction and improvement of houses in rural areas. In East Cirebon itself, the number of houses rose from three hundred and thirty-six in 1989 to four hundred and sixty in 1998. This is a much greater increase than would be expected from the growth in village population, and is the result of reduction in the average number of residents per house. Generations no longer tend to live together in the same house and even more than before the nuclear family has become the typical form of cohabitation. While this trend continues, there has been another significant change: brick is replacing wood and *bilik* (walls made of bamboo or woven mats) as the preferred choice of material for house building. We noted this trend ten years ago, and since then it has become even more pronounced. The prevalence of brick gives the rural architecture an 'urban' feel to it. This is reinforced by the bungalow-type houses built by those who have worked abroad for some years. The owners of brickworks told us that a significant proportion of their products are sold to contractors working for these clients in the wider surroundings of the village. They have the crisis to thank for these orders because, due to the fall in the value of the rupiah, the remittances coming from abroad have much increased in value.

In mid-1998 bricks were sold for sixty thousand rupiah per thousand, but two years later the price had increased to ninety thousand to one hundred thousand rupiah. The increase reflected a proportional increase in production costs. In 1998, a team of two adult workers were paid ten thousand rupiah for every thousand bricks they supplied to the kiln. By mid- 2000, this had risen to twelve thousand to fourteen thousand rupiah. To bake a thousand bricks twenty to twenty-five sacks of chaff are required, at a price of one thousand rupiah per sack. The kiln workers were paid five thousand rupiah per thousand bricks in 1998, and carriers received two thousand rupiah for every thousand bricks they removed from the kiln. These rates, too, had increased by 40% two years later. Taking into account all production costs – and assuming that the ratio of material to labour remained constant at 60:40 – a thousand bricks cost forty thousand to forty-five thousand rupiah to make in 1998. This amount was substantially higher two years later, but the sales price had risen more in relative terms. Consequently, the profit margin was higher than at the beginning of the crisis. The larger brick manufacturers benefited most from this development. Six of the smaller brickwork owners in East Cirebon went bankrupt through a shortage of capital. They were stuck with unsold stock and needed credit to be able to continue production. The interest rate had risen to such an extent that they were forced to seek other sources of funding for the purchase of rice chaff and to pay their wage bill. The larger manufacturers were prepared to lend them money in exchange for the supply of bricks at little more than cost price. Those who agreed to this in effect became employees of those who lent them the money.

The starting point for calculating the wages of the brick-makers is the ten thousand rupiah that they were paid per thousand bricks in 1998. The number of bricks they produce in a day depends heavily on weather conditions and does not exceed four hundred to five hundred in the rainy season. At the height of the monsoon, work in the brickfields can come to a standstill for days or sometimes weeks on end. The brick-makers try to supplement this loss of their regular income by finding work through the *ceblokan* system during the planting and harvesting of rice at the beginning and at the end of the rainy season. In the dry season they can make between six hundred and eight hundred bricks in a day, but this means that they have to be at the site from the early morning to late in the afternoon. Even with such long working days, their earnings were not high: around eight thousand rupiah in 1998, rising to ten thousand rupiah two years later. To earn this amount required the labour of two adults, often assisted by one or two children. The low pay is to a certain extent offset by the greater number of possible working days a year.

The low wages tend to discourage newcomers. It is half the daily wage of labourers who have worked in the building sector in Jabotabek. This explains immediately why most migrants show little enthusiasm for brick-making now they are back in the village again. Our informants gave unfamiliarity with the work as their main reason for not doing so, but when we continued the line of questioning, other reasons emerged, including the low pay. But, in the face of unremitting unemployment, a few of them have been forced to change their minds. In March 1999, one told us that in the preceding three days he, his wife and their ten-year-old son had been unable to make more than a thousand bricks. Because of his inexperience, the owner of the brickworks had only given him a small advance payment of two hundred thousand rupiah, while experienced workers could ask for a much higher *kontrak*, of five hundred thousand rupiah or more. The brick-makers do not perceive their poverty in terms of their daily production, or the fact that their wife and children have to help them with the work, but by the scale of the advance payment they can command. The *kontrak* ties them to an employer, effectively denying them freedom of movement. Apart from the extremely low pay – in 1998, even in the most productive part of the year, they did not earn more than four thousand rupiah per adult (and this is not taking into account the work performed by the children) – the heavy work and the long hours also encouraged those without work in the village to resist this source of income for as long as possible. The villagers describe undignified work as lacking prestige (*gengsi*). Brick-making is a clear and understandable example of such work. One young man told us that the girl who had agreed to marry him had said that she would change her mind if he signed a *kontrak* to work as a brick-maker. Nevertheless, several brickwork owners acknowledged that men who had worked in Jabotabek had visited their homes to ask for work as brick-makers, together with their wives. If the owners were in need of more workers, they would sometimes give these applicants a chance. But only if at least one of the couple had done such work before, and only then if there was no doubt about their willingness to exert themselves. Workers accustomed to earning a living in the city were known to be demanding and unreceptive to authority, character traits which the *bandar bata* certainly did not wish to see in his employees.

Transport and trade

7% of the workforce is active in the transport sector. Those with capital own large or small commercial vehicles, used to carry goods (chaff, bricks, and so forth), or minibuses (*angkotan*) which carry passengers. The minibuses have largely taken over from the motorbicycle (*ojeg*) and cycle (*becak*) taxis. The predominantly young men who own motorcycles earn a few thousand rupiah per day from pillion passengers. This is considered pocket money and they do not have to share it with their parents or other members of the household. The *becak* riders on the other hand do earn a living from carrying customers. They have bought their pedicabs for two hundred fifty thousand to five hundred thousand rupiah, depending on the age, and complain about the loss of business to the minibuses, which can take customers to the surrounding villages and market towns quickly and cheaply. Competition from the *angkot* has become so fierce that the minibus drivers are often confronted with angry *becak* riders. In early-1998 this even escalated into a regular fight and the destruction of vehicles. A compromise was reached: the minibuses would not work after five o'clock in the evening. But some *becak* owners in East Cirebon suffered such a loss of income that they were forced to sell their vehicles. We were told in 1998 that they were earning less than five thousand rupiah a day and the same amount was mentioned again on our return visit two years later. Some were unable to dispose of their cycles and we found them standing idle at the owners' houses.

Most owners of vehicles for the transport of goods or passengers capital-

Becak riders complain about lack of passengers

ize on these assets by renting them out on terms that are similar to tenancy or sharecropping agreements. The drivers pay them either a fixed rent or, in case of close relatives, 30% of their daily revenue. The drivers themselves have to take care of expenses for fuel, small repairs and 'fines' (they are regularly stopped by the police who collect two thousand rupiah for each 'inspection'). The owners are responsible for more costly repair work. The drivers also share a third of the daily income with the *kenek*, the driver's mate who accompanies them. A small delivery van or minibus should earn the owner between thirty thousand to thirty-five thousand rupiah in rent, while the driver can count on a net income of ten thousand to fifteen thousand rupiah a day. The driver's mate will make a half to a third of what the driver earns. Except for pushing prices up across the board, the crisis seems to have had little effect on business in the transport sector. Some owners said that they could no longer afford tyres or replacement parts imported from abroad. Lastly, we would like to point out that work in this branch of the economy continues to be an entirely male activity.

When *krismon* struck, East Cirebon had a total of thirty-six shops, the larger known as *toko* and the smaller ones as *warung*. Among their customers were members of the households whose men went to Jabotabek for work. These families depended on the earnings of the circular migrants for their daily subsistence. Shopkeepers were forced to sell a significant part of their wares, some 30 to 40%, on credit. The women would come and make their daily purchases, but could only settle the bill when their husbands returned with their savings every few weeks. This practice continued for years, but came to an abrupt end with the onset of the crisis. The men returned to East Cirebon with no prospects of getting a job and were sometimes unable to pay the debts their families had accumulated. This was a serious setback for the shopkeepers, which was exacerbated by the fall in purchasing power of most of the rest of their customers. Around twenty of the smaller traders – mostly women – went bankrupt, closing down their 'businesses', which often consisted of little more than a few planks on trestles or a table in front of the house, on which their limited assortment of wares were on display. They had little choice, because they were unable to pay the money they owed to their suppliers in the nearby market towns. The larger shopkeepers survived the crisis in better shape, but still suffered from the sale reduction because of rising prices. Customers now buy cheaper brands and smoke *kretek* instead of the more expensive cigarettes. After the subsidies on the price of rice were scrapped, the price of *beras* (polished rice) shot up to one thousand eight hundred to one thousand nine hundred rupiah a kilogram in July/August 1998, and to more than three thousand rupiah by the end of the year. The subsequent fall in price, firstly to two thousand five hundred rupiah in the spring

A *warung* owner holding out in the crisis

of 1999 and then to two thousand one hundred rupiah in mid-2000, offered some relief but was still more than double the price before the outbreak of *krismon*. Fearing that they themselves would be unable to pay their bills as a result of the fluctuating prices, shopkeepers tried to minimize credit buying. Only regular and, above all, customers with an untarnished credit rating were allowed this privilege, and even then only for the most common articles. To avoid this problem, some shops stopped selling rice altogether during the worst period of the crisis. As a result of all these factors, turnover fell by between a quarter and a third.

Among the migrants who were forced to leave Jabotabek are ten men and women who ran small food stalls or earned a living selling their wares on the streets in the informal sector of the urban economy. A slightly larger number of these *kaki lima* are still managing to survive in the city, despite a loss of turnover and much lower profit margins. Those who sell prepared food cannot increase their prices to compensate for the increased cost of ingredients such as cooking oil and *tahu*. They have therefore reduced the portions.

Four other men, who had worked in the building sector in Jakarta, have turned their hand to selling iced lollipops since their return to East Cirebon. A family member who owns two brickworks and a truck lent these men *peda-*

Ambulatory vendor with customer

gang keliling money to buy a handcart, which they use to ply their trade in the surrounding villages. In 1998, their net daily takings would have been between four thousand and seven thousand rupiah. Several men and women have taken up trading in second-hand goods, a type of business which has increased considerably since the outbreak of the crisis. They mostly trade in consumer durables – gold jewellery, televisions, parabolic antennas, audio equipment, sewing machines – but sometimes also in clothing or crockery. Most of the articles they buy are not sold to other households in East Cirebon but to traders in nearby market towns. Two other former circular migrants survive by collecting scrap metal, empty bottles, plastic and old rags. They take the waste to Sindanglaut every week and, in 1998, were making between three thousand and seven thousand rupiah a day. A woman who added to the earnings of her husband, a *becak* driver, by selling rice cookies (*serabi*) in the mornings told us in August 2000 that she never makes more than four thousand rupiah a day. That is what she has left if she sells all the cookies she has prepared using five kilos of *beras* (at two thousand two hundred rupiah a kilo) and one kilo of sugar (the price of which has risen from two thousand two hundred to three thousand six hundred rupiah). Of the working population 6% depend on trade for their subsistence. This figure has remained steady, with those dropped out the sector being replaced by newcomers trying their luck.

Other crafts and services, including government employment

The self-employed village artisans (a tailor and a bicycle mechanic) or those engaged as waged workers (a second tailor who travels back and forth to a shop in Cirebon, a maintenance engineer in a local sugar mill, a motorcycle mechanic in a repair shop, and two others who work in factories in Bekasi) are among them. In 1998, the average daily income of a reasonably experienced craftsman was between two hundred thousand and three thousand five hundred rupiah a month. Five workers in this category lost their jobs as a result of the crisis: three factory workers in Jabotabek and two technicians employed by the Karangsuwung sugar mill. The last two were part of the permanent core staff of ninety who worked in shifts and were among eighteen who lost their jobs. One of these two, a skilled worker with an employment record at the mill of thirty-seven years, told us in embittered tones that he had received a redundancy payment of one million one hundred thousand rupiah, a little less than four months' salary. He had to use the money to pay off some of his debts and was now working wherever he could as an unskilled hand. Most days he was unable to find anything to do at all. We also counted the *welitan* maker among the craftsmen. This old man made roof coverings from bamboo and sugarcane leaves, which he sold to the brickworks owners for the kiln sheds in the brickfields. He had to give the work up when he had no money to buy bamboo and rope. He now collects large stones from the river hammered by him and his wife into smaller pieces. When we spoke to him in 1998, there were three piles of stones next to his wretched hovel, waiting for a buyer. He told us that these heaps, the result of ten days' work, would be worth around twenty-eight thousand rupiah.

The service category comprises a varied range of practitioners, including a puppeteer (*tukang wayang*), a scissor and knife sharpener, a masseuse (*tukang pijit*) and a barber. It is the only sector in which women are more numerous than men. This is largely due to the fact that nine women work as housemaids. All of them are employed outside the village: two in Cirebon and five in Jakarta. In 1998, in addition to bed and board, they earned a monthly salary of between fifty thousand and eighty-five thousand rupiah. They generally return home only once or twice a year. Two of the women recently returned to the village for good, but it is not clear whether they lost their jobs because of the crisis. The remaining two have gone to Saudi Arabia. They were recruited by an agent in Cirebon and are overseas on two-year contracts. Converted into rupiah, their salaries are so high that they have become the best paid workers in East Cirebon. However, unlike many of the other local villages, it is still exceptional for inhabitants of East Cirebon to work abroad.

Those who are in government service enjoy a much higher status. With one exception – a guard-cum-messenger – they have all enjoyed a secondary, or even more advanced education. In this last category there are three officials (two men and a woman) who work outside East Cirebon, at the sub-district or district administration office. In 1998, their regular monthly salary varied from two hundred fifty thousand to four hundred thousand but, but this was supplemented by at least as much again in the form of semi-legal bonuses and illegal 'donations'. A midwife at the *puskesmas* (primary health care centre) had a monthly income of more than two hundred fifty thousand rupiah. A married couple, both teachers, earned six hundred fifty thousand and four hundred fifty thousand rupiah respectively, while another graduate had a teaching job at a local secondary school at five hundred fifty thousand rupiah. With one exception, the members of the village administration are all men, as are the remaining individuals in this category, retired military personnel and civil servants.

Although the lower ranking officials in the *aparat desa* receive an annual payment, considered to be a supplement to their main income from other work, the village head and his immediate staff are paid their salaries in the form of *bengkok*, communal fields which are at their disposal for the duration of their appointments. The *reformasi* movement which led to the collapse of the Orde Baru in 1999 also had an effect on the composition of the local administration. Under pressure from part of the local elite, which turned against him, the village head (*kuwu*) was forced to step down. It took a long time to find a successor, because he had rented his fields out to a sugar mill for many years. This meant that the new village head would only be paid his salary after the current rental contract had expired. This, together with uncertainty about the political future, explains why it was so difficult to fill this local power vacuum. Eventually, an official working at the regional administration was found willing to act as provisional head until a permanent appointment is made. Although, because of rising prices, the income of government employees has lost some of its purchasing power, these households have suffered less under the crisis than those in other sectors of employment. In combination, all those engaged in crafts and services account for some 10% of the working population in East Cirebon.

A residual category

Table 1, above, shows the breakdown of the working population in their spread over the various sectors of the economy. To arrive at 100%, however, it was necessary to include a residual category to record the workers who, as a result of the crisis, did not fall into any of the categories discussed. We clubbed this segment, which accounts for 9% of heads of households, together under the label of 'casual and unskilled labour'. The people in this category are men who try to survive at the bottom end of village economy and are forced to take on all kinds of unskilled work, most of which entails heavy physical labour. From one day to the next, or sometimes in a matter of hours, they will move from job to job without ever becoming closely identified with any specific occupation. Before the crisis, most of them worked as unskilled building labourers in Jabotabek; earth-moving, paving or asphalting roads, digging trenches for cables or pipelines, loading or unloading trucks, and the like. Returning to East Cirebon because there was nothing to do any longer in the city, they found that there was no regular employment for them in the village either. There are occasionally trucks to load or unload and go around with, but by far not enough to provide all of them with continuous work. They therefore have to be prepared to do any other jobs that come along, such as carrying fresh bricks from the kilns, or helping shopkeepers get their wares from the market. And of course there is digging work to be done, such as removing sand from the river, or work on the land of the farmers or in the sugarcane fields. They distinguish themselves from those who are clinging to such work more steadily, in their willingness to engage themselves in a wide range of jobs in a short period of time. They rush from place to place, often not knowing at the start of each day what work they will be doing, for whom, for how long and how much it will get them. And there are many days when they can find nothing at all. But when they do, their earnings vary widely. Driving around with a truckload of goods, such as bricks or sacks of rice chaff, is gang work. The daily wage will depend on the size of the group, the number of trips made and the distance covered. On a good day, these men could earn ten thousand rupiah in 1998 (this had risen to fifteen thousand rupiah in mid-2000), but it is often much less and sometimes they will earn nothing at all. It is not exceptional for them to be hanging around for hours at pickup points with nothing to do.

To describe this way of seeking employment as being engaged in multiple occupations does not accurately reflect the situation of socio-economic insecurity in which the large under-class in the village has found itself since the outbreak of the crisis. Their livelihood had all the features of those of an industrial reserve army. In the course of our investigations we discovered that this erratic movement back and forth between different kinds of work, interrupted by hours and days without any employment at all, was not restricted to this 9% of heads of households. The survey conducted in July 1998, during which we registered the basic details of the members of one hundred and seventy-nine households (almost 30% of the population), provided a more accurate picture of the intense and chronic lack of work and income at the bottom end of the village economy.

Work or no work and the state in between

The one hundred and seventy-nine households which we studied to determine the occupations of the heads and how these had been affected by the crisis counted a total of eight hundred and forty-three members. The average household size was therefore 4.7, the same as for the country as a whole. Two hundred and eighty-seven of these people were economically inactive. They included children below the age of twelve who were still at school, the elderly and disabled adults. Although people were assumed to be too old for the working population when they reached sixty, some carried on working after this, while a few others stopped working earlier. The other five hundred and fifty-six people (3.1 per household) were of a working age, and were therefore in principle available to work.

Table 3. Economically non-active and active members of 179 households in East Cirebon

Households	Economically	Economically non-active			Continually or regularly employed			Occasionally or not employed		
		m	f	total	m	f	total	m	f	total
179 with 843 members	287 members	287	269	556	255	97	352	32	172	304

Source: household survey Breman and Wiradi, July 1998.

Those who are economically active are divided into two categories: 63% (three hundred and fifty-two members) are continually or regularly employed, while the remaining 37% (two hundred and four) are occasionally employed or not at all. The four hundred and ninety-one household members who are economically non-active or who have no or only occasional employment are entirely or mainly dependent on the three hundred and fifty-two members in regular work (an average of two per household).

What immediately strikes the eye regarding the figures is the unequal access to gainful work between men and women. While four in every five men who are economically active actually find continual or regular employment, only one in three women are more than occasionally involved in income-generating activities. This very unequal division of paid labour is not a recent phenomenon. In the report on his fieldwork in 1989, Breman observed that the majority of women in East Cirebon were not engaged in paid employment outside their homes. This was so infrequent that they could not be considered as occupationally engaged. According to our informants, the wives of men who went to Jabotabek in search of work had no other choice than stay at home in order to care for the dependent members of the household, particularly young children. Nor is it common in East Cirebon for unmarried women without children to work as waitresses or maid servants outside the village. Only a relatively small number of young women were employed in such jobs. But the assumption that women's labour power is not sold unless out of economic necessity is not true in all cases. The women who run small businesses or, for example, buy rice and gold, or operate as moneylenders are very rarely from the poorer households. A few women with a higher education work as teachers or nurses. One young woman who worked as a secretary at a computer company in the subdistrict capital had to resign when she got married. Her husband, who used to earn a reasonably good income as a tiler in Jabotabek, did not want his wife to continue working. Conversely, lower-income households cannot afford to let their female members stop working. In the case of households which depend on farm labour or brick-making, the nature of the work makes it essential that the women take an active part.

The argument that women cannot go to work while their men folk are in Jabotabek is also no longer valid. Many migrants have after all returned to East Cirebon and a significant number of them have been unable to find regular work. With this loss of employment outside the village, not to exploit the large pool of unused female labour power in the village has become less and less a matter of choice. More importantly, however, is the structural lack of opportunities for women of a working age to make an active contribution to subsistence of the household by engaging in paid employment. As already noted, the number of women working in Jabotabek was a fraction of the total

Table 4. Occupational distribution of working members of 179 households in East Cirebon

Outside the village			In the village		
m	f	total	m	f	total
58	14	72	197	83	280
of whom working in:			of whom working in:		
building		49 (49 m)	agriculture		50 (31 m+19 f)
other branches of the informal sector		23 (9m+14 f)	brickmaking		84 (43 m+39 f)
			building		27 (27 m)
			trade + transport		41 (27 m+14 f)
			crafts + services		23 (12 m+11 f)
			casual labour		55 (55 m)

Source: Household survey Breman and Wiradi, July 1998.

number of male migrants. Of those women who have returned to the village, only one has been able to find work. This unequal distribution of unemployment also applies to women who had an independent source of income in East Cirebon. Our survey shows that nearly half of those who had petty businesses or who sold food from small stalls have, for the time being, been forced to close down.

Table 4 shows the enormous fall in unemployment outside the village. At the time of the survey, only 13% of the working population were still in continual employment in Jabotabek, compared to 34% (one hundred and eighty-nine men and women) a year earlier at the outbreak of the crisis. Of these one hundred and eighty-nine erstwhile migrants, one hundred and fifty-one (all men) used to work in the building industry, while the other thirty-eight (almost equally divided between men and women) had been involved in a wide range of other activities in the informal sector. The seventy-two migrants from East Cirebon who were still in Jabotabek in July 1998 (or who had gone back there included fifty men working in the building sector, eight men earning a living as street vendors, headloaders or factory hands and fourteen women working as maids, waitresses or in factories. The other one hundred and seventeen had returned to the village for an unknown period of time. Of these, thirty-seven (thirty-two men and five women) are no longer actively looking for work. They just wait at home until they are asked to do a job that is in some way related to their former occupation. Since this is more the exception than the rule we have included them among the unemployed. The remaining migrants who were unable to continue working in Jabotabek after the outbreak of the crisis keep on trying to seek paid work since their return, with varying degrees of success. Although some of them do the same work they did in the city (mostly in the building sector or as street vendors), the majority now do other kinds of jobs. The category which we have called casual labourers, for the sake of convenience, accounts for 20% of the working population and is thereby one of the largest segments within the local workforce. The people in this group are all men, of varying ages, in search of income opportunities, whatever, in order to satisfy not only their own needs but also those of the dependent household members. Their economic activities cannot be described in terms of the standard sectoral boundaries. They are as flexible as possible in the kind of work they are prepared to take on, yet are still unable to find paid work every day. The supply of these casual labourers so exceeds the moderate and fluctuating call on their services that, in our opinion, they can hardly be distinguished from the much larger group of working age to which the term labour reserve, in the stricter sense of the word, is applicable. On the basis of the findings of our survey we conclude that, of the five hundred and fifty-six people in the village of an age to be economically active, a little less than half (two hundred and fifty-five) have to earn enough to assure the subsistence of those dependent upon them. Furthermore, a fifth of those in this group (fifty-five) – in spite of their own belief that they have continual or regular work – have had such difficulty in finding employment since the crisis that they can be considered as making a gradual transition to the industrial labour reserve. Illustrative of this low level of economic activity were the responses we received in July 1998 to the question we posed to the heads of the one hundred and seventy-nine households, as to whether they had engaged in paid work in the past two days. Of them 39% said that they had not worked on that day and 47% responded negatively for the previous day.

The decreasing availability of gainful employment is most striking for the male working population, because they are expected – more than the women – to be the main providers for their households. As we have seen, thirty-two of these men make very little or no effort to find work, either in their own employment niche or in another. A number of them told us that they were waiting for the building industry to pick up again in Jabotabek. These are largely skilled or older workers, who do not want to join the army of those seeking whatever work happens to be available in or around East Cirebon and particularly not for a wage that is considerably lower than to which they were, until recently, accustomed.

As far as the men are concerned, open unemployment – *nganggur* – is a new phenomenon in East Cirebon. It is difficult to say with certainty whether women who did not work outside the home ever voluntarily placed restraints on their availability for work. Men for whom there was little or no work in the village were sent off to Jabotabek from an early age, where there was nearly always sufficient demand for their labour power. On their return to East Cirebon, by no means all of these migrants were reintegrated into the local economy. And those who were usually had to settle for a considerable loss, both of the number of days they were employed and of the income such activities generated.

As far as open unemployment is concerned, more prolonged investigations are required to determine whether and for how long the men in this category (thirty-two at the time of our survey) can afford to carry on without paid employment. A typical example of this category was the *mandur* who was confident that one of his former bosses would ask him to come back to complete an unfinished project. While he was waiting for the call, he sat at home, where members of crews he used to recruit would come from far and wide to bother him practically every day demanding to know if and when he would need them again. But the call never came. When we spoke to him again in March/ April 1999 he seemed to have lost his faith in the recovery of the building industry and told us that he was thinking of taking a job as a driver's mate on a minibus running between Karangsuwung and Cirebon.

The occupational change would mean a massive drop in income and status. Understandably, this downward mobility took some time, partly because the financial reserves which the *mandur* had built up enabled him to turn down job offers that he did not consider suitable. Unskilled workers did not have this choice and on their return to East Cirebon, they were forced to go straight to work loading and unloading trucks or, together with their wives, making bricks.

We saw little willingness among the migrants to return to farm work. Among the younger generation in particular, this option seemed completely out of the question. Lack of sufficient arable land is not the only obstacle to a revival of their involvement in agriculture. A large part of the population of East Cirebon already lost its affinity with farming as an occupation already several generations ago. Even for owners of arable land, it is not always a very attractive proposition to go and work in the fields themselves. A man who had returned to the village after being sacked from a building site in the city told us that he had sufficient food for the coming months because a sharecropper was working his land. We asked him if he was considering growing rice on the land himself, but he told us that he had never done it and would not know how to go about it.

Some of the people returning from Jakarta changed occupation several times in an attempt to make a new start. A number of building labourers who discovered that they were unable to earn enough in the building sector tried their luck as food vendors. Two are still in business, but three have given up after realizing that they were not cut out for it. One is now a driver's mate on a truck and the other two have joined the ranks of what we call the casual workforce. Changing one's occupation is costly, both in time and money. The savings of many households have been used in the more often than not unsuccessful quest for new income opportunities.

The very limited employment possibilities in the overcrowded village economy explains why many people, particularly the young men, had not given up hope in 1998 of finding work in or around Jakarta. They had learned from long experience that, when it was all said and done, the economic opportunities were still far better in the city than in the countryside. They refused to believe that, because of the crisis, the labour market in Jabotabek had become closed off to their likes, circular migrants from the hinterland. With the little money they were able to gather together to cover their expenses, they set off full of hope. One man we talked to had only worked four days during a month's stay and came back minus his savings and with an additional debt of twenty-five thousand rupiah. A friend of his had found a job immediately on arrival in Jakarta. He was paid the paltry sum of two thousand rupiah a day to make snacks for a small food stall. Although he was allowed to sleep in a nearby shed, the wage was not enough for him to sur-

Construction labourers pushed out of the urban economy at work in a nearby village

vive in the city and he returned to the village. But the conviction that there is always work to be found in Jakarta seemed to have lost none of its power, although everyone knows from experience that it is more expensive to live in the city than in the village. Yet neither this knowledge nor the premature return of a cousin or the neighbour's son could stop the young men of the village from trying their luck. This might be against their better judgement, but they told us that, since staying at home made them feel they had no future at all, the prospects outside the village must always be brighter. A year later, this situation seemed to have changed very little. Although some sectors of economic activity had recovered marginally, in the building sector in particular there was little or no improvement.

Is there no solution to walking the tight rope between insufficient economic prospects in East Cirebon and the costs and risks involved in trying to find an opening in the shrinking labour market in Jabotabek? It is the skilled workers among the unemployed building labourers who try to find an alternative. Carpenters, bricklayers, plumbers and tilers try to find patrons for their skills within a radius of several tens of kilometres around the village. Although they do not find enough work to keep them in full employment, it is enough to enable them to continue in their chosen occupations. Traders

House built from savings accumulated by a foreign-returned domestic servant

and the owners of vehicles can also operate in a wider area, but this rarely extends further than the boundaries of the district of Cirebon. The higher the standing of an occupational group is – usually measured by the combination of physical and social capital – the more room to manoeuvre it has for finding work. Travelling costs money and this explains why unskilled labourers have to try and make do with the limited possibilities offered by the local economy of East Cirebon. Carriers and earth-movers might find job work in Cirebon, but they need to be at the sites of activity early in the morning. That is not a problem in itself, but it costs them two thousand rupiah a day for the return journey – and five hundred rupiah more if they work late because the *angkot* do not operate after five p.m. With a daily wage (in 1998) of ten thousand rupiah, this might just be worthwhile, but not on days that their labour power is not required.

Some kinds of work, such as making bricks, has such a low status that many people put this off as long as they possibly can. For some, however, it can become the only option available. After all, as we were told by one informant, beggars cannot be choosers. But even if returning migrants overcome their strong aversion to working in the brickworks, the owners are not always prepared to take them on. As we have seen, the men who have spent many years working on the building sites of Jabotabek are reputed to lack compliance and as some of the brick manufacturers (*bandar bata*) made it clear to us – not without a certain satisfaction – they did not appreciate being considered employers of the last resort.

People began to leave East Cirebon in search of work many years ago, primarily because local demand for employment was rapidly outstripping supply. The massive push-back of casual labour from the urban conglomeration to the countryside was a direct result of the dramatic contraction of the urban economy after the outbreak of the crisis. The returning migrants know that there are insufficient means of existence in the village to absorb them all and make every effort to discover employment opportunities further afield. The assumed existence of such opportunities fires the imagination, despite the absence of any tangible evidence how to get access to employers far away from home. The hope of better times is fed by speculation about the imminent recruitment of large numbers of workers for jobs abroad. During our visit to East Cirebon in July 1998 there was a rumour that a *mandur* from a neighbouring village had been asked to contract thirty labourers for a building project in Saudi Arabia. Candidates would have to pay half a million rupiah towards the preparatory costs for their departure and their travelling expenses. The whole story was made up, but was not so absurd as to exceed the bounds of credibility. During a subsequent visit in the spring of 1999, we were told of a young woman who had just completed a course as a seamstress and had been recruited by an agency in Cirebon for a job in a garment factory in Malaysia. The awareness that, in adjacent villages, it is no longer the exception for people to go and work abroad for a few years on contract keeps wishful thinking alive in East Cirebon, particularly among young people equipped with a secondary school certificate, that better times are on the way. That this will take them far from home is not seen as a problem. The people of the village have a long-standing tradition to depart for greener pastures elsewhere.

Impoverishment and downward mobility

Between mid-1997 and the spring of 1999 we estimate that the total income generated by the economically active population of East Cirebon in or outside the locality fell by about 25%. The fall in the gross village product did not happen gradually but in a series of sudden drops caused by events which took place far from the village and were therefore difficult for the people to comprehend: the progressive fall of the rupiah at the end of 1997, the riots sparked off by the scrapping of state subsidies and the transition to market prices for food and transport in February 1998, the political unrest in May

1998 which heralded the eclipse of the New Order and lastly, as a direct result of these interruptions in normal everyday life, far-reaching social disruption which appeared to reach its deepest point at the end of 1998.

The substantial fall in production capacity has affected workers in the various sectors to varying degrees. The most heavily hit are, without doubt, those – all men – who worked as building labourers in Jabotabek. They were the largest group in the working population, accounting for 30% of the total. After the majority of these labourers had been summarily dismissed, they returned to East Cirebon, where there is little or no demand for their labour. If they do find regular work in their old occupations, the pay is lower than that to which they were accustomed. The crisis has had a much less visible effect on agriculture and in the brickworks, which are a significant source of rural employment, output has been maintained at not much below its pre-crisis level. But the considerable decrease in income of the more than a third of the households which were largely or entirely dependent on incomes earned outside the village (not only in the building sector, but also in other sectors of the informal economy in and around Jakarta) has been accompanied by a drop in turnover and work in the remaining sectors – trade, transport, other crafts and services – of the village economy. Generally speaking, those affected were mainly men and women who made a living with little capital or schooling, such as the keepers of small *warung* and *becak* riders.

The crisis has made itself felt not only through a substantial fall in income, but also in the sharp rise in prices across the board, especially of the basic necessities. This was caused by the dramatic drop in value of the rupiah against foreign currencies (forcing many industries to stop all activities for which imports were required) and by the government's decision, under pressure from the World Bank and the IMF, to slash public expenditure. The practice of ensuring that the price of daily necessities remained affordable for the mass of the population came to an abrupt end. The phasing out of the subsidies on rice (as well as other food products like cooking oil and sugar) and petrol (intended to keep the costs of transporting people and goods down) almost led to popular uprisings in various parts of the country. In February 1998, there were food riots in the immediate vicinity of East Cirebon. Several dozen Chinese shops were looted and set on fire in the market towns of Sindanglaut and Ciledug. Further disruption of daily life was prevented by the partial reversal of the price rises for petrol and electricity, but the government had insufficient budgetary resources to counteract the massive rise in food prices.

To understand this impact it cannot be emphasized enough that the economic life in the countryside is hardly less monetized than in the urban areas. Like the people living in Jakarta, the inhabitants of East Cirebon depend on the local shops for their daily necessities. Only during the rice harvest is it still customary for labour to be paid in kind rather than in cash. But the quantity of rice that the members of landless households manage to accumulate in this short period is by no means enough to provide them with food for the entire year. In addition, like the farmers themselves, they have to convert part of the proceeds of their labour sooner or later into cash in order to buy other daily or non-daily necessities. As mentioned above, the price per kilo of *beras* tripled between mid-1997 and March/April 1999. Wages also rose during this eighteen-month period, but at a much slower rate. Whereas in 1989 a daily wage of one thousand five hundred rupiah was sufficient to meet basic food requirements, farm labourers would need to earn at least seven thousand five hundred rupiah ten years later to buy the same quantity. With their daily wages significantly lower than that – at around five thousand and certainly no more than six thousand rupiah – their capacity to purchase even the most elementary necessities has fallen by at least a quarter. The fitful manner in which the price rises occurred meant that, for certain periods of time, other than the most basic of necessities were simply beyond the budget of many people. Cooking oil, for example, went from around one thousand six hundred to six thousand seven hundred rupiah per kilogram, and milk powder from three thousand to five thousand rupiah a tin. Some shopkeepers in East Cirebon even stopped replenishing their stocks of milk powder – an important component in the diet of young children – because demand fell so dramatically. Instead of pap, the children were fed with rice water and sweetened tea to fill their stomachs. An indication of the problems this caused was that some children went to live with family members who were better able to take care of them. That this was not always a success is illustrated by the case of a young girl who had to stop going to school in Cirebon because her grandmother, who lived there and who had taken the girl in, was forced to ask for money to cover the extra expenses. She came home where she got less food and now also deprived of further education. In August 2000, the plight of the average brick-makers' household was summed up for us by a man who said that, whereas they used to be able to earn enough in one day to buy enough food for two days, it now took two days' work to buy enough food for one day.

The people of East Cirebon adopted different strategies to survive this disruptive combination of falling income and rising prices. The first reaction was to use any monetary reserves they had and to call in any debts owed to them. For the poorer households in particular, this option was soon exhausted. The next step, a seamless continuation of the first, was to acquire as many as possible of their necessary purchases on credit. This could be achieved by not paying immediately and in full, and by borrowing money from those who were better off. As we have seen, shopkeepers – who were now also

Buying up ornaments offered for sale in the local market

under pressure to pay for their goods in cash – responded by refusing to sell to all but their most reliable customers unless they were willing and able to pay at least part of the bill up front. Employers were also reluctant to pay for work before it had been done. To obtain interest-free loans – to get the fare for a trip to Jakarta, for medical treatment, or for the purchase or repair of means of production – people would first try their immediate family or close friends. For smaller loans to buy daily necessities, they might ask their neighbours. With the need for credit greater than ever, the creditworthiness of the poorer people in the village in particular diminished. The very unequal access to livelihood resources meant that, as the crisis developed, the value of capital fell less rapidly than that of labour.

Once their savings had been used up, many households had little other choice than to sell off consumer durables that they had bought in more prosperous times. This strategy is less noticeable in the classes at the top and bottom end of the village economy than in those in between. As in previous times of adversity, the most well-to-do households have managed to finance the rise in the cost of living from a larger number of income sources, while the poorest had little of value in the first place. Our survey shows that, of the remaining households, almost a third have sold off gold jewellery, while one in six have been forced to sell stereo equipment, fans, refrigerators and other goods characteristic of the earlier upward trend in purchasing power. The last thing to go in the majority of these households is the television. But in the social class below this intermediate layer, it is means of production that have to be sold off: a motorcycle used as *ojeg*, a sewing machine for making clothes, a no longer lucrative *becak* and, in once case, a *dilman* (horse and cart). The sale of furniture, clothing or pots and pans raises little money, but shows just how desperate the situation has become in the lower echelons of the village economy. The pawnshop in Sindanglaut is rumoured to have been doing good business since the outbreak of the crisis, but we could not confirm this as we were not permitted to see the books. Pawning is one way of ensuring that you get your property back if you can afford to repay the debt, even though both parties know that while the crisis lasts this is a vain hope.

In addition to selling off or pawning possessions for cash, it is also crucial of course to keep expenditure to a minimum. As the level of prosperity falls, the daily cost of food takes up an increasingly large share of the available budget. The poorest households might spend three-quarters to four-fifths of their meagre income on food. The higher this percentage becomes, the greater the need to cut back on both quantity and, more usually, quality. Rice will be served only with *kecap*, rather than the fish, soy and other accompaniments (referred to as *lauk pauk*), which make it not only more tasty but also healthier. In many cases, families are forced to cut back not only on vitamins and protein, but also on the staple foods. First of all, they reduce the amount of rice per meal and then cut down from three meals a day to two. At the end of 1998, according to a female member of the village administration, around one-fifth of all households were eating only one meal a day. During our fieldwork it was not always easy to obtain a forthright answer to our questions regarding food consumption. Many informants told us that they still had sufficient stocks of food, even when this was obviously not the case, while some said that the reason they regularly missed meals was a sudden need to fast. The fact that many people do not realize the severity of the situation in which they find themselves may be related to the still vivid memory of *paceklik*, the quiet period in the agrarian cycle which traditionally preceded the rice harvest. Although, as a result of the more intensive use of arable land throughout the year, this regular period of scarcity is now a thing of the past, many people – especially those from farm labouring families whose members have never left the village to work outside the agricultural sector – are accustomed to the cycle of good and bad months. When we asked a woman from one of these landless households how *krismon* had affected her life, she answered: '*Krismon*? I've been living in *krismon* all my life!'

The majority of households have little left over for other purchases, no matter how badly they may be needed, after having bought food. This also applies to schooling, despite the fact that the inhabitants of East Cirebon are fully aware of the importance of a good education for their children as an investment in the future. At the start of the new school year in 1998, in the face of alarming predictions of declining attendance at the primary level, the government launched a campaign to urge parents to go on sending their children to school. Television commercials showed a typical middle class family, whose kids seemed to have little need of this urgent advice. From our survey and from talks with local teachers, we learned that primary school attendance in East Cirebon has not fallen radically. This is quite surprising, considering that, despite the official regulations, even primary education is not cost-free. In 1998, parents with a child at the village school were made to pay one thousand rupiah a month. And that was not all. At the beginning of the year, they had to pay a one-off sum of twelve thousand rupiah for 'maintenance' of the school building and it also was compulsory to buy two sets of school clothes worth for which fifteen thousand rupiah were charged. In mid-2000, the monthly fee had risen to one thousand five hundred rupiah a month.

The costs of secondary education, for which children have to go outside the village, are even higher. In 1998, junior high school (*smp*) pupils had to pay five thousand five hundred rupiah a month and seventy-five thousand rupiah at the start of the school year; for the senior high school (*sma*) the forced contribution to the salaries of the teaching staff was fifteen thousand rupiah a month and one hundred thousand rupiah once a year. And this did not include the costs of travel, books and clothes, which could amount to another seven thousand five hundred rupiah a month. Understandably most low-income parents were no longer able to afford such expenses. This explains the sudden reversal of the earlier trend for a larger number of children to go for higher education. The head of the primary school in East Cirebon told us that, in the year before the outbreak of the crisis, 60% of pupils went on to secondary school after completing the final year of primary school, while in 1998 only four of the twenty-seven did so. For the same reasons, there was a high dropout rate among pupils enrolled already at the *smp* or *sma*, more so among girls than boys. College education, which had at least been a possibility in the past, was now completely out of the question. Skilled craftsmen have to abandon their ambitions to send their sons to technical training schools (*stm*), while other forms of higher vocational education, such as senior high school (business) or smea, have become much too expensive even for middle class households. The high fees, together with the costs of travel and accommodation mean that the new generation, through lack of schooling, is destined to a working life of low and irregular wages in the informal sector.

Several kinds of diseases are both a cause and an effect of poverty, and poor households are confronted with more than their share of health problems. At seven thousand rupiah a visit, dental treatment is postponed even in cases of chronic toothache. The *puskesmas*, the primary health care centre located in the sub-district capital, recorded a drop in the number of patients attending surgery. Although the centre's staff insisted that a visit to the doctor and simple medication are free of charge, our informants told us that they never left without paying for something. Lack of money explains why people turn to paramedical practitioners working outside the formal circuit of hospitals and qualified professionals, even in cases where hospitalization or an operation is necessary.

Concern has been expressed in the media about the long-term negative effects of inadequate nutrition on the health of mothers and children. This concern is justified, but there is another vulnerable category that receives much less attention: the elderly. The normal health problems that occur with age are exacerbated by an acute and continual lack of proper nutrition. In the course of our study we visited several old people living alone who have to survive on one meal a day, and that was made of the simplest of ingredients. When we asked if they were not hungry in the evenings, the reply often given was that they would then drink a cup of tea or warm water. Keenly aware of their unproductivity and indigence, the elderly try their best not to be a burden to others and not to complain about their exclusion.

One area that it almost unexplored is the impact of *krismon* on the mental welfare of the rural population. Clearly, not all psychological complaints in East Cirebon are linked to the economic crisis, but in some cases the connection is undeniable. One woman, for example, has heart problems and has been advised to avoid stress. The doctor literally told her to avoid anything that she might associate with *krismon*. It was undoubtedly a well-intentioned warning but not very realistic considering the tension caused by the uncertainty as to whether her husband could earn enough for them to survive after losing his job. The most vulnerable households in a psychological sense are those in which the men work as casual labourers, constantly in search of petty jobs and roaming around different sectors of the economy, with many days of inactivity in between, wildly fluctuating incomes and debts left, right and centre which they are unable to pay off. The pressure under which these people live has increased enormously. A woman who spoke to us at her home early one morning asked us several times within a half an hour what the time was. If we heard someone coming, she would go outside to see who it was. She told us that she was so nervous because this was close to the time that she would know whether there would be money to buy food for the day. Her husband had left earlier that morning looking for work, and the longer he stayed away the more chance was there that he had found work somewhere in or near the village. In the previous few days, he had been unsuccessful. During other visits we witnessed the return home of a failed breadwinner.

Standing at the door, the females of the house were visibly upset to see the man return home and stopped talking to us. The man himself passed without saying anything and went and lay on the bed.

Undoubtedly, the most rigorous cutbacks in expenditure take place in the field of social obligations. The circumcision of a son is occasion for a festive ceremonial party (*slametan*) attended by relatives and neighbours. But even if such a public display is still arranged, fewer guests are invited. Funerals have become much more simple and instant affairs (with little or no expenditure in the follow-up mourning) and weddings are postponed or are celebrated with much less pomp, circumstance and hospitality than would normally accompany such rites of passage. It is far too simple to suggest that, because such ceremonies tend to be exceptionally expensive, it is easier for those directly involved and others to accept that they should be the first to be scrapped when times are hard. For the outsider, these events might seem instances of ostentation and wasteful consumption, often costing much more than the families themselves are actually prepared to expend. But such rituals must also be seen as investments in social capital and the pressure not to forgo them is difficult to withstand. It is at these times that the networks of contacts in which households participate become visible, networks on which they rely not only for respect from their neighbours, but also for work, income, credit and the opportunity to acquire such benefits for the new generation. The fact that that part of the dramatically reduced budget can no longer be spent for these life-cycle events can also be interpreted as a form of disaccumulation. One of the striking features of households that fall into poverty is that they also become socially marginalized.

The efforts made by the people of East Cirebon, as described here, to balance their expenditure against the sharp fall in income on the basis of carefully weighed up priorities, could create the impression that the majority of households have managed, albeit with considerable difficulty, to bring the effects of the economic crisis reasonably under control. Such a conclusion, however, underestimates the severity of the social disruption that has occurred.

One issue that has not been addressed, and to which we in fact devoted too little attention in the course of our fieldwork is the shift in the gender balance. At first glance, it could be argued that the increased vulnerability of men must have improved the social position of women. Yet the crisis seems to have hit women harder than men. While women's first concern is the care of the children, men tend to respond to the loss of their capability to provide the family with its basic necessities by putting their own interests and welfare first. They continue to travel to the city in search of work, in many cases without stopping to think how those they leave behind are to survive. The women often do not know where the men have gone, whether they have been able to find work, or when and, more importantly, with how much money they will eventually return. Family conflicts and arguments are common, between man and wife, and between adults and children, and are clearly sparked off by the dire economic straits in which they find themselves. In a few households, the men have walked out after fierce and recurrent quarrels. Divorce is by no means exceptional and it would be misleading to attribute all recent cases to the economic crisis. But poverty and unemployment has seriously disrupted family life, as we learned from a number of informants from households where the man had gone, ashamed that he could no longer provide for his wife and children. One woman added that her husband had returned to his parents in another village to wait for better times. Another young couple had resorted to similar tactics; unable to survive independently, each had returned provisionally to their separate parental homes.

In addition to tensions within the household, the growing socio-economic insecurity has caused more widespread disruptions in social life. One indication of this is rising crime. In discussions on this topic, our informants tended to blame the increase in theft and robbery, as well as the violence that accompanied it, on dark but external forces. These unfocused sentiments were a local reflection of the disintegration of the New Order but were expressed in more concrete terms through references to hold-ups on the main road from Cirebon to Semarang. Trucks had been forced to stop and their loads stolen. Young men held up private cars and minibuses on secondary roads and relieved the occupants of their money and jewellery. We have already referred to the food riots in the market towns of Cirebon district that made the streets unsafe for days on end. The people of East Cirebon, too, have had to put up with their share of crime, although it has not been so violent. One man, held up outside the village, had his motorcycle stolen. The impression that person and property were no longer safe was reinforced by the rise in petty theft in and around the home. Chickens disappeared, washing was stolen from the line and, in one case, a bowl of rice was taken from the front room of a house. Such criminal acts have more to do with an increasingly dire economic situation than with the dissolution of the Orde Baru. In July 1998, several long-term unemployed ex-migrant workers frankly told us that, once all their valuable possessions had been sold, they would have no other choice than to resort to crime in order to survive.

The prospects are particularly bad for young people. They do not want to involve themselves in farm work, even if there were more jobs available in agriculture. And in other sectors, too, there is insufficient expansion to offer them any gainful outlet. Their hopes lay in finding work in the urban economy but, with the contraction of economic activity in the city as a result of *krismon*, there is no longer any demand for fresh labour from the countryside.

The increase in the numbers of young people attending secondary school in recent years was an indication of their desire to qualify themselves for work and income in the formal circuit of the economy but few will succeed. Moreover, for many children, the crisis has meant that their formal education ends after primary school. Like their parents, they will never be able to make a living other than by unskilled and low-paid work. In landless and landpoor households, those who drop out from school are quickly forced to search for work. It is a different matter for households higher up in the social hierarchy, where the children are not expected to look for jobs immediately after having completed junior or senior high school. Parents are more tolerant of their children lazing around for a considerable length of time. These adolescents belonging to the better-off families think of themselves as being too highly qualified for *kuli* work but are unable to find employment that suits their aspirations for upward mobility. For girls this problem is to a certain extent solved by keeping themselves busy with chores in and around the house until they get married. It is, however, not unusual for young men to have nothing to do for years on end. They hang around in groups by the entry roads to the village, some disguising their idleness by waiting for passengers to carry around on their motorcycles. This intermittent work as *ojeg* and other odd jobs bring in a small amount of cash which they do not have to give up when they get home. It is pocket money for cigarettes, goods with brand labels, sweets, and for forbidden pleasures such as drink, drugs and blue movies, which are widely available in the nearby market towns. It is a consumption-oriented youth culture that combines a careless approach to money with aggressive behaviour, expressed in quarrels and fights both among themselves as well as in provoked encounters with outsiders.

Differentiating impact of the crisis on social classes

The previous section looked at the unequal impact of the crisis on the various sectors of economic activity. But the crisis has also had a differential effect on the various social classes in East Cirebon. Although this feature has already been referred to before, whenever we found such differences to be of relevance, the issue is examined in more detail below to underline its importance. In short, it can be said that the crisis has had less effect on the value and yield of capital than on the price of labour, in both relative and absolute terms. While the scale of economic activity has declined by something like a quarter, the total value of fixed or movable property owned – in which the factor capital is expressed – seems to have fallen only slightly or not at all in real terms. The rise in the market price of capital goods has kept apace with, or even exceeded, the fall in exchange rate of the rupiah. The decrease in the availability of work, on the other hand, has not been compensated by stability in wage levels, let alone a rise. On the contrary, the price of labour has fallen with the number of jobs on offer. This can be illustrated by changes that have come about in the factors of production specific to the brick-making industry. While the manufacturers sell the bricks for a much higher price, because they claim that production costs have risen sharply, wages have far lagged behind. Stated in other words, owners' profits have risen disproportionately in this significant branch of local industry. The net result of this trend in East Cirebon is that a minority of households lays claim to the lion's share of the means of acquiring wealth, while the great majority of households belonging to the landless or landpoor classes have further fallen back in their share of all income generated by economic activity.

During our visits in 1989 and in 1998-1999, we stratified the village population according to an elementary division into three classes: upper, middle and lower. While the number of households increased in the intervening decade from four hundred and ninety-five to five hundred and eighty-two, there was also a shift in the balance between the classes which we are inclined to attribute largely to the economic crisis that arose in 1997.

Over the ten year period, the upper class remained as good as unchanged in terms of scale and identity. The findings of our study do not provide sufficient information to determine the investments made by the local elite outside the village. Some operate as magnates (*cukong*), renting land from peasant farmers for the sugar mills for the coming years. The agro-industry pays two million three hundred thousand rupiah per hectare for a growing cycle of around fourteen months. But by entering into a rental agreement much earlier the *cukong* pay a little less than half, around one million one hundred thousand rupiah. The enormous difference between these two amounts is the

Table 5. Classification of households in East Cirebon according to level of prosperity, 1989-1998/1999

Social class	Proportional share		Share in internal and/or external means of subsistence	
	1989	1998/99	1989	1998/99
Upper	17%	13%	45%	50%
Middle	33%	20%	35%	30%
Lower	50%	67%	20%	20%
Of which almost-poor to				
Poor	35%	43%	16%	16%
Ultra-poor	15%	24%	4%	4%

Source: Household survey Breman and Wiradi 1998-1999.

interest which the *cukong* claims for advance payment of the lease to the owner for his land to be utilized in the near future for growing cane. The middlemen between the owners of farm land and the sugar mills are often the same people who provide loans to clients known as *bank keliling*. These are transactions with a forty day duration, on which the first repayment is deducted immediately from the principal. Because of the extremely high interest, this informal means of acquiring credit is popularly known as the 'devil's bank'. Not surprisingly, we had great difficulty in obtaining factual information from these loan sharks. The fact that many of the households belonging to the local nobility operate outside the confines of the village also made it difficult for us to get a clear picture of their business dealings. It was clear, however, that they engage in wide-ranging activities of accumulation. The case of *pak* A. (note: influential and respectable persons are addressed which the honourable *pak*) is a good example of these practices. This man has worked himself up from a simple village teacher to head of the education department at the office of the district council. He drives there everyday in his own car, but his civil servant's salary alone could never cover the purchase of such a vehicle and the costs of the spacious bungalow he lives in on the edge of East Cirebon. His incremental earnings include in any case the proceeds from the purchase of land in the local area, which he then splits up into smaller parcels and sells for the building of houses. The information he gathers in the course of his official duties is valuable to him in his extracurricular business activities. He also has a long-term tenancy on ten hectares of land, also divided in plots which farmers hire from him in sharecropping contracts to grow maize. In East Cirebon *pak* A. is the prototype of the *orang kaya baru*, the nouveau riche, who have emerged in the rural economy. His good fortune has not suffered from the crisis and illustration for this is his recent purchase of a station wagon (*kijang*), an investment that he is recouping by renting it out.

The broad middle class has displayed the greatest change in lifestyle. These households which belong neither to the top nor to the bottom responded to the policy change in the later phase of the New Order regime in favour of the urban economy with a dynamism expressed both in increased prosperity and upward social mobility. This class of the petty bourgeoisie included many households which became the main beneficiaries from the scale-enlargement in the labour market. They earned their more profitable incomes by offering their self-trained skills for hire outside the village economy. Indicative of the aspirations for upward mobility of many people in this class were the hopes of parents, who could afford to equip their children – especially the sons – by sending them to secondary school, that their offspring would enter the job market at a somewhat higher level, formally qualified for better paid and more permanent employment. The economic crisis has dashed these hopes of much better prospects for the next generation. The disappointment is temporarily overshadowed by a more immediate and drastic setback to the chances for consolidation of the economic and social progress attained by the, until recently, expanding middle class of East Cirebon: the consequences of their sharp drop in employment opportunities and levels of income. Many households, in which the male members belonged to the more elevated ranks among the circular migrants heading for Jabotabek, have found themselves sliding down the social ladder.

Two-thirds of the population is now stuck at the bottom end of the village economy. Such a large mass cannot be homogeneous and requires further differentiation. As Breman did in his 1989 fieldwork report, we distinguish the poor and the ultra-poor. Both of these subclasses have expanded by around one-third, a rate of increase which carries extra weight in the light of the ongoing natural growth of the population of East Cirebon. The majority of households are concentrated in the upper of the two subclasses, the almost-poor to poor. They lack both the capital resources and the more than minimal level of schooling, nowadays considered to be a necessary although not a sufficient precondition, to escape the poverty in which they live by increasing their productivity. The great demand for their low-skilled labour outside the village used to enable these households to acquire their daily necessities and pay for them later, but the economic crisis has put an end to their economic value. The army of circular migrants which has been driven back to the rural hinterland only manages to find irregular and sporadic work in the village economy. With growing unemployment and the price of the main daily necessities rising fast while wages lag behind, many household budgets seem to have become strained beyond the coping ability of the income-generating members. Like their parents, the children from this background seem fated to a life of unskilled, low-paid work in the informal sector and hopelessly stuck in a life of poverty at the margins of society.

Yet beneath the proletariat class, there is the under-class of ultra-poor. This social residue also existed ten years ago, but then it was much smaller. It consisted of the weakest households in East Cirebon in which the potential breadwinners were hardly economically active, or not all, because of age, physical disability, illness or social handicaps (widows or divorced women with young children). But this extremely vulnerable segment has now been joined by men and women who have the ability to work but who have been without employment for so long that they cannot, or can barely, assure their own subsistence. The ultra-poor have not only been denied access to the labour market, they are also unable to fulfil their own basic needs. Their degree of exclusion, both from the means of production and consumption, is nearly absolute and there seems little prospect of a change for the better. One

This old man and his bed-ridden wife had not eaten for the last three days

household we encountered illustrates the severity of the deprivation in which these people live. The elderly man and his wife are still employed as brick-makers. They have two sons who used to work as navvies in Jabotabek until recently and a daughter who works as a maid. In spite of their combined efforts they lead a thoroughly pauperized existence. Their house is in such bad state with the roof leaking to the extent that, during heavy rainfall, they have to take shelter under the neighbours' porch.

Our schematic overview of the changing shape and distribution of the social hierarchy in East Cirebon would be incomplete without a short discussion on the impact *krismon* has on the dynamics of inter-class interaction. Initial reports on the contraction of economic activity focused strongly on the consequences for urban work and labour. In the media the dominant opinion was that the loss of jobs resulting from the closure of offices and factories would predominantly affect the formal sector, which is strongly associated with the metropolitan economy. When it later appeared that the crisis extended further than this and had affected the large mass of casual labour recruited from the rural hinterland, their plight was still considered to be less severe. According to many observers, among policy makers as well as the general public, the exodus of building labourers and other segments of the informal sector workforce would liberate Jakarta and its satellites from a mass of people that had become superfluous. Vested interests expressed fears that in such tempestuous times these now labourless nomads might turn into a *Lumpenproletariat* to be mobilized against the established order. This was one of the reasons why the authorities actively encouraged the exodus by offering the migrants free travel back to their homes in rural Java. The national and international policy-makers – the IMF and the World Bank had by now taken over the formulation and implementation of policy to combat the crisis – did not concern themselves with the fate of the migrants once they had returned to their villages. The prevailing opinion was that, by leaving and seeking work in the city, they had not entirely broken their ties with the village economy. It would therefore be easy for them to resume the lives they had left behind. This view, which was not founded on any thorough knowledge of the situation in the countryside, saw *krismon* as a purely urban phenomenon. In the agricultural sector especially, it would be business as usual. In line with the wishful thinking that the migrants hailed from agricultural households, the received wisdom was that they would return to earning a simple living by working a small piece of land as small owner-cultivator, tenant or sharecropper. Those family members who had been dispatched to try their luck in the city were just earning a little extra, but this was seen as supplementary to what had always been their basic source of income: working in the fields.

Our study shows that this view of the situation painted a far too favourable picture of the village economy in rural Java. This optimistic and naïve view neglected the main incentive for migration, which was a large-scale and sustained expulsion of labour from the agricultural sector resulting from a grossly unequal distribution of land. Other branches of rural economic activity were unable to compensate for the increased pressure on the agricultural means of subsistence. Consequently, the expulsion of labour from the agricultural sector also meant expulsion from the village economy. These dynamics explain why large numbers of migrants who have been forced to leave the urban conglomeration of Jabotabek since the outbreak of the crisis have been unable to find sufficient means by which to assure their subsistence since returning to their villages of origin.

Policy-makers tend to see the crisis as being far more serious in the cities than in the countryside for yet another reason. This argument, unsubstantiated by empirical evidence, relates to the tenacious belief that the rural population is characterized by a high degree of economic and social homogeneity, expressed by more or less equal access to the means of subsistence and collective welfare. It is the misconception which has its roots in the myth of a traditional rural community, which may have suffered a certain amount of erosion with the passage of time, but not as much as in the cities, where capitalism has come to maturity leading to sharper divisions between social classes in terms of property, power and status. This principle of communality attributed to agrarian communities harks back to the old colonial notion that, without endogenous dynamic factors, rural social change is determined by static expansion rather than progressive differentiation among the peasantry. Geertz spoke of a pattern of shared poverty and introduced the now well-known concept of involution as the most striking structural and cultural factor in the transformation of the agrarian landscape in the plains of Java. His analysis was based on ideas put forward by the colonial economist and policy-maker Boeke, who outlined a model for the indigenous economy characterized by an unlimited but paralyzing elasticity, in which an increasingly large population can be absorbed into an economic space that remains stagnant in technological terms. The division of labour ensured a meagre existence for all members of the community.[2] Geertz called this strategy the traditional weapon of the poor, without elaborating on it further. The trend he described related to agriculture, and especially to wet-rice cultivation. He saw this milieu as the ideal-typical setting for the involution model.[3]

There is, however, no evidence of such a communal code in the pattern of agrarian production in East Cirebon, either now or in the past. The available arable land is certainly not divided into mini-plots belonging to all or even most households, nor is it common for land to be used for cultivation by farmers in the village. Yet this in itself does not mean that there may not have been an involutionary trend in the past. It could be argued that the colonial administration destroyed age-old practices based on communality in the early twentieth century when it displaced many small farmers by confiscating their land and giving it to the large landowners, with the intention of restructuring agriculture along more capitalist lines (Breman 1983). All speculation on the true nature of the 'ancien régime' and the reasons for its disappearance aside, the fact remains that a considerable proportion of the population of East Cirebon for a very long time has worked hardly or not at all in the agricultural sector and have been partly or entirely dependent on

2 For a general review of this notion and other aspects of Boeke's economic dualism, see Indonesian Economics (1966), which contains selections from his work, with essays by authors with disagreeing with the views that Boeke had expounded.

3 Geertz elaborated on this term in a wide variety of ways, including the following: 'the intricate institutional fretwork through which land and labor are actually brought together. In share tenancy and associated practices the ever-driven wet-rice village found the means by which to divide its growing economic pie into a greater number of traditionally fixed pieces and so to hold an enormous population on the land at a comparatively very homogeneous, if grim, level of living.' (Geertz 1963:99-100.) For a critical view on the involution concept and the related idea of shared poverty, see White 1983.

income from activities in the other-than-peasant economy. In our view, the shift from the countryside to the metropolitan economy is not a new phenomenon and, for that reason, it is impossible to speak of closed and separated circuits of economic activity with their own modes and patterns of operation. There is still a tendency to see the urban environment as more capitalist than rural areas, but this is based on a contradiction that simply does not exist, and probably never has. Summarizing a study in which Geertz described the social history of a small town in East Java, Wertheim concluded that the mechanism of shared poverty seems to have been relocated from the countryside to the city. In this passage he outlined what would later be referred to as the informal sector and what Geertz himself called the *kampong* sector. Hidden unemployment resulting in too little to survive and too much to die – this is how Wertheim described the lives of the men and women forced to leave their villages to eke out an existence at the lower end of economic life in 'Modjokuto' town:

> the lack of opportunity for employment in the town, the growing stream of impoverished rural inhabitants moving there, and the generally low standard of living lead to the available opportunities for work being spread over large numbers of applicants each of whom has too little to do and is living on the very margin of minimal subsistence. The innumerable street-vendors, pedicab drivers, 'peons' and little clerks in the offices all testify to the same system, in which social justice takes precedence over efficiency and a minimum output per head is put up with so that the available means of subsistence can be spread out over a maximum number of people. (Wertheim 1964:12.)

The transfer of the concept of shared poverty from the village to the city, as Wertheim pointed out, also involved a remarkable reduction in the scope of the term. The argument, made more implicitly than explicitly, was that it no longer related to the entire gamut of economic life but only testified to the increasingly dense mass of people congested at the lower end of urban society.[4]

But is this not the same view as that taken by present-day policy-makers when they suggest that the informal sector economy has a rationale and an ethic of its own? They are referring to the capacity of small-scale, unorganized economic activity to absorb the continual influx of unskilled and low-paid labour flowing into the city from the countryside. The never-ending

4 In a later publication Wertheim distanced himself somewhat from the idea of shared poverty and suggested that Geertz had failed to identify the strategy of the rural elite to exclude themselves from demands claiming for distribution of property and employment: '*in addition to* the shared poverty among the poorest groups, there was also a clear bifurcation, with rich and poor growing apart, an accumulation of land by the rich landowners, an increasing tendency to capitalist land exploitation by the richer farmers.' (Wertheim 1975:199.)

ability to make space for more newcomers, the perpetual willingness to allow them to join loosely structured occupational niches which, to outsiders, are already overfull, has been a much-discussed theme in the literature since the introduction of the informal sector concept. There is, however, good reason to doubt the accuracy of this analysis. The elasticity attributed to the lower economic zones does not exist within a closed circuit or a statically expanding arena, but presupposes a dynamism which never ceases to generate more work opportunities. The way in which the multitude of migrant workers who arrive in the city are recruited and deployed allows for portraying them as a floating reserve army of labour that can be expanded or contracted, without ominous consequences, as the situation requires.

The state of flux since the outbreak of the recent crisis can be seen as corroborating this kind of benign interpretation. The idea of shared poverty contributes to the firmly held notion that the expelled mass of migrant workers require little attention or care from policy-makers because both in the place where they found temporary employment – the city – and the place they originate from – the village – they are able to avoid exclusion by dividing up the available work and income, thereby helping each other to survive under difficult circumstances.

Is this indeed how migrants from Jabotabek returning to East Cirebon were reintegrated into the local economy? It would be difficult for us to reconcile this view with the results of our empirical investigations. But indeed, there are a number of employment arrangements that could be seen to fall within this category. In the agricultural sector, for example, farmers have for many years entered into *ceblokan* agreements with landless families to assure them of a share in the harvest. There has been a long debate on whether this closed field system is an expression of the willingness of the landowners to give the landless of the village a share in the yield from agrarian means of subsistence. Some authors interpret such contracts as exemplary of a patron-client relationship which does not deny the structural divide between those with and those without property, but which does make the class contradiction more palatable against a background of increasing stratification within the agrarian milieu (Hayami and Kikuchi 1981:215). Others see such exclusive working arrangements as an illustration of the subjection of the employees to the power of the employers. The latter are assured of a docile and cheap workforce, and use this employment modality – taking labourers on at the beginning of the planting cycle but only paying them at the very end – as a means of social control (Hart 1986a). More prudent analyses which try to avoid making a clear choice between these two extremes, emphasize the huge diversity within the rural landscape on Java and point out the importance of seeing institutions like *ceblokan* in a wider spatial and time-bound context (Pincus 1996). We place ourselves in the latter camp. In our opinion, the closed field system in East Cirebon is neither an accommodating gesture towards the descendants of those households that were excluded from access to land in the early years of the twentieth century, nor do we see in it a concerted effort on the part of farmers to ensure that the landless do not leave for better paid work in Jabotabek by tying them down to work contracts at home. Factual evidence is lacking to support the suggestion that one or both strategies can be merely related to changes in the local balance of supply and demand for labour, caused by increased population pressure.

Outside agriculture it is just as difficult to argue that the shortage of work caused by the cessation of the recurrent exodus from the village to Jabotabek is being solved by efforts to accommodate the circular migrants back into the village economy; or to come to the converse conclusion that those in a stronger economic position are taking advantage of the situation to make the weak even more vulnerable than they already are. The custom of giving brick-makers a *kontrak* to ensure that they can provide their own daily necessities is certainly not driven by any compassion on the part of the manufacturers regarding those at the bottom of village society. Payment of advance wages is one way of ensuring that work is performed at the lowest possible rate – not much higher than the cost for reproduction of the labour power. This mode of payment is not an isolated arrangement between employer and worker, but is part of a much longer chain of credit transactions, starting with urban-based suppliers of construction material who provide owners of brickfields with cash advances in exchange for which they lay claim to a large part of, or even the entire, production of bricks against attractive terms of delivery. Such practices seem to have much more to do with mercantile capitalism than with shared poverty.

The latter mechanism, which in our opinion smacks more of mercantile capitalism rather than shared poverty, is more than an arrangement only between providers and receivers of work to be done, but says something of the relationship between them. In East Cirebon, a truck or minibus may have one owner but several drivers. The drivers all hire the vehicle under the same terms without being allowed the right to drive it every day. They alternate with each other from day to day or every few days. This arrangement is similar to a sharecropping agreement, in which the owner decides who gets the benefit, on a rotational basis, for the exploitation of his means of production. The drivers are not able to decide among themselves who is eligible. In making the selection, owners give the impression of applying the principle of divide and rule.

The employment of the loading and unloading crews who ride on the trucks is more akin to the open-field system that is used during the rice harvest in other parts of Java (see Breman 1995 as well as a host of other authors). Neither the owner nor the driver concern themselves with the recruitment and size of the crews. On some days, only four men will turn up looking for this work, while on others there may be six or more. The price per load varies with the distance and the members of the crew receive an equal share in the revenue from the total number of trips. If more than the usual number of men show up, everyone earns a little less. The reaction to this, according to our informants, is rarely direct exclusion, although some of the men may step down voluntarily if the crew threatens to be too large. Just how this works in practice is unclear, not in the last place because of the different ways in which the rules were explained to us. A few of the older men told us that there were conditions attached to becoming a regular crew member that had little to do with a communitarian ethos. They said that they no longer join the truck crews because their physical strength was clearly and persistently weaker than that of the younger members. They were then so ashamed to receive the same pay that they had decided to stop doing the work. No one had asked them to stay away, but no one had come to ask them why they had not shown up either.

The young men who carry the fresh bricks from the kilns are also employed according to the open-field system. The *tukang obong*, who supervises this final stage of the process of production, wants the shed to be emptied as soon as possible so that newly made dried bricks waiting outside the

Lifestyle of a single-headed female household

Lifestyle of prosperous households

shed can be brought inside and stacked before firing the kiln. The carriers, many of whom used to be unskilled building labourers in Jabotabek, try to take out as many bricks as quickly as possible, because they are paid piecemeal. In their eagerness to earn more, they often burn their hands on the still hot bricks. They work in a state of frenzy and the atmosphere, although not marked by open hostility, just as at the time of the rice harvest under the open-field system, there is little evidence of collegiality, let alone solidarity between them. In fact, the people of East Cirebon seem to have responded to the crisis by withdrawing into their own households, rather than with any display of mutual concern or involvement in wider collective action. In such a context, the need for security and safety is maximized, but even this is not always successful and, as we have seen, as the crisis has progressed, even the household as the primary social unit has come under increasing pressure.

The state of open unemployment which affects particularly the older men within the village workforce shows that there are definite limits to the equal distribution of work. This economic exclusion affects women who are still of working age even more, and often leads to the social exclusion of single headed female households at the bottom end of the economy. They lack more than just the basic necessities to survive. Those among them who are also without the social contacts indispensable in the search for paid employment, appear to have become more or less invisible to their fellow villagers.

What prospects are there for the future? Much will depend on the speed with which the urban economy recovers. Public opinion wants so much to hear that the economic tide is turning again for the better, that signals – at least as numerous – of continued stagnation tend to get ignored. For the mass of low-skilled labour in rural areas, the most important thing is whether employment opportunities will expand again in the lower echelons of the urban economy in Greater Jakarta. In August 2000 many idle workers made new attempts to shuttle back and forth to Jabotabek but in many sectors, including the building industry, the supply of labour still far exceeded the demand. At the moment, unless the demand for labour is going to pick up elsewhere, it does not look as though the local means of subsistence will be sufficient to sustain the majority of households in East Cirebon. One immediate threat to the resource base within the village is that the land available for brick-making will soon be exhausted. More than one brick manufacturer told us that there was little hope for continuing the industry for longer than another two or three years. The bad relations between them must be seen against this background. They are competitors not only in recruiting workers but even more so in acquiring parcels of scarce land. In 1999, conflicts over the latter led to a number of baking sheds being set on fire. The owners suffered such a financial setback, especially as they were unable to obtain credit in the middle of the crisis, that they were hardly able to survive. A small number of the bigger owners took the opportunity to buy out the smaller and less fortunate manufacturers, thereby increasing their own production. But this strategy seems also in their case only a stay of execution. In a few years' time they, too, will have to stop production. Some are already looking for suitable land further away from the village. The vital question then becomes whether they would be prepared to continue to employ inhabitants from East Cirebon. The disappearance of this local industry, which has absorbed an increasing proportion of the working population over the years, will add to the pressure on the remaining means of subsistence in and around East Cirebon.

If the cultivation of sugar, which has dominated the local landscape for almost two hundred years, were to stop, there might be more opportunity for expansion in the farming sector. But even if the agro-industry were to withdraw from the area along the north coast of West Java completely, and the landowners were to use the land for other, more profitable agrarian purposes, it would offer insufficient work and income to assure the subsistence of the largely landless population. Population pressure, which has reached incredible proportions in this region, makes the future exodus of a large proportion of the labour force to the metropolitan economy absolutely imperative. Any delay in the recovery of the magnetic attraction of these urban growth poles will result in sustained poverty in the rural hinterland.

Need for and absence of a public social safety fund

The economy of East Cirebon, with its means of subsistence already under considerable pressure, has had no opportunity to adjust the division of labour within the village to absorb the large number of unemployed circular migrants that has returned from Jabotabek. But – to take the theory of shared poverty a little further – how willing are the better-off households to provide social support for those of their fellow villagers who are in economic dire straits?

A very common view which is often referred to in policy-making circles is that the traditional system of community provision is still more or less intact in rural Java. No one denies that the modern age has undermined the traditional cultural code, with its emphasis on co-operation and reciprocal exchange, also in rural areas, but the duty to help one's neighbour is considered to have survived much better in the countryside than among the much less cohesive population in the cities. Codes of conduct, it is argued, can be maintained much more easily in small-scale communities where patron-client relations and religious charity also have greater sway, than in the anonymity and transience of the big city. The authorities' relief when the migrant workers who had become redundant after the outbreak of the crisis left Jabotabek en masse was partly informed by the assumption that once they returned to their villages they would be able to call on the social safety framework of which they had been a part before their departure and with which they had always retained a strong link in spite of working far from home. In our view, this was plain wishful thinking. It should be pointed out that, with the growing diversification of the agricultural economy and a rapidly increasing orientation towards the outside world, much facilitated by the modernization of transport and communication, production, distribution and consumption in the village sphere have become almost as monetized as in city life. Consequently, in style and substance, social relations between the villagers have taken on a definite contractual character and monetary transactions play a pivotal role in structuring the local fabric. In addition, until recently, a large part of the working population had been used to spending most of the year outside East Cirebon and had little to do with the goings-on in the village, outside their own households. They took little part in the ceremonies and festivities that give a community its identity. The remark made at the beginning of this study that the village looks like an urban *kampung* extends to more than just its outward appearance. The lifestyle of the majority of the villagers also has little in common with that of a rural agrarian settlement.

As we have seen, the structure of relations between the members of the various classes are founded more on divergent than on congruous interests. This correlates with the absence of an institutionalized system of transfers through which the better-off households help to alleviate the need of those less fortunate. Nearly three decades under the New Order destroyed all the mechanisms of collective action and shared resilience at the local level. The authoritarian state apparatus tolerated no social formations or networks that challenged the monopoly of its supra-local exercise of power. In the strict top-down system of order imposed by the government there was no scope for the horizontal ties that characterized the earlier notion of a civil society. Collective arrangements and associations with a co-operative structure, which might offer some escape from the grip of the higher authorities or even contain the seeds of countervailing power from below were obstructed or simply forbidden. The *zakat* – under which landowners would surrender a percentage of their rice yield to be distributed among the needy – is no longer levied in East Cirebon and the *lumbung desa*, which offered the people of the village some solace under the colonial administration during hard times (such as a failed harvest), was replaced by a state-controlled cooperative (*kooperasi unit desa* or *kud*), over which the farming population had no say at all. The godown in East Cirebon, formerly a rice storehouse, is not any longer in use. Due to large-scale fraud and corruption, the local *kud* branch collapsed already more than ten years ago and closed down in a state of bankruptcy.

If there ever was in the past a close-knit village community with a code that prevented and counteracted the accumulation of wealth among a small elite, there is certainly no evidence of an undifferentiated peasant order in East Cirebon today. In the light of the economic, social and political dynamics outlined above, it is an illusion to believe that even the remains of any communitarian social safety net, which may have existed in the past, could have survived. This does not mean that villagers suffering from acute poverty cannot call on those around them to alleviate their distress. Households in acute misery can rely on help from those around them. Our study shows that it is very common for close family and friends to support each other. This, however, by no means extends to include a much wider circle, let alone the entire village population. With such support restricted to such a small radius, it is in most cases very modest, such as small 'loans' or helping out with some food. Further investigations could confirm our impressions that choice of marriage partner in East Cirebon is determined by class identity and that there is also a correlation, although somewhat weaker, between neighbourhood and social milieu. This would support the conclusion that poor households tend to be surrounded by family and neighbours in a similar economic position, who will therefore be unable to provide them with more than the minimum of material assistance. The resulting configuration explains, for example, why the elderly do realize that their married children can only spare a little food or money from time to time. How can they support their parents if they have hardly enough resources to provide sustenance for their own family?

We have observed that where poverty becomes pauperism, social exclusion increases. The most vulnerable households, where ultra-poverty is concentrated, typically lack the network through which assistance can be claimed and provided. This affects not only the elderly and single mothers with small children, but also large households in which the economically active members earn insufficient income to assure a basic subsistence for the entire family. In that severe state of deprivation, not only has the ability to be self-sufficient entirely disappeared, but the notion of mutual assistance – no matter how loosely defined – has lost all its meaning. The almost complete inability to invest in social obligations reinforces this process of progressive exclusion.

In response to alarming reports about the acute distress of the poor and impoverished in Java, both in the cities and in the countryside, the Jakarta office of the World Bank decided to lend the government large sums of money for the establishment of a social safety net. The aim was to enable the identified target groups to preserve their level of consumption and strengthen their productive capacity. The introduction of this programme at the end of 1998 was a delayed reaction to the combined effect of the loss of work and the explosive price rises that followed the scrapping of the subsidies on basic necessities, rice first and foremost. It entailed a wide range of measures designed to provide immediate relief for a large number of people who were unable to survive under their own steam and to pump new life into the economic activity that had been lost. The programme, known as JPS (Jaring Pengaman Sosial), was intended as a short, sharp shock and not as a long-term intervention which would become institutionalized. The high-ranking civil servant charged with implementing the programme described it as follows:

> subsidy and transfer programmes for the most vulnerable and severely affected parts of the population, in both rural and urban areas; basic nutrition assistance and support for continuing education for those negatively impacted families with small children; public work programmes for the rural landless, smallholders, and the urban poor (especially) who have lost their main sources of income (due) to the crisis; and micro-finance schemes for small and medium-sized businesses which have temporarily lost access to standard credit facilities [...] (Sumodiningrat 1999:10-1).

The various components of the JPS programme were not started everywhere at the same time and on the same scale. Our assessment of the structure, operation and implementation of the programme is of course limited to the nature of the social safety net in East Cirebon, and is based on data that we gathered in the spring of 1999.

Our main conclusion is that there was no substantial effort on the part of the government to provide effective assistance to the large number of households affected by *krismon*. The volume of funds available was too limited and the approach too mechanistic. In the first instance this was certainly true of the component known as Operasi Pasar Khusus, which involved the distribution of cheap rice to families living below the poverty line. Using lists drawn up by the local administrations, a register was made of needy cases eligible for a monthly ration of ten kilograms of rice at the subsidized price of one thousand rupiah per kilogram. This would not satisfy the entire primary food needs of the recipient households, but would certainly make a substantial contribution. During the period between our visits in July/August 1998 and March/April 1999 cheap rice was distributed in the village only twice. In both cases, the delivery was completely unannounced and the quantity that reached the village was different, giving the villagers the impression that part of their ration was being withheld. Nor was the rice distributed as planned. The hamlet heads proved unable to ensure that the rations were assigned only to the most needy households which, according to the village records accounted for 51% of al households. The better-off – and even some of the wealthy – villagers thought that they, too, had a right to a share. To avoid an escalation of conflict in an already tense situation, the village administration decided to apportion the rice in equal shares to all households that claimed to be eligible for a ration. This amounted to five kilograms a share the first time and three kilograms the second time. When we questioned informants several months later, many of them fervently denied ever having received a ration of this cheap rice. Some who would be considered most needy in any system of classification said that they had heard about the cheap rice but had not applied because they did not have the money to pay for it. The rice itself was of bad quality and the better-off recipients sold it to a local shopkeeper for a slightly higher price. He then resold it to his less well-off customers, with a profit although still below the market price.

Little seems to have come from plans to provide grants to stop children from dropping out of school. Only a few parents out of a much larger number who were eligible for these grants told us that they had ever received any money, and even then it was a one-off payment and far too small to cover the costs. Furthermore, the grants for the same type of education varied widely for reasons no one could understand. A decisive factor proved to be whether the application was supported by teachers, but they too often did not know how to make the application or from whom to get the amount concerned. As with other parts of the programme, the grant was seen as a favour, sanctioned or not on the basis of unclear grounds, instead of a right to which the targeted households were entitled. A year later, the grant facility no longer existed.

We can be very brief about assistance in the area of health care – at the time of our visit none had been provided. The office at the *puskesmas* in the sub-district capital had received a message that a nutrition programme for young mothers and babies to be funded by the World Health Organization (WHO) was being prepared, but there was no information on when exactly the programme would become operational. And although the medical staff we spoke to agreed that the elderly were undoubtedly one of the most vulnerable groups, no assistance was planned specifically for them.

We were able to obtain information on the results of public works carried out within the context of the JPS programme immediately on our return in the spring of 1999. We were told at the sub-district office that the surfacing of one country road in East Cirebon, which had provided work for a lot of men, had been completed the previous week. The complete lack of any projects aimed at women shows how much policy-makers consider unemployment merely as a male problem. There was no shortage of workers on the road project. In fact, so many former migrant workers claimed to be eligible to participate in the project because of being unemployed that the project leader, himself a subcontractor with many years of experience in Jabotabek, had to choose from the surplus of candidates. He divided the job into two phases of ten days each and recruited two teams of twenty-two and sixteen men from three different hamlets who did the work by rotation. The daily wage was set in advance at seven thousand rupiah. The road project, registered in the official accounts as a job creation scheme, had a budget of 20,769,550 rupiah. The lion's share of this went on administrative costs and materials (including the hire of a steamroller). Less than 10% (2,660,000 rupiah) was reserved for labour costs, while the number of days in which the construction was done totalled three hundred and eighty (10 x 38) – a drop in the ocean given the scale of unemployment in the village. In addition, a large proportion of the work on this already very modest project was not performed by those who most needed the income. This project was the entire extent of the public works undertaken in the village.

The final component of the JPS was the credit programme meant for restoring the vitality of small-scale producers and owners of capital. In East Cirebon this led to the setting up of three groups (*kelompok*) made up of farmers, brickworks owners and traders, with a total budget of 16,738,000 rupiah. When the groups were formed, an *animator* was appointed for each charged with extending the credit to the group members and to collect the repayments in instalments. The amount of credit depended on the number of members who registered. The traders' group attracted the most interest and each member received fifty thousand rupiah. The members of the farmers' group received eighty-seven thousand rupiah each and the brickworks owners the most: one hundred and twenty-six thousand rupiah. The allocation criteria were not clear and led to dissatisfaction among those who did not qualify for credit. Some informants said that they had used the credit – which was in some cases less than they had signed for – for its stated purpose: farmers bought artificial fertilizer or pesticide, while traders used the money to buy the goods they wanted to sell or, for example, a utensil in which to prepare *tahu*. The general complaint was that the credit was too limited to invest as working capital. No one worried unduly about repayments because paying off debts to the government was considered the lowest priority in their package of obligations. When we returned in August 2000, none of the *animators* were still performing the function.

As this summary review shows, the social safety net programme fulfilled a number of purposes but clearly failed to provide assistance to the target group that needed it the most: the poorest households in the village. This was not in the last instance because the better-off villagers felt that they had the same rights to government assistance as their less fortunate neighbours.

Since it was introduced, there has been constant criticism of the JPS programme in the media and there have been examples galore to confirm suspicions that the large sums of money pumped into the programme have been used neither efficiently nor effectively. Accusations of fraud were not difficult to substantiate. These accusations, part of the wider critique of what is known as *kkn* (corruption, collusion and nepotism), claim that the budget has been used to pursue party political aims. The Golkar party, which was still in power at that time, was said to have used the funds, through the government apparatus under its control, for consolidating its vote bank and thereby to ensure the continued domination of the party and its leaders after the elections in the early summer of 1999. The evidence provided in support of the allegations was sufficient for foreign sponsors of the JPS to suspend subsequent payments until the results of the election were known.

We found no evidence of such corrupt attempts to extend the power of the New Order in East Cirebon. The powerful and streamlined government apparatus that had until recently controlled the countryside from the district and sub-district headquarters had turned into a badly worn machine that could no longer keep abreast of social change and was starting to lose its grip at local level. As the perpetual flow of instructions from above – the capital of the nation where chaos and stalemate were gradually getting the upper hand – dried up, the provincial administration also found itself in a situation of near paralysis. In this twilight period for the New Order, authorities from high to low responded to this power vacuum with lethargy and hesitation. The breakdown of the direct line of command, of which the village administration was the final link, meant that these local officials too lost all legitimacy. The *asal bapak senang* (as long as father is happy) principle could no longer give drive and direction to administrative action, because the top bapak had been deposed and, at the other end of the scale, the village head of East Cirebon had also resigned. The latter told us that he had been forced to do so by the *reformasi*. On the way from the sub-district capital of Karangsuwung to East Cirebon in March 1999, we passed the village administration office. On the sign outside youngsters had written the slogan: down with the *aparat desa*!

The implementation of the social safety net programme at the end of 1998 already took account of the change in the political climate. The U-turn was expressed in the emphasis that was laid on the participation of the people and their active involvement in the allocation of the provisions on offer. The new modus operandi was described in the official directive as follows: 'the Social Safety Net Programme emphasizes the active and full participation of the community through counselling and partnership.' (Sumodiningrat 1999:30).

Execution of the programme was entrusted to a new body, the

Community Self-Reliance Development Institution (LPSM). This board comprised officials from the sub-district and a number of appointed representatives of the village community. There was also a representative from a non-governmental organization who was given the job of management consultant. The choice in favour of this policy brought to an abrupt end the monopoly that the government bureaucracy had enjoyed until then in organizing and controlling economy and society. This was also the explanation of the *camat*, the head of the sub-district, when we spoke to him in his office. He did not mince words in expressing his strong displeasure about the involvement of outsiders. 'We have been placed under guardianship, but to whom are the guardians held accountable?' he asked at the end of a meeting with him and his staff about the progress of the social safety net projects in East Cirebon. It was a pertinent question. A number of people had emerged in the village as *fasilitator* or *animator*, their only qualifications being that they did not belong to the clique formed by the village head and his immediate staff. The NGO agent, who came from LP3ES, a large voluntary organization based in Jakarta, had to be provided with a room in the office. The local staff considered him a peeping Tom. We tried to make an appointment with him to hear his views on running the JPS programme in East Cirebon, but our repeated efforts were in vain. We were told that he had little to tell us. His fee pushed up the budget's overheads, but his function, supposed to be countervailing to official and vested interests, remained unfulfilled.

What was presented as a concerted front involving NGOs and popular participation was in fact a façade behind which there was no genuine mobilization of forces to counter the dominant power structure. The depoliticization of the countryside under the New Order, as expressed in the concept of the 'floating masses', had left those at the base of society with little collective resilience. The people had learned the hard way to keep a low profile and to obey orders from above – or at best to ignore them with as little fuss as possible. The state strongly opposed all forms of social action that developed spontaneously and outside its own sphere of operation, using force if it suspected that joint claims, even when expressed mutely, were intended as a challenge to its power.

This example illustrates the absence of a social culture and structure which allows the villagers to express their opinions freely and to defend their own interests, especially when they are different to those of the policy-makers. The dismantling of the New Order regime that was under way at the time of our fieldwork may have provided more scope for the development of civil society, but this transition was still in its early stages in 1998-1999. It is not a coincidence that, in the prevailing situation of uncertainty, both the old and the new political leadership reverted to the tried and trusted recipe of the village community to preserve – and where necessary, restore – social

Reformasi comes to the village. Down with the *aparat desa* was the slogan with which the youth challenged the power of the local officials.

stability in rural areas. But the village is now less than ever a community based on close ties between the people who live and, to a greater or lesser extent, work in it. Society, and particularly rural society, will be organized along new lines and with new institutions. The myth of the village community conceals the existence of the now very extensive under-classes of poor and ultra-poor, who are only marginally integrated into the established order and who are becoming even more excluded as a result of the crisis.

Reformasi comes to the village

The reform movement (*gerakan reformasi*) which heralded the fall of the New Order started in the cities. When the movement gathered pace in 1998-1999 the urban biased media continued to focus strongly on the events in the cities where the resistance to Suharto's regime had initially surfaced. The countryside gave the impression of suffering the gradual transition of power rather than contributing to it. This prolonged passivity was illustrative of the way in which the New Order had put a stop to all political activity in rural areas, unless orchestrated by the state apparatus. It is therefore no coincidence that the new era announced its arrival in East Cirebon with the resignation of the village head, not voluntarily but under pressure. The man had always faithfully carried out the instructions he received from higher up and his loyalty to the Golkar party was beyond any doubt. He had certainly benefited from his official position, but he had not been guilty of excessive corruption or abuse of power. The village head justified his departure himself as a logical consequence of the fall of Suharto. When we talked to him he told us that the President of Indonesia had also been deposed by foes who had cleverly nestled themselves in his immediate entourage and who had taken advantage of the crisis to replace the leader of the nation. It was therefore not surprising that the same should now happen to him at village level. This interpretation did not strike us as being far from the truth. The man received a golden handshake of 1.5 million. This sum was the result of long negotiations and the sub-district office only agreed to it to prevent escalation of a conflict between the village head and his closest competitor, another fervent Golkar supporter. The smart money shelled out to the first among the *pamong desa* was taken from the budget for the social safety net programme. There were few candidates to take over his position, because it looked as though the new village head would have to survive without his primary source of income, the income from the official rice fields (*bengkok*). The deposed head had rented the land, some 7.5 hectares, to the sugar mill for several years to come and had no intention of surrendering the money he had received for this in advance. As explained earlier, this dilemma was solved temporarily by appointing a sub-district official as acting village head and continuing to pay him the salary that went was his former posting.

After the ban on the activities of political parties imposed by the New Order had been lifted, the campaign for the elections in June 1999 was conducted with great fervour. During our visit to East Cirebon in March/April of that year, the main street of the village was lined with red, yellow, blue and green flags of the leading political parties. From hastily constructed wooden platforms, the villagers were called upon by loudspeaker to cast their vote for *reformasi*. The passers-by did not appear very interested in this colourful and loud expression of their now restored political freedom. Those we talked to made a clear link between *krismon* and the political revolution that was taking place in Jakarta. Yet their response was more one of spectators watching a performance with an unknown ending, rather than that of actors getting involved in writing the script and staging the drama. This detachment was reinforced by the reporting, first censored and then gradually less so, on the successive events on the television: student demonstrations, riots in the streets, army and police action, declarations by government and opposition politicians. Villagers would watch all this at home or in the local *toko*, but would just as easily switch over to a boxing match or a popular soap opera. News of the unrest reached the villagers mostly in this verbal form. Not more than a handful would care to read newspapers or magazines, much less discuss their content.

In as much as there was any research in overt political activism to speak of it was conducted by the young people of the village. They felt inspired by their counterparts in the cities, mostly university and other higher education students who were at the forefront of the protests against the New Order. It were these youngsters who hung banners in front of the office of the local administration in the neighbouring village calling for a thorough shake-up of the *aparat desa*. Spokesmen for Golkar went around informing the people that it was their duty to vote for the government party, which had provided them with cheap rice and all the other facilities under the social safety net programme. Brickworks owners pressurized their workers to vote for the party of their bosses' choice, a kind of vertical pressure along economic lines of dependency which was a prominent feature of the campaign. In the run-up to the elections we asked the members of the village administration what results they expected. As agents of the government at grassroots level, their support for Golkar was beyond dispute, but their comments on the events in Jakarta showed that they understood that the party's monopoly of power at the centre was broken. At the same time, they were unable to imagine a future in which Golkar was not the major source and broker of power. They predicted that their party would remain the largest by far, albeit with a reduced majority. In the future, the state party would therefore have to take more account of other political ideologies and movements. Their misreading of the popular mood was typical of the extent to which even the lower echelons of the New Order overestimated their grip on the people. Events proved them wrong. Golkar received only one in ten of the votes cast in East Cirebon, while six out of ten voted for the PDI-S.[5] The electorate of East Cirebon had unambiguously voted against the regime that had been in power for almost three and half decades.

It is very tempting to interpret this result as a clear expression of the widespread discontent with the authoritarian style of politics and administration of the New Order. This is, however, only true to a certain extent. A major driving force behind the opposition was, after all, factions in the elite who hoped to bring to an end their exclusion from power in the village by identifying themselves with reform parties like the PDI-P or PKB. In our view, the election result reflects this factionalism and the unmitigated desire of a relatively small elite to safeguard its dominant position. To see the outcome of

5 The complete result was as follows: total number of votes: 1470; of which PDI-P 917, PKB 303, Golkar 155, PPP 51, PAN 35, PKP 5, PNI 4.

Campaign for the June 1999 elections in the village

the political head-count as signifying successful resistance on the part of the landless and landpoor to a social order that ignored the interests of the majority would, in our view, be wishful thinking. The result can hardly be attributed to a demonstration of allegiance by the voters to clearly spelled-out programmes or tangible policy aims of the various parties, because there are none. The votes must be seen as an expression of support for the main political actors on the national stage rather than loyalty to the political interests they happen to represent. The parties are loosely structured and are in practice based on networks of largely personal contacts, with as yet few transparent line of communication between the leaders at local, regional and national level. As leader of the PDI-P, Megawati in particular is undeniably popular in East Cirebon, but to suggest that the majority of ordinary people who have voted for her are convinced that she will alleviate their distress and fulfil their wishes is to assume that the new political élan has caught on really on a large scale. We found no evidence that this is indeed a widely spread belief.

Since Suharto seized power in 1965-1966, the exclusion of the poor was the direct outcome of the oppression and elimination to which all forms of overt and covert resistance from below were systematically exposed. The reform movement that emerged in 1998-1999 wanted to redress the balance of power to include those who were excluded and to destroy the highly centralized political regime based on military might. But the promised democratization is progressing very slowly and there are new rules of the game which appear to pre-empt any chance that the social classes with little or no economic, social and political capital are going to participate fully in the decision-making progress in the country at large or, for that matter in East Cirebon.

This conclusion can be illustrated by the administrative changes that have already come about in our fieldwork locality. Formerly, the members of the Lembaga ketahanan masyarakat desa, the local administrative council, were appointed by the district government. The LKMD has now been replaced by an elected village council, the Badan Perwakilan Desa (BPD). The first BPD elections were held in East Cirebon in July 2000. There were seventeen candidates for thirteen seats. The tasks and powers of the new board have not yet been decided, but for the moment the fresh members seem to be mainly preoccupied with finding out how much they are going to earn. Referring to the new spirit of *reformasi*, one of them told us hopefully: 'Perhaps we will be able to decide that ourselves'. Only allowed to contest were candidates with a secondary education certificate. This criterion effectively excluded from standing members belonging to the landpoor and landless households that make up the majority of the village population. The fact that only one member of the new council is a woman – who happens to be the wife of one of the *pamong desa* – shows that the gender balance also leaves much to be desired.

This is not a very promising start to the planned reform of the state system by shifting the centre of gravity away from the national centre. The intention is to designate the district as the locus of political power and government administration. Such executive devolution is assumed to make a radical break with the rigid top-down approach in which the New Order excelled. The proposed reform, however, ignores the fact that the mechanisms of inclusion and exclusion manifest themselves at all levels of policy implementation. It is not at all inconceivable that the announced political and administrative reforms will formally legitimize the exercise of power by an elite alliance operating between village and district. After having built up a privileged position as brokers of the higher authority, a small layer of powermongers now acquire more room to manoeuvre, which they will undoubtedly use to promote their own interests rather than those of the people to whom they are owe their election. Financial transactions in which a number of leading figures in East Cirebon have been involved are the kind of operations which, in our opinion, will have a bright future. With formal and affordable credit scarce as a result of *krismon*, members of the local elite arranged loans with speculators from outside the village so that they could themselves put out the money at much higher interest rates. The man who was the driving force behind the enforced resignation of the village head set himself up as agent for a shady conglomerate in Bandung which offered credit at extremely favourable terms. He told his clients that he was acting on behalf of large financial interests with a massive reserve of funds which it wanted to use to help small rural investors. It was not clear what reasons the backstage magnates of this scheme had for their generous business offer but the agent insisted that fraud was out of the question and that, once participants had made a small down payment for administrative costs, they would be party to an agreement which he assured them would be very lucrative. How this suspicious-sounding racket turned out we do not know, but further study of these kind of transactions could reveal the network of contacts between the village elite and wheeler-dealers active at regional and provincial level. Without extra guarantees to defend the interests of the less well-off, we foresee that the delegation of politics and authority will largely if not only benefit the wealthy rural elite.

This is not say that *reformasi* has not helped to open up a modicum of space also for the majority of people who were coerced into silence by the New Order regime. There is now more scope for building up countervailing power against the informal and formal domination of the rural elite. The *pamong desa* observe with concern that the people are less submissive and more articulate in their dissatisfaction. Now, when implementing orders from above, they are expected to explain it in detail. People are less willing than before just to do what they are told. But it is not the super-poor who are becoming increasingly vocal. Their extreme vulnerability precludes any show of opposition let alone acts of unambiguous resistance. The large number of circular migrants who have returned from Jabotabek are considered the most assertive. They are used to having to provide for themselves outside the village and their employment in the city has made them less pliable with respect to their bosses and authority in general. This recalcitrance, however, is strongly individual in character and has not yet crystallized into a collective expression of militancy. Pressure from below for a better future and a more equitable distribution of the means of subsistence remains for the time being limited to the weapons of the weak. The *reformasi* has only just begun and may also soon come to an end again.

CHAPTER VI

Epilogue

This study takes the form of a monograph of two villages located on the north coast of West Java. Both authors had in the past conducted fieldwork separately in these villages. In early 1998, after the outbreak of the economic crisis in Asia, they decided to return to the same locations together to study the impact of *krismon* on the work and welfare of the rural population. An exploratory visit early in 1998 reinforced their belief that the prevailing view among politicians and policy-makers – that the village economy had suffered little from the crisis – was misconceived and grounded in a strong urban bias.

Breman first visited East Cirebon in 1980 as part of a historical study he was preparing on the region (Breman 1983). Wiradi used to visit the village as a member of the Agro Economic Survey in the 1970s and 1980s, while studying changes in agricultural production in several parts of Java. In this context, he also came to North Subang, where he accompanied Kikuchi when the Japanese economist started the first round of his local-level research on which he and Hayami reported in 1981 (Hayami and Kikuchi 1981). Both villages had thus already been investigated in the past when Breman and Wiradi became involved in a comprehensive research project focusing on the dynamics of employment outside agriculture in rural West Java (White 1986). The fieldwork conducted by Breman in this context in 1989 and 1990 forms the basis of this monograph. His report on North Subang was made available some years later (Breman 1994, 1995), but the results of the same study in East Cirebon have not been published until now. Wiradi has, however, authored a number of papers on his research in East Cirebon (for example White and Wiradi 1989; Wiradi 1991).

The fieldwork locations: contrasts and similarities

Each village has, naturally, its own specific character and history. North Subang closely fits the conventional image of a typical *desa* on Java: a small-scale agrarian settlement with clusters of houses surrounded by rice fields on all sides. Administratively it is a *kampung*, falling under the jurisdiction of a village centre some distance away. The locality is situated alongside a canal, which keeps the fields irrigated during the dry season. Agriculture is the main means of subsistence for the inhabitants, who numbered just under nine hundred in 1998. Rice, planted twice a year, is practically the only crop. North Subang is still a relatively young settlement, dating back three generations to the early 1920s when the then sparsely populated Pamanukan and Tjiasem Estates, then the property of a private agribusiness enterprise growing perennial crops, were opened up to peasant colonists. The *kampung*, which slowly materialized in these backward parts, did not prosper much and could not be reached by motorized vehicles until recently. The journey to Bekasi, the capital of the district of the same name, now takes only three hours, bringing the urban belt around Jakarta into easy reach. The population all around in this fertile coastal plain is Sundanese, but some of the colonists who settled in North Subang came from the east and still pride themselves on their Javanese origin. The people of the region are predominantly strict Muslims who take their religious duties seriously. Parents that can afford it send their sons to a *pesantren* (religious boarding school) and can increase their status by undertaking the costly pilgrimage to Mecca. On their return they, of course, identify themselves as *haji*.

East Cirebon gives a completely different impression on a first visit. Although further away from Greater Jakarta – the bus journey takes at least six hours – this region has long been densely populated and has a definite urban character. Although the total surface area of East Cirebon is less than 50% larger than that of North Subang, it has three times as many inhabitants. In its present form East Cirebon has its own village administration. It was joined with the adjacent village until 1984. In that year the larger settlement was bifurcated because it had grown beyond the standard size of a village. The two localities run into each other, with no break between the built-up areas, bearing witness to the recent past when they were still amalgamated.

Food production plays a minor role in the total economic activity of the village. This is certainly related to the fact that a large part of the cultivable land is taken up by the agro-industry. Under a system introduced in the early decades of the nineteenth century, farmers had to surrender up to two-thirds of their holdings on a rotational basis to the sugar mills. This compulsory land transfer was replaced only a few years ago by voluntary leasing from owners in the surrounding villages the extensive acreage needed for the cultivation of a sufficient supply of sugarcane in the command area of each mill. Due to the liberalization of the economy, the agro-industry has declines. Most, if not all, mills in the district may soon stop growing and crushing cane, as they have already done in Central and East Java. Until the end of our research, however, the amount of land hired by the two local mills, Karangsuwung and Sindanglaut, remained as high as before and this means that the farmers have to grow their own crops, rice in particular, on barely one third of the cultivable area belonging to East Cirebon.

A rural industry that has expanded considerably in recent decades is brick-making. The production process is based on simple technology, explaining the high percentage of the workforce – nearly one third of the total – dependent for their livelihood on this mode of employment, provided in most cases by small-scale manufacturers. But this major activity too is under threat as the land which is available for brick-making has almost been exhausted. Consequently, the economic future of East Cirebon is very uncertain.

Our second village of research has a much longer history than North Subang. According to local tradition, East Cirebon was founded in ancient times by some notable families owing allegiance to the Sundanese kingdom of Pajajaran. Because of its proximity to the province of Central Java, the cultural influence of the latter is much more marked here than in North Subang. This affinity is not apparent in housing architecture and style of clothing, both of which have strong urban features, but finds expression in the language spoken in the village, a mixture of Sundanese and Javanese. The early industrialization of agrarian life has left its mark on this area, which was already well-known in the colonial era for the secular outlook of the people living here. During the struggle for national independence, radical left-wing groups had a base among the landpoor within the region in their resistance to Dutch colonial authority. This militancy lingered on until the advent of the New Order and a revival is not inconceivable.

The emphasis so far has been on the differences between the two locations of our study. But there are also similarities. The most striking feature that North Subang and East Cirebon have in common is a very high level of landlessness. Eight to nine in every ten households have no cultivable land of their own. The sharp inequality in landownership is somewhat, although certainly not significantly, mitigated by making agrarian resources in the villages available to tenants or sharecroppers. Farm labourers constitute a much larger class among the economically active in agriculture but, because of lack of regular and full-time employment, this is the sole or main source of income in only a few cases. The extremely unequal distribution of agrarian property means that more and more people are forced to seek work and income in other economic sectors. While the brick industry in East Cirebon has been able to absorb a growing segment of both male and female labour power, in North Subang no other branches of employment outside agriculture have emerged locally. In both villages, the availability of work has lagged behind the steady growth in the population. Consequently, the search for livelihood opportunities outside the locality has become inevitable. The solution has been found not in departure in order to settle down in other rural areas or in urban destinations. The structural, rather than seasonal, redundancy in the rural economy has led to large-scale labour nomadism. It is a pattern of migration that has necessitated young males above all to leave home for variable periods, unspecified in advance but lasting for several weeks or months. They usually go to a wide range of work-sites in or close to urban growth poles. Greater Jakarta and the satellite townships that circle it, Jabotabek for short, act like magnets for a massive army of circulatory workers from far and wide in the hinterland of Java. Distance is clearly not a factor, since these migrants left East Cirebon earlier and in greater numbers than those from North Subang. The landless and the landpoor in North Subang succeeded in finding work in agriculture or in other sectors of the rural economy for much longer than their counterparts in East Cirebon. But ultimately, for them too the cyclical trek to Jabotabek has become increasingly important. Only a few men and women from both villages have managed to gain access to the formal sector of employment in the urban economy. This is true even of the simplest form of factory work, which may not offer much in the way of protection against the vicissitudes of fate, but at least provides relatively fixed employment with regular working hours and a reasonably steady income.

Most of the migrant labourers from the two villages are unskilled and therefore have little chance of finding regular, reasonably well-paid work. Because they are only employed as cheap and casual labourers, they cannot bring their families to settle permanently in the city. The costs of even the most minimal accommodation and subsistence would simply take up nearly all of their earnings. The state of flux is therefore not a first stage in the transition from rural-agrarian to urban-industrial employment, but is more structurally inherent to the conditions under which they continue to live. They are destined to shuttle back and forth interminably, leaving their families in the village. These circular migrants are concentrated in a number of occupational niches. The majority of the men who migrate from East Cirebon work as unskilled labourers in the building industry. The migrants from North Subang include a large group of petty traders, mostly street vendors who earn a living selling food on the streets. Of late it has become quite common for young women, from North Subang in particular, to sign up with recruitment agencies for a two-year contract to work as a maid in Saudi Arabia or Malaysia.

A longitudinal perspective

The research carried out earlier in both North Subang and East Cirebon was an important motivation to go back to these localities nearly ten years later. Village studies, which were quite fashionable in the 1960s and 1970s to account for processes of development at the local level in the post-colonial era of what were called peasant societies, seem to have become much less popular since then. Unfortunately so, as stated in the introduction to a recent volume bringing together various reports on the restudy of rural communities in different parts of Asia. In the opinion of the editors:

> the village study has been rightly defended as providing an appropriate framework for the investigation of rural society and social change using a holistic approach which requires a study not just of the position of individual households but also of relational dimensions and their multi-faceted nature. While an extensive defence is hardly necessary, it is worth noting that all too frequently, investigators with different disciplinary backgrounds or ideological approaches display wide-ranging differences with regard to what constitutes the form and substance of village-level dynamics. (Breman, Kloos and Saith 1997:4.)

In other words, the make-up of the village is in the eye of the beholder. The same can be said for the interpretation of local-level dynamics. But whatever the reasons may be for differences in opinion about the substance, shape and direction of change over time, it would be futile to deny that restudies of earlier research sites do provide meaningful insights in processes of transformation, irrespective of whether they are internally or externally driven. This is precisely the reason why the Survey Agro Ekonomi, which had close links with the Bogor Agricultural University, set up a Rural Dynamics Research Programme for assessing both agrarian and non-agrarian changes in the rural economy. Wiradi was one of the senior staff members of this agency who made several return visits to a variety of small-scale settlements in different agro-ecological zones of Java which had been surveyed before. The series of reports published over many years helped in building up a massive bank of benchmark data.

The time span is important not only to be able to understand the nature of the forces at work but also for monitoring their impact on the economic, social and political balance of all those who belong to the unit of analysis. After having investigated agrarian relationships in West India at the beginning of the 1960s, Breman went back a quarter of a century later to find out about change and continuity in the two localities of his initial fieldwork in South Gujarat (Breman 1974, 1993, 1997). This experience whetted his appetite, so to say, to adopt the same approach in his investigations of work and life in rural Java. Return visits to villages for renewed research seem to have gained again popularity in Indonesia as well. The fact that Hayami and Kikuchi had selected North Subang towards the end of the 1970s for one of their case studies, motivated Breman as well as Pincus, as mentioned in the introductory note to the first part of Section I, to locate themselves more than ten years later in the same kampung. Another example is the monograph in which the anthropologist Hüsken reported on his findings in the late 1970s in a Central Javanese village. The choice of his fieldwork baseline was partly inspired by the availability of local-level reports for the same area dating back to the end of the nineteenth and to the middle of the twentieth century (Hüsken 1988). Then there is the follow-up to the research, initially carried out by Singarimbun and Penny, on poverty conditions in a village to the south of Yogyakarta at the beginning of the 1970s (Penny and Singarimbun 1973). Singarimbun himself went back a few years later to do the first repeat study (Singarimbun 1976) and a young anthropologist has once again selected Sriharjo as the base for his fieldwork which is still going on (for a first and tentative report, see Kutanegara 2001). White has also returned to the location of his fieldwork in the early 1970s in the Central Javanese village of Kali Loro and is presently engaged in writing its post-colonial history from a political economy perspective. And finally, when we decided to investigate the impact of *krismon* in rural Java, our intention right from the start to contextualize the consequences of this economic crisis on work and welfare in a longer time perspective naturally took us back to the sites of our own earlier fieldwork. The comparison between North Subang and East Cirebon gave us the opportunity to assess the changes that have taken place in both villages over the last ten years and to understand the local manifestation of *krismon*, which had its origin in the urban milieu, in the light of the history and socio-economic specificity of each of the two villages.

Crisis as a recurrent experience

Our reports on two localities in West Java discuss what has happened to the livelihood of its inhabitants since the outbreak of *krismon*. The description of the evolution of the crisis covers a period of more than two years and is based on data gathered during three rounds of fieldwork. This has enabled us to study the malaise as a process unfolding itself in successive stages rather than as a static momentary phenomenon. Furthermore, the time span covered by the monograph is not limited to the crisis period. The point of departure for our recent investigations was the outcome of Breman's earlier fieldwork in the same villages. The inclusion of this benchmark material, gathered in East Cirebon in 1989 and in North Subang in 1990, gives the monograph a longitudinal dimension. The diachronic comparison of the situations at the beginning and at the end of the final decade of the last century, based on our own direct observations, is supplemented by a summary outline of the nature and direction of the process of change that has taken place in the intervening years. This method has made us even more aware that the villagers themselves tend to place their fluctuating fortunes in a long-term perspective and have made us more alert also to inter-generational changes. For the older inhabitants the adversity of recent years is no new experience. *Krismon* brings back memories of earlier threats to their survival. The oldest of these, the economic recession of the 1930s, has all but disappeared from local history, but later crises – such as the famine during the Japanese occupation and food shortages in the early 1960s as a result of drought and the political turmoil a few years later ending in the installation of the New Order – were recalled by the older age groups among our informants as examples to show that *krismon* has certainly not been their only experience with a sudden turn for the worse, forcing them to tighten their belts. The cyclicality of good times and bad times is a fact of life that is deeply imprinted on the collective memory.

The young people do not want to listen to these stories and seem to be more upset about the return of bad times. Most members in the new generation have turned their backs on agriculture not only because of its declining importance in the village economy, but also because of a clear preference for an urban-industrial way of life. The prospects for attaining that cherished life-style more fully in the near future have largely been frustrated by *krismon*. Young people from the better-off households prepared themselves for the leap forward into the formal sector economy by getting a secondary education and vocational training. Even in earlier, more prosperous times only a few were successful in finding regular and well-paid work in the somewhat elevated echelons of the economy outside the village. Now that the chance of acquiring such work has as good as disappeared, these youngsters seem even more hesitant to join the labour process. So far, parents have shown remarkable restraint – especially where boys are concerned – in accepting this unwillingness on the part of their children to earn a living. The reluctance is in effect a protest by these educated young people against having to perform work for which they consider themselves to be overqualified on the basis of their, actually quite modest, level of formal schooling. Their contemporaries from the landpoor and landless households that constitute the large majority of the village population cannot allow themselves such luxury. Economic distress forces them to seek paid employment from an early age. Any aspirations they themselves or their parents may have had for the continuation of their education after primary school often have to be abandoned in the face of shrinking household budgets. Consequently, the new generation will not have the opportunity to raise the status of their working life above that of their parents. It is almost a foregone conclusion that they will end up joining the lowest echelons of the informal sector in the countryside and in the city, performing low-paid and irregular work for a constantly changing series of short-time employers. The prospects of any improvement in the lot of these migrant workers are more pessimistic than optimistic, even now that the worst of the recession is over.

Differential impact

There can be no denying that the large segment of circular migrants from both villages who constitute the floating mass of working people at the bottom of the urban economy have been hit heavily by *krismon*. At the end of 1997, practically all building activity in Jabotabek came to a halt and the *kaki lima*, the street vendors operating at their own cost and risk, not only lost their customers, but the sharp increase in the price of their raw materials reduced their profit margins. Having become redundant in the informal sector, many were forced to leave. This led to an exodus of the army of labour nomads that had flocked to the cities in the heyday of the Asian miracle, but who had failed to establish themselves permanently in the urban environment. Many of these sojourners instantly dismissed from their casual jobs have been unable to reintegrate fully or even partly into sectors of employment at home. They have responded to their structural redundancy in the village economy by continuing to undertake sorties to the city areas with which they had grown familiar in search of work, with varying degrees of success. Other segments of the working population in the rural hinterland that continued to depend on means of agrarian and non-agrarian subsistence have also suffered, particularly households with little or no means of production of their own. According to our calculations, loss of work and welfare resulted in a contraction of by least a quarter of the gross village product of East Cirebon and by at least a sixth in North Subang between mid-1997 and 1999. There have been some indications of a slight economic recovery from mid-2000 onwards, but this good news seems to be based more on the success of efforts to control inflation than growing employment or a rise in real wages. For the time being there is not much factual evidence of recovery in the substantially diminished standards of living.

There is little thorough empirical or comparative inter-sectoral research to support the conclusion that workers in the formal sector have suffered more from the crisis than those in the informal sector. It is founded on the assumption that elasticity is one of the most striking features of informal economic activity and that the men and women who are forced to eke out a living in this sector will therefore continue to do so during hard times. From this viewpoint, the informal sector expands and contracts like the tides. The reassuring message is that the enormous reserve army of labour knows best itself what it should do and where it should go – in terms of both location and sector – in response to a temporary surplus in some or all areas of economic activity. This theory does not, however, hold up in practice. After being sacked on the spot, most circular migrants from East Cirebon had little other choice than to retreat from their employment niches in the metropolitan economy. The same was true for these labour nomads from North Subang.

Back in the village their plight can be described as a state of limbo, characterized by a mixture of concealed and open unemployment.

We also contest the often-voiced claim that *krismon* has had the greatest impact on the prosperity of the non-poor, and that the position of those without property has not worsened to any significant degree. Once again, there are insufficient reliable and comparative figures to defend or dispute this biased assertion. On the basis of our fieldwork we conclude that, as a consequence firstly of loss of employment and secondly of the rising prices of basic necessities, poverty did worsen after the outbreak of the crisis, expanding to embrace two-thirds of the inhabitants of both villages by the start of 1999. We estimate that the households with no or very little property that make up this large majority receive only a fifth of all the income generated. Of particular concern is the advanced degree of exclusion in which the under-class of the ultra-poor – around a quarter of all the inhabitants – find themselves.

Macro- versus micro-studies

Most of the studies published on the repercussions of the Asian crisis for the work and welfare of the people concerned were in the nature of macro-level analyses based on statistics generated by huge sample surveys and conducted at the regional or national level. Policy-makers, by and large, showed little or no interest in more detailed local-level restudies of earlier research locations as a method to find out about the immediate impact of *krismon*. In a seminar that brought economists and anthropologists together to talk to each other about the pros and cons of their respective research methodologies, a leading representative of the first discipline claimed that:

> there is nothing inherent in the survey method that precludes it from generating the same information as a village study based on participant-observation. Given infinite resources, highly trained and motivated investigators, very carefully designed and pre-tested schedules of enquiry, et cetera, large-scale sample surveys can in principle replicate the richness, the intensity and the comprehensiveness of micro studies. But at usual levels of practicality even our best sample surveys clearly miss many important features of economic change and yield, in some respects systematically biased results. (Bardhan 1989:3-4.)

From the other side the argument was put forward that macro-surveys are particularly weak in capturing dynamics, processes and relations for which, in addition to the quantitative techniques of data collection, qualitative methods of investigations such as practiced by anthropologists are more suitable. In the measurement of rural change there are limitations to the standard approaches that are pursued by both disciplines. While we would be in favour of multi-level research, allowing for a combination of various methodologies, an optimal mixture cannot be found in the kind of rural rapid appraisals that do not add up to much more than quick hit-and-run missions which fall short on adequate quantification as well as qualification.

We certainly do not want to suggest that the results of our fieldwork in North Subang and East Cirebon can be read as representative of the situation in rural Java as a whole. It is not advisable to capture the great variety of conditions that exist in a few simple and generalized statements. It is our belief also that the reliability of large-scale data banks, accumulated by questionable statistical techniques, relating to widely diverse regions and inspired by a preconceived political agenda, is highly questionable. In our experience, most national and international policy agencies ignore or even deny the relevance and usefulness of micro-level restudies in examining economic, social and political dynamics. The resulting distortion helps to explain the lack of insight that policy-makers have – and would appear to want to have – concerning those who were to a large extent excluded from the benefits of economic growth under the New Order and who have suffered most from the current malaise. In contrast to macro-level directed studies which allow for researchers to remain detached from the subjects of their research, anthropological fieldwork based on constant and close encounters with people who then transcend the status of mere 'respondents' makes it less plausible to disregard the notion that poverty is more than just a matter of deprivation. It is not only a situation in which people find themselves but also defines how they are integrated, or not, in society.

In the presentation of our findings we have drawn attention to the social differentiation caused by *krismon* on the basis of the various consequences it has had for the different classes into which the village population can be divided. Again, there is no reason to assume that this impact has been the same throughout Java. Nor should it be concluded that the results of our case studies are valid only for the locations under study. We chose East Cirebon and North Subang because we presumed that a number of important common characteristics of the two villages would also tend to apply in other areas characterized by: growing pressure on the rural means of subsistence caused by demographic growth, the declining importance of agriculture, a very unequal distribution of agrarian property, and the migration of members of landpoor and landless households to the urban economy in response to a lack of local employment and income opportunities. This set of factors is bound to manifest itself in a socio-economic configuration analogous to the two cases we have discussed.

Village tigers

One of the hallmarks of the Orde Baru was excessive state control. The method of regimentation that this involved permeated all levels and areas of social life. Our analysis focuses on the social and economic ramifications. The ideology on which the legitimacy of the regime rested suggested that the rural population was distinguished by a high degree of homogeneity. Propaganda was aimed to promote the façade of an undifferentiated community marked by shared or congruent rather than conflicting interests. This pretension denied the realities of a situation in which the concerns of the capital-owning elite were furthered at the expense of a much larger mass with had little or no means of production. The internationally acclaimed model of development that portrayed Indonesia as one of the New Asian Tigers was back up by high rates of economic growth between the 1970s and the mid-1990s. The fruits of this prosperity, however, were largely enjoyed by those in the upper income brackets. The conventional view, which became the received wisdom, that these privileged groups were an urban phenomenon is inaccurate. The progressive tilting of the balance between capital and labour also occurred in the countryside, widening the gap that already existed between the elite and the mass of the people even more during the last quarter of the twentieth century.

In the villages in which we conducted our fieldwork, the elite consists of large landowners, traders and owners of rice mills, shopkeepers, brickworks manufacturers, owners of trucks or pick-ups, teachers, sub-district and district officials. The senior members of the *aparat desa* are also rooted in this milieu. The most successful among the elite are characterized by a lifestyle that explains why they are referred to as the *orang kaya baru*, the nouveau riche. With physical and social capital concentrated in their hands, they were the key to the exercise of power by the New Order in the countryside. In exchange for formal access to the lower ranks of the state apparatus or their proven willingness to collaborate, they were the first to be allowed to cream off a share of the funds and facilities with which the Suharto regime established and later consolidated its legitimacy at village level. The top-down political and administrative structure was based on a military model of social organization in which the local agents of the higher authorities had to preserve peace and stability at the broad base of rural economy and society. Their task was to ensure unconditional loyalty to the regime and acceptance of the extreme inequality that not only lay at the base of the development process, but was also reinforced by it.

The triumph of this local complex of political power and public authority was facilitated by the elimination, immediately after the coup in 1965-1966, of all associations and networks that could have mobilized any kind of resistance. Not only were the national leaders of trade unions, youth organizations and farmers' associations which represented the aspirations of the landpoor and landless masses in the countryside taken out of circulation, but also their lower-ranking cadre and active members. The organizations themselves were decreed subversive, and banned. Suspicion of being a supporter of radical-left goals such as land reform, or even being sympathetic to such subversive ideas, was enough to be rounded up, placed in long-term detention or even killed on the spot. The campaigns of brutal violence in the early years of the New Order, carried out by the army and the police, together with gangs defending the interests of the local rural elites, also claimed victims in the two villages in which we conducted our fieldwork. Our informants refused to speak up at their own initiative about these events and replied to our cautious questioning with vague and evasive answers. This reluctance, which still holds sway despite the fall of Suharto, is indicative of the atmosphere of terror and intimidation that dominated rural life for many years. The despotic regime put an end to all political activity which was not stage-managed from the centre of the New Order apparatus. Those in power ensured that the *massa bodoh*, the poor, uneducated country-folk that so easily fell victim to radical influences, were protected against their own ignorance. This viewpoint resulted in the notion of the 'floating mass', which meant that no political propaganda was allowed in the villages unless approved and directed by the authorities.

Reformasi

The reform movement (*gerakan reformasi*) that started to gather momentum in 1998 brought this long period of political demobilization to an end. With freedom only re-established so recently, it is too early to judge what socio-economic effects it will have. The elections of June 1999 resulted in a crushing defeat for Golkar, the party that orchestrated the New Order regime, in both North Subang and East Cirebon. It would, however, be a gross exaggeration to see this hopeful outcome as an expression of a successful revolt against the machinations from higher up to stifle the voice of opposition. The campaign in favour of *reformasi* in the two villages was not led by representatives of the landpoor and landless majority, but by leaders from the dissenting faction among the local elite who saw an opportunity to turn the table against those who had kept them out of power and who used to monopolize the gains attached to it. The election results might optimistically be read as heralding a major change in the local balance of power, but there is no evidence for such a fundamental shift. What seems to be at stake is fierce competition among the local power contenders in a continuation of rivalries that have existed for generations. It would be wishful thinking to suggest that the manner in which the have-nots in our fieldwork villages were allowed to cast their votes, relatively free from state control, is much more than a first and necessary step to bring their political exclusion to an end.

Without creating more space for assertion from below, including tolerance for the articulation of collective grievances, it will be impossible to break through the conspiracy of silence that has been maintained since 1965 about a class conflict that provided a fertile breeding ground for the turnaround in the political tide of that moment: the call for land reform, which was driven from below and opposed from above. The need to finally put into effect the 1960 Basic Agrarian Law, and especially the provisions imposing a maximum on the size of private landholdings, could be seen as part of a policy change aimed at giving this primary economic sector, after a long period of neglect, a powerful boost to help increase production and productivity. The appeal is now for making a fundamental choice between a mode of owner-cultivator based agriculture and a new type of agribusiness run along lines of corporate management with the use of cheap farm labour. The supporters of the latter option appear to have gained the upper hand.

But even a more equitable distribution of cultivable land among the large segment of the working population that continues to be involved in the prime sector of the economy would, certainly on Java, offer insufficient solace for the enormous increase of pressure on the agrarian means of subsistence. Nor does it appear likely that the urban economy will be able to provide permanent employment to the steadily growing part of the labour force that can no longer be fully and continuously accommodated in an agrarian way of life. A fundamental restructuring of the political economy, involving the diversification of rural economic activity by promoting small-scale farm enterprises is frustrated by the supporters of the development model that prevailed under the New Order, the key features of which are the free flow of foreign capital and the opening up of industrial and non-industrial branches of activity to multinational investment. The monetary reconstruction policy imposed by the IMF and the World Bank is an extension of essentially the same policy and pre-empts the choice of an economic strategy that would better serve the interests of Indonesia and its people. The labour market scenario that this implies points to a continuation of the pattern of circulatory migration, both between city and countryside and between economic sectors. It is a policy script that leaves little scope for improving the lot of the working population.

In addition to accepting the unfortunate separation between home and work for the large army of labour nomads, their constant coming and going also has negative effects on the family and the household left behind in the rural hinterland. The costs of alienation imposed on the elementary formation at the basis of society are generally not taken into account in weighing the advantages and disadvantages of various strategies of social development.

In our analysis we have devoted considerable attention to the intensity and scale of poverty in rural Java, both before and after the outbreak of the economic crisis. The acute deprivation suffered by a substantial part of the rural working population is a consequence of their exclusion from ownership of means of production and of depriving them from earning incomes that would at least enable satisfaction of their basic needs. We think that the discussion should not remain limited on how to measure poverty, by what percentage this phenomenon has increased and since when and where exactly, whether a series of case-studies at the micro-level or investigations in a macro-perspective and based on large-scale surveys provide the best possible insight in the dynamics at work. Without denying the relevance of such questions, it would be much more important to address ways of improving the social safety and economic resilience of a huge workforce living in poverty, however defined, and armed with little more than their unskilled labour power for their survival.

Protection against immiserization

The expulsion for the time being of many migrant labourers from the lower echelons of the urban economy after the outbreak of the crisis expressed the failure on the part of the state to provide basic support to this industrial reserve army. With political unrest gathering momentum policy-makers and politicians were afraid that this redundant mass was about to fulfil its historic destiny as *'la classe dangereuse'*. Its expulsion from the urban environment was justified with the argument that, once back in their villages, the migrants would be able to benefit from the traditional mechanisms of social security that had tenaciously survived in the agrarian-rural milieu. During our fieldwork, we found no evidence to support this brand of wishful thinking which is so popular among politicians and policy-makers. There is no reason to assume that the situation that we encountered in North Subang and East Cirebon – advanced monetization of the local economy and the hegemony of contractual relations – was an exception to a general pattern in which the organic principles of what is obstinately referred to as the traditional Javanese culture could still be identified.

We found no evidence that the wealthy upper class households were prepared to spend even a minor part of their surplus to mitigate the misery of their less fortunate fellow villagers. Nor are there any collective arrangements designed to counteract the (increasingly) unequal distribution of wealth. Contractual relations have gradually replaced the former patron-client transactions, in which the wealthy would pledge assistance and protection in exchange for the labour and loyalty of the poor. Under the New Order the elite no longer needed the dependence inherent in the system of patronage to bolster their superiority. The *orang kaya baru* themselves, however, increasingly became 'clients' of those in authority at district and sub-district level. In exchange for their support in preserving the social order based on social inequality and political exclusion, they were rewarded by their patrons in the form of preferential drawing rights on the resources of the state.

Would it be possible to detect a culture of shared poverty among the people coping for survival at the congested base of rural society, in an effort to distribute the available work and the income as equally as possible, through collective action and mutual solidarity? In neither of our two research localities did we find institutionalized arrangements to tie in one's fate with households in similar circumstances. As we have seen, during the New Order era, there was no social and political space in which an awareness of common interest could develop among the landpoor and landless classes. The sustained strategy of fragmentation is most likely one of the main reasons why the outbursts of protest that accompanied the deepening crisis did not develop into open and violent class warfare.

In our view, another reason why this did not occur was the increasing opportunity for escape to the urban growth poles. The rapid expansion of employment niches, at shorter or longer distances away from home, helped to lower the pressure building up in the rural economy. Large masses of migrant labourers flocked to these growth poles from the hinterland of Java without making a definite break with their milieu of origin. As a result the bond with the village remained intact, but it has been weakened. The constant mobility of these circulatory workers, most of whom belong to the subordinated classes, has made them less susceptible to the economic and social power of village elites. This is expressed in a recalcitrance that is a source of irritation to both rural employers and officials. Having become street-wise in the urban economy, the labour nomads enjoy a reputation for being demanding and less malleable than their classmates who remain stuck in the villages. In mobilizing opposition from below in support of the process of political reform, greater account will have to be taken than before of the 'floating mass' of the people and, moreover, in a much more literal sense than when the term was coined by the powers that be during the Suharto regime.

The very many households that play a marginal role in the economic process have little more to fall back on during times of crisis than their own resilience. They of course ask for and receive help from those around them, particularly close kinsmen and immediate neighbours. But given the fact this assistance also comes largely from other poor households, such transfers are limited in scale, regularity and substance. To alleviate the economic distress of those most severely affected, the government could in the end not avoid introducing what it had consistently tried to neglect: a social safety net. This scheme, intended as a temporary solution only, produced little in the way of concrete results. Even the emergency food relief and public works projects, aimed at the poorest of the poor, largely benefited others than those in the ill-defined target groups. The local authorities in North Subang and East Cirebon defended their decision to distribute the emergency provisions to all the villagers by saying that everyone had equal rights to government support. It is our conclusion that this argument, too, was a logical consequence of the political and bureaucratic myth of the village as a community.

The crisis in Indonesia has stopped being a purely monetary-economic recession and has escalated into a far-reaching disruption of society as a whole. The political instability and the threat to national unity may jeopardize all chances of economic recovery for many years to come. Reforms will only have the desired effect if, at the same time, the people are given more say in all matters affecting the quality of their lives. The proposals to shift the focus of political and administrative activity from national to regional level must be assessed in this light. These plans are at an advanced stage and a start has already been made with their implementation We would like to point out that, without guarantees that the very weak bargaining position of the rural poor in North Subang and East Cirebon will be strengthened, the devolution of political and executive power will result only in a legitimation of the informal supremacy of the district and village elites. It is the old principle of 'betting on the strong' that has always been at the forefront of Indonesia's development model.

The colonial theory of dualism saw an irreconcilable opposition between two economic systems in rural Java, caused by the penetration of capitalist forces of production and their clash with a static precapitalist society. The main criticism of this dichotomy of stagnation versus dynamism was that it had its origins in foreign domination. Later versions of the same dualistic model – firstly of city against countryside, and then of the formal and informal sectors in the urban economy – proved to be just as much a product of their age, enjoying popularity in analyses of the development process in the second half of the twentieth century. The current debate on inclusion and exclusion within the context of the globalization of political economy can be seen as a new variant of the old theme of dualism. The scale enlargement in terms of production, consumption and distribution has a strongly differential impact on the social classes that become, actively or passively, involved in the global transformations. Since the fall of Suharto, Indonesia has taken the first hesitant steps towards the transition to a civil society based on a democratic order. The progress made on this route will depend largely on whether the far-reaching social exclusion of the subaltern classes, of which the landpoor and landless in North Subang and East Cirebon are such striking examples, will take a turn for the better at the start of a new century. That this conclusion must be seen in a broader context than just the two villages in which we conducted our fieldwork needs no further explanation.

Glossary, abbreviations and acronyms

akseptor	person meant to practice birth control techniques provided by government agencies
anak buah	client
angkot	minibus
aparat desa	village administration
ani-ani	knife for cutting rice ears
asal bapak senang	as long as father is happy
asrama	hostel
babinsa	village-level agent of the military administration
bahasa Indonesia	Indonesian language
bahu	land measure: 0.7096 hectare
bajaj	three-wheeler motor-taxi
bakul	petty trader
balai desa	village hall
bandar bata	owner of brickworks
bank keliling	non-formal moneylending
bapak pembangunan	father of development
baso	soup
bata	land measure: 0.14 hectare; 500 bata is one bahu
bawon	harvest share
becak; tukang becak	pedicab; pedicab rider
bengkok	salary land given to senior village officials
beras	polished rice
bilik	house with bamboo walls and thatched roof
BKKBN, Badan Koordinasi Keluarga Berencana Nasional	National Family Planning Co-ordinating Board
bon	to buy on tick, credit extended by shopkeeper
borongan	job work, contract labour
BPD, Badan Perwalikan Desa	Elected Village Council
BPS, Badan Pusat Statistik	Central Statistics Agency
bubur	porridge
bulgur, zaman bulgur	famine, years of famine
BULOG, Badan Urusan Logistik	state-run food procurement agency,village

	co-operative
buruh liar	casual labourer
calo	commission agent, broker
camat	head of the subdistrict
ceblokan	closed field system under which labour is contracted in advance for harvest and pre-harvest operations
colt	minibus
cukap	sufficient, enough (for livelihood)
cukong	rural magnate
dagang keliling	perambulatory vendor
desa	village
dilman	passenger horse-carriage
DOLOG, Depot Logistik	food procurement agency at district level
dukun	traditional healer
dusun	hamlet, sub-village
es campur	sweet drink
fasilitator kecamatan	facilitator at the sub-district level
fasilitator, animator	facilitator supposed to guide villagers in self help
foya	to spend money freely
gabah	unhusked rice
gadai	mortgage of land for a loan
gado-gado	mixed cooked vegetables with groundnut sauce
gadu	cultivation cycle of paddy in dry season
gajar	advance wage payment
gensi	status, prestige
gerakan reformasi	reform movement
Golkar, Golongan Karya	state-supported and ruling party under the New Order
goreng	fried (food)
gotong royong	mutual help
grobak	handcart
haji	Mecca-returned pilgrim
harian	daily wages
ibu picit	masseuse
Idul Fitri	feast at the end of the fasting month
ilmu burung	augury
inpres (instruksi presiden)	Presidential decree; special fund for District--based development projects
IPB, Institut Pertanian Bogor Jabo-zone	Bogor Agricultural University urbanized
tabek (Jakarta, Bogor, Tangerang, Bekasi)	of districts around Jakarta
jaipong	Sundanese song and dance group
Jamsostek, Jaminan Sosial Tenaga Kerja	Workers' Social Security Agency

jodoh	affinity with work performed
JPS, Jaring Pengaman Sosial	Social Safety Net
juragan	patron, boss
k'neg	helper of skilled labourer
kaki lima	unlicensed street vendors
kampung	hamlet, also Sundanese name for village; a neighbourhood in the urban context
kartu sehat	special health card
kasikepan	village land shared among peasant-cultivators
kecap	soy sauce
kedeleh	soy beans
kelompok	group
kepala dusun	head of hamlet (sub-village)
kepala kampung	head of kampung
kepala rombongan	leader of transplanting gang
ketua kelompok	group leader
kijang	station wagon
KKN, Korupsi, Kolusi & Nepotisme	corruption, collusion and nepotism
KODAMIL, Komando Daerah Militer	Army Territorial Command
kontrak	contract, advance wage given to team of brick-makers
kretek	clove-spiced cigarette
krismon (krisis moneter)	monetary crisis
kristal (krisis total)	total crisis
KS, kurang sejahtera	poor
KUD, kooperasi unit desa	village cooperative unit
kuli	unskilled, casual labourer
kuli (biasa, macul, apa saja)	unskilled and casual labour
kuli gali	navvy
kulikang	regular farm servant
kurang	lack of basic means required for livelihood
kuwu	village head (Javanese)
laukpauk	side-dishes to staple
lebaran	festive end of fasting month
Masyarakat Desa	Village Community Resilience Board
lumbung desa	village grain bank
lurah	village head
madrasah	Islamic religious school
mandur	jobber, gang boss, foreman
mantri	head clerk in
maparo	tenancy contract dividing cost and yield in 1:2 ratio
maro	sharecropping arrangement (1/2)
masih bodoh	ordinary people (derogatory term)
masjid	mosque
menumpang	landless peasant
mertelo	tenancy contract dividing cost and yield in

	1:3 ratio
milik	property
Muslim asli	authentic Muslim
ngadugdag	commuters returning home in the evening
nganggur	open unemployment
ngasak	gleaning rice field after harvest
ojeg	motorbike carrying pillion passenger
ongkos	expenses
OPK, Operasi Pasar Khusus	Special Market Operation (public distribution of cheap rice)
orang kaya	well-to-do people
orang kaya baru	newly rich people
Orde Baru	New Order
p'rik	gleaning rice fields after harvest
pabrik bata	brickworks
paceklik	slack season of food scarcity between - harvests
pacul	hoe
padat karya	public work
padi	rice sheaves
pak	Mr.
pamong desa	body of village officials
pasar	market, bazaar
patok	share in what used to be communal land
PDI-P, Partai Demokrasi Indonesia Perjuangan	Indonesian Democratic Party – (of Struggle)
PDM-DKE, Program Pemberdayaan Daerah dalam Mengatasi Dampak Krisis Ekonomi	Regional Empowerment Programme to Overcome Economic Crisis
pembantu	maid servant
pemborong	(sub-)contractor in building industry
penebas	rice harvest contractor
pengobongan	brickworks
perang desa	village war
perkerja tidak tetap	doing work which is not permanent or steady
pesantren	religious boarding school
phk (permuhusan hubungan kerja)	instant dismissal
picis	copper coins used in colonial time
pikulan	carrying pole with baskets or loads hanging on either side
PKB, Partai Kebangkitan Bangsa	Party of the National Awakening
pokmas (kelompok masyarakat)	group formation for local-level economic co-operation
polowijo	secondary food crops grown after main rice harvest
pondok	boarding house
PPK, Program Pengembangan	Sub-district Development Program

Kecamatan	
Pra-KS	ultra-poor
proyek	project
puskesmas	primary health centre
real	Saudi Arabian currency
reformasi	reform
rendangan	cultivation cycle of paddy in wet season
revolusi colt	rapid increase in motorized transport by minibus
ringgit	Malaysian currency
RSS, Rumah Sangat Sederhana	low-cost public housing
RT, Rukun Tetangga	neighbourhood, lowest administrative vil-lage unit
rujak	mixed fruit (sweet and sour)
RW, Rukun Warga	neighbourhood consisting of two to three RT
serabi	rice cookies
SAE, Survey Agro Ekonomi	Agro Economic Survey
safari	official dress for civil servants
sawah	irrigated rice field
sejahtera, kurang sejahtera (KS)	prosperity (KS = still lacking prosperity)
sekdes (sekretar desa)	village secretary
sewa	land lease, tenancy arrangement
sikep	shareholder in communal land
singkong	fried cassava chips
slametan	ceremonial meal to mark life-cycle or religious events
sma	senior high school
smea	business college
smp	junior high school
sponsor	labour recruitment agent for overseas employment
stm	industrial training school
tahu	soy cake
tangkung	peasant holding no share in communal land
titisara	communal land used to cover village expenses
TKPD, Tim Pelaksana Kegiatan Desa	Executive Team for Village Activity
TKW, Tenaga Kerja Wanita	state-run employment agency for female workers going overseas
toko; toko mas	shop; shop selling and buying gold ornaments
tris or tri (tebu rakyat intensifikasi)	mode of smallholder sugarcane cultivation
tukang	craftsman
tukang obong	brick firer
tukang pacul, tukang macul	agricultural labourer
tukang picit	masseur
tukang rail	worker employed to lay and rails for lorry

	van
tukang wayang	puppeteer
warteg (warung tegal)	food stall
wartel (warung telpon)	telephone shop
warung	food stall, small village shop
welitan	woven mats of sugarcane leaves used for roof thatching
zakat	collection of alms (on Lebaran)

Bibliography

Ahmed, I. and S. Dhanani
1999 *Indonesia's recovery; Employment optimism or statistical illusion?* Jakarta: ILO. [Occasional Discussion Paper Series 2.]

Antlöv, H.
1999 'The new rich and cultural tensions in rural Indonesia', in: M. Pinches (ed.), *Culture and privilege in capitalist Asia*, pp. 188-207. London/New York: Routledge.

Arndt, H.W. and H. Hill (eds)
1999 *Southeast Asia's economic crisis; Origins, lessons and the way forward.* Singapore: Institute of Southeast Asian Studies.

Bardhan, P. (ed.)
1989 *Conversations between economists and anthropologists; Methodological issues in measuring economic change in rural Java.* Delhi: Oxford University Press.

Boeke, J.H.
1952 'Dorpsherstel' [later included in abridged form in: *Indonesian economics; The concept of dualism in theory and policy*, pp. 303-15. The Hague: Van Hoeve, 1966].

Boomgaard, P.
1991 'The Javanese village as a Cheshire cat; The Java debate against a European and Latin American background', *Journal of Peasant Studies* 18: 228-304.
1999 *Labour in Java in the 1930s.* Amsterdam: IIAS/IISG. [Working Papers on Asian Labour.]

Booth, A.
2000a 'Poverty and inequality in the Soeharto era; An assessment', *Bulletin of Indonesian Economic Studies* 36-1:73-104.
2000b 'The impact of a severe economic crisis on poverty and distribution; An Indonesian case study, 1977-99'. Revised and expanded version of an earlier draft, London.

Breman, J.
1974 *Patronage and exploitation; Changing agrarian relations in South Gujarat.* Berkeley: University of California Press.
1978 'Seasonal migration and co-operative capitalism; The crushing of cane and of labour by the sugar factories of South Gujarat', *Economic and Political Weekly* 13-31/33:1317-60.

1980 *'The informal sector in research'; Theory and practice.* Rotterdam: Erasmus University, Comparative Asian Studies Programme. [CASP Series 3.]

1983 *Control of land and labour in colonial Java; A case study of agrarian crisis and reform in the region of Cirebon during the first decades of the 20th century.* Dordrecht: Foris. [KITLV, Verhandelingen 101.]

1985 *Peasants, migrants and paupers; Rural labour circulation and capitalist production in West India.* Oxford: Oxford University Press, Delhi: Clarendon Press.

1990 'Ontwikkeling op commando', *Onze Wereld* 33-7/8:10.

1993 *Beyond patronage and exploitation; Changing agrarian relations in South Gujarat.* Delhi: Oxford University Press.

1995 'Work and life of the rural proletariat in Java's coastal plain', *Modern Asian Studies* 29-1:1-44. [Published in 1994 in Indonesian translation: 'Kerja dan kehidupan buruh tani di Pesisir', *Prisma* 21:3-34.]

1996 *Footloose labour; Working in India's informal economy.* Cambridge: Cambridge University Press.

1997 'The village in focus', in: J. Breman, P. Kloos and A. Saith (eds), *The village in Asia revisited*, pp. 15-76. Delhi: Oxford University Press.

1999a 'Politics of poverty and a leaking safety net', *Economic and Political Weekly* 34-20:1177-8.

1999b 'Monetary crisis in rural Java; The exclusion of the poor from the social safety net programme'. Paper, P.E.P. LIPI-ISI Seminar, Jakarta, April.

Breman, J. and B. White

1995 'Coercion and quality in Indonesian family planning; A response to Anke Niehof', *Bijdragen tot de Taal-, Land- en Volkenkunde* 152:144-7.

Breman, J. and G. Wiradi

1999 'The impact of krismon in two villages along the northern coast of West Java; Report of fieldwork in progress'. Workshop on the Economic Crisis and Social Security in Indonesia. Nijmegen.

Breman, J., P. Kloos and A. Saith (eds)

1997 *The village in Asia revisited.* Delhi: Oxford University Press.

Conter, J.M.

1981 Pendapatan dan kesempatan kerja buruh migran di Mariuk dan Tambakdahan, kecamatan Binong-Subang. [MA thesis, Fakultas Pasca Sarjana, Institut Pertanian Bogor.]

Daukes, W.

1942 *The P&T lands; An agricultural romance of anglo-dutch enterprise.* London: Eden Fisher.

Dhanani, S. and I. Islam

2000 'Poverty, inequality and social protection; Lessons from the Indonesian crisis'. Working Paper 00/001, United Nations Support Facility for Indonesian Recovery, Jakarta.

Dirkse, Jean-Paul, Frans Hüsken and Mario Rutten (eds)

1993 *Development and social welfare; Indonesia's experiences under the New Order.* Leiden: KITLV Press. [Verhandelingen 156.]

Djumhono, D., T. Sunarminto, S. Soedarsono and G. Wiradi
1988 *Laporan studi desa/puklutan – desa Curug, kecamatan Karangsembung, kabupaten Cirebon*. Bogor: Institut Pertanian Bogor.

Ernaini, N.
1991 *Pembentukan modal, sistem perkreditan dan koperasi; Kasus desa Curug, kecamatan Karangsembung, kabupaten Cirebon*. Bogor: Institut Pertanian Bogor. [Seri Working Paper A-8.]
1999 Evaluasi I proyek PDM-DKE, tahun 1998-1999. Kecamatan Binong, Kab. DI II Subang 1999.

Feridhanusetyawan, T.
1999 *The impact of the crisis on the labour market in Indonesia*. Report prepared for the Asian Development Bank, Manila.

Geertz, C.
1963 *Agricultural involution; The processes of ecological change in Indonesia*. Berkeley: University of California Press.
1965 *The social history of an Indonesian town*. Cambridge, Mass.: MIT Press.

Hardjono, J.
1999 'The micro data picture; Results of a SMERU social impact survey in the Purwakerta-Cirebon corridor'. Final report, Social Monitoring and Early Response Unit, Jakarta.

Hart, G.
1986a *Power, labor and livelihood; Processes of change in rural Java*. Berkeley: University of California Press.
1986b 'Exclusionary labour arrangements; Interpreting evidence on employment trends in rural Java', *Journal of Development Studies* 22:681-96.
1989 'Agrarian change in the context of state patronage', in: G. Hart, A. Turton and B. White (eds), *Agrarian transformations; Local processes and the state in Southeast Asia*, pp. 31-49. Berkeley: University of California Press.

Hart, G., A. Turton and B. White (eds)
1989 *Agrarian transformations; Local processes and the state in Southeast Asia*. Berkeley: University of California Press.

Hayami, Yujiro and Masao Kikuchi
1981 *Asian village economy at the crossroads; An economic approach to institutional change*. Tokyo: University of Tokyo Press.

Hill, H.
1999 *The Indonesian economy in crisis; Causes, consequences and lessons*. Singapore: Institute of Southeast Asian Studies.

Hugo, G.
1985 'Structural change and labour mobility in rural Java', in: G. Standing (ed.), *Labour circulation and the labour process*, pp. 46-88. London/Sydney: Croom Helm.

Hugo, Graeme J., Terence H. Hull, Valerie J. Hull and Gavin W. Jones
1987 *The demographic dimension in Indonesian development*. Singapore: Oxford University Press. [East Asian Social Science Monographs.]

Hüsken, F.
1988 *Een dorp op Java; Sociale differentiatie in een boerengemeenschap, 1850-1980.* [PhD thesis, Universiteit van Amsterdam.]
1989 'Cycles of commercialization and accumulation in a Central Javanese village', in: G. Hart, A. Thurton en B. White (eds), *Agrarian transformations; Local processes and the state in Southeast Asia*, pp. 303-31. Berkeley: University of California Press.
1999 '"Crisis, what crisis"; The village community of Gondosari during the krismon'. Workshop on the Economic Crisis and Social Security in Indonesia, Nijmegen.

Hüsken, F. and B. White
1989 'Java; Social differentiation, food production, and agrarian control', in: G. Hart, A. Thurton and B. White (eds), *Agrarian transformations; Local processes and the state in Southeast Asia*, pp. 235-65. Berkeley: University of California Press.

International Labour Organization
1998 *Employment challenges of the Indonesian economic crisis.* Jakarta: ILO/UNDP.

Islam, I. and S. Nazara
2000 *Minimum wage and the welfare of Indonesian workers.* Jakarta: ILO. [Occasional Discussion Paper Series 3.]

Jellinek, L. and B. Rustanto
1999 'Survival strategies of the Javanese during the economic crisis'. Consultancy report to the World Bank. Jakarta.

Koning, J.
1999 'Krismon and Reformasi: Life goes on; Some first impressions from Rikmokeri village, Central Java'. Workshop on the Economic Crisis and Social Security in Indonesia, Nijmegen.

Kunio, Y.
1988 *The rise of ersatz capitalism in South-East Asia.* Singapore: Oxford University Press.

Kutanegara, P.M.
2001 'Working hard and living simple; Coping strategies of poor households in Sriharjo, Central Java'. Paper, Workshop International Institute of Social History, Amsterdam.

Kutunegara, P. M. and G. Nooteboom
2000 *Forgotten villagers; The effects of the crisis and the role of government in rural Java.* Nijmegen: Research Project on Social Security and Social Policy in Indonesia, Department of Anthropology, University of Nijmegen.

Manning, C.
1988 'Rural employment creation in Java; Lessons from the green revolution and oil boom', *Population and Development Review* 14:47-80.
1998 *Indonesian labour in transition; An East Asian success story?* Cambridge/Melbourne: Cambridge University Press.

2000 'Labour market adjustment to Indonesia's economic crisis; Context, trends and implications', *Bulletin of Indonesian Economic Studies* 36-1:105-36.

Manning, C. and P. van Diermen
1999 'Introduction to social dimensions of *reformasi* and crisis', in: C. Manning and P. van Diermen (eds), *Indonesia in transition; Social aspects of reformasi and crisis*, pp. 143-5. Singapore: Institute of Southeast Asian Studies.
1999 (eds) *Indonesia in transition; Social aspects of reformasi and crisis*. Singapore: Institute of Southeast Asian Studies.

Mehta, J. and S. Venkataraman
2000 'Poverty statistics; Bermicide's feast', *Economic and Political Weekly* 35-27:2377-82.

Mishra, S. and I. Islam
2000 'Towards a poverty reduction strategy for Indonesia'. Seminar on Renewing Poverty Reduction Strategy in Indonesia, Badan Perencanaan Pembangunan Nasional, Jakarta.

Mubyarto
1999 'Poverty in Indonesia before and after the crisis', in: *Poverty reduction; What's new and what's different? Report of a seminar organized by the Asian Development Bank in conjunction with the 32nd annual meeting of its Board of Governors; Manila, Philippines 29 April 1999*. Manila: Office of Environment and Social Development, Asian Development Bank.

Niehof, Anke
1996 'Family planning research in Indonesia; A source of far-reaching controversy, a rejoinder to Breman and White', *Bijdragen tot de Taal-, Land- en Volkenkunde* 152:148-51.

Olken, B.A., M. Nabiu, N. Toyamah and D. Perwira
2001 'Sharing the wealth; How villages decide to distribute OPK rice'. [SMERU Working Paper, Jakarta.]

Papanek, G. and B.S. Handoko
1999 'The impact on the poor of growth and crisis; Evidence from real wage data'. Paper presented to the LPEM-FEUI/PEG-USAID conference 'The economic issues facing the new government', Jakarta, 18-19 August.

Penny, D.H. and M. Singarimbun
1973 *Population and poverty in rural Java; Some economic arithmetic from Sriharjo*. Ithaca, NY: Department of Agricultural Economics, New York State College of Agriculture and Life Sciences, Cornell University. [Cornell International Agricultural Development Mimeograph 41.]

Pinches, M. (ed.)
1999 *Culture and privilege in capitalist Asia*. London/New York: Routledge.

Pincus, J.
1996 *Class, power and agrarian change; Land and labour in rural West Java*. London: Macmillan.

Poppele, J., S. Sumarto and L. Pritchett
1999 'Social impacts of the Indonesian crisis; New data and policy implications'. [SMERU Report, Jakarta.]

Pradhan, M., A. Suryahadi, S. Sumarto and L. Pritchett
2000 'Measurements of poverty in Indonesia: 1996, 1999 and beyond'. [SMERU Working Paper, Jakarta.]

Schweitzer, Th.
1989 'Economic individualism and the community spirit; Divergent orientation patterns of Javanese villagers in rice production and the ritual sphere', *Modern Asian Studies* 23-2:277-312.

Singarimbun, M.
1976 'Sriharjo revisited', *Bulletin of Indonesian Economic Studies* 12-2:117-25.

Skoufias, E., A. Suryahadi and S. Sumarto
2000 'Changes in household welfare, poverty and inequality during the crisis', *Bulletin of Indonesian Economic Studies* 36-2:95-112.

Suhendar, Endang
1999 'Villages in the crisis; From poor to poorer'. Workshop paper, Akatiga. Bandung.

Sumarto, S. and A. Suryahadi
2001 'Principles and approaches to targeting; With reference to the Indonesian social safety net'. [SMERU Working Paper, Jakarta.]

Sumarto, S., A. Suryahadi and W. Widyanti
2001 'Designs and implementation of the Indonesian social safety net programs; Evidence from the JPS module in the 1999 SUSENAS'. [SMERU Working Paper, Jakarta.]

Sumodiningrat, G.
1999 'Economic stabilization and social safety net; Achieving public prosperity'. Contribution to Seminar on Social Safety Net Programs in Indonesia, JICA Institute for International Cooperation, Tokyo, 16 February 1999.

Sunarminto, T. and A. Sadelie
1989 *Profil desa Curug dan Curug Wetan, kecamatan Karangsembung, kabupaten Cirebon, Jawa Barat*. Bogor: Pusat Studi Pembangunan Lembaga Penelitian, Institut Pertanian Bogor.

Suryahadi, A., Y. Suharso and S. Sumarto
1999 'Coverage and targeting in the Indonesian social safety net programs: evidence from 100 village survey'. [SMERU Working Paper, Jakarta.]

Suryahadi, A. and S. Sumarto
1999 'Update on the impact of the Indonesian crisis on consumption expenditures and poverty incidence; Results from the December 1998 round of 100 village survey'. [SMERU Working Paper, Jakarta.]
2001 'The chronic poor, the transient poor, and the vulnerable in Indonesia before and after the crisis'. [SMERU Working Paper, Jakarta.]

Suryahadi, A., S. Sumarto, Y. Suharso and L. Pritchett
2000 'The evolution of poverty during the crisis in Indonesia, 1996 to 1999'. [SMERU Working Paper, Jakarta.]

Wertheim W.F.
1964 'Betting on the strong?', in: *East-West parallels; Sociological approaches to modern Asia*, pp. 259-77. The Hague: Van Hoeve.

1964 *East-West parallels; Sociological approaches to modern Asia.* The Hague: Van Hoeve.
1975 *Elite en waan; Een bijdrage tot ontmaskering van de elitewaan.* Amsterdam: Van Gennep.

Wertheim, W.F. and G.H. van der Kolff (eds)
1966 *Indonesian economics; The concept of dualism in theory and policy.* The Hague: Van Hoeve. [Selected Studies on Indonesia 6.]

Wetterberg, A., S. Sumarto and L. Pritchett
1999 'A national snapshot of the social impact of Indonesia's economic crisis', *Bulletin of Indonesian Economic Studies* 35-3:145-52.

White, B.
1983 '"Agricultural involution' and its critics; Twenty years after', *Bulletin of Concerned Asian Scholars* 15-2:18-31.
1986 *Rural non-farm employment in Java; Recent developments, policy issues and research needs.* The Hague: Institute of Social Studies Advisory Services.
1993 'Indonesia's population problems and policies; A non-Malthusian view', in: Jean-Paul Dirkse, Frans Hüsken and Mario Rutten (eds), *Development and social welfare; Indonesia's experiences under the New Order*, pp. 105-13. Leiden: KITLV Press. [Verhandelingen 156.]

White, B. and G. Wiradi
1981 *Land tenure in West Java; A regional overview, with some historical notes and a case study from the Cimanuk river basin.* Bogor: Agro-Economic Survey.
1989 'Agrarian and nonagrarian bases of inequality in nine Javanese villages', in: G. Hart, A. Thurton en B. White (eds), *Agrarian transformations; Local processes and the state in Southeast Asia*, pp. 266-302. Berkeley: University of California Press.

White, B. and I. Abdullah
1999 'Rural development and household welfare; 25 years of change in a Javanese village, 1973-1998'. Paper, Workshop on the Economic Crisis and Social Security in Indonesia, Nijmegen.

Widyanti, W., S. Sumarto and A. Suryahadi
2001 'Short-term poverty dynamics; Evidence from rural Indonesia. [SMERU Working Paper, Jakarta.]

Wiradi, G.
1991 *Industri gula di Jawa dalam perspektif model inti-satelit; Kasus di kabupaten Cirebon, Jawa Barat.* Bogor: Pusat Studi Pembangunan, Institut Pertanian Bogor. [West Java Rural Nonfarm Sector Research project, Working Paper Series A-31.]

World Bank
1990 *Indonesia; Poverty assessment and strategy report.* Washington: World Bank. [Report no. 8034-IND.]
1996 *Indonesia; Dimensions of growth.* Washington: World Bank. [Report no. 15383-IND.]
1998 *Indonesia in crisis; A macroeconomic update.* Washington: World Bank.

1999 *Indonesia; Country assistance strategy.* Washington: World Bank. [Progress report no. 18963-IND.]

2000 *World Bank poverty assessment; Revised new outline.* Washington: World Bank. [Draft for discussion.]

Index